T0348663

Blender Scripting with Python

Automate Tasks, Write Helper Tools, and Procedurally Generate Models in Blender 4

Isabel Lupiani

Apress®

Blender Scripting with Python: Automate Tasks, Write Helper Tools, and Procedurally Generate Models in Blender 4

Isabel Lupiani
Orlando, FL, USA

ISBN-13 (pbk): 979-8-8688-1126-5   ISBN-13 (electronic): 979-8-8688-1127-2
https://doi.org/10.1007/979-8-8688-1127-2

Copyright © 2025 by Isabel Lupiani

Managing Director, Apress Media LLC: Welmoed Spahr
Acquisitions Editor: Spandana Chatterjee
Editorial Project Manager: Kripa Joseph
Desk Editor: James Markham

Distributed to the book trade worldwide by Springer Science+Business Media New York, 1 New York Plaza, Suite 4600, New York, NY 10004-1562, USA. Phone 1-800-SPRINGER, fax (201) 348-4505, e-mail orders-ny@springer-sbm.com, or visit www.springeronline.com. Apress Media, LLC is a California LLC and the sole member (owner) is Springer Science + Business Media Finance Inc (SSBM Finance Inc). SSBM Finance Inc is a **Delaware** corporation.

For information on translations, please e-mail booktranslations@springernature.com; for reprint, paperback, or audio rights, please e-mail bookpermissions@springernature.com.

Apress titles may be purchased in bulk for academic, corporate, or promotional use. eBook versions and licenses are also available for most titles. For more information, reference our Print and eBook Bulk Sales web page at http://www.apress.com/bulk-sales.

Any source code or other supplementary material referenced by the author in this book is available to readers on GitHub. For more detailed information, please visit https://www.apress.com/gp/services/source-code.

If disposing of this product, please recycle the paper

For James, Zoe, and Caleb

Table of Contents

About the Author

Isabel Lupiani is a software engineer by day and a maker by night, who enjoys handcrafting 3D models as much as procedurally generating them. She received her MS in Computer Science from Georgia Tech and has worked at several game studios in the past as an AI engineer for PC/Xbox games. Most recently, Isabel was a lead AI engineer in the simulation industry.

About the Technical Reviewer

 **Ajit Deolikar** is a mechanical engineer from Pune, India, and has experience in new product design and development. His work area involves designing aesthetic accessories for four wheelers and two wheelers (motorcycles as well as scooters), structural systems, power parts, bodywork, etc. He is also involved in designing and engineering of farm equipment and other testing equipment.

He is passionate about art and started using the open source software Blender as a hobby many years ago. He likes to create short animations as well as explanatory videos of various training modules for educational purposes.

He extended Blender experience in his professional work for preparing product styling surfaces and CAD construction using hard surface modeling. In addition, he has used it to solve complex mechanical motions using a physics engine and for various other tasks. With Blender Python scripting, he has created specific add-ons for simplifying and automating many repetitive tasks. He has even taken efforts to customize the project workflow for improving product quality to shorten delivery schedules. His product marketing videos and brochure, made using Blender, make him stand out from the competition.

In his spare time, he likes to play chess and analyze game strategies played by the world's great Grandmasters. He would someday love to write at least one book on those approaches. He can be reached at ajitb502@gmail.com.

Acknowledgments

I've always found the thought of anyone willing to read my work incredibly humbling and flattering. Thank you to all the readers out there, whether you've supported the previous incarnations of the book or are picking it up for the first time—the book exists (and lives on) because of you. I'd also like to express my gratitude to Spandana Chatterjee, Shobana Srinivasan, Kripa Joseph, James Markham, Joseph Quatela, Jessica Vakili, Sowmya Thodur, and the rest of the Apress team, for your support and guidance throughout the publishing process. Thank you to the technical reviewer for taking the time to read the chapters, dotting my Blender i's, and crossing my Python t's. Last but not least, thank you to my husband James, my daughter Zoe, and my son Caleb, for your eternal love and support, and not to forget Tiddles, the red-footed tortoise, for graciously modeling for the Chapter 8 photos.

Introduction

Art, games, and I go way back. My kindergarten teacher folded a paper crane in class one day, and I was hooked. By the time I was in first grade, I was designing and making my own pop-up cards. To this day, I love telling the story of the day the stars aligned and I won a Sega Genesis in an art competition—henceforth my indoctrination to the fascinating world of video games. You could call it fate, since my parents probably never would've bought me a game console!

Fast forward to 2007, I was a year into the game industry as an AI programmer and had picked up Blender in my spare time to communicate with artists at work better and to fuel my own creative outlet. It would take another 10 years, however, when I took on a project to port Blender to room-scale VR that I finally attempted to work with Blender Python—and boy, was that difficult! Even though I'd been using Blender for years and programming professionally, getting one thing to work in Blender Python would sometimes mean days of trial and error plus digging through documentation and poring over online posts. It may be cliché when authors say they wanted to write a book they wished had existed—in my case, I honestly did. This book is the accumulation of everything I learned working with Blender Python over the years, with solutions to problems that'd only come up when you try to write tools for a real production environment.

The book will show you how to write extension add-ons for Blender 4 from start to finish. Chapter 1 opens with a hands-on tour of the Scripting workspace with basics like loading and running scripts and turning hand modeling steps into Python by capturing them in the Info Editor. Chapter 2 explains the structure of operators and add-ons and shows how to use various input widgets to create user interfaces. You'll learn various strategies for finding the Python equivalent of Blender menu options and hotkeys in a systematic way. In addition, you'll dissect add-ons shipped with Blender to see how they work and take advantage of built-in templates to quickly create new scripts.

With a firm grasp of scripting basics, in Chapters 3, 4, and 5, you'll find out how to create add-ons for editing and generating 3D models. In Chapter 3, you'll learn the basics of using modifiers and the bmesh module to edit meshes in Python and then write your own script to generate barrels from scratch with interesting variations. In Chapter 4, you'll add more advanced mesh editing functionalities to your add-ons, like extrude/bridge edge loops, loop cut-and-slides, plus all the essentials for manipulating vertices, edges, and faces like merge, rip, join, rotate, scale, bevel, and inset. You'll also write functions for cleaning up meshes and correcting normals. In addition, you'll learn how to handle imports (i.e., scripts that reference functions defined in one another) for both scripts meant to run in the Text Editor as well as packaged add-ons.

The second half of the book takes you through developing a series of practical and production-quality add-ons, inspired by various stages of a 3D modeling pipeline. In Chapter 5, you'll develop an add-on to procedurally generate stylized fire hydrant meshes with parametric controls. In Chapter 6, you'll create a suite of helper tools that collect user inputs from Grease Pencil strokes marked directly on sculpted meshes, for carving and in/outsetting selected regions as well as retopologizing them. In Chapter 7, you'll learn to write Python functions that automate key steps of the UV mapping process. Building on skills from Chapter 7, in Chapter 8, you'll create tools for projection painting textures by sampling from the same reference photos used to model the mesh. After mastering add-on development, in Chapter 9, you'll find out how to package, distribute, and market your extension add-ons through different channels. With the help of modal operators, you'll also create time-lapsed and interactive demos to showcase your procedural generation algorithm building a mesh gradually in the viewport with 3D text as captions.

Who This Book Is For

The intended audience of this book are 3D artists and programmers who want to create custom Blender add-ons to automate part of their workflow. Readers are assumed to have a high-level understanding of the 3D art pipeline, and either already use Blender or have experience with other CAD software such as 3Ds Max, Maya, or Rhino. Knowing basic Python is immensely helpful, although it is possible for motivated readers to learn it along the way by supplementing with resources outside the book.

Suggested Reading Road Map

The book is designed for a linear read through from Chapters 1 to 9. However, if you already have experience with Blender Python or are only interested in certain stages of the 3D modeling pipeline, it is possible to skip some chapters. In this section, I will suggest some alternative road maps through the book.

Chapters 1 and 2 provide a comprehensive overview of operators and add-ons, along with a plethora of strategies for systematically converting Blender edits by hand into Python. I suggest you read Chapters 1 and 2 regardless of any prior experience with Blender Python, as they'll serve as good refreshers and likely offer tips you've not seen elsewhere.

If you are primarily interested in mesh editing or procedural generation but not UV mapping or texturing, you can read Chapters 1–5 and safely skip Chapters 7 and 8. If the reverse is true, you can read Chapters 1, 2, 3, 7, and 8 and refer to Chapter 4 for an explanation on how to handle imports for both scripts run from the Text Editor and packaged add-ons. If you are not concerned with sculpting or retopology, you can safely skip Chapter 6; however, Chapter 6 does cover how to configure the Grease Pencil and process Grease Pencil input using Python.

If you are not looking to sell your add-ons, you can skip the parts of Chapter 9 that discuss marketing, promotion, and pricing strategies. Even if you are not concerned with making time-lapse demos like those mentioned in Chapter 9, they are built with modal operators that only run when certain type(s) of events are detected (like timer ticks or keystrokes), which may still be of interest and worth a read through.

CHAPTER 1

Getting Started on Blender Scripting

Just about any action you perform by hand in Blender can be automated with a script. In this chapter, I'll introduce you to Blender's built-in scripting interface, which includes the *Python Console* and the *Text Editor*. The Python Console is a convenient way to experiment with individual commands and see their effects in real time, whereas the Text Editor is great for editing and running scripts from files. We'll start by playing with API functions from the Python Console and observe immediate feedback happening in the viewport, followed by running one of Blender's built-in Template scripts in the Text Editor and observing its effects. Along the way, I will show you a variety of developer features that will help you discover which Python operator is behind a Blender menu item or hotkey and how to easily look up its implementation.

Introduction to Blender's Scripting Interface

Blender comes equipped with a *Scripting workspace*, which can be accessed by clicking the "Scripting" tab at the top of the screen as shown in Figure 1-1. The Scripting workspace contains a Text Editor for editing and running scripts from files, as well as an interactive Python Console that has been customized around the Blender Python API.

I. Lupiani, *Blender Scripting with Python*, https://doi.org/10.1007/979-8-8688-1127-2_1

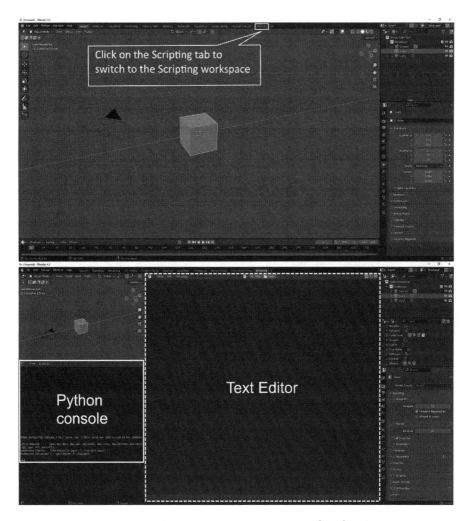

Figure 1-1. *Accessing the Scripting workspace (top). The Text Editor and Python Console within the Scripting workspace (bottom)*

Convenience Variables

Blender's built-in Python Console is customized specifically around Blender's scripting API and provides many features not found in a native Python installation. The first of these are *convenience variables*, which are shorthand aliases for certain Blender modules. For example, the two convenience variables C = bpy.context and D = bpy.data are already defined for you inside the console.

A convenience variable is declared with the syntax <new alias> = <name of variable>. So, any time you find the need to type bpy.context at the prompt, you can enter C instead, which is a lot shorter and quicker to type.

Automatic Imports and Autocomplete

Another feature of the built-in console is that some of the frequently used Blender modules like mathutils as well as Python libraries like math are automatically imported for quicker access.

Yet another feature (which is also my favorite) is *Autocomplete*. If you're not sure what the name of a command is or are curious about what functions are under a module, you can enter a partial command at the prompt and use *Console* ➤ *Autocomplete* to search for a list of options for completing that command, as shown in Figure 1-2.

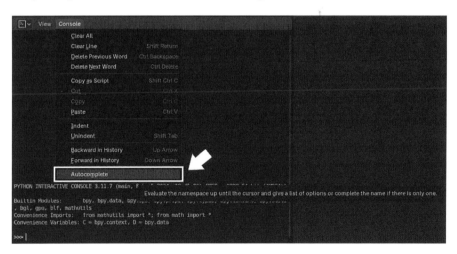

Figure 1-2. *The Autocomplete feature of the Python console*

Let's try this in an example. Inside the Python Console, type `import bmesh`, and hit the *enter* key to import the `bmesh` module (which is a built-in Blender Python module for mesh editing we'll go over in Chapters 3, 4, and 5). At the following prompt, type `bmesh.utils.`(be sure to include the dot at the end), then, without hitting *enter*, click *Console ➤ Autocomplete*. You should see the list of available functions under `bmesh.utils.` automatically brought up, as shown in Listing 1-1.

Listing 1-1. Retrieving the list of functions under `bmesh.utils` using Console ➤ Autocomplete

```
>>> import bmesh
>>> bmesh.utils.
                edge_rotate(
                edge_split(
                face_flip(
                face_join(
                face_split(
                face_split_edgenet(
                face_vert_separate(
                loop_separate(
                vert_collapse_edge(
                vert_collapse_faces(
                vert_dissolve(
                vert_separate(
                vert_splice(
>>> bmesh.utils.
```

Tip   If the list of results returned by *Autocomplete* is too long to read without scrolling, you can use *View ➤ Area ➤ Toggle Maximize Area* (Ctrl-Spacebar) to maximize it, then either hit Ctrl-Spacebar a second time or click the "Back to Previous" button along the top menu bar to bring it back down to size when you're done. This functionality is available in many other screen areas such as the 3D Viewport, Text Editor, and so on.

If you have an idea of what a function or property's name might be but are unsure of the exact wording, you can type in a partial name as the search term and utilize *Autocomplete* as a search tool. For instance, if you remember that some of the debug settings are under the bpy.app module, you can find their precise names by typing bpy.app.debug at the prompt, and without pressing the enter key, click *Console ➤ Autocomplete*, as shown in Listing 1-2.

Listing 1-2. Searching for debug options under bpy.app using Console ➤ Autocomplete

```
>>> bpy.app.debug
                    _depsgraph
                    _depsgraph_build
                    _depsgraph_eval
                    _depsgraph_pretty
                    _depsgraph_tag
                    _depsgraph_time
                    _events
                    _ffmpeg
                    _freestyle
                    _handlers
```

```
                    _io
                    _python
                    _simdata
                    _value
                    _wm
>>> bpy.app.debug_events
False
```

The results from *Autocomplete* in this example suggest that bpy.app.
debug_events is a valid variable in the Blender API (note that you can
tell it's a variable as opposed to a function, since its name does not have
a trailing pair of parentheses). To find out more about bpy.app.debug_
events's usage, you can type it at the next prompt in the console and hit
enter. The console returns False, which indicates that bpy.app.debug_
events is a boolean property with its current value set to False. If you had
typed bpy.app.debug_Events instead, which is the same term but with the
wrong capitalization (notice the E instead of e for event), *Autocomplete*
will fail to return any results and display an AttributeError instead:

```
>>> bpy.app.debug_Events
Traceback (most recent call last):
  File "<blender_console>", line 1, in <module>
AttributeError: 'bpy.app' object has no attribute
'debug_Events'
```

If you spell out the full name of a function and hit *Autocomplete*, the
console will bring up that function's entry in the documentation where
available. This is helpful for learning the correct usage of a function, like
the types and ordering of its input parameters and what values it returns.

If you need more information on how to use a method, you can always
look it up in the Blender Python API online documentation at https://
docs.blender.org/api/current/index.html. Notice, however, since

Blender is continuously in development, you might not see the same level of support for all parts of the API, particularly those that are newer or have recently undergone changes.

Caution   *Autocomplete*'s search capabilities are rather limited since the partial term's capitalization and the ordering of the words both need to be correct.

Example: Move Mesh Vertices in the Viewport with the Python Console

Playing with commands at the built-in console with the help of *Autocomplete* is a great way to learn your way around the Blender API. Let's try this with an example. You'll run a series of commands at the console to move a corner vertex of the cube in the default startup blend file.

Switch to the *Scripting workspace*, and go over to the Python Console. At the prompt, enter the following command:

```
>>> cube = bpy.context.scene.objects["Cube"]
```

This retrieves a reference to the cube by its name (*"Cube"*) from the current list of scene objects and stores that reference in a variable called cube. Later on, you'll make edits to the cube with script commands through the cube variable.

We're going to use the built-in Blender module bmesh to manipulate cube's mesh data. As shown in the previous example, since bmesh is not imported to the console by default, you'll need to explicitly import it by entering the command

```
>>> import bmesh
```

Next, switch cube to *Edit mode* in the *3D Viewport*, which will let you create a bmesh instance bm based on the cube's mesh data, cube.data, with the following command:

```
>>> bm = bmesh.from_edit_mesh(cube.data)
```

Through bm, you'll have access to the edges, faces, and vertices of cube's mesh data. For example, bm.verts is a sequence containing all of cube's vertices. Since a cube has eight corners, you can verify that the length of bm.verts is 8 with len(), which is a built-in Python function that tells you how many items are in a container, like this:

```
>>> len(bm.verts)
8
```

Next, you'll randomly pick one of cube's vertices and experiment by moving it through script commands. Enter the following command to select one of cube's vertices—let's say the vertex with index 3—and store a reference to it in the variable v. You can verify that v's index is 3 by printing it to the console with v.index.

```
>>> v = bm.verts[3]
>>> v.index
3
```

Note   Sequences in Python (such as a list) use zero-based indexing, which means the first item of a sequence has index 0, the second item has index 1, and so on. The last item has an index that is one less than the total number of items in the sequence. For example, if a sequence has five items, the last item has index 4.

The numerical indices of vertices, edges, and faces in Blender reflect the order in which they are created (elements with smaller indices are created first). Note that unlike editing meshes in the 3D Viewport by hand, where you have to select a portion of the mesh with the mouse or keyboard first, many script operations allow you to directly manipulate part of a mesh without explicitly making a selection.

Next, we'll move v through commands at the console and verify its movement in the viewport. v.co is a trio of X, Y, and Z coordinates (a Vector) that represents v's location in 3D. v.co[0] is its X coordinate, v.co[1] its Y coordinate, and v.co[2] its Z coordinate. Enter v.co at the prompt to display its current location:

```
>>> v.co
Vector((1.0, -1.0, -1.0))
```

To move v, you can edit one or more components of v.co or assign a new Vector to v altogether. Enter the following command to add 1 to v.co[1], which moves v in the positive Y direction by one unit:

```
>>> v.co[1] += 1
>>> v.co
Vector((1.0, 0.0, -1.0))
```

In general, when you edit a mesh through a bmesh instance, the changes are queued up on the bmesh instance and not reflected on the mesh until you call the method bmesh.update_edit_mesh(<name of mesh>). Ensure that the cube is in *Edit mode*, then, type the following line into the console to flush the change to v.co from bm to cube's mesh data:

```
>>> bmesh.update_edit_mesh(cube.data)
```

You can verify v's movement in the 3D Viewport, which should look like the right-hand side of Figure 1-3.

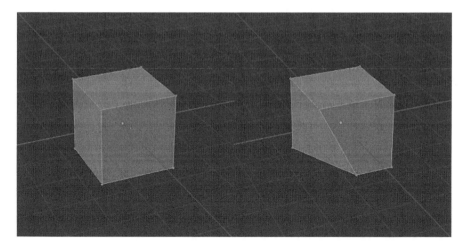

Figure 1-3. *Left: The cube in the viewport in its original state. Right: After its vertex at index 3 has been moved 1 unit in the positive Y direction*

Tip   The Python Console in Blender acts very much like a typical command line interface. If you are already familiar with one, you'll pleasantly discover that many common shortcuts like the Up or Down Arrow keys for cycling through command history also work in the Python Console.

Transferring Console Contents into a Script

After experimenting with some commands in the console, you might find yourself arriving at a pretty solid basis for a script or add-on. To copy the console session in its entirety, with lines automatically formatted according to Python syntax, go to the top of the console window and select *Console* ➤ *Copy as Script* (***Shift-Ctrl-C***), then, paste (***Ctrl-V***) into any text editor. This will remove the >>> prompts and convert the console output lines to Python comments by prepending them with "#~".

Notice that within the Console menu, there are several additional options for editing commands at the prompt, such as *Indent/Unindent* for formatting a multiline function definition, *Clear Line* for erasing the current line, and *Clear All* for erasing the entire console history so far.

Editing and Running Script Files

You can quickly load, edit, and run existing scripts as well as create new ones in Blender's built-in *Text Editor*. It provides some basic Python programming support like line numbers and syntax highlighting. The main advantage of using the Text Editor is you can quickly run a script, observe its effects in the 3D Viewport or another area of Blender, make revisions to the script as necessary, and repeat, without having to switch back and forth between an external editor and Blender. Figure 1-4 shows the *Text Editor's* user interface when it first starts up without a file loaded.

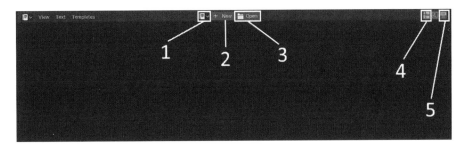

Figure 1-4. *Text Editor at startup without a file loaded. (1) Click the button to show the list of newly created files or files loaded from disk. (2) Create a new script file. (3) Open an existing script file on disk. (4) Toggle the display of line numbers in scripts. (5) Toggle syntax highlighting*

Let's open one of Blender's built-in template script files in the Text Editor. On the top menu bar, click *Templates ➤ Python ➤ Ui Panel Simple*. You'll see the contents of the file ui_panel_simple.py linked in as a new text data block and displayed inside the Text editor, as shown in Figure 1-5.

11

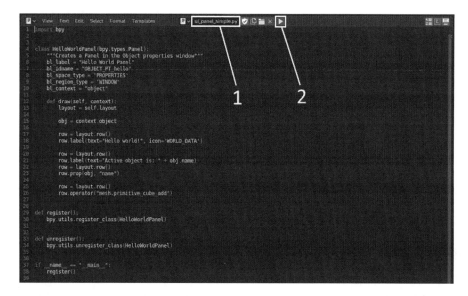

Figure 1-5. *(1) The built-in template file* ui_panel_simple.py *loaded as a text data block in the Text editor. (2) After the file is open, a Run Script button appears, which looks like a "play" button*

Try running the script you just opened, ui_panel_simple.py, by clicking the *Run Script* button (which appears to the right of the *Open Text* button after at least one script is loaded or created, as shown in Figure 1-5). You should see a new panel titled *Hello World Panel* pop-up under the *Properties Editor* ➤ *Object tab*, as shown in Figure 1-6. The Properties Editor is by default located at the lower right corner of the Scripting workspace. Note that you may need to scroll down in the *Object tab* to make the panel visible.

Figure 1-6. *Running the built-in sample script* ui_panel_simple.py *creates a new panel titled Hello World Panel in the Properties Editor* ➤ *Object tab*

Multiple text data blocks can be linked in the Text Editor simultaneously; however, only *one* can be active at a time to be edited or run. To select a different block as active and show its contents in the Text Editor, click the Text button to expand the list of currently linked blocks, then, click the name of any block in the list to make it active, as shown in Figure 1-7. The list of linked blocks includes any script files loaded from disk as well as new blocks created during your current Blender session.

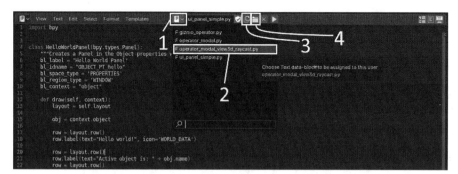

Figure 1-7. *Text Editor with several scripts in memory. (1) Click the Text button to expand the list of currently linked data blocks, which may include newly created blocks as well as files loaded from disk. (2) You can click the name of any block in the list to make it the current active block. (3) Click the New Text button to create a new text data block. (4) Click the Open Text button to select and load a script file from disk*

Displaying Operator Calls in the Info Editor

Most of the actions you perform in Blender are implemented as operators under the hood, which means they can be either carried out by hand (e.g., by clicking a menu item or using a hotkey) or invoked via the Blender Python API by executing a Python script, running an add-on, or entering a command in the built-in Python Console.

In the Scripting workspace, the *Info Editor* is displayed in the lower left corner by default, as shown in Figure 1-8. Regardless of how an action is initiated, Blender automatically logs the corresponding operator call in the Info Editor, along with any associated error or warning messages. Observing the operator call log is a great way to learn how to automate tasks in Python, since you can perform an action by hand and watch which operator gets called in the log to find out how you can emulate the same action in a script. The operator log is also a great resource for debugging a script, since it records the sequence of operator calls leading up to the error that causes the script to fail or exit unexpectedly.

Note that to streamline the amount of traffic in the *Info Editor*, by default, Blender only logs calls of operators with the REGISTER option enabled. To enable logging of all operator calls, you can either use the option --debug-wm when starting Blender from the command line or set bpy.app.debug_wm to True in the Python Console, like this:

```
>>> bpy.app.debug_wm = True
```

Let's run a built-in Python operator and verify it gets logged in the Info Editor. An **operator** in Blender is a tool that does one unit of work. Generally speaking, when you press a button, click a menu item, or use a hotkey in Blender, you are accessing an operator under the hood. For example, one of the most common tasks during mesh modeling is scaling an object. Select a mesh object in the viewport, and switch that object to *Edit mode*. Press *A* to select all of the object's vertices, then *s*, *Z*, and *2*, followed by a left mouse click to confirm. You should see the mesh scaled to 200% in the Z direction and find the corresponding operator call appear in the Info Editor, as shown in Listing 1-3.

Listing 1-3. Operator call corresponding to scaling an object by 200% in the Z direction logged in the Info Editor

```
bpy.ops.transform.resize(value=(1, 1, 2), ↵
orient_type='GLOBAL', ↵
orient_matrix=((1, 0, 0),(0, 1, 0),(0, 0, 1)), ↵
orient_matrix_type='GLOBAL', ↵
constraint_axis=(False, False, True), ↵
mirror=True, use_proportional_edit=False, ↵
proportional_edit_falloff='SMOOTH', ↵
proportional_size=1, ↵
use_proportional_connected=False, ↵
use_proportional_projected=False,
snap=False, snap_elements={'INCREMENT'}, ↵
use_snap_project=False, snap_target='CLOSEST', ↵
use_snap_self=True, use_snap_edit=True,
use_snap_nonedit=True, ↵
use_snap_selectable=False)
```

This means that when you press the *s* key, you are really accessing the `bpy.ops.transform.resize()` operator behind the scenes. Pressing the *z* key constrains scaling to the Z axis by setting the operator's `constraint_axis` parameter to `(False, False, True)`. Pressing the 2 key sets the scaling factor to 200% by setting the operator's `value` parameter to `(1, 1, 2)`.

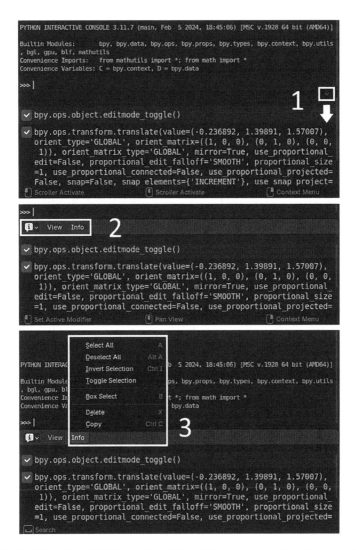

Figure 1-8. *The Info Editor is by default located in the lower left corner of the Scripting workspace. Every operator call, whether initiated via a user clicking a menu, executing a script, or entering a command in the Python Console, gets logged inside the Info Editor. (1) The top menu bar of the Info Editor is hidden by default. To reveal it, click and hold LMB on the little tab on the upper right and drag it down. (2) The top menu bar of the Info Editor appears. (3) Clicking the "Info" menu expands the list of options for selecting and copying logged calls*

Note   In the Blender Python API, you will see many parameter values expressed in the form of a three-tuple, which is a sequence of three values enclosed by parentheses. The three values usually correspond to settings for the X, Y, and Z axes, respectively.

Let's say you want to reuse this operator call along with its parameter values in a Python script. You can do so easily by copying the content of the *Info Editor* onto the clipboard. Start by left-clicking an operator call in the *Info editor* to toggle its selection (if a single call spans multiple lines, all lines will be automatically selected). Then, press Ctrl-C on Windows or Cmd-C on Mac to copy the lines, followed by Ctrl-V (Cmd-V) to paste.

Experimenting by reusing and modifying calls copied from the *Info Editor* is a great way to learn how different operators work in Blender. Let's try this with an example. Ensure that a mesh object is selected and in *Edit mode* in the 3D Viewport. Copy the call to bpy.ops.transform.resize() from the Info Editor, paste it into the Python Console at a prompt, then press enter. You should see the selected object scale to 200% in the Z direction, as if you have just pressed the key sequence *s*, *Z*, and *2* to scale it by hand.

If you want to copy multiple items logged in the Info Editor at a time, you can hold down Shift while left-clicking the calls you wish to select, or use the A key to toggle selection of the entire history.

Tip   Left-click an operator call logged in the *Info Editor* to select it (hold down Shift to select multiple), then, copy it to the clipboard with *Ctrl-C (Cmd-C on Mac)* or *RMB* ➤ *Copy*. You can also select the entire log history at once with the A key.

As you experiment with different parts of the Blender Python API, it might be more convenient to open the *Info Editor* under other workspaces than Scripting. You can do so by selecting Info as the Editor type in any view area as shown in Figure 1-9.

Figure 1-9. *You can switch to the Info Editor in any view area. (1) Left-click the Editor type at the top left corner of any view area. (2) Left-click Info to switch to the Info Editor*

Displaying Native Python Output in the System Console

As you become more familiar with Python scripting, you might find it helpful to have the System Console open alongside Blender, since it displays additional output from your script not shown in the *Info Editor*, including print statements and the full Python stack trace, which will help you pinpoint the cause of errors. Moreover, if a script runs too long or gets caught in an infinite loop, you can stop its execution by pressing *Ctrl-C* or *Ctrl-Z* in the System Console.

If you're a Windows user, you can open or dismiss the System Console with *Window ➤ Toggle System Console* or by calling the following operator in the Python Console:

```
>>> bpy.ops.wm.console_toggle()
```

When summoned, the System Console will appear in its own separate window, as opposed to being nested as a view area inside Blender. The history inside the System Console will be retained throughout a Blender session even if you were to toggle it on and off.

If you are on Linux or OSX, you must start Blender from an open terminal, and that same terminal doubles as your Python System Console.

Using an IDE to Write Your Scripts

If you're an experienced Python programmer, you probably already have a favorite *IDE* (*Integrated Development Environment*). If you're just starting out, once you get a bit more comfortable with Python, it's usually a good idea to start using an IDE as well, instead of the built-in Text Editor.

Although you could write all of your scripts in the built-in Text Editor, IDEs are tailored around software development and therefore offer many functionalities such as intelligent code completions, refactoring tools, call hierarchy searches, and debugging and profiling options that are not available in the Text Editor. As you develop add-ons with increasing complexity, potentially spanning several files, you'll likely find managing your add-ons easier with an IDE.

There are many open source as well as commercial Python IDEs available online. The choice ultimately comes down to your personal preference, as any Python IDE can be used to develop Blender scripts.

Finding the Corresponding Script Function to a Command

One of the things you'll often find yourself doing while making add-ons (which we'll start doing in Chapter 2) is figuring out which Blender API function corresponds to a given action. In this section, I'll show you some tricks I use to speed along the process.

Finding Script Functions or Properties Through Tool Tips

If you hover over any button or menu entry in Blender and pause, a tool tip appears that shows a description of the item, followed by its corresponding Python API function or property (as shown in Figures 1-10 and 1-11, respectively). If this feature is not enabled by default in your particular version of Blender, you can enable it by going to *Edit* ➤ *Preferences…* ➤ *Interface* ➤ *Display* and check the *User Tooltips* and *Python Tooltips* boxes (make sure both boxes are checked). The *User Tooltips* box toggles the display of tool tips, while the *Python Tooltips* box toggles whether the corresponding Python operators are shown inside the tool tips.

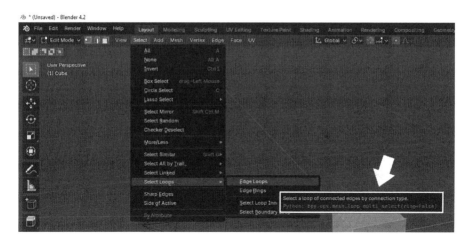

Figure 1-10. *The tool tip displayed for the menu option Select* ➤ *Select Loops* ➤ *Edge Loops, which shows its corresponding Blender Python operator, bpy.ops.mesh.loop_multi_select(ring=False)*

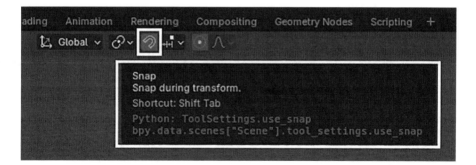

Figure 1-11. Hover over the Snap button in the 3D Viewport to display its tool tip, which shows a description of its functionality along with its corresponding Blender Python variable, bpy.data. scenes["Scene"].tool_settings.use_snap

Example: Python Operator Behind a Menu Option

Figure 1-10 shows the tool tip for *Select* ➤ *Select Loops* ➤ *Edge Loops*, which is a menu option available for a mesh object in *Edit mode* in the 3D Viewport. Based on the tool tip, the option corresponds to the bpy operator bpy.ops.mesh.loop_multi_select(ring=False). You could see right away that this is a function as opposed to a variable from the parentheses. Furthermore, ring=False tells you that the operator takes one argument named ring, with the default value False when none is given.

bpy.ops, Context, and Context Override

bpy.ops is a module under the Blender Python API which contains many of the most commonly used operators that perform tasks based on the user *context* (what the user has currently selected in a particular area of Blender). You may have noticed that bpy.ops.mesh.loop_multi_select(ring=False) does *not* let you specify which mesh or where on a mesh to select the edge loop. When a user manually interacts with Blender, the operator infers where to make the loop selection based on what the user has currently selected in the 3D Viewport.

If the same operator is invoked from a Python script or add-on, there are two possibilities: the first being the Python script is purposed as an interactive tool, such that it expects the user to make the appropriate selection before running it. The second being the script automates some task on its own without human input and therefore has to create a proper context for the operator to act upon.

Depending on the nature of the operator, having the "right context" could mean many things, such as having the right type of object selected in the right area, having the active or selected object in a certain mode, or having access to a certain editor type (like the 3D Viewport or the UV Editor). "Faking" the context in which an operator runs from Python is called ***context override***, which we'll see many examples of throughout the book.

Example: Python Variable Behind a Setting

Figure 1-11 shows the tool tip displayed when you hover over the *Snap* button in the top menu bar in the *3D Viewport.* The button's corresponding Blender Python item is bpy.data.scenes["Scene"]. tool_settings.use_snap. You could tell right away that this is a variable since there are no trailing parentheses. Because a button is either pressed or not pressed, you would have probably guessed that bpy.data. scenes["Scene"].tool_settings.use_snap is a boolean value which is either True (pressed) or False (not pressed). Testing this by entering bpy. data.scenes["Scene"].tool_settings.use_snap in the Python console confirms this:

```
>>> bpy.data.scenes["Scene"].tool_settings.use_snap
False
```

If you start with the *Snap* button unpressed, the console will show that `bpy.data.scenes["Scene"].tool_settings.use_snap` is `False`. If you then set its value to `True` in the Python console, you will see the *Snap* button become pressed in the 3D Viewport:

```
>>> bpy.data.scenes["Scene"].tool_settings.use_snap = True
```

Although this feature is not available for all menus and buttons, while a tool tip is showing, you can sometimes press Ctrl-C to copy the Python function displayed inside that tool tip to the clipboard. For example, if you hover over *Select* ➤ *Select Loops* ➤ *Edge Loops* from Figure 1-10 and hit Ctrl-C (Cmd-C on Mac), the line `bpy.ops.mesh.loop_multi_select(ring=False)` will be copied to the clipboard. You can then use Ctrl-V (Cmd-V on Mac) to paste it in the Python console or Text Editor to run it or use it as a search term to look it up in the Blender Python API documentation. On the other hand, hitting Ctrl-C while the Snap button's tool tip is showing (Figure 1-11) does *not* copy anything.

Secondary Scripting Helper Menu

A secondary context-sensitive menu with additional scripting related options could be brought up by right-clicking a menu item or button. If this feature is not enabled by default in your particular version of Blender, you can enable it by going to *Edit* ➤ *Preferences...* ➤ *Interface* ➤ *Display* and checking the *Developer Extras* box. Depending on the menu item or button, the additional options may include some or all of the following:

- Copy Data Path (*Shift-Ctrl-C*), which copies the RNA datapath of the item to the clipboard. As you will see in the upcoming chapters, you can use the RNA datapath of a UI element to determine how to access and manipulate its value in Python.

- Online Manual (F1), which opens a web browser tab showing the item's page in the Blender Reference Manual (`https://www.blender.org/manual/`).

- Online Python Reference, which opens a browser tab that shows the item's corresponding Python function in the Blender API documentation (`https://docs.blender.org/api/current/index.html`).

- Edit Source, which automatically loads the menu item's source (*.py) file into the built-in Text Editor for inspection, such as the example shown in Figure 1-12.

Figure 1-12 shows an example of how to load a menu item's Python source file via *Edit Source* in that item's secondary context menu (right-click) using the following steps:

1. Switch to the Modeling workspace: Find the *Snap* button located at the top of the *3D Viewport.*

2. Right-click the *Snap* button to bring up its context menu: Left-click *Edit Source.*

3. You'll see the notification "See 'space_view3d.py' in the text editor" appear at the bottom of the 3D Viewport (note that the notification will disappear after a few seconds): This tells you the Python source file containing the implementation for the *Snap* button has been loaded into the Text Editor and the name of the file is space_view3d.py.

4. Switch to the Scripting workspace: Go to the Text
    Editor. Click the *Text* icon at the top to expand the
    drop-down of all currently linked text data blocks.
    Click the block named `space_view3d.py` in the
    drop-down to make it active. Refer to Figure 1-7
    under the section "Editing and Running Script Files"
    for more detail.

5. The contents of `space_view3d.py` will be shown
    inside the Text Editor with the cursor (colored in
    blue) automatically scrolled to the part of the code
    that implements the *Snap* button.

Figure 1-12. *Loading the Snap button's Python source file in the Text Editor via "Edit Source". (1) Find the Snap button in the top menu bar in the 3D Viewport. (2) Right-click the button to expand its secondary context menu, and left-click "Edit Source". (3) The notification "See 'space_view3d.py' in the text editor" will appear at the bottom of the 3D Viewport, letting you know that the Python source file implementing the operator for the Snap button has been loaded in the text editor. (4) Go to the Text Editor, and click the Text button to expand the list of currently linked text data blocks. Click "*`space_view3d.py`*" to make it active. (5) You should see the contents of* `space_view3d.py` *appear in the Text Editor, with the cursor automatically scrolled to the portion of the code that implements the Snap button. If line numbers are not showing, you can toggle it with the Line Numbers button on the upper right*

Context-Sensitive Search Box

If you're not sure where a menu item is located or what its exact name is, Blender has a search box that lets you type in a partial search term and retrieve a list of matches based on the current context. Since the search box is context-sensitive, given the same search term, you could get different results depending on which workspace and/or object interaction mode you are in.

The search box will match any menu entries, settings, or hotkeys available to the user while interacting with Blender based on the current context. In addition, you could look up any operator you are developing. As long as you have run the Python script to register the operator with Blender, the search box will find it, whether you've added the operator to the Blender UI or not. We will see several examples of how to register operators with Blender in Chapter 2.

If you have *User Tooltips* and *Python Tooltips* enabled in *Edit ▶ Preferences...* as described in the earlier section "Finding Script Functions or Properties Through Tool Tips," when you hover over an item in the search results, a tool tip will pop up showing that item's corresponding Python function or property.

Moreover, if you left-click an item in the search results, Blender will execute it and automatically log any associated Python calls in the *Info Editor*, provided that you have set `bpy.app.debug_wm` to `True` as described in the earlier section "Displaying Operator Calls in the Info Editor."

Let's try looking up an operator and running it through the search box. Navigate to the 3D Viewport, select a mesh object, and switch it to *Edit mode*. Select all of the mesh's edges with the *A* key. Then, bring up the search box, and type in "sub" as a partial search term, as shown in Figure 1-13. If you hover over one of the entries marked "Subdivide", you will see a tool tip showing its corresponding `bpy.ops` operator, `bpy.ops.mesh.subdivide()`.

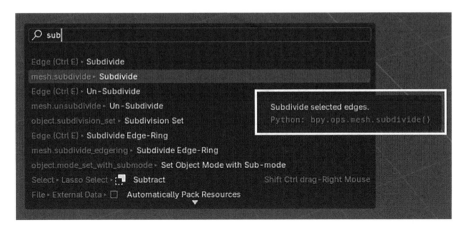

Figure 1-13. *With a mesh in Edit mode selected in the 3D Viewport, enter the partial term "sub" in the search box to look up Subdivide. Hovering over one of the matching entries in the results will show the tool tip containing Subdivide's corresponding operator,* bpy.ops. mesh.subdivide()

Left-click Subdivide in the search results to execute it. You should see your selected mesh subdivided in the 3D Viewport. You could also verify that the call to *bpy.ops.mesh.subdivide()* has been logged in the Info Editor.

If you have written an operator of your own that deforms a mesh, you could test it in a similar way as Subdivide, by bringing up the search box in the 3D Viewport, searching for your operator by name, then running it, and checking the log in the Info Editor.

Configuring Key Bindings for the Search Box

There are multiple ways that you can configure key bindings for the search box. If you are used to using the spacebar to bring up the search like in older versions of Blender, you could go to *Edit* ➤ *Preferences...* ➤ *Keymap* ➤ *Preferences* ➤ *Spacebar Action* and left-click *Search* to select it, as shown in Figure 1-14.

Figure 1-14. *You can configure the spacebar to bring up the search box, by going to Edit ➤ Preferences... ➤ Keymap ➤ Preferences ➤ Spacebar Action, and left-click Search to select it*

You could specify a different key than the spacebar for calling up the search box by going to *Edit ➤ Preferences... ➤ Keymap* and enter "search" in the "Search by Name" field at the top, as shown in Figure 1-15. You will then see at least one entry for "Search Menu" that is available for customization. The example in Figure 1-15 creates a key mapping to *Shift-Alt-S*. If you have previously set the *Spacebar Action* to *Search*, you'll notice that an additional key binding to the search box has been created for you, which allows you to now call up the search box in two ways: with both the key you customized and the spacebar.

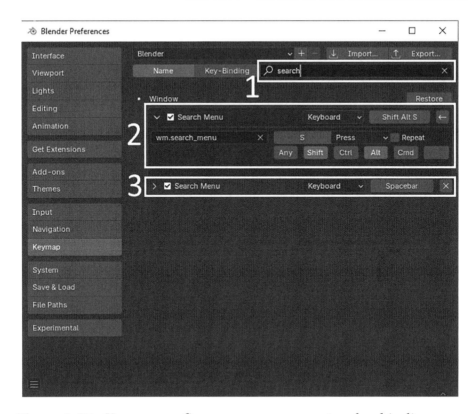

Figure 1-15. *You can configure one or more custom key bindings for calling up the search box, by going to Edit ➤ Preferences... ➤ Keymap. (1) Enter "search" at the "Search by Name" field at the top. (2) You should see at least one key binding to Search Menu that could be customized. The example shown in the figure sets the key to Shift-Alt-S. (3) If you have previously set the Spacebar Action to Search, you'll notice that an additional key binding to the search box is created for you*

Summary

In this chapter, you learned how to interact with Blender's Scripting workspace, through editing a mesh by entering commands in the built-in Python Console, as well as loading and running scripts in the Text Editor. You also learned about resources to help you develop and debug your scripts, such as the built-in Template Files, which can be used as starting points of scripts, and Developer Extras, which provide additional features for looking up Python implementation behind an operator. Along the way, you picked up many strategies for finding out the corresponding Python operators for menu items and hotkeys you see in Blender, such as the Python tool tips and context-sensitive search box. Coming up in Chapter 2, you'll learn the basic structures of Blender add-ons and operators and how to make your own operator and add it to a menu and create your first add-on with an UI panel in the Properties Editor.

CHAPTER 2

Getting Started with Operators and Add-Ons

In this chapter, you'll build your first add-on from the ground up. We'll cover everything from where to look for inspiration, how to formulate designs, to writing operators and assembling them into add-ons. By the end of the chapter, you'll have created a simple add-on complete with a custom UI panel.

The first part of the chapter will show you how to formulate add-on designs at a high level and explain ways to automate the same tasks you would perform by hand with Python. The second part of the chapter will walk you through putting together your first add-on step by step. We'll start with the basic structure of a Blender operator, which is a Python class that performs a basic unit of work, then go over how to compose add-ons using one or more operators. We continue the discussion with different types of add-on user interfaces and ways to implement them. Finally, we'll conclude by reviewing how to prepare an add-on for publication.

© Isabel Lupiani 2025
I. Lupiani, *Blender Scripting with Python*, https://doi.org/10.1007/979-8-8688-1127-2_2

Formulating a Plan to Automate a Task

From a user's perspective, add-ons roughly fall into two categories: helper tools and generation tools. *Helper tools* make life easier by performing mundane or repetitive tasks for you or automating jobs that are tricky to get right by hand. *Generation tools* create partial or complete pieces of assets on their own from input data, with or without user-configured parameters—for example, rigs from existing models or textures from photos.

A great way to come up with inspiration for designing new tools is to observe either your own or a fellow artist's workflow and look for tasks that tend to be repetitive and have predictable inputs. Once you see a pattern emerge, think about how you would reproduce the actions you'd do by hand with Python operators (see the section "Finding the Corresponding Script Function to a Command" from Chapter 1). Try to separate the parameters or settings from the actions themselves. For example, if the task at hand is scaling a mesh to 80% of its size, then *scale* is the action, and the 80% is the *parameter*. This step will help you decide which settings you should make configurable to the users of your add-on.

Here is a summary of how to approach add-on building at a high level:

1. Think about the series of steps you go through when performing a task by hand.

2. Look up the Blender Python API functions or variables that correspond to these steps.

3. Experiment by calling these functions or assigning values to these variables in the built-in Python Console with a sample set of parameters.

4. Think about how different values for the parameters change the outcome of the tasks, and consider which of them you want the users of your add-on to be able to change.

5. Implement an add-on based on the sketch you made with steps 3 and 4.

6. Run, debug, and confirm that the add-on has the desired behaviors and produces the correct results.

Accessing Add-Ons

We'll start with an overview of the types of add-ons, how to install/ uninstall and enable/disable them, how to locate source files that implement an add-on, and the general types of files making up an add-on.

Legacy vs. Extension Add-Ons

We refer to add-ons prior to Blender 4.2 as legacy add-ons, which include built-in add-ons that can be enabled under *Edit* ➤ *Preferences...* ➤ *Add-ons*, as well as add-ons implemented by third-parties or users themselves that are installed locally from *.zip files.

Blender 4.2 introduces extensions, which include add-ons and themes that an end user can install from online repositories (though it's also possible to install them from a local repository on the user's disk or from zip files).

Legacy and extension add-ons differ in the way their metadata are authored. A legacy add-on has a bl_info struct inside __init__.py with its id, version, name, description, etc., whereas an extension add-on stores such data in a blender_manifest.toml file. In addition, an extensions repo must host a *.JSON file which lists all the packages available based on their blender_manifest.toml files.

We will look at how to write a bl_info struct for a legacy add-on and convert that to a blender_manifest.toml file for an extension later in this chapter.

Enable Built-In Legacy Add-ons

You can find legacy add-ons shipped with your version of Blender under
Edit ➤ *Preferences...* ➤ *Add-ons*, as shown in Figure 2-1. To enable
(disable) an add-on, simply check (uncheck) its check box. You can also
find the link to the add-on's online documentation and the button to
uninstall it, by clicking the angle bracket preceding the add-on's check box
to expand its listing.

Figure 2-1. *You can find built-in legacy add-ons under Edit ➤
Preferences... ➤ Add-ons. (1) Click the angle bracket to expand an
add-on's listing for more info. (2) Each add-on's listing includes a link
to its online documentation. Even though the button only says "docs.
blender.org", it actually takes you to the page specific to the add-on
under the manual of the current Blender version. (3) To enable an
add-on, simply check its check box*

Installing Extensions

You can find extensions under *Edit ➤ Preferences... ➤ Get Extensions*, as shown in Figure 2-2. Use the drop-down at the top to filter the type of extensions shown (which is either Add-ons or Themes). The installed extensions are listed first, followed by those available to install, based on the repositories configured under the Repositories drop-down at the upper right. You can uninstall an extension by expanding its entry in the installed list, then clicking the "v" at the upper right corner, and clicking the Uninstall option in the menu.

Figure 2-2. *You can install extensions under Edit ➤ Preferences...*
➤ Get Extensions. (1) Select Add-ons to filter the type of extensions
shown. (2) Click the Repositories drop-down to edit the list of
repositories used to populate the list of available extensions. (3) List
of already installed extensions. (4) To uninstall an extension, click the
"v" at the upper right-hand corner of an extension's listing, followed
by Uninstall. (5) List of extensions available. Click the Install button
(6) to install an extension

Caution   If you install an extension add-on via *Edit ➤ Preferences...*
➤ *Get Extensions*, it will also show up under *Edit ➤ Preferences...*
➤ *Add-ons*. However, you will only be able to uninstall it from *Edit ➤*
Preferences... ➤ Get Extensions.

Examining Add-On Source Files

One of the best ways to learn how to write scripts is to study an existing add-on, by taking apart its source files and examining the code in parts, especially if you're already familiar with the add-on's behavior.

The source files for legacy and extension add-ons are structured the same way except for their metadata. In addition, many well-reputed and popular add-ons are still yet to be converted to extensions at the time of writing; therefore, it is worth familiarizing yourself with both types of add-ons.

Locating Built-In Legacy Add-On Source Files Under a Blender Installation

We'll start by locating the source (`*.py`) files for add-ons listed under *Edit* ➤ *Preferences...* ➤ *Add-ons*. Let's call the directory that you've installed Blender to <Blender dir>. For example, if you're a Windows user and have installed Blender 4.2 to the default directory, your <Blender dir> will be a path similar to the following:

```
C:\Program Files\Blender Foundation\Blender 4.2
```

You can then find the add-on source files under

```
C:\Program Files\Blender Foundation\Blender 4.2\4.2\scripts\addons_core
```

In other words, the add-on source files will be in the folder

```
<Blender dir>\<Blender version>\scripts\addons_core
```

Structure of a Legacy Add-On Package

Let's do a case study on one of the legacy add-ons shipped with Blender, *VR Scene Inspection*. Its source files are located in the folder, `<Blender dir>\<Blender version>\scripts\addons_core\viewport_vr_preview`, as shown in Figure 2-3. You'll notice that the add-on's name *VR Scene Inspection* under *Edit* ➤ *Preferences...* ➤ *Add-ons* is a human-friendly name, which does not necessarily match the add-on's Python package name (which is also the name of its folder).

Python code that spans multiple files is organized into a hierarchy of *packages* and *modules*. You can intuitively think of a package as a folder that contains an `__init__.py` file as its entry point, plus (optionally) other `*.py` files that implement modules used by the package, with each `*.py` file corresponding to a module of the same name.

Note   In general, `__init__.py` files are used to mark directories as containing Python packages. This is true whether you are working with Blender Python or Python in general (outside of Blender).

Name	Date modified	Type	Size
configs	7/17/2024 12:24 AM	File folder	
__init__.py	6/5/2024 9:01 PM	Python Source File	2 KB
action_map.py	6/5/2024 9:01 PM	Python Source File	6 KB
action_map_io.py	6/5/2024 9:01 PM	Python Source File	13 KB
defaults.py	6/5/2024 9:01 PM	Python Source File	75 KB
gui.py	6/5/2024 9:01 PM	Python Source File	10 KB
operators.py	6/5/2024 9:01 PM	Python Source File	17 KB
properties.py	6/5/2024 9:01 PM	Python Source File	8 KB
versioning.py	6/5/2024 9:01 PM	Python Source File	2 KB

Figure 2-3. *The source files for the built-in legacy add-on VR Scene Inspection. The add-on's Python package name is viewport_vr_preview, which also matches the name of the folder containing its* `__init__.py` *file*

In the case of *viewport_vr_preview*, its package is one-level, with a single folder containing an __init__.py plus other *.py files implementing its modules, as shown below:

```
viewport_vr_preview          (top-level folder name and Python
                              package name)
↳   __init__.py                    (entry point to the
                                    package)
↳   action_map.py                  (implements the module named
                                    action_map)
↳ action_map_io.py           (implements the module named
                                    action_map_io)

↳   ...
```

Most add-ons spanning multiple *.py files are packaged this way, with an __init__.py containing the main structure of the add-on, which in turn references operators and functions defined in other *.py files located in the same folder. (Though the latter is optional, it's possible for __init__.py to implement the entire add-on on its own without referencing other *.py files.)

In addition to housing the main structure and serving as the entry point to the add-on, __init__.py will contain code for registering/unregistering the add-on with Blender and initializing and destroying bpy. Scene variables used by the add-on.

To structure more complex add-ons, you can use nested packages of several levels, with an __init__.py at each level, like the following:

```
package
↳   __init__.py
↳   module_1.py
↳   ...
↳   sub-package_1
```

```
↳    ↳    __init__.py
↳    ↳    module_1_1.py
↳    ↳    ...
```

The built-in add-on *Edit ➤ Preferences... ➤ Add-ons ➤ glTF 2.0 Format*
is an example of an add-on that uses nested Python packages, with
io_scene_gltf2 as its top-level package and an __init__.py for each
subpackage nested under. You can find io_scene_gltf2's source files in
the directory:

```
<Blender dir>\<Blender version>\scripts\addons_core\io_scene_gltf2
```

We will take a closer look at the inner working of *.py files that make up
an add-on as we work through this chapter.

Locating Extension Add-On Source Files on Disk

Let's look at an add-on installed from extensions.blender.org to see how
we can locate its source files on disk. To demonstrate, I have installed the
extension *GeoNode Shape Keys* to the default directory. After installation,
I can find the add-on under *Edit ➤ Preferences... ➤ Get Extensions ➤
Installed*, as shown in Figure 2-4. If I click the ">" next to the extension's
name, I can expand its listing to show "Path", which tells me where the
extension is installed on disk:

```
C:\Users\<your user name>\AppData\Roaming\ ↵
Blender Foundation\Blender\ ↵
<Blender version>\extensions\blender_org\geonode_shapekeys
```

Under this directory, I will find *GeoNode Shape Keys*'s source files,
as shown in Figure 2-5, which consists of an __init__.py file and other
*.py files, plus a blender_manifest.toml file, which replaces bl_info in
a legacy add-on. The name of the folder geonode_shapekeys matches the
extension's Python package name.

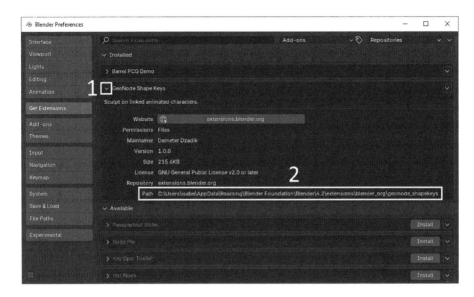

Figure 2-4. *Locating the path to the source files of an installed extension. Go to Edit ➤ Preferences... ➤ Get Extensions. Locate the add-on in the "Installed" section at the top. (1) Click the ">" to the left of the extension's name to expand its listing. (2) The path to the add-on's source files is the last entry in the listing*

Name	Date modified	Type	Size
__pycache__	7/30/2024 12:42 PM	File folder	
__init__.py	7/30/2024 12:42 PM	Python Source File	2 KB
blender_manifest.toml	7/30/2024 12:42 PM	Toml Source File	1 KB
geonodes.blend	7/30/2024 12:42 PM	Blender 4.2	1,421 KB
operators.py	7/30/2024 12:42 PM	Python Source File	22 KB
prefs.py	7/30/2024 12:42 PM	Python Source File	3 KB
props.py	7/30/2024 12:42 PM	Python Source File	3 KB
README.md	7/30/2024 12:42 PM	Markdown Source...	3 KB
ui.py	7/30/2024 12:42 PM	Python Source File	4 KB

Windows (C:) › Users › isabe › AppData › Roaming › Blender Foundation › Blender › 4.2 › extensions › blender_org › geonode_shapekeys

Figure 2-5. *The source files for the extension GeoNode Shape Keys, which are located in a directory named geonode_shapekeys, matching its Python package name. Notice that the package contains a* `blender_manifest.toml` *file*

Tip   To change the directory the extensions from a repo are installed to on disk, go to *Edit* ➤ *Preferences...* ➤ *Get Extensions*. Expand the "Repository" drop-down at the upper right, click the repository you want to modify the installation path for, then go to the "Advanced" section at the bottom to change the directory.

Template Files

Another great resource for learning Python scripting is Blender's built-in template files. In the Text Editor under the Scripting workspace, click *Templates* ➤ *Python* to reveal the list of all available script templates. The templates cover a few different areas of script development, including various UI (user interface) elements, file input/output, modal operators, mesh editing, game logic, and so on. Each template file is a runnable sample script that performs a simple task.

For example, if you click *Templates* ➤ *Python* ➤ *Operator File Import* to load the template file operator_file_import.py into the Text Editor and click the *Run Script* button, it'll open up a file import dialog. As you can see, the template by itself doesn't do much, but that's okay—because it's not meant to be a complete add-on but rather show an example of how you can use file input as part of a script.

A great way to poke your head around the templates is to open one up, run it, observe the output (if there is any), modify parts of the script, and run it again to see if its behaviors adjust like you anticipated. If you have a specific idea in mind for an add-on or script, you can also use one of the related template files as a starting point.

You can find the template source files on disk under your Blender installation in the following directory:

```
<Blender dir>\<Blender version>\scripts\templates_py
```

Once you're more comfortable with scripting, you can create and copy your own *.py template files to this directory and make them accessible inside the Text Editor under Templates ➤ Python alongside the built-in template files.

Overview of Built-In Modules of the Blender API

Before diving into operators and add-ons, let's look at some of the most frequently used API modules and what they do. Most of the functionalities you'll use will be in the module bpy (which, you've probably guessed, stands for Blender Python!). Importing bpy in your script will give you access to all the submodules under bpy.

The bpy.ops submodule contains most of the built-in operators. An operator is a tool that does a small unit of work in Blender, such as bridging two edge loops, scaling an object by a factor, and so on. The bpy.ops submodule is further divided into more modules, such as bpy.ops.mesh which contains mesh editing-related operators, bpy.ops.armature which provides the operators for manipulating armatures, and so on.

The bpy.context module provides access to the current context. A context in Blender contains information such as the scene, objects, screen space, and tool settings related to the area of Blender the mouse cursor is currently hovering over, like the 3D Viewport, UV/Image Editor, and so on. Some operators will only work in certain contexts.

The bpy.data module gives you access to all the data contained in the current *.blend file, including textures (bpy.data.textures), materials (bpy.data.materials), meshes (bpy.data.meshes), images (bpy.data. images), and so on. You can see a complete list of the types of data accessible via bpy.data by using the Autocomplete feature in the Python Console (by typing bpy.data. at the prompt, followed by Console ➤ Autocomplete) or by looking up the bpy.data module in the Blender API documentation.

There are several other API modules that we'll learn about as we proceed through the book.

Basic Structure of Operators

Let's take apart one of the built-in template files to study the basic structure of an operator. Open a default startup `.blend` file, then open the Operator Simple template file from the Templates ➤ Python menu in the Text Editor.

If you are using Windows and don't have a System Console window open, invoke one with Window ➤ Toggle System Console. If you are on Linux or OSX, you must start Blender from an open terminal window.

Rather than diving directly into code, let's first run the script and find out what it does. Click the Run Script button at the top of the Text Editor. Nothing seems to have happened in the 3D Viewport. However, if you look at the System Console, you'll notice some messages similar to the following have been printed:

```
<bpy_struct, Object("Cube") at 0x000001D3D6740820>
<bpy_struct, Object("Light") at 0x000001D3D6740120>
<bpy_struct, Object("Camera") at 0x000001D3D6743220>
```

The script lists the objects in the current scene along with their addresses in memory (the strings above that start with "0x"). The memory addresses will likely look different on your system.

Now that you know what the operator does, let's go back to the script `operator_simple.py` to see how it's implemented. First, you'll notice that the module `bpy` is imported at the top of the file via the line:

```
import bpy
```

Let's take a look at `class SimpleOperator`, which is partially reproduced in the following code snippet. This is the portion of the script responsible for the operator's behavior.

```
class SimpleOperator(bpy.types.Operator):
    """Tooltip"""
    bl_idname = "object.simple_operator"
    bl_label = "Simple Object Operator"
```

The SimpleOperator class derives from the base class bpy.types. Operator. Every operator derives from bpy.types.Operator, which is a built-in Blender API type that defines the common set of methods and data all operators must provide to function properly. Operators can derive from additional bpy types, if their functionality depends on them.

In addition to defining its behavior, an operator's class specifies how the operator appears in menus and tool tips and (optionally) the valid context the operator runs in. Notice that the first line inside the class is a comment starting and ending with three double quotes. This comment defines the text shown inside the tool tip displayed when you hover over the operator's menu entry or UI element (for example, its button).

The bl_idname property stores the name you would use to uniquely identify the operator internally. For example, if you're making an add-on by compositing several operators together into a group of buttons, you would use bl_idname to control which button invokes which operator. The bl_label property specifies the name displayed in menus or on the UI element for accessing the operator. For instance, if you create a button that runs the operator with each press, bl_label will be the text displayed on that button, unless specified otherwise. Note that bl_label does not need to be unique across different operators.

You can bring up the search box inside the 3D Viewport and enter "simple" to look up SimpleOperator by name. You should see the name "Simple Object Operator" come up, which matches the value assigned to its bl_label. Try assigning a different string to bl_label, click the Run Script button, then look up the operator in the search box again—you should see the entry coming up in the search this time matching the string you just changed bl_label to.

Tip   Recall in Chapter 1 you learned that you can configure the key mapping for calling up the context-sensitive search box via *Edit* ➤ *Preferences...* ➤ *Keymap*.

Next, scroll down in operator_simple.py and take a look at SimpleOperator's poll method, as reproduced here:

```
@classmethod
def poll(cls, context):
    return context.active_object is not None
```

The poll method is derived from bpy.types.Operator and determines whether the required conditions for the operator to run have been met. poll should return True if the conditions are met and False otherwise. poll is also used by Blender to determine whether to enable or disable (gray out) the operator in the menu. If you omit the poll method in your operator class, Blender will allow your operator to run at all times.

SimpleOperator's poll method checks whether the current context (such as the 3D Viewport) has a valid active object. If not, SimpleOperator is disabled and will not show up in the search box until you add a new object.

If you scroll down a little further in operator_simple.py, you'll find the SimpleOperator class' execute method, as reproduced here:

```
def execute(self, context):
    main(context)
    return {'FINISHED'}
```

The execute method is where an operator does the majority of its work. Like poll, it is also inherited from bpy.types.Operator and can be overridden. Since SimpleOperator prints the names of the scene objects to the System Console, you might reasonably expect its execute method to do just that—well almost, in this case, the task is delegated to the main method through the call to main(context), which in turn prints the scene objects in a for loop (the main method, which is reproduced in the next snippet, is located near the top of operator_simple.py).

Notice that execute returns a set containing the string 'FINISHED' to let Blender know the script ran successfully. It's customary for a Blender operator to return a set containing a string that indicates its status at the end of execution, such as {'FINISHED'} (success), {'RUNNING_MODAL'} (keep the operator running), {'CANCELED'} (no action taken), {'PASS_THROUGH'} (event is passed on to other parts of Blender), and {'INTERFACE'} (handled event as an interface, such as displaying a pop-up menu).

Note   You'd use PASS_THROUGH if you have a modal operator that does something whenever the user presses a certain key, and you want the rest of Blender to be notified of the same key press. Otherwise, your operator would "capture" the key press and prevent other parts of Blender from getting it. For instance, you'd use PASS_THROUGH if your add-on displays a message when the user presses the "K" key, and you still want the Knife tool to be triggered in Edit mode.

The next two methods you'll see in operator_simple.py are register and unregister, as shown in the following code snippet. register calls the built-in method bpy.utils.register_class to register the SimpleOperator class with Blender and make it available to users as an operator, while unregister does the opposite.

In the Blender 4.2 version of operator_simple.py, register and unregister also add and remove the SimpleOperator to the end of the Object menu in Object mode. Since adding an operator to a menu is quite involved, I will defer the discussion to the next few sections.

```
def register():
    bpy.utils.register_class(SimpleOperator)
    bpy.types.VIEW3D_MT_object.append(menu_func)

def unregister():
    bpy.utils.unregister_class(SimpleOperator)
    bpy.types.VIEW3D_MT_object.remove(menu_func)
```

The register method typically takes care of any one-time, installation related setup necessary for the add-on or operator to work properly. Depending on the add-on or operator, this might include registering various components with Blender, inserting things into menus, and so on. When you enable an add-on in the *Edit* ➤ *Preferences...* menu, Blender automatically looks up and calls the register method inside that add-on's script file. Similarly, when an add-on is disabled (or uninstalled), Blender calls the unregister method inside the add-on's script to reverse everything done by register.

Caution   register and unregister are the only two methods in your operator that Blender will directly call.

Finally, the last block of code in operator_simple.py is provided for testing purposes so you can run the script from the Text Editor and register the operator. This is to get around the fact that operator_simple.py is missing metadata required for it to be installed via *Edit* ➤ *Preferences...* (bl_info for legacy add-on or blender_manifest.toml for extension add-ons). __main__ is the name of the top-level environment in which your code is run (which might be the Text Editor, the Python Console, etc.). Therefore, the block of code is simply saying "Wherever you are running the code from, do this...". It first calls `register()` to register the `SimpleOperator` class and make it show up in Blender as a valid operator, then runs the operator by calling `bpy.ops.object.simple_operator()` (this is also how you would call `SimpleOperator` inside the Python Console or from inside another script). Notice that `SimpleOperator` is classified under the module `bpy.ops.object`. This is the default module that operators are filed under, unless otherwise specified.

```
if __name__ == "__main__":
    register()

    # test call
    bpy.ops.object.simple_operator()
```

Now that you've learned the basic structure of operators, let's think about how we can use them as building blocks to make add-ons.

Adding an Operator or Add-On to a Menu

Once you have an idea of what you want your add-on to do, you'll need to decide where to put it in the Blender interface. Depending on factors such as how an add-on interacts with the user, if it needs input, as well as the context under which it operates, you'll find certain add-ons make more sense in some menus or workspaces than others.

When deciding where to place an add-on, I like to think about it from a user's standpoint: if I were a user, where would I expect a tool to be? A mesh editing tool would most likely fit under the Mesh (or Vertex, Face, Edge) menu in Edit mode. If a tool is run repeatedly, then a keyboard shortcut would probably be convenient. If a tool functions under multiple interaction modes (e.g., in both Edit and Object modes) or requires users to enter data or configure settings before it is run, then the properties panel where the tool can be "sticky" (not go away after a menu click or mode switch) would be ideal.

The following three steps are required to add an operator or add-on to a Blender menu:

1. Define a method that creates the menu entry for the operator or add-on with the desired (and context appropriate) icon, if any.

2. Find the name of the Python class that implements the intended menu in the Blender Python API.

3. Add the menu entry created in the first step to the desired menu found in the second step in the register() method of the operator or add-on.

We'll revisit SimpleOperator and see how it is added to the Object menu as an example.

#1: Write a Method to Create the Menu Entry

The first step is to write a method that creates the menu entry. Inside the method, you'll call the built-in function self.layout.operator to create the entry. For SimpleOperator, we'll create a method called menu_func which creates a menu entry with the display text "Simple Operator" and an icon, as shown in Listing 2-1.

Listing 2-1. Adding menu_func(self, context) to operator_simple.py

```
def menu_func(self, context):
    self.layout.operator(SimpleOperator.bl_idname, ↵
    text="Simple Operator", icon="OBJECT_DATA")
```

The first parameter to `self.layout.operator` is always the `bl_idname` of your operator, which by default is also the text displayed in its menu entry (recall from the "Basic Structure of Operators" section, `bl_idname` is a string variable required for uniquely identifying each operator class). If you want to change the menu text to something else, you can supply the optional second argument `text` with a string you want displayed instead, as shown here.

You can use the optional third argument `icon` to specify an icon to be displayed next to the text of the menu entry. The value of `icon` can be any one of several Enum strings listed under the `icon` parameter of `bpy.types. UILayout.prop` in the Blender Python documentation. In this example, `OBJECT_DATA` is used to select the Object Data icon.

To help you discover which icons are available in Blender and learn which Enum string is associated with each icon, I've prepared a sample script `sample_builtin_icons_popup_display_operator.py` which implements an operator that when run displays every Blender icon with its Enum value. **The source code for this book is available on GitHub via the book's product page, located at www.apress.com/979-8-8688-1126-5.** Once downloaded, open the script in the Text Editor, click the Run button, then go over to the viewport, and press the *Space* key to bring up the search box. Type in the word "icon" in the search box to look up the operator, and click its name, `Built-in Icons Pop-up Display Operator`, to run it (as shown at the top of Figure 2-6). You should see a large window pop-up containing all the icons and their associated Enum strings (as shown at the bottom of Figure 2-6).

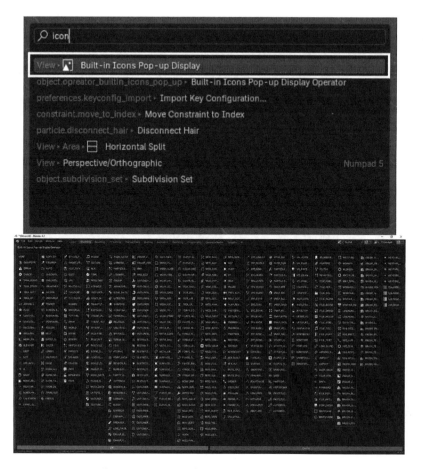

Figure 2-6. *Visualizing Blender's built-in icons. Top: After running the script in the Text Editor, call up the search box, and type in the search term "icon" to look up Built-in Icons Pop-up Display, and click it in the search results to run. Bottom: Running the operator displays a pop-up dialog showing Blender's built-in icons and their names*

#2: Find a Menu's Corresponding Python Class in the Blender Python API

If you hover over any top-level (unexpanded) menu item with the mouse cursor, the Python class that implements the menu will appear in a tool tip. For example, if you hover over *File* along the top bar, a tool tip will pop up showing the string TOPBAR_MT_file (Figure 2-7). Therefore, the *File* menu's Python class is

bpy.types.TOPBAR_MT_file

Figure 2-7. *Hover the mouse cursor over any unexpanded menu item, such as File, to bring up the tool tip containing the name of the Python class that defines the item*

Once you know the class of an unexpanded menu, the class of any of its submenus can generally be derived by appending an underscore followed by that submenu's name in lowercase. For example, using this pattern, the Python class for the submenu *File* ➤ *Import* is therefore

bpy.types.TOPBAR_MT_file_import

Unfortunately, there are some exceptions to this rule. For example, in Edit mode, the Python class for the *Mesh* menu is

bpy.types.VIEW3D_MT_edit_mesh

However, the Python class for the submenu *Mesh* ➤ *Snap* is

bpy.types.VIEW3D_MT_snap

Which is not what you'd expect based on this rule. But that's okay—later in this chapter, in the section "Finding the Python Class for a Menu Item from Its Source File," I'll show you an alternative way of finding the Python class for a menu by peeking into the source file that implements that menu's parent. It's a slightly more complicated trick, but should help in situations where this simple rule doesn't apply.

Going back to our `SimpleOperator` example, let's look at how we can add `SimpleOperator` to the *Object* menu in Object mode, which is the class

```
bpy.types.VIEW3D_MT_object
```

#3: Add the Entry to the Desired Menu

The last step is to add the newly created entry for your operator to the menu. Menus are organized as lists, so to add an entry to the *bottom* (or end) of a menu, you would call append from the menu's class (found in step #2) in the `register` method of your operator, as shown in Listing 2-2.

Listing 2-2. Adding an entry to the bottom (end) of a menu by calling append() in register()

```
def register():
    bpy.utils.register_class(<Your operator's class>)
    bpy.types.<menu's Python class (from step ↵
        #2)>.append(<menu method (from step #1)>)
```

If you want to add the entry to the *top* (or beginning) of the menu instead, you would call that menu's prepend method:

```
bpy.types.<menu's Python class (from step #2)>.prepend( ↵
    <menu method (from step #1)>)
```

The built-in `simply_operator.py` script adds the operator to the bottom of the Object menu. We'll experiment here by changing it to the *top* (beginning) of that menu instead, as shown in Figure 2-8. To do this, simply change the call from `bpy.types.VIEW3D_MT_object.`**append**`(menu_func)` to `bpy.types.VIEW3D_MT_object.`**prepend**`(menu_func)`, as shown in Listing 2-3.

Listing 2-3. Adding SimpleOperator to the top (beginning) of the Object menu by calling prepend()

```
def register():
    bpy.utils.register_class(SimpleOperator)
    bpy.types.VIEW3D_MT_object.prepend(menu_func)
```

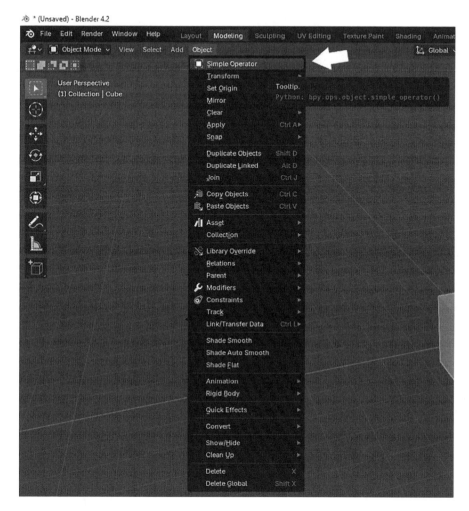

Figure 2-8. *Adding SimpleOperator to the top of the Object menu in Object mode*

Lastly, you'll need to remove the same menu entries previously added via `register` in the `unregister` function, so that when a user disables the add-on or operator, it doesn't leave behind any invalid menu entries or cause an `AttributeError` or a `ValueError` (if you do run into these issues, restarting Blender will generally fix them).

To remove menu entries, you'll call the remove method in the place of append or prepend. Listing 2-4 shows an example where SimpleOperator's menu entry is removed in the unregister method.

Listing 2-4. Removing SimpleOperator from the Object menu by calling remove() in unregister()

```
def unregister():
    bpy.utils.unregister_class(SimpleOperator)
    bpy.types.VIEW3D_MT_object.remove(menu_func)
```

Adding a Pop-Up Dialog to the Simple Operator

SimpleOperator currently prints the names of scene objects to the System Console. While this is a valid way of displaying output, users who are unfamiliar with Blender scripting will likely miss it. In this section, we'll look at how to show the same output via a different and arguably more accessible method—a pop-up dialog. You can modify your copy of operator_simple.py to follow along. You can also download the script operator_simple_popup_dialog.py which will contain all the modifications from this section in one file. **The source code for this book is available on GitHub via the book's product page, located at www.apress.com/979-8-8688-1126-5.**

To add a pop-up dialog to SimpleOperator, we need to make two changes to the SimpleOperator class. First, we need to add an invoke method to initiate the dialog and, second, a custom draw method to display the information we want inside that dialog.

The invoke method is inherited by all operators through bpy.types. Operator. When an operator is run, Blender first calls its invoke method, followed by a call to its execute method. Therefore, you would override and place all necessary prep work to get the operator ready inside invoke, then implement the operator's main task inside execute. For instance, if you're making an operator that automatically unwraps a selected mesh object, you would switch the object to Edit mode inside the operator's invoke method (since you can only unwrap in Edit mode), then unwrap the object in the operator's execute method.

Like poll, invoke, and execute, the draw method is inherited from bpy.types.Operator and is automatically called by Blender when an operator is run to render its UI (user interface) elements.

Try adding the invoke method as shown in Listing 2-5 to the SimpleOperator class just below execute, in operator_simple.py.

Listing 2-5. Adding an invoke method to the SimpleOperator class

```
def invoke(self, context, event):
    return context.window_manager.invoke_props_dialog(self)
```

context.window_manager is an object that keeps track of the windows that are currently open as well as other UI-related data for context. The call to invoke_props_dialog creates a new pop-up dialog that contains an OK button.

Run the script again in the Text Editor, then look up Simple Object Operator in the search box, and click its name to run—a dialog that looks like Figure 2-9 with the name of the operator across the top (which Blender has automatically inferred from SimpleOperator's bl_label) should appear.

Figure 2-9. *Making SimpleOperator pop up an empty dialog*

The dialog is empty since we haven't told Blender what to display yet. We'll fix this by adding a custom `draw` method to the `SimpleOperator` class to show the names of the scene objects inside the dialog. Listing 2-6 creates a layout consisting of a single box nestled inside a single column, with the list of object names printed inside the box.

Listing 2-6. Adding a custom draw() method to SimpleOperator to show names of scene objects

```
def draw(self, context):
    layout = self.layout
    col0 = layout.column()
    box0 = col0.box()

    # Display the names of the current scene objects.
    box0.label(text="Scene Objects:", icon='OBJECT_DATA')
    for ob in context.scene.objects:
        r = box0.row(align=True)
        r.label(text=str(ob.name))
```

All subclasses of `bpy.types.Operator` (`SimpleOperator` included) have a `self.layout` variable through which the organization of the operator's UI elements are defined. We start by creating a single column and assigning it to the `col10` variable. A column is a sublayout such that UI items placed in it are stacked vertically. Next, we create a box inside that column. A box is another type of sublayout, such that UI items in it are stacked vertically and there is a single box-like background enclosing all the items.

The next four lines of code print the list of scene object names inside `box0`. First, we create the label at the top of the box: the first argument being the text to display on the label, `"Scene Objects"`, and the second argument the optional icon shown next to the text (in this case, the `Object Data` icon). The following `for` loop iterates through the list of objects in the current scene. At each iteration of the loop, a new row is created inside the box, and a label is created to display the name of the object (ob.name) on that row.

Figure 2-10 shows the result of running the modified Simple Object Operator to display the list of scene object names in a pop-up dialog.

Figure 2-10. *Modified Simple Object Operator that displays the names of scene objects inside a pop-up dialog*

Creating a Custom UI Panel in the Properties Shelf

When you click the menu entry for an operator or add-on, it runs immediately based on the current context. For example, when you click *Bridge Edge Loops* in the *Edge* menu in Edit mode, it runs right away based on the currently selected mesh in the viewport. This solution is great for the types of add-ons that require responsiveness, need to be run repeatedly (back to back), or don't need to prompt users for input before they are run.

If your add-on needs to allow users to calibrate its settings before its run, you can create a UI panel for the add-on to be placed inside areas such as the Properties shelf (*N* key in viewport). For example, in the Modeling workspace, if you click Annotate on the tool shelf to activate the grease pencil, a horizontal panel of options will appear just beneath the top bar, allowing you to configure settings such as stroke color before drawing. An additional panel appears under the Properties shelf (N key) ➤ Tool tab ➤ Active Tool which duplicates the same options in the top bar.

Another circumstance appropriate for a UI panel would be if your add-on needs to run under several object interaction modes (Object mode, Edit mode, and so on). Unlike menus that disappear when a user switches from one mode to another, you can make UI panels retain their settings and remain visible under multiple modes. For example, in the Modeling workspace, if you change the stroke color of the Annotate tool to green in Object mode, the setting persists when you switch to Edit Mode, Vertex Paint Mode, etc.

Let's go through a concrete example of how to organize and assemble a UI panel for user interaction. You can download the complete script `sample_panel_properties_shelf_tool_tab.py` which will contain all the modifications from this section in one file. **The source code for this book is available on GitHub via the book's product page, located at www.apress.com/979-8-8688-1126-5.**

The bpy.types.Scene Data Block and Scene Variables

The `bpy.types.Scene` data block contains objects, animation data, and render settings for a Blender scene. Unlike variables defined within an operator class, which can only be accessed by that operator, when you declare variables under `bpy.types.Scene` in a script—which I will refer to as *scene variables*—they are accessible to all add-ons and operators that also live in that script.

When you design an add-on that is made up of several operators, you'll often need to share data between them—this is where scene variables come in handy. For example, you might need these operators to share access to the same input image, so that each operator can perform a different unit of work on it. You can define a variable under `bpy.types.Scene` like this:

```
bpy.types.Scene.<variable name> = <value>
```

For example, to make a scene variable named input_image to keep track of an image loaded into Blender (an image data block), you can do this:

```
bpy.types.Scene.input_image = <some image data block>
```

Next, I'll show you how to define properties for handling some of the most common types of user input. You'll store these properties as scene variables so they can be shared between different operators that make up an add-on. Later, I'll also show you how to consolidate these properties to be neatly displayed inside a custom UI panel.

Defining Properties as Scene Variables

The built-in Blender module bpy.props has a number of property types that you can use in your add-on to accept and store data of different types from users—IntProperty, FloatProperty, StringProperty, EnumProperty, and BoolProperty—to name a few. Each is designed to handle its designated data type in an intuitive way. For example, a property for integers or float values allows you to impose constraints like a minimum and a maximum to prevent a user from dragging a widget beyond its limits.

Properties can be hooked up directly to a UI panel and ready to receive user input. Based on each property's data type, the most intuitive widget will automatically be displayed, such as a check box for a BoolProperty, a drop-down list for an EnumProperty, and so on.

We'll create seven commonly used widgets: a text input, a dialog to open a file, a check box, a drop-down list, an integer slider, a percentage slider, and a floating point number slider. To make use of the bpy module and its property types, you need to import them at the top of the script file to bring them into scope, as shown in Listing 2-7.

Listing 2-7. Import bpy properties

```
import bpy
from bpy.props import (
    StringProperty,
    BoolProperty,
    EnumProperty,
    IntProperty,
    FloatProperty)
```

Now that the properties are imported, we'll create scene variables for each of them next.

Creating Text Input with **StringProperty**

First, you'll create a function named init_scene_vars(), in which you'll set up the various scene variables. The first property you'll create in init_scene_vars() is a StringProperty instance with the subtype 'NONE', as shown in Listing 2-8, which will become a text input widget in the UI for a user to type in a string, like the one shown in Figure 2-11.

Note that at this point in time, we have yet to add code to draw the widgets in the UI, so when you run the script, you will not yet see the text input in Figure 2-11. For now, the figures are meant to give you an idea of how the widgets will look and interact with the user. At the end of this chapter, I will show you how to assemble all the widgets you'll create in the next few sections into a panel and make it show up in the UI.

Listing 2-8. Initialize a StringProperty instance with 'NONE' subtype to create a text input field

```
def init_scene_vars():
    bpy.types.Scene.sample_text = StringProperty(
        name="Text",
```

```
description="Sample text input",
maxlen=1024,
subtype='NONE')
```

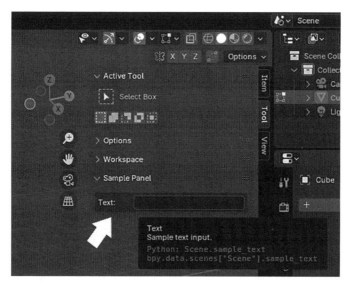

Figure 2-11. *The text-input widget implemented by* bpy.types. Scene.sample_text *from Listing 2-8, which is an instance of* StringProperty *with subtype* 'NONE'. *The user can type or paste a string into the widget*

Note   Blender follows PEP8 for styling Python code, with some customizations, one of which being that string literals for specifying Enum values should be surrounded by single quotes, while all other strings should be surrounded by double quotes.

For example, in Listing 2-8, the value 'NONE' assigned to the argument subtype for StringProperty is one of several Enum values and therefore should be surrounded by single quotes. The value "Text" assigned to the argument name is a non-Enum string literal and therefore should be surrounded by double quotes.

A text input field is useful when you need the user of your add-on to enter any kind of text, such as a name for a mesh. Notice that the value you pass to name is the text displayed to the *left* of the text box and the value passed to description is the text displayed *inside the tool tip* when you hover over the text box (notice that a period is automatically added to the end of each of these strings inside the tool tip, as shown in Figure 2-11). The argument maxlen specifies the maximum number of characters that can be entered into the box. If it's set to 0, the length is unlimited. The subtype specifies the type of input the text box is expecting, which when set to 'NONE' means plain text. Using different subtypes, you can create text boxes tailored for file names (subtype 'FILE_NAME'), passwords ('PASSWORD'), and so on.

In general, all property types have a name and a description variable that work very much the same way, with name displayed to the left of a property's widget and description shown inside the tool tip when you hover over the widget with the mouse cursor.

The next property we'll create in init_scene_vars() is an open file dialog, which is almost identical to the previous example, except with a different subtype and additional options related to loading files. Add the block of code shown in Listing 2-9 to the end of init_scene_vars() to create a StringProperty instance named bpy.types.Scene.sample_ filename.

Listing 2-9. Initialize a StringProperty instance with 'FILE_PATH' subtype to create a text input field with an open-file button

```
bpy.types.Scene.sample_filename = StringProperty(
    name="Filename",
    description="Sample filename input",
    maxlen=1024,
    subtype='FILE_PATH',
    options={'SKIP_SAVE'})
```

The subtype 'FILE_PATH' creates a text input box with a button to its right which opens a file dialog when pressed. After the user selects a file through the dialog, the path to the file is automatically copied into the text box (alternatively a user can also type in a filepath). This type of input is useful for add-ons that deal with import/export or add-ons that require users to load images or other types of files. The argument options is a set of built-in Enum strings you can use to configure file opening-related options. 'SKIP_SAVE' specifies that the filepath shouldn't be saved in presets. You can see what the open-file widget created by Listing 2-9 looks like in Figure 2-12.

Figure 2-12.   *Text input widget with open-file button, implemented by* bpy.types.Scene.sample_filename *in Listing 2-9, which is a* StringProperty *instance with subtype* 'FILE_PATH'

Creating Check Boxes with **BoolProperty**

For simple on/off type settings, check boxes are your best bet. You can easily create custom check boxes with BoolProperty instances. Add the code shown in Listing 2-10 to the end of your init_scene_vars() method to initialize a BoolProperty instance named bpy.types.Scene.sample_ checkbox

Listing 2-10. Initialize a `BoolProperty` instance to create a check box widget

```
bpy.types.Scene.sample_checkbox = bpy.props.BoolProperty(
    name="Checkbox",
    description="Sample checkbox",
    default=True)
```

Unlike other property types, the name of a `BoolProperty` instance is displayed to the right of the check box as opposed to its left, as shown in Figure 2-13. If the `default` variable is set to `True`, the check box is checked when it is first loaded.

Figure 2-13. *Check box widget implemented by* `bpy.types.Scene.` `sample_checkbox` *in Listing 2-10, which is a* `BoolProperty` *instance. Since the* `default` *argument is set to* `True`, *the check box is checked when first loaded*

Creating Drop-Down Lists with `EnumProperty`

If you need the user of your add-on to configure a setting by selecting one from a list of several options, you can create a drop-down list by defining an `EnumProperty` instance with the available options as its items. For example, to set up a drop-down list with three options `Apple`, `Pear`, and `Banana`, you would create an `EnumProperty` instance as shown in Listing 2-11.

Listing 2-11. Initialize an `EnumProperty` instance to create a drop-down list widget

```
bpy.types.Scene.sample_enum = bpy.props.EnumProperty(
    name="Enum",
    items=(('Apple', "Apple", "First fruit"),
        ('Pear', "Pear", "Second fruit"),
        ('Banana', "Banana", "Third fruit")),
    description="Sample enum",
    default='Apple')
```

If you take a closer look at the `items` argument, you'll notice that each item of the drop-down is designated by a three-tuple that holds that item's internal ID, its display name (if you want the drop-down to show something different than the ID), and the content of its tool tip, as shown in Figure 2-14.

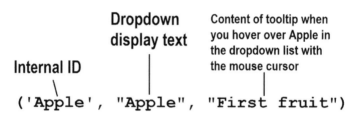

Figure 2-14. *Each item in the drop-down list is designated as a tuple of three values*

The `default` argument specifies which item is selected by default when the drop-down is first loaded (if no default value is explicitly given, the first item in the list becomes the default). You can see what the resulting drop-down looks like in Figure 2-15.

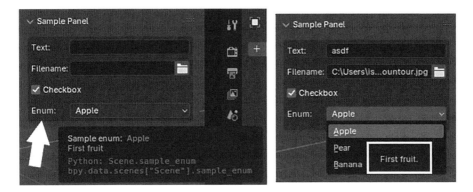

Figure 2-15. *Drop-down widget implemented by* `bpy.types.Scene.` `sample_enum` *in Listing 2-11, which is an* `EnumProperty` *instance. Left: When first loaded, the drop-down shows the value specified by the* `default` *parameter (in this case,* `'Apple'`*). Right: Clicking the widget expands the list. Notice that when you hover over* `'Apple'`*, the tool tip shows the string* `"First fruit"` *from the third position (index 2) of its three-tuple in* `items`

Creating a Slider Widget with **IntProperty** or **FloatProperty**

Sometimes, it makes sense to let users specify a setting in whole number increments, such as the number of subdivisions or number of edge loops to cut. IntProperty is designed for this very purpose. When displayed inside a UI panel, an IntProperty instance shows up as a slider widget which doubles as an input box that optionally lets you type in a number, as shown in Figure 2-16. Listing 2-12 shows how you can initialize an instance of IntProperty:

Listing 2-12. Initialize an `IntProperty` instance to create an integer slider widget

```
bpy.types.Scene.sample_int = bpy.props.IntProperty(
    name="Integer",
    description="Sample integer input",
    default=30,
    min=20,
    max=40)
```

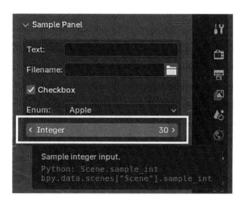

Figure 2-16. *Slider widget implemented by `bpy.types.Scene.sample_int` in Listing 2-12, which is an instance of IntProperty. Since the `default` argument is set to 30, the slider is at 30 when first loaded and will only slide between 20 and 40, as specified by `min` and `max`, respectively, in whole number increments*

You'll see that when the slider is first loaded, it is at the value of 30, as specified by the `default` argument. The `min` value of 20 and `max` value of 40 are not displayed on the widget itself, but when the user drags the (implicit) slider, the farthest it will go to the left is 20, and the farthest it will go to the right is 40. If the user tries to enter a number out of bounds, it will automatically be clamped.

In addition to having min and max values, which are referred to as hard minimum and hard maximum values, the slider can have soft minimum and maximum values that are set with the variables soft_min and soft_max. You might be wondering what the difference is between the two. The soft_min and soft_max values show up as the lower and upper constraints on the slider widget so the user can't slide it past either end; however, the user can still type in a value outside this range to forcefully set a number lower or higher than the range. For example, if you set soft_min = 20 and soft_max = 40, users can't slide the widget to the left past 20 or to the right past 40; however, they can still type in 55. On the other hand, min and max pose rigid limits—a user can't slide the widget past either end nor enter a number outside that range. For example, if you set min to 20 and max to 40, and a user enters 55, the entered value would be automatically clamped to 40, which is the nearest limit. The min/max and soft_min/soft_max values don't have to be specified in pairs—you can specify only one end of the range and leave the other open.

It's worth mentioning that you can create a percentage slider widget just by adding the subtype 'PERCENTAGE' to an IntProperty instance, as shown in Listing 2-13.

Listing 2-13. Initialize an IntProperty instance with subtype 'PERCENTAGE' to create a percentage slider widget

```
bpy.types.Scene.sample_int_pcrt = bpy.props.IntProperty(
    name="Percentage",
    description="Sample integer percentage input",
    default=50,
    min=10,
    max=100,
    subtype='PERCENTAGE')
```

Code-wise, this widget is set up exactly like bpy.types.Scene.sample_ int from Listing 2-12, except that there is an additional subtype specified as 'PERCENTAGE', which adds a percentage sign (%) to the right of the input field in the widget. The widget displays a blue "progress bar" that grows from the left toward the right as the percentage increases, as shown in Figure 2-17.

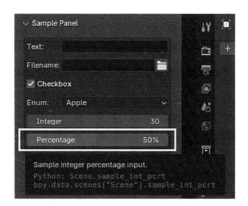

Figure 2-17. *Slider percentage widget implemented by* bpy.types. Scene.sample_int_pcrt *in Listing 2-13, which is an instance of* IntProperty *with* subtype *set to* 'PERCENTAGE'

Instead of whole number increments, sometimes, it makes sense for users to enter decimal values for a setting, such as the strength of a sculpting brush, or the scaling factor for a mesh. Listing 2-14 shows an example of a FloatProperty instance which creates a slider widget that supports decimal numbers, as shown in Figure 2-18.

Listing 2-14. Initialize a FloatProperty instance with subtype 'PERCENTAGE' to create a slider widget for decimal numbers

```
bpy.types.Scene.sample_float = bpy.props.FloatProperty(
    name="Float",
    description="Sample float input",
    default=0.0,
    soft_min=-5.0,
    soft_max=5.0)
```

You'll notice that both the arguments and appearance of a FloatProperty's widget are nearly identical to those of an IntProperty's. The only difference is that a FloatProperty's numerical arguments and user input can have decimal points.

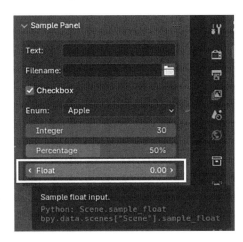

Figure 2-18. *Decimal number slider widget implemented by bpy. types.Scene.sample_float in Listing 2-14, which is an instance of* FloatProperty

Next, we'll create an empty UI panel under the Tool tab in the Properties shelf (*N* key to bring up in the 3D Viewport), which you'll later use to assemble all the widgets you've created in this chapter.

Creating an Empty UI Panel at a Desired Screen Location

To create an empty UI panel, we'll start by writing a class SAMPLE_PT_Shelf that derives from the built-in type bpy.types.Panel. Listing 2-15 shows the beginning of the class.

Listing 2-15. Create a class that derives from bpy.types.Panel to create your own UI panel

```
class SAMPLE_PT_Shelf(bpy.types.Panel):
    bl_label = "Sample Panel"
    bl_space_type = 'VIEW_3D'
    bl_region_type = 'UI'
    bl_category = 'Tool'
```

There are several metadata fields that must be defined for the panel to render and function properly. bl_label specifies the name shown at the top of the panel. bl_space_type, bl_region_type, and bl_category define a nested hierarchy of screen spaces (from outer to inner and from largest to smallest), respectively, which together define the location of the panel.

For example, in Listing 2-15, you've set bl_space_type to 'VIEW_3D' (the 3D Viewport), which encloses the Properties shelf (bl_region_type = 'UI'), which in turn encloses the Tool tab within the Properties shelf (bl_category = 'Tool'), as illustrated in Figure 2-19.

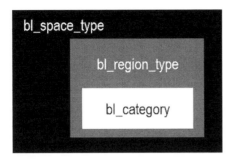

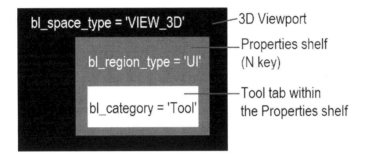

Figure 2-19. *How different types of screen areas nest inside one another.* bl_space_type *encloses* bl_region_type, *which in turn encloses* bl_category

Another Example: Revisiting `ui_panel_simple.py`

In the section "Editing and Running Script Files" in Chapter 1, you ran one of Blender's built-in template scripts, ui_panel_simple_.py, which produced a panel in the Properties Editor ➤ Object tab (as shown in Figure 1-6). I've reproduced the snippet from ui_panel_simple.py that defines the panel's screen location in Listing 2-16.

Listing 2-16. Snippet from `ui_panel_simple.py` that sets up the HelloWorldPanel's location

```
class HelloWorldPanel(bpy.types.Panel):
    """Creates a Panel in the Object properties window"""
    bl_label = "Hello World Panel"
    bl_idname = "OBJECT_PT_hello"
    bl_space_type = 'PROPERTIES'
    bl_region_type = 'WINDOW'
    bl_context = "object"
```

You can see from this example the panel is in the Properties Editor (`bl_space_type = 'PROPERTIES'`), which encloses a window with multiple tabs (`bl_region_type = 'WINDOW'`), one of which being the Object tab (`bl_context = "object"`).

Assembling Properties Inside the Empty Panel

The next step for completing the UI panel is to organize the properties into a layout inside the panel. To do this, we'll add a custom `draw` method to the `SAMPLE_PT_Shelf` class, as shown in Listing 2-17.

Listing 2-17. Custom draw() method for the `SAMPLE_PT_Shelf` class

```
def draw(self, context):
    layout = self.layout
    col0 = layout.column()
    box0 = col0.box()

    r = box0.row(align=True)
    r.prop(context.scene, "sample_text")
    r = box0.row(align=True)
    r.prop(context.scene, "sample_filename")
    r = box0.row(align=True)
```

```
r.prop(context.scene, "sample_checkbox")
r = box0.row(align=True)
r.prop(context.scene, "sample_enum")
r = box0.row(align=True)
r.prop(context.scene, "sample_int")
r = box0.row(align=True)
r.prop(context.scene, "sample_int_pcrt")
r = box0.row(align=True)
r.prop(context.scene, "sample_float")

box1 = col0.box()
box1.label(text="User Entered Values:", icon='TEXT')
r = box1.row(align=True)
r.label(text="Text: "+str(context.scene.sample_text))
r = box1.row(align=True)
r.label(text="Filename: "+ ↵
    +str(context.scene.sample_filename))
r = box1.row(align=True)
r.label(text="Checkbox: "+ ↵
    str(context.scene.sample_checkbox))
r = box1.row(align=True)
r.label(text="Enum: "+str(context.scene.sample_enum))
r = box1.row(align=True)
r.label(text="Integer: "+str(context.scene.sample_int))
r = box1.row(align=True)
r.label(text="Percentage: "+ ↵
    str(context.scene.sample_int_pcrt)+"%")
r = box1.row(align=True)
r.label(text="Float: "+str(context.scene.sample_float))

box2 = col0.box()
box2.label(text="Scene Objects:", icon='OBJECT_DATA')
```

```
for ob in context.scene.objects:
    r = box2.row(align=True)
    r.label(text = str(ob.name))
```

Listing 2-17 creates a column (col0), then stacks three boxes vertically inside the column, box0, box1, and box2. The top box (box0) houses the seven properties we defined in the previous sections and lays each out sequentially in its own row.

The middle box (box1) displays the user-entered value for each property in its own row, in the same order the corresponding properties are displayed. Notice that to access the current value of a scene variable, you have to use the syntax

context.scene.**\<scene variable name\>**

For example, to access the current value of the scene variable bpy. types.Scene.**sample_text**, you would use context.scene.**sample_text**.

The bottom box (box2) displays the names of the objects in the current scene, again each in its own row. The completed UI panel is shown in Figure 2-20.

Figure 2-20. *The completed* SAMPLE_PT_Shelf. *(1)* box0 *in Listing 2-17 contains the seven input widgets we've defined throughout the chapter. (2)* box1 *displays values currently entered into the widgets. (3)* box2 *displays the names of objects currently in the scene, using the same layout from the section "Adding a Pop-Up Dialog to the Simple Operator"*

Setting Up and Cleaning Up Scene Variables Systematically

When initializing a large number of scene variables, I find it neatest to group all the initializations into one function, such as how `init_scene_vars()` is set up earlier in the chapter. Then, all you have to do is call `init_scene_vars()` in `register()` like in Listing 2-18, and all the properties will be initialized at once and ready to go before your add-on is run.

Listing 2-18. Register all classes and init all scene variables in register()

```
classes = [SAMPLE_PT_Shelf]
def register():
    for c in classes:
        bpy.utils.register_class(c)
    init_scene_vars()
```

Analogously, you can create a method that deletes all the scene variables in one place, which we'll do in `del_scene_vars()`, as shown in Listing 2-19.

To delete a variable, you would use `del <name of variable>`. For example, `del bpy.types.Scene.sample_text` deletes the scene variable `bpy.types.Scene.sample_text`.

Listing 2-19. Create a function called del_scene_vars() to delete all scene variables in one place

```
def del_scene_vars():
    del bpy.types.Scene.sample_text
    del bpy.types.Scene.sample_filename
    del bpy.types.Scene.sample_checkbox
    del bpy.types.Scene.sample_enum
```

```
del bpy.types.Scene.sample_int
del bpy.types.Scene.sample_int_pcrt
del bpy.types.Scene.sample_float
```

Then, for cleanup, you'll simply call del_scene_vars() in unregister() as shown in Listing 2-20 to ensure that no invalid or unused scene variables are left behind.

Listing 2-20. Unregister all classes and delete all scene variables in unregister()

```
def unregister():
    for c in classes:
        bpy.utils.unregister_class(c)
    del_scene_vars()
```

Testing the Sample UI Panel

Similar to operator_simple.py discussed earlier in the chapter, you can add Listing 2-21 to sample_panel_properties_shelf_tool_tab.py to run it in the Text Editor and register it with Blender to test it, without having to set up the metadata required to install it via Edit ➤ Preferences... (which is either bl_info for legacy add-ons or blender_manifest.toml for extension add-ons). Recall that __main__ is the name of the top-level environment in which your code is run, so Listing 2-21 simply means, wherever you are running the code from, call register().

Listing 2-21. Setup call to register() for testing a script in the Text Editor

```
if __name__ == "__main__":
    register()
```

Finding the Python Class for a Menu Item from Its Source File

Earlier in this chapter, in the section "Find a Menu's Corresponding Python Class in the Blender Python API," you learned that if you knew a menu's Python class, you could derive its submenu's class by adding an underscore followed by the submenu's name in lowercase. While this trick works well in many cases, there are unfortunately some exceptions. In this section, I'll show you an alternative way of finding the Python class for a submenu—by peeking into the source file that implements its parent menu in the Blender Python API.

Let's revisit the example of finding the Python class for the Edit mode *Mesh* ➤ *Snap* menu. The first step is to ask Blender to retrieve the source file that implements the parent menu—*Mesh*. Right-click *Mesh*, then click *Edit Source*. You should see the message *"See 'space_view3d.py' in the text editor"*, which is the name of the source file containing the implementation for *Mesh*, appear at the bottom of the 3D Viewport. The same message is also logged in the Info Editor. Switch to the Scripting workspace. Select `'space_view3d.py'` from the drop-down at the top of the Text Editor to make it active. In Blender 4.2, you should see the cursor automatically scrolled to the line:

```
layout.menu("VIEW3D_MT_edit_" + edit_object.type.lower())
```

Note   Recall from the section "Secondary Scripting Helper Menu" in Chapter 1, once you have the option *Edit* ➤ *Preferences* ➤ *Interface* ➤ *Developer* Extras checked, you'll have access to the *Edit Source* feature in the right-click context menu of any item in the UI, which allows you to view the Python source (*.py file) that implements that item.

The next step is to use the Text Editor's search tool to locate the portion of the code within space_view3d.py that implements the *Mesh* ➤ *Snap* submenu. Press *Ctrl-F* while the mouse cursor is inside the Text Editor to bring up the Find & Replace panel on the right. Type in the search term "snap" in the text box. Make sure that Match Case is toggled off to make the search case-insensitive (so "snap" will match "Snap," "SNAP," and so on—since we don't yet know what the capitalization will be in the code block we're looking for). Make sure to toggle on Wrap, so that when the search (which goes in the forward direction) reaches the end of the file, it'll automatically start from the top again.

Now you're ready to start the search. If you press the "Find Next" button, it will take you automatically to the next match in the file, which lands on the following line in Blender 4.2:

```
class VIEW3D_MT_snap(Menu):
```

Congrats! You've just found the class that implements the *Mesh* ➤ *Snap* submenu. To double-check this, take a look inside the class—you'll see some strings that match the options under *Mesh* ➤ *Snap* in the UI (for example, "Selection to Grid"), which confirms that this is the class you're looking for.

Preparing Your Add-On for Publication

There are two more items to be completed to get your add-on ready for publication. The first is metadata, in the form of a Python dictionary called bl_info for legacy add-ons, and a blender_manifest.toml file for extension add-ons. The second is a license comment block detailing the add-on's licensing requirements.

Creating Metadata for Your Add-On

We'll first go over how to create metadata for legacy add-ons.

Creating Metadata for Legacy Add-Ons in `bl_info`

Metadata for legacy add-ons is stored in `bl_info`, which is a Python dictionary summarizing the properties of an add-on for proper identification and installation. For each add-on, Blender reads its `bl_info` to populate an entry under *Edit ➤ Preferences... ➤ Add-ons.*

Blender requires `bl_info` for a legacy add-on to be submitted to the official Blender repository, but even if you don't plan on officially publishing an add-on, it's still a good idea to include it since it communicates important information such as what the add-on does and the minimum Blender version it requires to run. Include `bl_info` at the top of your legacy add-on's __init__.py file.

An example of how `bl_info` is filled out for sample_panel_ properties_shelf_tool_tab.py from the previous section is shown in Listing 2-22.

Listing 2-22. How to create a bl_info for sample_panel_properties_ shelf_tool_tab.py

```
bl_info = {
    "name": "Sample UI Panel in the Properties Shelf >
    Tool tab",
    "author": "Isabel Lupiani",
    "version": (2, 0, 0),
    "blender": (4, 2, 0),
    "location": "Properties Shelf > Tool > Sample Panel",
    "warning": "",
```

```
        "description": "This add-on creates a sample UI Panel in ↵
            the Properties Shelf > Tool tab",
        "wiki_url": "",
        "category": "Object"
}
```

The "name" is the name of your add-on as a string, and "version" is the version of the add-on in case you release updates and need a version number to differentiate between them. The value in "blender" is the *minimum* version of Blender required for the add-on to work (the third digit specifies the subversion of the Blender release, which isn't relevant to add-ons and can just be left as 0). The "location" field specifies the menu or screen area the add-on can be found. The "warning" field is usually left blank unless you need to inform users of a potential bug or problem with the add-on. When "warning" is set to a non-empty string, a warning icon is shown with the add-on's entry under *Edit* ➤ *Preferences...* ➤ *Add-ons*, and the warning message is shown alongside the add-on's "description", which is a short string describing what the add-on does. The "wiki_url" is the link to the add-on's page in the Blender wiki and is required if the add-on is to be listed in the official Blender repository. The "category" denotes which category the add-on is to be filed under *Edit* ➤ *Preferences...* ➤ *Add-ons*.

Creating Metadata for Extension Add-Ons in blender_manifest.toml

Starting in Blender 4.2, the metadata for extension add-ons is defined in a file named blender_manifest.toml, which lives in the same folder as the top-level __init__.py for the add-on. You can see a sample blender_manifest.toml file prepared for the sample UI panel add-on in Listing 2-23.

Listing 2-23. Contents of a sample `blender_manifest.toml` file prepared for the sample UI panel add-on

```
schema_version = "1.0.0"

id = "sample_ui_panel"
version = "2.0.0"
name = "Sample UI Panel in the Properties shelf > Tool tab"
tagline = "This add-on creates a sample UI Panel in the ↵
    Properties shelf > Tool tab"
maintainer = "Isabel Lupiani <a@b.com>"
type = "add-on"

tags = ["3D View"]
blender_version_min = "4.2.0"

license = [
  "SPDX:GPL-2.0-or-later",
]

copyright = [
  "2018-2024 Isabel Lupiani",
  "2024 Apress",
]
```

The first six fields (`id`, `version`, `name`, `tagline`, `maintainer`, and `type`), as well as `license`, are required, whereas `tags`, `blender_version_min`, and `copyright` are optional. You can easily see that the field `tagline` was `"description"` in `bl_info`, `maintainer` was `"author"`, and `tags` corresponds to "category", except that `tags` allows a list of multiple (you can find a list of available tags at `https://docs.blender.org/manual/en/dev/advanced/extensions/tags.html`). Note that `type` is either "add-on" or "theme," as those are the only types of extensions supported.

Listing 2-23 only shows a subset of the optional fields available to a blender_manifest.toml file. You can find a complete list at https:// docs.blender.org/manual/en/latest/advanced/extensions/getting_ started.html#manifest.

Converting Metadata from a Legacy Add-on to an Extension Add-On

To convert the metadata from a legacy add-on to an extension add-on, you would remove bl_info from the legacy add-on's top-level __init__.py file, fill out an blender_manifest.toml file based on the values in bl_info, and place the blender_manifest.toml file in the same directory as the __init__.py file.

Adding a License

Blender 4 uses GNU GPLv3, 29 June 2007, and will only allow add-ons compatible with GNU GPL v3.0 or later to be submitted to the official extension platform. Before submitting your add-on, you should prepare a license block and add it to the top of the __init__.py file for your add-on. You can find an example in Listing 2-24, where I've customized a GNU GPLv3 block for the sample UI add-on discussed earlier in this chapter.

Listing 2-24. GNU GPLv3 license block customized for the sample UI panel add-on

```
# ##### BEGIN GPL LICENSE BLOCK #####
#
# GNU GPLv3, 29 June 2007
#
# Examples from Ch2 of the book "Blender Scripting with
```

```
# Python" by Isabel Lupiani.
#
# This add-on creates a UI Panel in the Properties shelf
# > Tool tab.
# Copyright (C) 2024  Isabel Lupiani, Apress.
#
# This program is free software: you can redistribute it
# and/or modify it under the terms of the GNU General
# Public License as published by the Free Software
# Foundation, either version 3 of the License, or (at
# your option) any later version.
#
# This program is distributed in the hope that it will
# be useful, but WITHOUT ANY WARRANTY; without even the
# implied warranty of MERCHANTABILITY or FITNESS FOR A
# PARTICULAR PURPOSE.  See the GNU General Public License
# for more details.
#
# You should have received a copy of the GNU General
# Public License along with this program.  If not, see
# <https://www.gnu.org/licenses/>.
#
# ##### END GPL LICENSE BLOCK #####
```

You can find other types of license acceptable for official extension submissions for the current version of Blender at

```
https://docs.blender.org/manual/en/dev/advanced/extensions/
licenses.html.
```

Tip   You can start a single-line comment in Python with # or enclose a multiline comment block with triple quotes.

Summary

In this chapter, you've learned that add-ons mostly fall into one of two categories. The first is helper tools which automate repetitive tasks or perform jobs for you that are tricky to get right by hand. The second is generation tools that generate partial or complete assets automatically, with or without user input. You learned how to come up with new tool ideas by examining your own or a fellow artist's workflow, then go from design to add-on by converting the steps you'd normally perform by hand to operator calls.

You then learned the difference between legacy add-ons and extension add-ons (>= Blender 4.2) and how they differ in package structure. You also learned how to locate the source files for examples of both types of add-ons for further study.

The next part of the chapter took you on a deep dive of the inner working of an operator, then showed you how to compose an add-on from one or more operators and set up scene variables to share data between them. You created several common types of UI widgets using properties under the `bpy.props` module, such as text input, file open, check box, and number sliders, and how to assemble them into a UI panel with a custom layout, to draw at a desired screen location.

Finally, you learned how to prepare your add-on for publication: first by creating metadata (as `bl_info` for legacy add-ons and as `blender_manifest.toml` files for extension add-ons), followed by adding the appropriate license compatible with Blender's requirement for add-on submission.

## CHAPTER 3

Mesh Modeling Basics

Mesh modeling is an intricate and often time-consuming process. If you find yourself repeating the same steps each time you make a new model, like configuring a certain sequence of modifiers or creating the same material stack, automating these tasks can save you time and make the process more enjoyable.

Taking advantage of the Blender Python API, you can quickly automate the creation of low-poly assets for prototyping game levels or film projects. If you're an indie developer with limited access to artists, editing or generating models programmatically can help you get the basic assets you need to get a project up and running.

In this chapter, I'll show you how to access, create, and edit mesh objects using the Blender Python API's built-in modules `BMesh` and `bpy.ops`. By the end of this chapter, you'll have generated your own custom barrel meshes from scratch using Python and produced many interesting variations by changing script parameters.

Accessing a Mesh Object

When you want to create scripts for manipulating meshes, the first step is to obtain references to the objects that you want to edit. Each time an add-on is run, it is passed a `context` variable, which contains background

I. Lupiani, *Blender Scripting with Python*, https://doi.org/10.1007/979-8-8688-1127-2_3

information such as the screen area from which the add-on is invoked and data related to the objects accessible from the current workspace. For example, if you have the default startup *.blend file open, you can get a reference to the object named "Cube" from the current scene through context and store that reference in a variable named cube, with which to access the object later.

```
cube = context.scene.objects["Cube"]
```

If there is no object by the name you're trying to look up, however, you'll get a KeyError. It is therefore a good idea to use the find method first to verify that an object with a given name exists in a container and only then proceed to retrieve it, as shown in Listing 3-1. (Remember that if you were to try these two lines of code outside of an operator class (e.g., in the built-in Python Console), you would have to use bpy.context instead of just context.)

Listing 3-1. Checking whether an object by a name exists before accessing it

```
if context.scene.objects.find("Cube") >= 0:
    cube = context.scene.objects["Cube"]
```

If an object with the given name is found, find returns the object's index among the objects in the scene (which is a number starting at 0). If there is no match, find returns -1.

While using find is a great way to verify an object's existence—you should **not** store an object's index returned by find and use it to access the object at a later time, because an object's index can change while Blender is running, for example, when other objects are added, renamed, or removed from the same container.

The safest way to reference an object is to call find to verify the object's existence, then use either the object's name or the index returned by find to get a reference to that object *immediately after* calling find and

94

assigning the reference to a variable, through which to access or modify the object for the remainder of your add-on or operator's call.

Once you've obtained a reference to an object, you can access its properties through that reference, such as its name using dot notation, like cube.name. An important property is <object>.type, which tells you the kind of data the object holds. For example, an object that holds mesh data will have the type 'MESH'. Other possible types are 'CURVE', 'CAMERA', 'EMPTY', and so on. Basically everything you see in the *Add* menu (*Shift-A*) in Object mode is a possible object type in Blender.

You can access objects via the bpy.data module very much the same way as you would through bpy.context.scene, as shown in Listing 3-2.

Listing 3-2. Checking whether an object by a name exists before accessing it

```
if bpy.data.objects.find("Cube") >= 0:
    cube = bpy.data.objects["Cube"]
```

bpy.data contains everything from the blend file, including those that are not currently in use, like materials not currently applied to any model. In contrast, bpy.context.scene only contains objects you are currently interacting with in the scene.

The choice between using bpy.data or bpy.context.scene to access objects will therefore depend on what you need your script to accomplish. For example, if you are making an add-on to help users edit objects interactively in the 3D Viewport, you'll want to use bpy.context.scene to access objects. On the other hand, if you're making an add-on that generates meshes which the user can add to the scene at a later time, you'll save the mesh objects under bpy.data.

Watching Out for Invalid References

Keep in mind you cannot assume that the reference to an object will stay valid beyond an add-on or operator's current call, because a user or some other script could delete the object, move it elsewhere, or modify it in such a way that it no longer holds the data your operator or add-on expects.

For example, if each call to your add-on unwraps a selected mesh—after verifying the mesh's validity at the beginning of the call and getting a reference to it—you can assume that the reference will remain valid until the call returns. However, there is no way to know after that whether the user would delete the mesh from the scene, rename the UVs the add-on had unwrapped, or unwrap another set of UVs to the same slot the add-on had used. Therefore, when the add-on is called again, it cannot depend on any references or data used by the previous call.

Another thing to watch out for is if your add-on creates new objects or data blocks (or renames them), the requested name may not be honored if something with that name already exists, or if the name is invalid or too long. If you assume that the naming had gone through (when it hadn't) and try to look up the object or data block by that name, you'd get an error or possibly end up with a reference to the wrong thing.

For example, if your add-on generates a mesh object with a name entered by the user (let's say it's "my_mesh"), but something with that name already exists. If your add-on proceeds anyway, the generated object will have the name "my_mesh.001", "my_mesh.002", and so on. If the user enters an empty string, Blender 4.2 will default to naming the object "Object" instead. If the user enters a string that is too long, Blender 4.2 will truncate the string to the maximum length allowed. In any case, the object does *not* end up with the name the add-on asked for. If the add-on assumes that the naming was successful and tries to look up the generated object with the name "my_mesh", it will reference the wrong object and edit it by accident.

You can use `find` to check whether an object or data block with a certain name already exists. If so, you have to decide whether it's appropriate for your add-on to go ahead anyway and end up with "<name>.001", "<name>.002", etc. for object names. Other possibilities include renaming the existing object, overwriting existing data, generating an alternative name that does not collide with existing names, or not to go through with the data creation at all and alert the user.

To safeguard against invalid names, you can use `len(<name>)` to get the <name> string's length and check if it is empty (with length 0) or too long. Similar to the scenario with duplicate names, in the event of an invalid name, you'll have to decide whether to replace it with a valid alternative or abort the operation altogether and inform the user.

Selecting Objects and Setting Object Interaction Modes

During a modeling session, sometimes you have to switch between interaction modes in order to access different sets of features in Blender, such as *Edit mode* for loop cuts or *Sculpt mode* for adding multi-res details. In addition, some modeling tasks can only be carried out in certain modes; for example, you can only apply modifiers or transforms in Object mode. Therefore, it's important to know how to switch between modes in Python while developing an add-on.

A simple way to change an object's interaction mode is to use the operator `bpy.ops.object.mode_set(mode=<mode>)`, where <mode> is an Enum string indicating which mode to switch to, such as `'EDIT'`, `'OBJECT'`, `'SCULPT'`, and so on. The `bpy.ops.object.mode_set` operator, like most `bpy` operators, operates on the active object plus any other objects currently selected in the scene.

The function change_obj_to_edit_mode in Listing 3-3 shows how you can set the mesh object with the given name as the active object and switch it to *Edit mode*. You can download the script file change_obj_mode. py which contains this function. **The source code for this book is available on GitHub via the book's product page, located at www.apress.com/979-8-8688-1126-5.**

Listing 3-3. Setting the mesh object with the given name as active and switching it to Edit mode

```
def change_obj_to_edit_mode(mesh_obj_name: str):
    for obj in bpy.context.scene.objects:
        obj.select_set(False)

    if mesh_obj_name and ↩
        bpy.context.scene.objects.find(mesh_obj_name) >= 0:
        mesh_obj = bpy.context.scene.objects[mesh_obj_name]
        if mesh_obj.type == 'MESH':
            bpy.context.view_layer.objects.active = mesh_obj
            bpy.ops.object.mode_set(mode='EDIT')
```

Since bpy.ops.object.mode_set(mode=<mode>) will attempt mode switching on the active object plus any other objects currently selected, we must iterate through all objects in the scene and toggle each object's selection off via obj.select_set(False).

Next, with if mesh_obj_name, we check that mesh_obj_name is not None, before calling bpy.context.scene.objects.find(mesh_obj_name) to see if an object by that name already exists (in the scene)—if so, the index returned by find will be >= 0, in which case, we proceed to get a reference to that object and store it in the variable mesh_obj.

Before switching mesh_obj to Edit mode, we need to check if it is a mesh object (mesh_obj.type == 'MESH'), because attempting to change a nonmesh object to Edit mode could result in TypeError.

Once we know `mesh_obj` is a mesh object, we set it as the active object and call `bpy.ops.object.mode_set(mode='EDIT')` to change it to Edit mode.

Caution   Calling `find` with a None argument will result in `SystemError`; therefore, you must check if a string is None before calling `find` with it.

You'll notice that it is *not* possible to switch an object to a mode it does not have through Blender's UI (which is a good thing). For example, in the default startup `*.blend` file, if you select Light, which is a light object, the only mode available in the mode dropdown is Object mode; therefore, it's not possible to switch Light to Edit mode.

However, in Python, there is nothing stopping you from calling `bpy.ops.object.mode_set(mode='EDIT')` on objects that do not have Edit mode; therefore, you must check the object's type before calling `bpy.ops.object.mode_set`.

Similarly, it falls on you to check that an object is compatible with other `bpy.ops` operators before calling them (e.g., the object is of the appropriate type, is in a mode that can be edited by that operator, etc.).

For a mesh object, you could use `bpy.ops.object.editmode_toggle()` to switch back and forth between the mode it is in and Edit mode. This is handy when you need to go back and forth between these two modes during modeling, such as switching to Object mode to apply a modifier, then back to Edit mode to make more edits to the mesh, and so on.

You could of course generalize change_obj_to_edit_mode into a function that will set an object to *any given mode*, not just Edit mode, by introducing two additional arguments, obj_type (type of the object to switch mode on) and mode_to_set (the mode to switch to), as the example shown in Listing 3-4.

Listing 3-4. Set the object of the given name and type as active, and switch it to the desired mode

```
def change_obj_to_mode(obj_name: str, obj_type, mode_to_set):
    for obj in bpy.context.scene.objects:
        obj.select_set(False)

    if obj_name and ↩
        bpy.context.scene.objects.find(obj_name) >= 0:
        obj = bpy.context.scene.objects[obj_name]
        if obj.type == obj_type:
            bpy.context.view_layer.objects.active = obj
            bpy.ops.object.mode_set(mode=mode_to_set)
```

Instead of checking the object to switch mode on is of type 'MESH', you'd check that it is of the type passed in. Instead of calling bpy.ops. object.mode_set with mode='EDIT', you'd call it with mode=**mode_to_set** instead.

You can look up the list of possible values for obj_type in the Blender Python API documentation, under *Object Type Items*, at https://docs. blender.org/api/current/bpy_types_enum_items/object_type_items. html#rna-enum-object-type-items. The possible values for mode_to_set are under *Object Mode Items* at https://docs.blender.org/api/current/ bpy_types_enum_items/object_mode_items.html#object-mode-items.

Caution   You should avoid using the operator `bpy.ops.object.select_all` to toggle selection of all objects in the scene, since it requires a very restrictive context to run (all objects in the scene have to be in Object mode).

Adding Built-In Primitive Shapes

Sometimes, it's more convenient to start a modeling session with one of Blender's built-in primitive shapes than to start from scratch. For example, when you're modeling an object whose underlying structure resembles a primitive, such as a fire hydrant that is roughly cylindrical or a Christmas ornament that is mostly spherical, it might save you some work to start with one of these basic shapes as you begin to block out a model. The primitives are also handy when you're just looking to test out materials with simple shapes or when you need to throw together some rough assets to populate a prototype game level.

The built-in operator to add a primitive is

```
bpy.ops.mesh.primitive_<type>_add()
```

You can use any of the shapes available under *Add (Shift-A)* ➤ *Mesh* menu in Object mode or the *Mesh (Shift-A)* menu in Edit mode, by replacing <type> with the type name in all lower case.

For example, you can use the following operator call to add a *Suzanne* mesh (the Blender mascot monkey) to the current scene:

```
bpy.ops.mesh.primitive_monkey_add()
```

When the call is made in Object mode, a new mesh object is created alongside new mesh data with a matching name—for example, adding a monkey shape with `bpy.ops.mesh.primitive_monkey_add()` creates the

101

object `bpy.context.scene.objects["Suzanne"]` with mesh data `bpy.data.meshes["Suzanne"]`. In contrast, no object is created when the call is made in Edit mode and the primitive is added to the mesh data of the current active object as additional geometry.

Since primitive-add operators have default values for all of their parameters, when you call them with no argument given, such as in the previous example, the mesh is created at its default size and configuration and added at the current location of the 3D cursor in the viewport (the same as when you add a shape by hand via either *Add (Shift-A)* ➤ *Mesh* in Object mode or *Mesh (Shift-A)* in Edit mode).

As you'll see later in this section, supplying optional arguments to some of these operators will give you greater control over the contours and sizes of the shapes created, such as the inner and outer radii of a torus. Just remember to use keyword arguments in this case, as in `location=(1, 2, 3)` instead of `(1, 2, 3)`.

Two of the parameters that are common across different primitive-add operators are `location` and `enter_editmode`. For example, you would make the following operator call to add an ico sphere (a sphere made of triangular faces) with the name `"Icosphere"` and default radius, centered at `(1, 2, 3)` to the scene:

```
bpy.ops.mesh.primitive_ico_sphere_add(location=(1, 2, 3), ↩
    enter_editmode=True)
```

The `location` parameter takes the X, Y, and Z coordinates of where the mesh is to be created, as either a tuple of three numbers, like `(1, 2, 3)`, or a `Vector` instance, like `Vector((1, 2, 3))` (`Vector` is a type under the Blender Python built-in module `mathutils`). When the operator is called in Object mode with `enter_editmode` set to `True`, the mesh is switched to Edit mode right after its creation. With these two parameters, you can create a primitive at a desired location and start editing it right away with one operator call, which is really handy.

Some of the operators have optional parameters for controlling the size and density of the geometry. Here are two examples for creating a cylinder named "Cylinder" and a uv sphere named "Sphere" with various optional parameter values:

```
bpy.ops.mesh.primitive_cylinder_add(vertices=8, radius=2.0, ↵
    depth=0.5, end_fill_type='NGON')

bpy.ops.mesh.primitive_uv_sphere_add(radius=3.5, ↵
    segments=16, ring_count=8)
```

The first line creates a 0.5-unit-tall cylinder (depth=0.5) that has N-gon end-caps each with eight vertices and radius of 2. The second line creates a uv sphere with radius 3.5 made up of 16 longitudinal and 8 latitudinal segments.

You can see from the examples so far that Blender unfortunately does not follow a consistent naming convention for primitives—ico sphere is by default named "Icosphere", whereas uv sphere is by default named "Sphere"—so be cautious of making assumptions about referencing them. Luckily, you can just as easily find out what the primitives' default names are by adding them to the viewport in Object mode from the Python Console and checking what names pop up in the Scene Collection.

Remember you can also add primitives to the 3D Viewport with either *Add (Shift-A)* ➤ *Mesh* in Object mode or *Mesh (Shift-A)* in Edit mode and check the Info Editor to see which operators were called along with their keyword arguments' names and the default values used.

If the same primitive-add operator is called multiple times in Object mode with the created objects left in their default names, the instances after the first will default to the naming convention <name of primitive>. xxx, with the xxx being a three-digit number starting from 001. For example, if you add a cube three times in a row without renaming them, the first cube will be named "Cube", the second "Cube.001", the third "Cube.002", and so on.

Preventing Addition of Duplicate Primitives

Let's create a new script file named creating_and_editing_mesh_objs.
py and type in the code from Listing 3-5. We will continue to reference
and build up this script for the rest of the chapter. Alternatively, you can
download the complete version of the script to follow along. **The source
code for this book is available on GitHub via the book's product page,
located at www.apress.com/979-8-8688-1126-5.** To start off, we'll import
various modules we'll need for add_cone_once() (Listing 3-5) as well as
other functions we'll write throughout the chapter.

Listing 3-5. Checking whether an object named "Cone" exists in the
scene before adding a cone primitive

```
import bpy
import bmesh
from mathutils import Vector
from math import cos, pi, radians, sin

def add_cone_once(context, location=(0, 0, 0), vertices=8, ↵
    radius1=2.0, depth=3.0):
    if context.scene.objects.find("Cone") < 0:
        if context.view_layer.objects.active is not None:
            bpy.ops.object.mode_set(mode='OBJECT')
        bpy.ops.mesh.primitive_cone_add(location=location, ↵
            vertices=vertices, radius1=radius1, depth=depth)
```

The add_cone_once function adds a cone primitive to the scene if there
isn't already an object named "Cone". The function starts off by calling
find and checking whether the returned index is < 0 (indicating no object
by that name exists)—in which case, it goes on to check whether there is
an active object and, if so, switches it to Object mode, so it can call
bpy.ops.mesh.primitive_cone_add next to create a new cone object

(as opposed to adding more geometry to the active object). `bpy.ops.mesh.primitive_cone_add` is called with the keyword argument `vertices` (which specifies the number of vertices making up the cone's bottom), `radius1` (which specifies the radius of the cone's bottom), and `depth` (which specifies the cone's height).

Caution You can only call `bpy.ops.object.mode_set(mode='OBJECT')` if there is a valid active object in the scene, with Object mode as one of its available interaction modes, otherwise you'll get the error `RuntimeError: Operator bpy.ops.object.mode_set.poll() Context missing active object`.

You can create a 5.0-unit-tall cone at location (1, 2, 3) with a bottom made up of 16 vertices and a radius of 3.0, by calling add_cone_once like this:

```
add_cone_once(bpy.context, (1, 2, 3), 16, 3.0, 5.0)
```

Note The keyword argument for the primitive cone's bottom radius is `radius1`, with the 1 at the end—this is not a typo. A cone is a degenerative case of a cylinder, so it has one radius instead of two.

Accessing Object Locations and Moving Objects

Sometimes, you might find yourself needing to build a scene with multiple objects positioned relative to one another. For example, you might use the location of a coffee table model as the reference point for placing sofa

105

and lamp models around the room. To animate a hard surface model like a spacecraft or fighter jet, you might use a combination of constraints and relative offsets between objects to set up a mechanical rig.

In this section, I'll show you how to use Python to access object locations, move objects around, and calculate directional offsets and midpoints between objects.

Let's head over to the Scripting workspace and make sure the viewport is in Object mode. Type the following code into the built-in Python Console to add a cone primitive to the scene, and display its `location`:

```
>>> bpy.ops.mesh.primitive_cone_add(location=(0, 0, 0),
radius1=4, depth=5)
{'FINISHED'}

>>> cone = bpy.context.scene.objects["Cone"]
>>> cone.location
Vector((0.0, 0.0, 0.0))
```

The location of an object is stored under its `location` variable as a `Vector`. The three elements of a `Vector` refer to its X, Y, and Z coordinates, respectively. The built-in Python Console automatically imports the `Vector` type for you. If you scroll to the top in the Python Console, you'll see the line

```
Convenience Imports:   from mathutils import *; from math
import *
```

If you're using `Vector` in a script, however, you'll need to import it yourself at the top of the file, like this:

```
from mathutils import Vector
```

Note Based on Blender Python's official recommendation, you should import only the types you need from a module. For example, the module `mathutils` consists of various types such as `Euler`, `Matrix`, `Vector`, etc. If you only need `Vector` for your script, you should write `from mathutils import Vector` to import only the `Vector` type, instead of using the wildcard import `from mathutils import *`, which imports everything from `mathutils`.

You can access individual elements of a `Vector` like you do a Python list. For example, the first element of a `Vector` v is v[0], the second v[1], and the third v[2]. Taking advantage of this, you can move an object by adding an offset to its `location` on a per-axis basis.

Enter the following lines into the Python Console, which move the cone object 1.5 units in the X direction, -2.0 units in the Y direction, and 3.0 units in the Z direction. As you enter each line, observe its effect in the viewport:

```
>>> cone.location[0] += 1.5
>>> cone.location[1] -= 2
>>> cone.location[2] += 3
```

Let's see what the cone's location is after the movement. Typing a variable name at the prompt (without an assignment) and hitting Enter simply prints its current value:

```
>>> cone.location
Vector((1.5, -2.0, 3.0))
```

You can do arithmetic calculations on `Vector` instances just like you do numbers. You can add `Vector` instances together, subtract them from one another, or even multiply a `Vector` by a number to scale the length of the `Vector` by that number. Let's create two `Vector` instances and store them in the variables v1 and v2, then do some math on them. Continue at the Python Console, and type in the following lines to see their effects:

```
>>> v1 = Vector((1, 2, 3))
>>> v2 = Vector((4, 5, 6))
>>> v1 + v2
Vector((5.0, 7.0, 9.0))

>>> v1 - v2
Vector((-3.0, -3.0, -3.0))

>>> 5 * v1
Vector((5.0, 10.0, 15.0))
```

You'll notice that v1 + v2 adds the two Vector instances element-wise, as in (1+4, 2+5, 3+6), as do v1 - v2, which results in (1-4, 2-5, 3-6), whereas 5 * v1 multiplies each element of v1 with 5, as in (1*5, 2*5, 3*5).

A Vector instance is initialized with a three-number tuple as a single argument. Because of this, when you create a Vector, you have to use two sets of parentheses—the inner set defining the tuple and the outer set defining the Vector.

Note   Tuple is a Python type for storing a collection of data. Just like a Python list, a tuple is ordered and allows duplicate elements. The difference is you can modify a list (add or remove elements) once it's initialized, but you cannot do so with a tuple. A tuple starts/ends with parentheses, for example, my_typle = (1, 2, 3). A list starts/ends with square brackets, for example, my_list = [1, 2, 3]. You can access an element in either a tuple or a list with its index. The first element has index zero, e.g., my_tuple[0]. The last element has index <length of tuple or list> - 1, e.g., my_tuple[2], but can also be accessed with my_tuple[-1].

Taking advantage of the fact that when two Vector instances are added together, their elements combine on a per-axis basis (zeroth element of one Vector is added to the zeroth element of the other, and so on), you can define a displacement Vector to move an object along all three axes at once:

```
>>> cone.location
Vector((1.5, -2.0, 3.0))
```

```
>>> cone.location += Vector((-1.5, 2, -3))
>>> cone.location
Vector((0.0, 0.0, 0.0))
```

Now that you've learned the basics of vector manipulation, you can use vector math to find the midpoint between two objects' locations. Enter the following code into the Python Console to add a second object to the scene (a primitive uv sphere), and try this out:

```
>>> bpy.ops.mesh.primitive_uv_sphere_add(location=(1, 2, 3))
{'FINISHED'}
```

```
>>> sphere = bpy.context.scene.objects["Sphere"]
>>> cone.location = Vector((4, 5, 6))
>>> mid_point = (sphere.location+cone.location)/2.0
>>> mid_point
Vector((2.5, 3.5, 4.5))
```

You've created a uv sphere at position (1, 2, 3) and moved cone to position (4, 5, 6). You then calculated the midpoint of the two objects by adding and averaging their location vectors.

The next example shows how you can find the distance between two objects, by calculating the length of their offset Vector (which is the result of subtracting one object's location from that of the other). Start by adding a primitive cylinder object to the scene at (-4, -5, -6), move cone to (3, 2, 1), then subtract cylinder's location from cone's location to get the offset Vector v between the two objects:

```
>>> bpy.ops.mesh.primitive_cylinder_add(location=(-4, -5, -6))
{'FINISHED'}
```

```
>>> cylinder = bpy.context.scene.objects["Cylinder"]
>>> cone.location = Vector((3, 2, 1))
>>> v = cone.location - cylinder.location
>>> v
Vector((7.0, 7.0, 7.0))
```

The distance between cone and cylinder is then equal to the Vector v's length. Nifty, isn't it?

```
>>> distance = v.length
>>> distance
12.12435565298214
```

Since v is also the offset (or displacement) vector *from cylinder to cone*, you can add v to cylinder's location to move cylinder to the same location as cone:

```
>>> cylinder.location += v
>>> cylinder.location
Vector((3.0, 2.0, 1.0))
```

```
>>> cone.location
Vector((3.0, 2.0, 1.0))
```

Note that when you subtract vectors, for example, v3 = v1 - v2, the resultant vector v3 has the direction *from v2 to v1*.

Let's move `cylinder` back to where it was, by subtracting `v` from its location:

```
>>> cylinder.location -= v
>>> cylinder.location
Vector((-4.0, -5.0, -6.0))
```

We'll now compute the displacement `Vector v_opp` from `cone` to `cylinder`:

```
>>> v_opp = cylinder.location - cone.location
>>> v_opp
Vector((-7.0, -7.0, -7.0))
```

`v_opp` has the opposite direction of `v`. You can then add `v_opp` to `cone`'s location, to move `cone` to the same location as `cylinder`:

```
>>> cone.location += v_opp
>>> cone.location
Vector((-4.0, -5.0, -6.0))
```

Adding Modifiers to Objects and Changing Modifier Settings

Modifiers are essential tools for modeling in Blender which allow you to nondestructively edit mesh objects and preview changes before committing to them. There are several different categories of modifiers for different types of tasks, such as generating additional geometry, deforming meshes, and simulating particles like cloth and fluids. You can add a modifier to a mesh object in Python like this:

```
modifier_instance = <object>.modifiers.new( ↵
    <name of modifier instance>, <MODIFIER TYPE>)
```

<object> is the mesh object you're adding the modifier to, <name of modifier instance> is a string to name the modifier instance so you can reference it later, and <MODIFIER TYPE> is an all-capitalized Enum string indicating the modifier type, such as 'MIRROR', 'SUBSURF', and so on. You can find <MODIFIER TYPE> in the tool tips brought on by hovering the mouse cursor over the menu items under *Properties editor* ➤ *Modifier tab* ➤ *Add Modifier*, as shown in Figure 3-1.

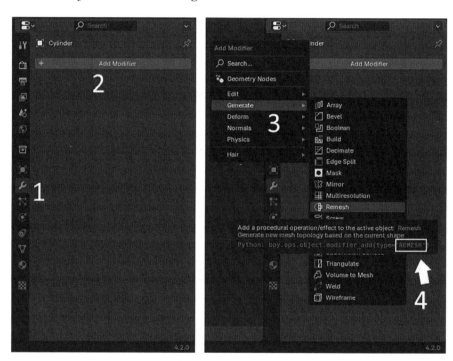

Figure 3-1. *Finding the* <MODIFIER TYPE> *Enum string for a modifier. Start by selecting a mesh object as active, then (1) go to Properties editor* ➤ *Modifier tab. (2) Click Add Modifier. (3) Hover the mouse cursor over "Generate" to expand it. (4) Hovering the mouse cursor over Remesh will bring up the tool tip containing its* <MODIFIER TYPE> *Enum string, in this case* 'REMESH'

Once a modifier instance is created, every setting visible in *Properties editor ▶ Modifier tab* can be changed through a Python script. Figure 3-2 shows an example of finding the Python variable corresponding to the *Merge Distance* of the Mirror modifier.

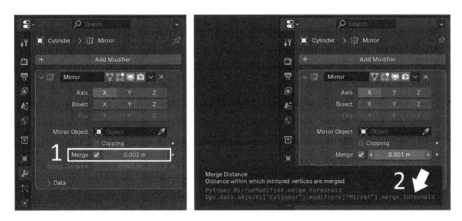

Figure 3-2. *Finding the corresponding Blender Python API property to a modifier setting. (1) Take example of the Merge Distance setting under the Mirror modifier; if you hover the mouse cursor over the slider to bring up its tool tip, (2) you'll find that its bpy property name is* merge_threshold

Let's work through a couple examples of creating and configuring modifiers using Python. A *Mirror modifier* instance creates a mirrored duplication of a mesh across either another object or across one or more given axes. It is commonly used for modeling subjects with some degrees of symmetry.

Starting with the default *.blend file, open the Scripting workspace, make sure that the 3D Viewport is in Object mode, then enter the following commands into the Python Console to add a primitive cone object to the scene and a Mirror modifier to the cone:

```
>>> bpy.ops.mesh.primitive_cone_add(location=(0, 0, 0),
radius1=4, depth=5)
{'FINISHED'}

>>> cone = bpy.context.scene.objects["Cone"]
>>> cone_mirror_mod = cone.modifiers.new("mirror_mod",
'MIRROR')
```

You can head over to the *Properties editor* ➤ *Modifier tab* to verify that a Mirror modifier instance named `mirror_mod` has been added to `cone`.

Since you assigned the modifier instance to the variable `cone_mirror_mod`, you can change the modifier's settings through it. Let's try this next. Keep an eye on `mirror_mod` under *Properties editor* ➤ *Modifier tab* as you enter each of the following commands into the Python Console. You should see the corresponding setting in the UI update immediately as you enter each command.

```
>>> cone_mirror_mod.show_in_editmode = False
>>> cone_mirror_mod.use_clip = True
>>> cone_mirror_mod.use_axis[0] = False
>>> cone_mirror_mod.use_axis[1] = False
>>> cone_mirror_mod.use_axis[2] = True
```

Through `cone_mirror_mod`, you turned off the option to display the modifier's effects in Edit mode. You then checked the "Clipped" check box to turn on clipping so the two mirrored halves don't go through the mirror and instead get clipped at their midline. In addition, you set the modifier to mirror about the Z axis but not the X or Y axis.

Another ubiquitous modifier used for mesh modeling is the Subdivision Surface modifier (Subsurf). Subdivision Surface is a technique for calculating a smooth surface from a coarser mesh through recursive subdivision. Here is an example of how you might set up a Subsurf modifier instance on the `cone` object from the previous exercise and configure its settings:

```
>>> cone_subsurf_mod = cone.modifiers.new("subsurf_mod",
'SUBSURF')
>>> cone_subsurf_mod.subdivision_type = 'SIMPLE'
>>> cone_subsurf_mod.levels = 2
>>> cone_subsurf_mod.render_levels = 3
>>> cone_subsurf_mod.show_on_cage = True
```

We add a Subsurf modifier named `"subsurf_mod"` to the object `cone` and assign the modifier instance to the variable `cone_subsurf_mod` so we can reference it later. The subdivision algorithm is set to "Simple". The number of subdivisions for previewing in the 3D Viewport ("Levels Viewport") is set to 2, and for rendering, it is set to 3 ("Render"). The option to adjust the edit cage to modifier results is turned on.

Now that you're familiar with the basics of working with existing objects and built-in primitives, I'll show you how to create new mesh objects using Python.

Creating New Mesh Objects

Sometimes, it makes sense to create a new object from a copy of an existing mesh such that the new object can be edited independently without affecting the original. A scenario where you might use this kind of setup is when you want to create several similar but nonidentical objects and you need the ability to edit each of these objects independently. For instance, let's say you're creating a library of game props that includes several swords with a similar underlying shape but different handles and decorations. You might start by making a simple sword mesh, then model a more complex variation that uses a copy of the simple sword as its starting point, and so on.

The function get_object_hard_copy shown in Listing 3-6 returns a new object created from a hard copy of the passed-in object's mesh data. Subsequently, the new object can be edited without affecting the original object. Add this function to your copy of creating_and_editing_mesh_objs.py, or look it up in the downloaded version.

Listing 3-6. Create a hard copy of a given mesh object (which can be edited independently), and link it to the given context's collection

```
def get_object_hard_copy(context, obj):
    context.view_layer.objects.active = obj
    bpy.ops.object.mode_set(mode='OBJECT')
    obj_copy = bpy.data.objects.new( ↵
        name=(obj.name+"_hard_copy"), ↵
        object_data=obj.data.copy())
    context.collection.objects.link(obj_copy)
    return obj_copy
```

Before copying its mesh data, the function sets the passed-in object obj as the active object, so it can be switched to Object mode—this is because if obj has been in Edit mode prior, all the edits will get forced through when obj is switched to Object mode, which ensures that its mesh data is up-to-date when it's copied.

Next, we call obj.data.copy() to create a copy of obj's mesh data and use it to construct a new object named after obj with the suffix "_hard_copy". The new object is linked to the given context's collection so it shows up in the viewport. Finally, the hard copy of the object is returned.

Note that obj.data is of type bmesh.types.BMesh; therefore, when you're calling obj.data.copy(), you're calling bmesh.types.BMesh.copy (not to be confused with Python's copy.copy()).

For example, in your script, you can add a primitive cone object, then call get_object_hard_copy to make a hard copy of it, like this:

```
add_cone_once(bpy.context)
cone_hard_copy = get_object_hard_copy(bpy.context, ↵
    bpy.context.scene.objects["Cone"])
```

Right after its creation, cone_hard_copy will look identical to cone. However, if you try editing either cone or cone_hard_copy, you'll see that the two objects are independent and changes made to one do not affect the other.

In some cases, you might want to create multiple objects that point to the same mesh data. When you edit the mesh through any one of these objects, the changes are automatically propagated to the rest of the objects that also use this mesh data.

For example, let's say you have a lamp mesh that you intend to place in various spots within an interior scene. You want to produce a consistent look for the room, so all instances of the lamp should look the same. By creating multiple lamp objects that share the same mesh data, you'll be able to edit the lamp mesh once to reflect the same changes on all the lamp objects in the scene.

You can modify Listing 3-6 to use the given object's mesh data directly to construct a new object (as opposed to using a copy of it), as shown in Listing 3-7.

Listing 3-7. Create a soft copy of a given mesh object (such that it shares the same mesh data) and link it to the given context's collection

```
def get_object_soft_copy(context, obj):
    context.view_layer.objects.active = obj
    bpy.ops.object.mode_set(mode='OBJECT')
    obj_copy = bpy.data.objects.new( ↵
        name=(obj.name+"_soft_copy"), ↵
        object_data=obj.data)
```

```
context.collection.objects.link(obj_copy)
return obj_copy
```

Notice that obj.data (which is obj's mesh data) is used directly as the object_data argument in the call to bpy.data.objects.new. This creates a new object that uses the same mesh data and looks identical to obj. Any edits you make to the new object's mesh will automatically be carried over to obj, and vice versa.

Getting Started with BMesh

In this section, I'll show you three different ways to use the Blender API's built-in module BMesh. The first way is to edit existing mesh data so you can continue building onto a model you already have. The second way is to create a mesh from scratch so you can generate a model procedurally or for when you don't have mesh data to borrow from. The third way is to use a stand-alone BMesh instance as a sketch pad to queue up edits without applying them to a mesh right away or as a shortcut for quickly replacing the mesh data of multiple objects at once.

Accessing or Editing an Existing Mesh

I'll first show you how to initialize a BMesh instance based on existing mesh data. You can add and remove geometry or perform other types of edits to a mesh through a BMesh instance created this way.

Listing 3-8 defines a function bmesh_from_existing() which adds a primitive cone object to the scene, makes a hard (independent) copy of it, then scales the copy via a BMesh instance bm. Add Listing 3-8 to your creating_and_editing_mesh_objs.py file, or locate the function in the downloaded script.

Listing 3-8. Add a primitive cone object to the scene, make a hard (independent) copy, then scale the copy via a BMesh instance bm

```
def bmesh_from_existing():
    add_cone_once(bpy.context, (2, 3, 3), 16, 1.5, 5.0)
    cone = bpy.data.objects["Cone"]
    cone_copy = get_object_hard_copy(bpy.context, cone)
    cone_copy.location = cone.location + Vector((0, -6, 0))

    if bpy.context.view_layer.objects.active is not None:
        bpy.ops.object.mode_set(mode='OBJECT')
    bpy.context.view_layer.objects.active=cone_copy
    bpy.ops.object.mode_set(mode='EDIT')

    bm = bmesh.from_edit_mesh(cone_copy.data)

    bmesh.ops.scale(bm, vec=(1, 2, 0.5), verts=bm.verts)

    bmesh.update_edit_mesh(cone_copy.data)
    bpy.ops.object.mode_set(mode='OBJECT')
```

The function starts by adding a primitive cone object to the scene using add_cone_once (from Listing 3-5), then creates a hard copy of cone with get_object_hard_copy (from Listing 3-6). If there is already an active object, it is switched to Object mode first, before cone_copy is made active.

Next, cone_copy is switched to Edit mode, and a BMesh instance bm is created from its mesh data (note that an object must be in Edit mode before you can call bmesh.from_edit_mesh with its mesh data). You can perform any type of edits on cone_copy's mesh through bm. We test this by scaling cone_copy through bm using the BMesh operator bmesh.ops.scale with scale factors 1, 2, and 0.5 in the X, Y, and Z directions, respectively. The vertices to be scaled are specified through the operator's verts argument, which is set to bm.verts (the sequence of *all* of cone_copy's vertices), to scale cone_copy as a whole.

119

The changes to cone_copy made through bm are cached on bm until you call bmesh.update_edit_mesh to flush the changes through to cone_copy. data (which is cone_copy's mesh data). You can call bmesh.update_edit_ mesh incrementally while editing a mesh or call it once you are finished with all the changes.

The results of calling bmesh_from_existing() are shown in Figure 3-3. The cone object is shown on the left, and the scaled cone_copy is shown on the right.

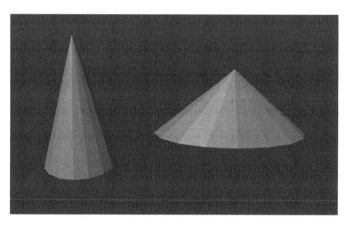

Figure 3-3. *Results of calling* bmesh_from_existing() *from Listing 3-8. Left: The original cone object. Right: A hard copy of cone scaled 200% in Y and 50% in the Z direction through a BMesh instance*

Building a Mesh from Scratch

In addition to editing an existing mesh, you can use BMesh to generate a mesh from scratch. To do this, you'll need to create an object containing an empty placeholder mesh, create a BMesh instance based on that placeholder mesh, then add geometry to the mesh through the BMesh instance—you can think of this as setting up a canvas (the mesh data) on an easel (the object), then adding paint strokes (vertices, edges, or faces) to the canvas by using a paint brush (the BMesh instance).

This technique is a lot like when you want to create a model by hand by laying down individual vertices and edges—you start by adding a built-in primitive object, then delete all of its vertices and edges to set up a blank object so you can add vertices one by one.

We'll write a function get_placeholder_mesh_obj_and_bm(), which creates an object with an empty placeholder mesh, along with a BMesh instance for modifying it, as shown in Listing 3-9.

Listing 3-9. Creating a placeholder mesh object and a BMesh instance for editing it

```
def get_placeholder_mesh_obj_and_bm(context, name, ↵
    location=Vector((0, 0, 0))):
    mesh_placeholder = bpy.data.meshes.new(name=name)
    obj_placeholder = bpy.data.objects.new(name=name, ↵
        object_data=mesh_placeholder)
    obj_placeholder.location = location
    context.collection.objects.link(obj_placeholder)
    for o in context.scene.objects:
        o.select_set(False)
    context.view_layer.objects.active = obj_placeholder
    bpy.ops.object.mode_set(mode='EDIT')
    bm = bmesh.from_edit_mesh(mesh_placeholder)
    return bm, obj_placeholder
```

get_placeholder_mesh_obj_and_bm() starts by creating an empty mesh data block mesh_placeholder, then uses it to create a new object obj_placeholder with the name and location that had been passed in.

Next, the function links obj_placeholder to the scene, deselects all, then sets obj_placeholder as active, and switches it to Edit mode, so it can create a BMesh instance bm for editing its mesh data. After that, bm and obj_placeholder are returned.

With a function to create a placeholder mesh object and a BMesh instance to edit it, we can now write another function, bmesh_from_ scratch(), to build mesh objects from scratch, as shown in Listing 3-10. bmesh_from_scratch() demonstrates how you can add geometry to a placeholder object via its BMesh instance.

Listing 3-10. Creating a placeholder mesh object and a BMesh instance for editing it

```
def bmesh_from_scratch():
    bm, obj_scratch = get_placeholder_mesh_obj_and_bm( ↵
        bpy.context, "from_scratch", Vector((0,0,0)))
    bpy.ops.mesh.primitive_monkey_add(location=(0,-5,-5), ↵
        rotation=(0,0,0), size=2.5)
    bpy.ops.mesh.primitive_monkey_add(location=(0,0,0), ↵
        rotation=(0,0,radians(45)), size=2)
    bpy.ops.mesh.primitive_monkey_add(location=(0,5,5), ↵
        rotation=(0,0,radians(90)), size=1.5)
    bmesh.update_edit_mesh(obj_scratch.data)
```

bmesh_from_scratch() starts by calling get_placeholder_mesh_obj_ and_bm() from Listing 3-9 to create a blank mesh object obj_scratch and a BMesh instance bm for editing it. Then, through bm, it adds three of the monkey primitives to obj_scratch's mesh data at various locations and rotations with calls to bpy.ops.mesh.primitive_monkey_add.

Note that since the three calls to bpy.ops.mesh.primitive_monkey_ add are made in Edit mode, they add geometry to the active object (obj_scratch). The rotation of each monkey is specified as a tuple of three radian values indicating rotation around the X, Y, and Z axes, respectively. radians(<deg>) is a function under Python's built-in math module, which you must import via from math import radians to gain access.

radians(<deg>) takes an angle in degrees and returns the equivalent in radians. The results of calling bmesh_from_scratch() are shown in Figure 3-4.

Figure 3-4. *Results of calling* bmesh_from_scratch() *from Listing 3-10, looking down the +X axis in the 3D Viewport*

Using BMesh As a Mesh Sketch Pad

You can also create a stand-alone BMesh instance without referencing any existing mesh data by calling bmesh.new(). Unlike a BMesh instance created using bmesh.from_edit_mesh(<some mesh data>), which can only be used to edit *that particular mesh*, a BMesh instance created using bmesh.new() acts like a sketch pad where you can add geometry and make edits without affecting any existing mesh. Once you're done with the edits, the contents of the stand-alone BMesh instance can be used to replace *any* object's mesh data.

The function bmesh_as_scketch_pad() shown in Listing 3-11 demonstrates this technique by using a stand-alone BMesh instance containing the geometry of a circle to replace the mesh data of two cone objects.

Listing 3-11. Using a single stand-alone BMesh instance to replace the mesh data of multiple objects

```
def bmesh_as_sketch_pad():
    add_cone_once(bpy.context, (2, 5, 3), 16, 1.5, 5.0)
    cone = bpy.data.objects["Cone"]
    cone_copy_1 = get_object_hard_copy(bpy.context, cone)
    cone_copy_1.location = cone.location + Vector((0,-4,0))
    cone_copy_2 = get_object_hard_copy(bpy.context, cone)
    cone_copy_2.location = cone.location + Vector((0,-9,0))

    bm = bmesh.new()
    bmesh.ops.create_circle(bm, cap_ends=True, ↵
        segments=8, radius=1)
    bm.to_mesh(cone_copy_1.data)
    bm.to_mesh(cone_copy_2.data)
```

bmesh_as_sketch_pad() first adds a cone object to the scene by calling add_cone_once (Listing 3-5), then creates two hard copies of it using get_object_hard_copy (Listing 3-6). A stand-alone BMesh instance bm is created using bmesh.new() without referencing any existing mesh data, then, the geometry of a circle is added to bm via the built-in operator bmesh.ops.create_circle. Next, bm is used to replace both cone_copy_1 and cone_copy_2's mesh data, causing both objects to turn into circles (note that the receiving object must be in Object mode when bm.to_mesh is called). You can see the result of calling bmesh_as_sketch_pad() in Figure 3-5, with the original cone object on the left and the two cone object copies with their mesh data replaced shown in the middle and the right, respectively.

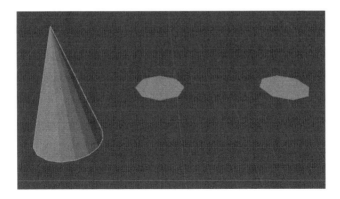

Figure 3-5. *Results of calling* bmesh_as_sketch_pad() *from Listing 3-11. Left: Original* cone *object. Middle and right: Two hard copies of the cone object with their mesh data replaced using a stand-alone* BMesh *instance*

Editing and Generating Meshes with BMesh

In this section, you'll delve deeper and learn how to work with individual vertices, edges, and faces. I'll start by showing you how to display indices of mesh elements in the viewport so you can visualize the order in which they're being laid out on a mesh and verify that a mesh generation script is working as intended.

Next, I'll show you how to add, remove, and look up vertices, edges, and faces on an object via a BMesh instance, as well as deform a mesh by moving vertices around. Putting all the concepts together, you'll try your hand at generating barrel meshes from scratch and creating interesting variations by changing parameter values.

Configuring Mesh Selection Modes

When you make a mesh editing add-on, it's often the case that you'll prompt users for a selection on a mesh for the add-on to modify. Depending on the nature of the add-on, it might make more sense to select

125

by a certain type of mesh element over another—for example, add-ons that manipulate edge loops should prompt users for edge selections.

The Vertex, Edge, and Face Select Mode buttons at the top of the viewport (in Edit mode) let you configure the type of elements that are selected when you click on a mesh. For example, if Edge select is enabled, then the closest edge(s) under the cursor are selected when you left-click or use box (B key) or circle (C key) select.

You can Shift-click multiple Select Mode buttons to enable more than one type of element to be selected simultaneously. For example, in Figure 3-6, both Vertex and Edge select are toggled on, so both the closest vertices and edges would be selected when you click a mesh.

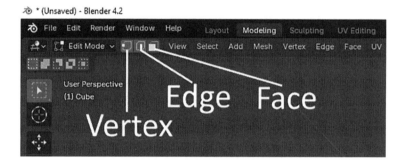

Figure 3-6. *Select Mode buttons in Edit Mode, for selecting the nearest vertex, edge, or face(s) when clicking a mesh with the mouse cursor. You can Shift-click more than one of the Select Mode buttons at once to enable multiple modes of selection. As shown, both the Vertex and Edge Select Modes are toggled on*

The mesh selection mode(s) can be configured using Python via the built-in variable `bpy.context.tool_settings.mesh_select_mode`, with a list of three boolean values, given in the order of vertex, edge, and face, with `True` to select a mode and `False` to deselect it. For example, to set the selection mode to vertex and edge, you would set the variable as follows:

```
bpy.context.tool_settings.mesh_select_mode = ↵
    [True, True, False]
```

126

Adding, Removing, and Looking Up Vertices, Edges, and Faces

In this section, I'll show you how to add and remove vertices, edges, and faces from a mesh object through a BMesh instance and look up edges or faces using their boundary vertices. Open the Scripting workspace, and make sure the 3D Viewport is in Object mode.

Using the concepts you've learned so far, create a blank mesh object test_obj and an associated BMesh instance bm for editing it in the Python Console, like this:

```
>>> import bmesh
>>> test_mesh = bpy.data.meshes.new(name="test_mesh")
>>> test_obj = bpy.data.objects.new(name="test_obj", ↵
    object_data=test_mesh)
>>> test_obj.location = (0, 0, 0)
>>> bpy.context.collection.objects.link(test_obj)
>>> bpy.context.view_layer.objects.active = test_obj
>>> bpy.ops.object.mode_set(mode='EDIT')
{'FINISHED'}

>>> bm = bmesh.from_edit_mesh(test_mesh)
```

Next, add a new vertex to test_obj via bm at location (1, 2, 3), like this. (You'll see the new vertex appear in the viewport right after you call bmesh.update_edit_mesh(test_mesh).)

```
>>> v1 = bm.verts.new(Vector((1, 2, 3)))
>>> bmesh.update_edit_mesh(test_mesh)
```

This creates a new vertex of type BMVert. Internally, bm adds newly created vertices to the end of the list of existing vertices. A single parameter, (1, 2, 3), which is a tuple of three numbers, is used to create a Vector instance, which is in turn used to create the vertex v1.

Note   Remember that the Python Console imports the Vector type for you. To use Vector in a script, you must import it yourself via from mathutils import Vector.

We'll create a few more vertices so we can use them to make edges and faces later:

```
>>> v2 = bm.verts.new(Vector((1, 2, 4)))
>>> v3 = bm.verts.new(Vector((2, 2, 4)))
>>>
>>> bmesh.update_edit_mesh(test_mesh)
```

To create a new edge between the two vertices, v1 and v2, you can use bm.edges.new, like this:

```
>>> e = bm.edges.new([v1, v2])
>>> bmesh.update_edit_mesh(test_mesh)
```

This creates a new edge e of type BMEdge between v1 and v2. Equivalently, you could have created e with bm.edges.new([v2, v1]), since the order of the two end vertices doesn't matter. However, make sure you only create an edge once. If you call bm.edges.new multiple times with the same vertices, even if they're in different vertex orderings, you'll get an error.

e's end vertices are stored in e.verts, with one end vertex as e.verts[0] and the other e.verts[1], which corresponds to the order in which the vertices are passed to bm.edges.new when e is created (in this case, e.verts[0] is v1, and e.verts[1] is v2). You can access e's index using e.index.

A new face is created with a boundary defined by a sequence of three or more vertices. For example, the following code creates a face f of type BMFace with the four boundary vertices, v1, v2, v3, and v4.

```
>>> f = bm.faces.new([v1, v2, v3, v4])
>>> bmesh.update_edit_mesh(test_mesh)
```

The face f is equivalent to a face created by selecting each vertex in the sequence by hand in the viewport and filling it by pressing the *F key*. The vertices in a face's boundary sequence can be ordered *clockwise* or *counterclockwise*, with the start and end vertices positioned anywhere along the cycle that makes up the boundary of the face. Hence, f's boundary can also be specified as [v3, v4, v1, v2], [v4, v3, v2, v1], [v3, v2, v1, v4], and so on, as shown in Figure 3-7. The difference is with each variation, the resultant face's internal ordering of vertices is different.

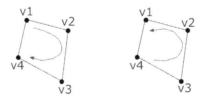

Figure 3-7. *Equivalent ways of defining face boundary verts in a sequence. Left: Clockwise, [v1, v2, v3, v4], or [v2, v3, v4, v1], and so on. Right: Counterclockwise, [v4, v3, v2, v1], or [v3, v2, v1, v4], and so on*

Make sure you only create the same face once. If you create the same face twice, even if the boundary vertex orderings are different, you'll get an error.

You can also access f's index using f.index and get the list of its boundary vertices using f.verts. You can find out how many vertices f has using the len function:

```
>>> len(f.verts)
4
```

To ensure that the internal lookup table for bm.verts is properly initialized and stays up-to-date, you need to call the built-in method bm.verts.ensure_lookup_table() before referring to vertices by their numerical indices for the first time, as well as after adding or removing any vertices.

```
>>> bm.verts.ensure_lookup_table()
```

Similarly, remember to call bm.**edges**.ensure_lookup_table() and bm.**faces**.ensure_lookup_table() before referring to edges and faces by numerical indices for the first time and after you've added or removed any edges or faces.

```
>>> bm.edges.ensure_lookup_table()
>>> bm.faces.ensure_lookup_table()
```

You can access vertices, edges, and faces with their numerical indices like this:

```
>>> v = bm.verts[0]
>>> e = bm.edges[0]
>>> f = bm.faces[0]
```

This assigns the first vertex, the first edge, and the first face we created to the variables v, e, and f, respectively. When you create an element, you can store it in a variable with a meaningful name so you can refer to it more easily later, like this:

```
>>> v_eyebrow_L_tip = bm.verts.new(Vector((2, 4, 6)))
>>> bmesh.update_edit_mesh(test_mesh)
>>> bm.verts.ensure_lookup_table()
```

You can retrieve an edge by its end vertices by calling bm.edges.get(<list of end verts>), like this:

```
>>> edge_between_v1_and_v2 = bm.edges.get([v1,v2])
>>> fallback_edge = bm.edges[0]
>>> edge_between_v1_and_v2_with_fallback = ↵
        bm.edges.get([v1,v2], fallback_edge)
```

Similar to bm.edges.new, the two end vertices can be given in either order. bm.edges.get returns None if the edge in question isn't found. Sometimes, it's a good idea to provide a fallback value, such as a nearby substitute edge, if you're not sure the edge you are looking for exists. The fallback value can be optionally specified as the second parameter to bm.edges.get, as in the last two lines of the previous example.

Like edges, you can retrieve a face using the list of its boundary vertices and specify a fallback value with the call to bm.faces.get(<list of boundary verts>):

```
>>> face_v1234 = bm.faces.get([v1,v2,v3,v4])
>>> fallback_face = bm.faces[0]
>>> face_v1234_with_fallback = bm.faces.get([v1,v2,v3,v4], ↵
        fallback_face)
```

To remove a vertex <vert>, you can call bm.verts.remove(<vert>). Let's try removing the vertex v_eyebrow_L_tip that you created earlier in this section:

```
>>> bm.verts.remove(v_eyebrow_L_tip)
>>> bmesh.update_edit_mesh(test_mesh)
```

Keep in mind that *removing a vertex will also remove any edges or faces that vertex is a part of*, so be careful! As you might've guessed, you can remove an edge or face in a similar fashion, using bm.edges.remove(<edge to remove>) and bm.faces.remove(<face to remove>), respectively.

Enabling Debug Option to Display Indices of Selected Vertices, Edges, and/or Faces

Another useful debug option in Blender is show_extra_indices, which lets you display the numerical indices of selected vertices, edges, and/or faces in the viewport. If you have multiple *Select Mode* toggled on in Edit mode (via Shift-click), e.g., vertex and edge, edge and face..., or all three, all those selected (regardless of type) will have their indices displayed.

To access the show_extra_indices option through Blender UI, first ensure that you have *Edit* ➤ *Preferences...* ➤ *Interface* ➤ *Display* ➤ *Developer Extras* checked. Then, in Edit mode, click the Mesh Edit Mode Overlays button at the upper right corner of the 3D Viewport, as shown in Figure 3-8; in the menu expanded, you'll find a Developer *Indices* check box near the top. Checking this check box will enable show_extra_ indices. Figure 3-9 shows an example of the default cube object's vertex and edge indices displayed.

If you hover the mouse cursor over the Developer *Indices* check box, the tool tip that pops up shows the following Python property:

bpy.data.screens["Modeling"].overlay.show_extra_indices

If you try setting this property in the Python Console, however, you'll get the following error:

```
>>> bpy.data.screens["Modeling"].overlay.show_extra_
indices = True
Traceback (most recent call last):
  File "<blender_console>", line 1, in <module>
AttributeError: 'Screen' object has no attribute 'overlay'
```

The Python tool tip isn't helpful here, unfortunately. You'll find out how to access show_extra_indices via Python in the next section.

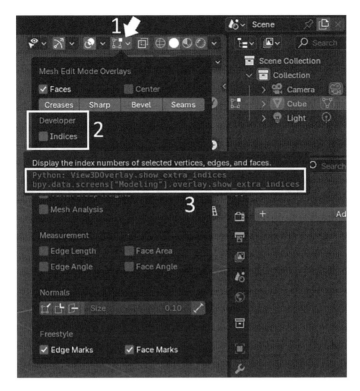

Figure 3-8. *Accessing the Developer Indices check box in the Mesh Edit Mode Overlays menu. (1) Click the button shown to expand the menu. (2) Check the Indices check box to enable the display of mesh element indices in the viewport. (3) The Indices check box's tool tip shows* bpy.data.screens["Modeling"].overlay.show_extra_indices

Note Recall from Chapter 2, you must go to *Edit* ➤ *Preferences...* ➤ *Interface* ➤ *Display* ➤ *Tooltips* and check both the *User Tooltips* and *Python Tooltips* check boxes, if you want to see the names of Python functions or properties that a menu item corresponds to in its tool tip.

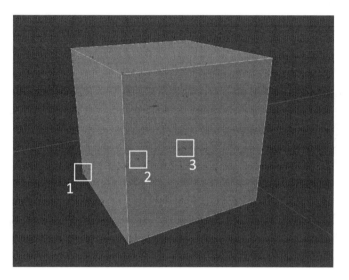

Figure 3-9. *Display of vertex and edge indices for the default cube object. (1) Vertex with index 7. (2) Edge with index 0. (3) Vertex with index 5. In other words, edge0 has vertex7 and vertex 5 as its two endpoints*

Locating the 3D Viewport Overlay Under Context

To access the show_extra_indices field, you have to write a function like display_mesh_element_indices shown in Listing 3-12, to iterate through the nested window structure under the current context to locate the 3D Viewport overlay.

Listing 3-12. Setting the value for View3DOverlay.show_extra_ indices, which is part of the overlay nested under the 3D Viewport

```
def display_mesh_element_indices(context, status):
    for a in context.window.screen.areas:
        if a.type == 'VIEW_3D':
            for s in a.spaces:
                if s.type == 'VIEW_3D':
                    s.overlay.show_extra_indices = status
                    return
```

Recall that context keeps track of where the user is currently interacting with Blender. Since the user can be using any of the workspace types at any given moment (or even a custom workspace), you cannot make assumptions about which screen areas may be currently open or what their ordering under the window may be like, which is why you have to iterate through each level of the nested structure under the current screen to locate the 3D Viewport.

A visualization of the nested window structure under context is shown in Figure 3-10. Under context.window.screen are a number of areas, with each area in turn having a number of spaces under it. Some space types have an overlay.

The 3D Viewport has an area of type 'VIEW_3D', with a space of type 'VIEW_3D' under it, which in turn owns an overlay (of type View3DOverlay), with a show_extra_indices property.

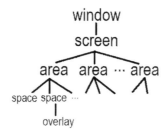

Figure 3-10. *Nested window structure under a given context. Under context.window.screen are a number of areas, with each area in turn having a number of spaces under it. Some types of spaces also have an overlay*

Tip   The `show_extra_indices` option to display edge, vertex, and face indices in the viewport is a great tool for debugging mesh generation scripts since you can easily visualize the order in which elements are added and removed.

Moving Vertices, Edges, and Faces

Now that you're familiar with how to add vertices, edges, and faces to a mesh via a `BMesh` instance, I'll show you how to move them around. Before continuing into this section, make sure you have a cube object in your scene named "Cube", either by using the default startup `*.blend` file or by adding one via *Add (Shift-A)* ➤ *Mesh* ➤ *Cube* in Object mode. Switch the cube to Edit mode, click to deselect all, and change the Mesh Select Mode to vertex and edge by holding down Shift while left-clicking the vertex and edge buttons.

We'll start by moving the cube object to the origin (if it isn't there already) and creating a `BMesh` instance `bm` to access it in the Python Console, like this:

```
>>> cube = bpy.context.scene.objects["Cube"]
>>> cube.location = (0, 0, 0)
>>> import bmesh
>>> bm = bmesh.from_edit_mesh(cube.data)
```

Next, you'll enable show_extra_indices as described in the previous section "Locating the 3D Viewport Overlay Under Context," to more easily visualize the movement of cube's vertices and edges.

Since we'll be referring to cube's vertices and edges by their numerical indices, we need to make sure the BMesh instance's internal lookup tables for vertices and edges are properly initialized and ready to be indexed, by calling:

```
>>> bm.verts.ensure_lookup_table()
>>> bm.edges.ensure_lookup_table()
```

With the lookup tables ready to go, you can make a vertex or edge's index show up in the viewport by selecting it in the Python Console. Type in the following commands while keeping an eye on the viewport. You'll see the vertex with index 2 become highlighted as its index appears next to it, as shown on the left of Figure 3-11.

```
>>> v = bm.verts[2]
>>> v.select = True
>>> bmesh.update_edit_mesh(cube.data)
>>> bm.verts[2].select
True
```

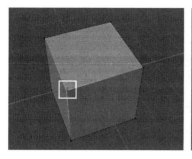 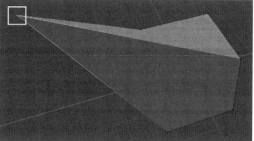

Figure 3-11. *Moving a vertex through a BMesh instance and visualizing it in the 3D Viewport with the help of* show_extra_ *indices. Left: The vertex at index 2 at its original location of (1.0, -1.0, 1.0). Right: The same vertex (index 2) moved to (2.0, -3.0, 4.0)*

You can access a BMesh vertex's location using its co variable. Try this with v.co:

```
>>> v.co
Vector((1.0, -1.0, 1.0))
```

Next, try moving v by adding an offset Vector to v.co, like this:

```
>>> v.co += Vector((1, -2, 3))
>>> v.co
Vector((2.0, -3.0, 4.0))

>>> bmesh.update_edit_mesh(cube.data)
```

You'll see that the vertex with index 2 has moved by that amount in the viewport, as shown on the right of Figure 3-11.

Another way to move v is by assigning a Vector to v.co, hence overwriting its location:

```
>>> v.co = (2.5, -1, 2)
>>> bmesh.update_edit_mesh(cube.data)
>>> v.co
Vector((2.5, -1.0, 2.0))
```

Note that v.co = (2.5, -1, 2) is a shorthand for v.co = Vector((2.5, -1, 2)).

A BMesh edge (of type BMEdge) has two end vertices of type BMVert. You can find the coordinates of the two end vertices of an edge—verts[0] and verts[1]—like this:

```
>>> bm.edges[10].verts[0].co
Vector((-1.0, 1.0, 1.0))
```

```
>>> bm.edges[10].verts[1].co
Vector((1.0, 1.0, 1.0))
```

As a result, you can find the direction of an edge by subtracting one end vertex's location from that of the other:

```
>>> edge_direction = bm.edges[10].verts[1].co - ↵
        bm.edges[10].verts[0].co
>>> edge_direction
Vector((2.0, 0.0, 0.0))
```

edge_direction is therefore the direction from bm.edges[10].verts[0] to bm.edges[10].verts[1].

The length of the edge bm.edges[10] is equal to the length of edge_direction:

```
>>> edge_direction.length
2.0
```

Using the same process, you can find the Vector from any vertex to any other vertex—which is useful for many purposes, such as measuring the distance between any pair of vertices or determining the offset to extrude an edge (or face) loop based on neighboring geometry.

Moving, scaling, or changing the orientation of an edge can be achieved by moving one or both of that edge's end vertices. For example, to scale an edge by 50%, you can move one of its end vertices to the edge's midpoint. Enter the following code to scale the edge bm.edges[2] to 50% its length by moving its second end vertex to its midpoint:

```
>>> bm.edges[2].verts[1].co = (bm.edges[2].verts[0].co + ↵
        bm.edges[2].verts[1].co) / 2.0
>>> bmesh.update_edit_mesh(cube.data)
```

We calculate bm.edges[2]'s midpoint by averaging the coordinates of its two end vertices, then use the midpoint to replace bm.edges[2]'s second end vertex's coordinates.

To make an edge twice as long, you can offset one end of the edge using the displacement Vector between that edge's two end vertices, like this:

```
>>> bm.edges[6].verts[1].co += (bm.edges[6].verts[1].co - ↵
        bm.edges[6].verts[0].co)
>>> bmesh.update_edit_mesh(cube.data)
```

You can also slide one end vertex of an edge along a given axis. For example, you can slide the second end vertex of the edge bm.edges[4] along the X axis, by incrementing that vert's X coordinate, verts[1].co[0] by 1:

```
>>> bm.edges[4].verts[1].co[0] += 1
>>> bmesh.update_edit_mesh(cube.data)
```

If you apply the same offset to both ends of an edge, the edge is moved, but the length and orientation of that edge is preserved:

```
>>> offset = Vector((0, 0, -0.5))
>>> bm.edges[11].verts[0].co += offset
>>> bm.edges[11].verts[1].co += offset
>>> bmesh.update_edit_mesh(cube.data)
```

Similarly, you can manipulate faces by moving one or more of a face's boundary vertices. For example, to align a corner or a side of the face with another face in preparation for merging.

There is also a built-in BMFace method for calculating face area, which returns the face's area as a decimal number:

```
>>> bm.faces[3].calc_area()
5.153882026672363
```

Generating Simple Barrel Meshes from Scratch

Now you know the basics of mesh manipulation by Python; in this section, you'll put your skills to the test by generating simple barrel meshes from scratch with BMesh. You'll start by generating circles to lay out the barrel's cross-sections, followed by forming the barrel's silhouette using a handful of built-in operators.

Generating the Circular Top, Bottom, and Cross-Sections of the Barrel

Many familiar shapes are defined by mathematical formulas that can be easily adapted into part of a mesh generation script. The parameters of these formulas can be exposed as user-inputted values through UI widgets or values read from a file which are then passed as arguments into a script function.

Let's see an example of this. The function add_circle in Listing 3-13 approximates the shape of a circle with the passed-in radius, by walking along the circle's perimeter, adding one "pie slice" at a time to create the given number of segments (num_segments). A visualization of this process is shown in Figure 3-12.

add_circle uses a list to keep track of the vertices as they're added to the circle so the vertices can be returned and used later to fill in the end caps of the barrel with faces. The completed circle mesh is added to the passed-in BMesh instance bm, with a Z offset specified by the argument z.

Listing 3-13. Function to add a circle mesh parallel to the XY plane to the given bmesh instance. The circle is constructed based on the passed-in radius, number of segments, and Z offset

```
def add_circle(bm, radius, num_segments, z):
    verts_added = []
    v_prev = None
    v0 = None
    for segment in range(num_segments):
        theta = (segment/num_segments)*2*pi
        v = bm.verts.new(Vector((radius*cos(theta), ↵
            radius*sin(theta), z)))
        verts_added.append(v)
        if segment == 0:
            v0 = v
        if v_prev:
            bm.edges.new([v_prev, v])
        if segment == num_segments - 1:
            bm.edges.new([v, v0])
        v_prev = v
    return verts_added
```

Let's look at add_circle's implementation in more detail. To create the circle, the function walks along the circle's perimeter and creates one edge at a time. Based on the total number of segments (num_segments), the coordinates of each vertex along the perimeter are calculated using the angle theta at the point of its "slice of pie." If you imagine the circle in Figure 3-12 as sitting parallel to the X (red)-Y (green) plane, then each vertex on the circle's perimeter will have the coordinates

```
(radius*cos(theta), radius*sin(theta), z),
```

where z is the Z axis offset passed into the function. The function stores the first vertex in a variable v0 so it can connect the last vertex of the circle back around to the beginning at the end. Each step of the way, the function makes an edge to connect the newly created vertex to the vertex created in the previous step. The very last vertex also connects back to the first vertex.

Note that because the circle's vertices are being added to an existing object through a BMesh instance, Blender automatically offsets their coordinates based on the location of that object.

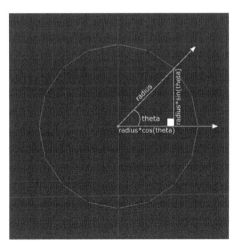

Figure 3-12. *Finding the coordinates of a vertex on a circle. You can see that if the radius is the hypotenuse of the right triangle (which is the side opposite the right angle), then the side opposite theta is radius * sin(theta), and the side adjacent to theta is radius * cos(theta)*

Procedurally Generating a Barrel Using Circular Cross-Sections

Next, we'll add the function generate_barrel, as shown in Listing 3-14, which generates barrel meshes, by using the outputs of add_circle (Listing 3-13) to create edge loops as the barrel's cross-sections, then bridging the edge loops to form the barrel's overall silhouette.

Listing 3-14. Generating barrel meshes from scratch using BMesh

```
def generate_barrel(context, name, radius_end, radius_mid, ↵
    height, num_segments, center=Vector((0, 0, 0))):
    bm, barrel_obj = get_placeholder_mesh_obj_and_bm( ↵
        bpy.context, name, center)

    bottom_cap_verts = add_circle(bm, radius_end, ↵
        num_segments, -height/2.0)
    add_circle(bm, radius_mid, num_segments, 0)
    top_cap_verts = add_circle(bm, radius_end, num_segments, ↵
        height/2.0)

    bm.faces.new(top_cap_verts)
    bm.faces.new(bottom_cap_verts)

    bmesh.ops.bridge_loops(bm, edges=bm.edges)
    bmesh.ops.recalc_face_normals(bm, faces=bm.faces)
    bpy.ops.mesh.select_all(action='SELECT')
    bpy.ops.mesh.subdivide(smoothness=1.1)

    bmesh.update_edit_mesh(barrel_obj.data)
    bpy.ops.object.mode_set(mode='OBJECT')
    context.view_layer.update()
```

First, generate_barrel creates a blank mesh object barrel_obj and a BMesh instance bm for editing it by calling the function get_placeholder_mesh_obj_and_bm from Listing 3-9. Then, three edge loops defining the bottom, middle, and top cross-sections of the barrel are added via bm using the outputs of add_circle from Listing 3-13.

The end cap faces are filled in next, and the three cross-sections are bridged together using the built-in operator bmesh.ops.bridge_loops. Then, the normals are recalculated to ensure that they're consistent (all facing outward). Finally, we subdivide the barrel using bpy.ops.mesh.subdivide with a smoothness of 1.1 (by first selecting all since the operator performs the subdivision based on the current selection).

Let's experiment by calling generate_barrel with several different sets of argument values, to see what kinds of variations we'd get. The first set of values uses radius_mid=5 which is larger than radius_end=3, and height=10 (twice of radius_mid), as shown in Listing 3-15. This proportion makes a traditional barrel shape with a rounded silhouette that is widest in the middle and tapers smoothly to two wide ends. The generated mesh is shown in Figure 3-13.

Listing 3-15. Generating a traditional barrel shape with generate_barrel

```
generate_barrel(bpy.context, "test_barrel", radius_end=3, ↵
    radius_mid=5, height=10, num_segments=16, ↵
    center=Vector((0,0,5)))
```

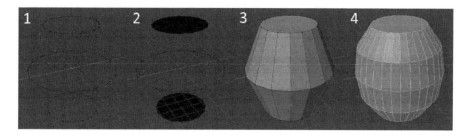

Figure 3-13. *Results of calling* generate_barrel *with* radius_
end=3, radius_mid=5, height=10, num_segments=16
(Listing 3-15). Steps 1–4 show the progression of the generation

The next set of values we'll try is shown in Listing 3-16, with radius_
mid=2, which is only slightly larger than radius_end=1.5, and height=15,
which is much larger than radius_mid. This proportion makes a tall
slender column shape. The generated mesh is shown in Figure 3-14.

Listing 3-16. Generating a tall slender column shape with
generate_barrel

```
generate_barrel(bpy.context, "test_tall_slim_barrel", ↩
    radius_end=1.5, radius_mid=2, height=15, ↩
    num_segments=16, center=Vector((0,12,7.5)))
```

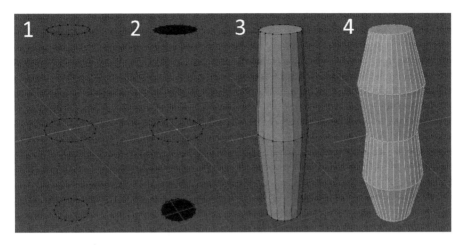

Figure 3-14. *Results of calling* generate_barrel *with* radius_
end=1.5, radius_mid=2, height=15, num_segments=16
(Listing 3-16). Steps 1–4 show the progression of the generation

The third set of values we'll try, as shown in Listing 3-17, is radius_
mid=2, which is smaller than radius_end=5, and height=7. This proportion
makes a bar stool shape as opposed to a barrel shape. The generated mesh
is shown in Figure 3-15.

Listing 3-17. Generating a bar stool shape with generate_barrel

```
generate_barrel(bpy.context, "test_bar_stool", radius_end=5, ↵
    radius_mid=2, height=7, num_segments=16, ↵
    center=Vector((0,24,3.5)))
```

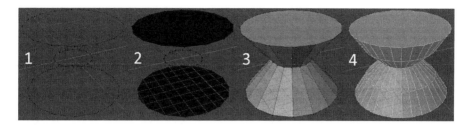

Figure 3-15. *Results of calling* generate_barrel *with* radius_
end=5, radius_mid=2, height=7, num_segments=16 *(Listing 3-17).*
Steps 1–4 show the progression of the generation

Figure 3-16 shows the results of calling Listing 3-15, Listing 3-16, and
Listing 3-17 side by side. You can see that by implementing a single procedural
generation function and strategically exposing several key arguments that
control the mesh's silhouette, you are able to create interesting variations that
are also vastly different, simply by changing the values of the arguments in
creative ways. This concept is called parametric modeling.

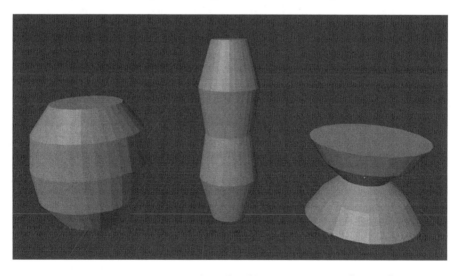

Figure 3-16. *Comparing results of calling* generate_barrel
(Listing 3-14) with different argument values. From left to right are
results of Listing 3-15, 3-16, and 3-17, respectively

Summary

In this chapter, you learned how to access, create, and edit mesh objects with the built-in modules BMesh and bpy.ops. You started with the basics like looking up objects by name, switching objects between modes, and selecting objects using Python as if you were selecting them by hand in the 3D Viewport.

You then learned how to utilize bpy.ops operators to quickly populate a scene with a variety of built-in primitives with custom proportions and sizes and practiced moving objects and configuring modifiers using these primitives.

Once you became familiar with manipulating existing mesh objects, you learned how to create new objects and use BMesh to edit and add geometry to them. You then delved deeper and looked at modifying individual vertices, edges, and faces and how to display their indices in the viewport so you can visualize how mesh elements are added to a model over time.

Putting it all together, you wrote your first procedural generation script to produce barrel meshes and learned to use the techniques of parametric modeling to expose arguments that control key aspects of the generation process to create purposeful and varied outputs.

CHAPTER 4

Advanced Mesh Modeling

In Chapter 3, you learned how to automate the prep work for a modeling session by setting up and organizing objects with Python, plus the basics of accessing and editing verts, edges, and faces. In this chapter, you'll learn how to automate steps for contouring and refining a mesh, as well as perform cleanup tasks in Python after wrapping up a model.

I'll show you how to write Python functions for building up the general structure of a mesh using edge loops and automate common modeling tasks like merging, splitting, rotating, and scaling parts of a mesh. You'll also practice adding detail and fine-tuning a mesh by beveling and insetting mesh elements in Python. To conclude the chapter, you'll learn how to write script functions for performing cleanup tasks such as correcting a model's normals and removing doubles and loose vertices.

Running This Chapter's Examples

The source code for this book is available on GitHub via the book's product page, located at `www.apress.com/979-8-8688-1126-5`). I've prepared this chapter's examples in two versions. The first version is meant to run in the Text Editor and the second version installed as an extension add-on. Both versions contain the same Python mesh editing examples.

© Isabel Lupiani 2025

I. Lupiani, *Blender Scripting with Python*, https://doi.org/10.1007/979-8-8688-1127-2_4

The trade-off is with the Text Editor version, you can change argument values (e.g., the distance of loop slides) and see how they influence the outcome, but it's cumbersome to change which function(s) to call and the order they are called, unless you modify the script.

With the extension version, it's easy to access the examples since you press buttons in the UI to invoke them as operators; however, you cannot change their argument values (they are too numerous to set up and attempting to do so detracts from the purpose of the chapter).

First, I'll walk you through how to install and run each version, then, I'll go over the high-level differences between the two. Finally, we'll look at how the two versions handle importing script files differently.

Setting Up/Running the Script Version

Go to the Scripting workspace and open /Ch4/text_editor/mesh_ editing_ops.py in the Text Editor to run it. There is a block already set up at the bottom of the file (with an excerpt shown in Listing 4-1) that calls the functions for testing the mesh editing examples in this chapter. You can selectively comment them in and out to control which functions are called.

Listing 4-1. Excerpt of testing block from /Ch4/text_editor/mesh_ editing_ops.py

```
if __name__ == "__main__":
    test_create_loop_stack(bpy.context)
    test_create_cylinder_bmesh(bpy.context)
    test_create_cone_bmesh(bpy.context)
    # ---- SNIPPED ----
```

Installing/Running the Extension Add-On Version

Go to Edit ➤ Preferences… ➤ Get Extensions, click the blue downward "v" at the upper right to expand the menu, and click *Install from Disk….* Navigate to the Ch4/extension/test_mesh_editing/ folder in the downloaded source, and choose the file test_mesh_editing-2.0.0.zip. The add-on containing this chapter's examples will be installed and automatically enabled, as shown in Figure 4-1.

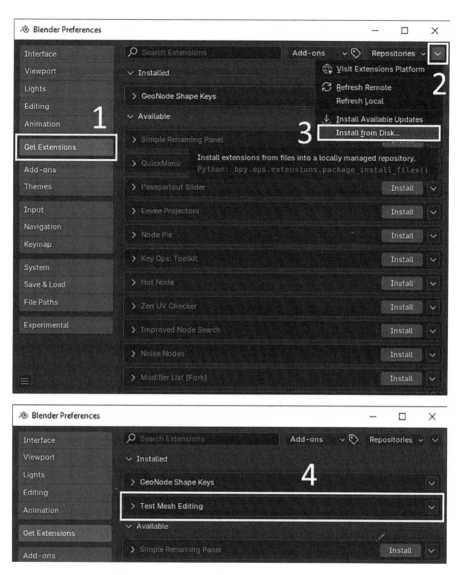

Figure 4-1. *Installing the Test Mesh Editing extension which contains this chapter's examples. Go to Edit ➤ Preferences…, (1) click Get Extensions on the left, then (2) click the "v" at the upper right to expand the menu, (3) click Install from Disk…, and navigate to the /Ch4/extension folder in the downloaded source, and pick* test_mesh_editing.zip. *You should see "Test Mesh Editing" appear in the Installed list*

Once installed, you can access the add-on "Test Mesh Editing" in the 3D Viewport *Properties* shelf (N key) ➤ *Tool* tab, as shown in Figure 4-2. Each button invokes a different category of mesh editing examples in this chapter.

Figure 4-2. *You can access the Test Mesh Editing add-on in the viewport Properties shelf (N key) ➤ Tool tab*

156

Script vs. Add-On at the Source Level

If you open both Ch4/text_editor/mesh_editing_ops.py and Ch4/
extension/test_mesh_editing/__init__.py and compare the two, you'll
notice they only differ in two major ways. The first is how they import
creating_and_editing_mesh_objs.py. The second is mesh_editing_ops.py
uses Listing 4-1 to call the test functions when you click run in the Text
Editor, whereas __init__.py contains operator classes (which call the test
functions) that are assembled into a UI panel.

Importing Functions from Other Scripts

To help with setting up geometry for the mesh editing experiments, we
import the function get_placeholder_mesh_obj_and_bm from creating_
and_editing_mesh_objs.py (a script from Chapter 3. There are separate
copies of this file under both Ch4/text_editor/ and Ch4/extension/
test_mesh_editing/ for both versions of the examples to import from).

We call get_placeholder_mesh_obj_and_bm to create placeholder
objects with empty mesh data, then use various bmesh.ops functions to
fill them with primitives, and practice mesh editing in Python on these
meshes, like cutting and sliding edge loops along a cylinder.

Importing for Running in the Text Editor

When running in the Text Editor, Blender's built-in Python does not
automatically look in the directory your active *.py file is for imports. You
have to derive the directory's path and add it to the list of paths Blender's
built-in Python will scan, as shown in Listing 4-2.

Listing 4-2. Importing other *.py files in the active file's directory when running from the Text Editor

```
import os, sys
script_dir = ""
if bpy.context.space_data and bpy.context.space_data.text:
    script_filepath = bpy.context.space_data.text.filepath
    if script_filepath:
        script_dir = os.path.dirname(script_filepath)
        if not script_dir in sys.path:
            sys.path.append(script_dir)
from creating_and_editing_mesh_objs import ↵
    get_placeholder_mesh_obj_and_bm
```

Since you're running the script in the Text Editor, bpy.context.space_data is the Text Editor, bpy.context.space_data.text is the active text data block, and bpy.context.space_data.text.filepath is the filepath of the active text data block (note that this path may not be valid yet—if you create a new data block and haven't saved it to disk, this will be a zero-length string).

You can call os.path.dirname to extract the directory portion of bpy.context.space_data.text.filepath. If this directory is not in sys.path yet (where Blender's built-in Python will scan for imports), you append it. (Note that you will need to import os, sys at the top of the script to use os.path.dirname and sys.path).

With the active block's directory appended to sys.path, you can import any *.py file from that directory as a module. To import a function named ‹function› from the file ‹module›.py, you'll do from ‹module› import ‹function›.

For example, to import the function get_placeholder_mesh_obj_and_bm from creating_and_editing_mesh_objs.py, you'll do:

```
from creating_and_editing_mesh_objs import ↵
    get_placeholder_mesh_obj_and_bm
```

You can then call the imported function in the active script as if it's in the same file.

Importing Scripts in an Add-On to Be Packaged

As discussed in the section "Script vs. Add-on at the Source Level," when Ch4/text_editor/mesh_editing_ops.py is converted to an add-on, it's renamed to __init__.py and moved under /test_mesh_editing/ (a directory named after the add-on). creating_and_editing_mesh_objs.py is unchanged and copied to /test_mesh_editing/ alongside __init__.py.

Listing 4-3 shows how you can import *.py files at the top of __init__.py. The code checks if Blender is already running (if "bpy" in locals()), and if so, it reloads the previously imported module to reflect any changes. Otherwise, it simply imports the module from the same directory (from . import creating_and_editing_mesh_objs).

Listing 4-3. Importing other *.py files at the top of the __init__.py file for an add-on

```
if "bpy" in locals():
    import importlib
    importlib.reload(creating_and_editing_mesh_objs)
else:
    from . import creating_and_editing_mesh_objs
```

Within __init__.py, you can then call the imported function with <module>.<function>. For example, creating_and_editing_mesh_objs. get_placeholder_mesh_obj_and_bm.

Turning a Script into an Add-On

To develop your own operator, you'd often start by writing a Python function and running it in the Text Editor. After you are confident the function works, you turn it into an operator class and possibly integrate it (along with other operators) into an add-on. In this section, I'll use this chapter's extension to briefly explain this process. You can find more detail about how to structure operators and add-ons in Chapter 2.

For example, to turn the function `test_extrude(context)` from Ch4/extension/test_mesh_editing/__init__.py into an operator, you'd create an operator class like the one shown in Listing 4-4, which derives from `Operator` (`bpy.types.Operator`) with a `bl_idname` (unique identifier for the operator) and a `bl_label` (name for the operator to display in the UI) and overrides the `execute(self, context)` method, in which you'd call `test_extrude(context)`.

Listing 4-4. Turning the function `test_extrude(context)` into the operator class `TestExtrusionOperator`

```python
class TestExtrusionOperator(Operator):
    bl_idname = "mesh.test_extrusion"
    bl_label = "Test Extrusion"
    """Test Extrusion"""

    def execute(self, context):
        test_extrude(context)
        self.report({'INFO'}, "Test Extrusion")
        return {'FINISHED'}
```

Tip   You have the option of calling multiple functions in your operator's execute(self, context) method. You can also implement your operator's action directly in execute (instead of calling a function). The advantage of delegating the action to a function is you can reuse that function elsewhere.

Listing 4-5 shows an excerpt of the panel class from Ch4/extension/ test_mesh_editing/__init__.py. Blender expects the panel class' name and bl_idname to contain the substring "_PT_". Since the panel is to be inserted into the *Properties* shelf ➤ *Tool* tab, the class has the bl_space_ type = 'VIEW_3D', bl_region_type = 'UI', and bl_category = 'Tool'.

To turn an operator into a button (such that when you press the button it invokes the operator), you'd simply do:

```
<box>.operator(<operator's bl_idname>, icon=<icon Enum string>)
```

For example, to create a button for TestExtrusionOperator from Listing 4-4, you'd call:

```
box0.operator("mesh.test_extrusion", icon='MESH_DATA')
```

as shown in Listing 4-5. At the start of the panel's draw method, it creates a layout containing a column (col0) with a box under it (box0). The button is inserted into this box.

Listing 4-5. Exposing an operator as a button in the UI as part of a Panel

```
class TEST_MESH_EDITING_PT_ToolPanel(bpy.types.Panel):
    bl_idname = "TEST_MESH_EDITING_PT_ToolPanel"
    bl_label = "TEST_MESH_EDITING"
    bl_space_type = 'VIEW_3D'
    bl_region_type = 'UI'
```

```
bl_category = 'Tool'
"""Test Mesh Editing Tool"""

def draw(self, context):
    layout = self.layout
    col0 = layout.column()
    box0 = col0.box()
  # --- SNIPPED ---
    box0.label(text="Test Extrusion")
    box0.operator("mesh.test_extrusion", icon='MESH_DATA')
    # --- SNIPPED ---
```

As discussed in Chapter 2, to complete an add-on so it can be installed by Blender, you have to create `register()` and `unregister()` functions to register and unregister classes that are part of your add-on, as well as `init_scene_vars()` and `delete_scene_vars()` functions to initialize and delete any scene variables the add-on uses.

BMesh vs. bpy.ops.mesh Operators for Mesh Editing

The Blender API provides two modules for programmatically generating and editing meshes: `BMesh` and `bpy.ops.mesh`. In this section, we will look at some of the pros and cons of using each module.

`BMesh` is Blender's mesh editing system since 2.63, with major improvements such as support for N-gons, knife tools (K key in Edit mode) that utilize N-gons, and cleaner topologies from loop cuts and subdivision. The `BMesh` module is exposed through Blender's Python API and allows script access to mesh elements (verts, edges, faces) along with their connectivity data. Mesh editing functions like split, join, dissolve, and so on are also available through the `bmesh.ops` module.

Alternatively, you can use the `bpy.ops.mesh` module, which contains the same mesh editing operations you invoke by hand through hotkeys or menu clicks in the viewport. As is the case with other `bpy.ops` operators, `bpy.ops.mesh` operators only return a set containing a flag indicating their exit status, like `{'FINISHED'}`, `{'CANCELLED'}`, and so on. Because `bpy.ops.mesh` operators don't return references to any additional geometry it might have created, such as from the results of ripping vertices or subdividing faces, you can't perform several edits in a row on the same part of a mesh by calling these operators back to back, by using the return value of one operator as the input to the next operator. For example, the operator `bpy.ops.mesh.rip_move` which rips and moves a vertex does *not* return the two vertices resulting from the rip; therefore, you wouldn't know which two vertices to select if you want to subsequently create an edge between them.

In addition, since `bpy.ops.mesh` operators are designed to work interactively based on user input, you have to explicitly select the portion of the mesh you intend for the operators to edit. Looking at a mesh in the viewport and making a selection by hand is straightforward; however, making the same selection in script can be challenging, especially if the mesh boundary isn't defined by clear-cut rules.

The benefit of using `bpy.ops.mesh` operators is that they behave and produce the same results in script as when you use the respective commands when modeling by hand. This can make them easier to learn and more intuitive to use than `BMesh` functions in some cases.

Unlike `bpy.ops.mesh` operators, `BMesh` functions like split, join, and dissolve return references to the newly created or destroyed mesh data, so you can chain up a sequence of `BMesh` method calls, with each referencing and building on the results of its predecessor.

`BMesh` methods let you pass in a list of input mesh elements (verts, edges, or faces) that you intend for the methods to make edits to, rather than having to select them one by one beforehand as in the case of `bpy.ops.mesh` operators.

In addition, bmesh.ops and bmesh.utils modules provide most of the same mesh editing operations as bpy.ops.mesh. You can use bmesh.utils to manipulate mesh elements on an individual basis, such as splitting edges, ripping verts, and so on, while bmesh.ops gives you higher-level routines that act on larger portions of a mesh at a time, like bridging loops, smoothing verts, insetting regions, and so on.

The good news is you can use both bpy.ops.mesh and bmesh in the same script; however, be mindful that bpy.ops.mesh operators can occasionally invalidate some of the references bmesh relies on, which would require the bmesh instance be updated or reinitialized altogether.

Using bmesh.ops Operators to Create Primitives

In this section, we'll look at using bmesh.ops functions to generate primitives like cylinders, cones, circles, grids, and cubes. If you are following along from the Text Editor, you can modify mesh_editing_ops.py to run each Listing. If you are using the extension version of the examples, simply press the "Test Create Primitives BMesh" button to run all the listings from this section in one go.

In the first example, we'll write a function create_cylinder_bmesh as shown in Listing 4-6 to generate a cylinder primitive. create_cylinder_bmesh accomplishes this by calling get_placeholder_mesh_obj_and_bm to create a placeholder object with empty mesh data, along with a bmesh instance bm for editing it, then add a cylinder to the object through bm by calling bmesh.ops.create_cone.

Listing 4-6. Generating a cylinder primitive using bmesh.ops.
create_cone

```
def create_cylinder_bmesh(context, name="cylinder_bmesh", ↩
    location=(0, 0, 0), radius1=1.5, radius2=1, ↩
    segments=16, height=1):
    bm, obj = get_placeholder_mesh_obj_and_bm(context, ↩
        name, location)
    bmesh.ops.create_cone(bm, cap_ends=True, ↩
        cap_tris=False, segments=segments, ↩
        radius1=radius1, radius2=radius2, depth=height)
    bm.edges.ensure_lookup_table()
    return bm, obj
```

Let's look at the arguments for bmesh.ops.create_cone in more detail.
cap_ends is True so the two ends of the cylinder are filled in with faces
(instead of being left open). cap_tris is False so the ends are filled with
n-gons instead of triangles. segments controls how-many-sided polygons
are used to approximate the circular end caps, with radius1 and radius2
determining their sizes. depth controls the height of the cylinder.

Since the caller of create_cylinder_bmesh will likely access the
cylinder's edges post creation, bm.edges.ensure_lookup_table() is
called here to ensure bm's lookup table for edges (bm.edges) is initialized
and ready to be indexed. (Recall that bm.edges.ensure_lookup_table()
must be called before the first time you use bm.edges[<index>] to retrieve
an edge as well as after you've made edits through bm so you don't get an
IndexError.)

You can generate a cone by calling create_cylinder_bmesh with 0 as
the argument value for either radius1 or radius2, as the example shown
in Listing 4-7.

Listing 4-7. Generating a cone primitive using bmesh.ops.create_ cone, by setting radius2 to 0

```
def create_cone_bmesh(context, name="cone_bmesh", ↵
location=(0, 0, 0), radius=1, segments=16, height=1):
    bm, obj = create_cylinder_bmesh(context, ↵
        name=name, location=location, ↵
        radius1=radius, radius2=0, ↵
        segments=segments, height=height)
    return bm, obj
```

You can also write a function that makes circles by replacing the call to bmesh.ops.create_cone with a call to bmesh.ops.create_circle, like this:

bmesh.ops.create_circle(bm, cap_ends=True, segments=segments, ↵
   radius=radius)

The parameter cap_ends when set to True fills the circle with an n-gon.

Similarly, you can create a grid by calling bmesh.ops.create_grid in bmesh.ops.create_cone's place. For example, the following call makes a 5-by-10 grid from a 12-by-12 Blender-unit square:

bmesh.ops.create_grid(bm, x_segments=5, y_segments=10, size=6)

The size argument for the grid here is analogous to the radius of a circle, which is the distance from the grid's origin to any one side. x_segments and y_segments specify the number of grid cells in each direction. With a size of 6, each side of the grid has 12 vertices, so each grid cell is 12/5 by 12/10 units or 2.4 by 1.2 units.

Lastly, to generate cubes, you'd call bmesh.ops.create_cube in lieu of bmesh.ops.create_cone. For example, you can create a cube with four Blender units per side like this:

bmesh.ops.create_cube(bm, size=4)

Editing Meshes with Edge Loops

An *edge loop* is a serially connected path of edges, as shown on the left of Figure 4-3. Each vertex in an edge loop has a valence (or degree) of four (having four edges connected to it). *Edge loops* are terminated by *poles*, which are vertices with an odd valence. *Face loops* are formed by the faces between two adjacent edge loops. *Edge rings* are similar to edge loops but consist of parallel instead of serial edges. Note that even though they're called loops and rings, these terms are more of a convention than definition, since the paths of edges or faces do not have to come back around into a closed circle. You can see examples of what an edge loop, edge ring, and face loop look like in Figure 4-3.

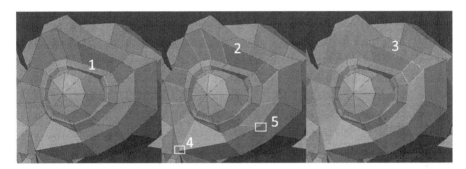

Figure 4-3. *Examples of (1) edge loop, (2) edge ring, (3) face loop, (4) pole, and (5) vertex of valence (degree) 4. The mesh used here is Suzanne and can be found under Add (Shift-A) ➤ Mesh ➤ Monkey in Object mode or Mesh ➤ Monkey in Edit mode*

With mesh Select Mode set to edge, you can select an edge loop with Alt-click and an edge ring with Ctrl-Alt-click. With Select Mode set to face, you can select a face loop with Alt-click.

When modeling organic forms, especially those that are meant to be animated like humans and animals, structuring edge loops to follow the natural contours and muscle flows of your subjects will allow the meshes to deform more cleanly and naturally. For example, arranging concentric edge loops around a human mesh's mouth will allow the mouth to expand and contract more easily to mimic lip movements in a speech animation.

Edge loops also allow a modeler (or script!) to quickly select and isolate a portion of a mesh for editing. For example, if you have loops surrounding the eye sockets, as in the case with Suzanne in Figure 4-3, you can select the loops by Shift-Alt-clicking one edge on each loop followed by Smooth to smooth the area. You can also use Loop Cuts (Ctrl-R) to create additional edge loops between existing ones to add more detail.

Additionally, you can systematically grow a structure by selecting the loops framing its cross-section and repeatedly extruding from them. For example, you can create an arm by selecting loops at the shoulder hole and Extrude (E key) along the length of the arm.

In this section, I'll show you how to automate several mesh editing tasks using edge loops in Python, starting with selecting edge loops, followed by bridging adjacent loops, extruding from selected loops, and cutting and sliding loops.

Selecting Edge Loops and Rings

While it's possible to select an edge loop by selecting one edge at a time (e.g., by iterating a sequence of BMesh vertices and their link_edges), it's much easier to call the built-in operator bpy.ops.mesh.loop_multi_select to select a desired edge loop or ring in one go.

You can write a function like select_edge_loops shown in Listing 4-8, which selects all the edge loops (or rings) each edge in the given list ref_edges is a part of.

Listing 4-8. Selecting edge loops with bpy.ops.mesh.loop_multi_select

```
def  select_edge_loops(bm, ref_edges, select_rings=False):
    bpy.ops.mesh.select_all(action='DESELECT')
```

```
for re in ref_edges:
    re.select = True
bpy.ops.mesh.loop_multi_select(ring=select_rings)

loop_edges = []
for e in bm.edges:
    if e.select:
        loop_edges.append(e)

return loop_edges
```

Recall that you can Alt-click one edge belonging to an edge loop to select that loop (or Ctrl-Alt-click to select the edge ring). Holding down Shift will allow you to select multiple loops or rings or add to an existing selection. select_edge_loops behaves as if you've Shift-(Ctrl)-Alt-clicked each of the edges in ref_edges.

select_edge_loops starts by deselecting all (A key), then selects each of the edges in ref_edges, before calling bpy.ops.mesh.loop_multi_select to select all loops the edges currently selected are part of. Note that the operator will select edge loops when ring is False and edge rings otherwise.

Although bpy.ops.mesh.loop_multi_select does not return the edges belonging to the selected loops, you can get around this by iterating through all the edges after the bpy.ops.mesh.loop_multi_select call and accumulate the ones that are selected in a list.

The example in Listing 4-9 shows how you can use select_edge_loops to select the edge loops at the two ends of a cylinder generated with create_cylinder_bmesh from Listing 4-6. If you're running the extension version of the examples, press the "Test Get and Select Edge Loops" button to run Listing 4-9 and 4-10.

Listing 4-9. Selecting the edge loops at the two ends of a cylinder

```
def test_select_edge_loops(context):
    context.tool_settings.mesh_select_mode = ↵
        [False, True, False]
    bm, obj = create_cylinder_bmesh(context, ↵
        name="test_select_edge_loops", ↵
        location=(0, 0, 0), radius1=1.5, ↵
        radius2=1, segments=8, height=2)
    loop_edges = select_edge_loops(bm, ↵
        ref_edges=[bm.edges[0],bm.edges[1]], ↵
        select_rings=False)
    bmesh.update_edit_mesh(obj.data)
```

Since edge #0 is part of the loop going around the bottom of the cylinder and edge #1 is part of the loop going around the top, select_edge_loops will select these two loops, as shown on the left of Figure 4-4. You can select the edge ring around the barrel of the cylinder instead (as shown on the right of Figure 4-4) by using one of the vertical edges and select_rings=True:

```
select_edge_loops(bm, ref_edges=[bm.edges[2]], ↵
    select_rings=True)
```

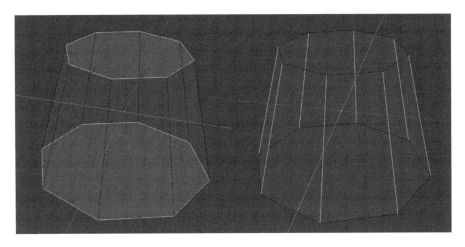

Figure 4-4. *Edge loops (left) and edge ring (right) selected as the results of running Listing 4-9*

Tip   Recall from Chapter 3 that once you have Edit ➤ Preferences… ➤ Interface ➤ Developer Extras checked, you'll have access to the option for enabling the display of indices of selected vertices, edges, and/or faces (this option is under Mesh Edit Mode Overlays ➤ Developer ➤ Indices). We also discussed in Chapter 3 how to use Python to enable this option.

You can use select_edge_loops to select parts of a mesh framed by edge loops (e.g., Suzzane's eye sockets) in preparation of calling another operator that acts on the currently selected portion of a mesh, like bpy. ops.mesh.vertices_smooth(). You can also manipulate the selected edges returned by select_edge_loops directly, such as scaling them.

select_edge_loops returns an unsorted list of all edges that are part of the selected loops; however, you don't know which edges belong to which loop. This poses a problem since sometimes you need to edit on a per-loop basis instead of all the loops at once.

You can write a function like get_edge_loops in Listing 4-10, which selects one loop at a time so it can record which edges are in each loop.

Listing 4-10. Retrieving the constituent edges of edge loops on a per-loop basis

```
def get_edge_loops(bm, ref_edges, select_rings=False):
    loops = []
    for re in ref_edges:
        bpy.ops.mesh.select_all(action='DESELECT')
        re.select = True
        bpy.ops.mesh.loop_multi_select(ring=select_rings)
        this_loop = []
        for e in bm.edges:
            if e.select:
                this_loop.append(e)
        loops.append(this_loop)
    bpy.ops.mesh.select_all(action='DESELECT')
    return loops
```

For each edge that's part of a loop you want to find, deselect all before selecting that edge to make sure it's the only thing selected, then, use bpy.ops.mesh.loop_multi_select to select the loop (or ring) that edge belongs to. Since at this point the loop is the only thing selected, finding the edges in the loop is the same as finding selected edges—hence, we do so by iterating through all the edges and accumulating the selected ones in a list (this_loop). We then add the loop (this_loop) to the list of all loops (loops) and repeat the process for the rest of the given edges (ref_edges).

The following example (Listing 4-11) shows how you can use get_edge_loops (Listing 4-10) to retrieve and print the indices of the edges making up the loops around the top and bottom of the cylinder created by create_cylinder_bmesh from Listing 4-6.

Listing 4-11. Using get_edge_loops to get the indices of the two edge loops at the ends of a cylinder

```
def test_get_edge_loops(context):
    bm, obj = create_cylinder_bmesh(context, ↵
        name="test_get_edge_loops", ↵
        location=(0, 0, 0), radius1=1.5, radius2=1, ↵
        segments=8, height=2)
    bmesh.update_edit_mesh(obj.data)
    loops = get_edge_loops(bm, ref_edges=[bm.edges[0], ↵
        bm.edges[1]], select_rings=False)
    for l in loops:
        print(str([e.index for e in l]))
```

After running Listing 4-11, you should see something similar to the following printed to the System Console (Window ➤ Toggle System Console):

```
[0, 4, 7, 10, 13, 16, 19, 22]
[1, 5, 8, 11, 14, 17, 20, 23]
```

You can verify that these two lists of indices match the two selected edge loops shown on the left of Figure 4-4, in the order of bottom to top.

By retrieving a group of edge loops on a per-loop basis, you have control over how each loop is adjusted individually as well as relative to each other while maintaining the proportion of the region represented by the group of loops as a whole. For example, when you're shaping an arm on a character, you can fine-tune the contour of the biceps, forearm, and wrists by editing the loops around each area while maintaining the relative proportion of the whole arm.

Bridging Edge Loops

Often, with a more complex model, you'd break down the subject into parts and model the pieces separately. A common way to stitch two constituent meshes together is to adjust the number of verts on the boundary of each piece to match, then connect the two pieces by bridging edge loops. In this section, we'll look at how to write script functions for bridging edge loops by utilizing built-in operators from the bpy.ops and bmesh.ops modules.

Generating a Stack of Edge Loops

To set up the geometry for bridging loops, I wrote a function called create_loop_stack which generates vertical stacks of circular edge loops, as shown in Listing 4-12.

Listing 4-12. Generating a stack of edge loops

```
def create_loop_stack(context, name="loop_stack_bmesh", ↵
location=(0, 0, 0), radius=1, num_loops=2, ↵
loop_segments=16, level_height=1):
    bm, obj = get_placeholder_mesh_obj_and_bm(context, ↵
        name, location)
    for i in range(num_loops):
        bmesh.ops.create_circle(bm, cap_ends=False, ↵
            segments=loop_segments, radius=radius)
    bm.verts.ensure_lookup_table()
    for i in range(1, num_loops, 1):
        for v in bm.verts[loop_segments*i:loop_segments*(i+1)]:
            v.co[2] += level_height*i
    bm.edges.ensure_lookup_table()
    return bm, obj
```

The function uses get_placeholder_mesh_obj_and_bm to create a placeholder object with empty mesh data and a bmesh instance bm for editing it, then adds the specified number of unfilled circles to the object through bm, each with the given number of segments (loop_segments) and radius.

The circles are all at the same location overlapping each other right now, so the next step is to separate them and arrange them into a vertical stack. We'll leave the first loop (circle at index 0) where it is, and move the rest up by offsetting the Z coordinate (v.co[2]) of the vertices in each loop according to which level the loop is (i) in the stack and how tall each level should be (level_height).

The loops (circles) are added sequentially through bm, so their constituent vertices are also listed in order in bm.verts. Since each loop has the same number of segments, we can infer the indices of each loop's constituent vertices using the loop's index. For example, if each loop has eight segments, then the first loop (index i = 0) has bm.verts[0] through bm.verts[7] or bm.verts[0:8], the second loop (index i = 1) has bm.verts[8] through bm.verts[15] or bm.verts[8:16], and so on. Finally, bm.edges.ensure_lookup_table() is called to ensure bm.edges is initialized and ready for lookup.

Listing 4-13 shows an example of how you can use create_loop_stack to create a mesh made up of five edge loops, such that each loop has a radius of 1.5 Blender units and eight segments and each pair of adjacent loops are two Blender units apart. If you are running the extension version of the examples, you can press the "Test Create Primitives BMesh" button to run Listing 4-13. The results of Listing 4-13 are shown in Figure 4-5.

Listing 4-13. Example of generating a stack of edge loops by calling
create_loop_stack

```
def test_create_loop_stack(context):
    _, obj = create_loop_stack(context, name="loop_stack_bmesh", ↵
        location=(0, 0, 0), radius=1.5, num_loops=5, ↵
        loop_segments=8, level_height=2)
    bmesh.update_edit_mesh(obj.data)
```

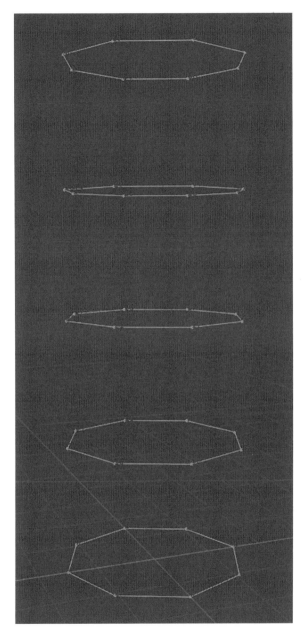

Figure 4-5. *Results of calling Listing 4-13 —a mesh object consisting of five edge loops that are two Blender units apart. Each loop has a radius of 1.5 Blender units and 8 segments*

Once you've generated a stack of loops, you can bridge the loops to make a cylinder as the basis for all kinds of models with an underlying cylindrical silhouette, like architectural columns, barrels, coke bottles, hour glasses, arms and legs, etc. You can also modify create_loop_stack to use shapes other than circles as units for the stack or add X and Y offsets to each loop instead of just stacking them straight up, to make spirals, cascades, and so on.

Bridging Edge Loops with bmesh and bpy Operators

Blender provides built-in operators for bridging edge loops through both the bmesh and bpy modules. We'll look at an example using bmesh first. The function bridge_loops_bmesh in Listing 4-14 uses bmesh.ops.bridge_loops to bridge edge loops and retrieve the newly created geometry.

Listing 4-14. Bridging edge loops by calling bmesh.ops.bridge_loops

```
def bridge_loops_bmesh(bm, ref_edges):
    edges_in_loops = select_edge_loops(bm, ref_edges)
    new_geom = bmesh.ops.bridge_loops(bm, edges=edges_in_loops)
    return new_geom['faces'], new_geom['edges']
```

bridge_loops_bmesh takes two arguments—the first is bm, the BMesh instance for the object you want to edit; the second is ref_edges, the list of edges indicative of the loops you want to bridge (with at least one constituent edge per loop).

Here, the select_edge_loops function from Listing 4-8 is used to select the loops and retrieve their edges, which are in turn passed to bmesh.ops.bridge_loops to perform the bridging.

bmesh.ops.bridge_loops returns the new geometry created by the bridging process in a Python dictionary (new_geom), where new_geom['faces'] is the list of new faces and new_geom['edges'] the list of new edges.

Listing 4-15 shows how you can use bridge_loops_bmesh to turn a loop-stack object generated with create_loop_stack (Listing 4-12) into an open-ended cylinder. If you're running the extension version of the examples, you can press the "Test Bridge Loops" button to call both Listings 4-15 and 4-16.

Listing 4-15. Using bridge_loops_bmesh to bridge the loops generated by create_loop_stack

```
def test_bridge_loops_bmesh(context):
    num_loops = 5
    num_segments = 8
    bm, stack_obj = create_loop_stack(context, ↵
        name= "test_bridge_loops_bmesh", location=(0, 0, 0), ↵
        radius=1.5, num_loops=num_loops, ↵
        loop_segments=num_segments, level_height=2)
    loop_ref_edges = [bm.edges[i*num_segments] for i in ↵
        range(num_loops)]
    resulted_faces, resulted_edges = bridge_loops_bmesh(bm, ↵
        loop_ref_edges)
    bmesh.update_edit_mesh(stack_obj.data)
```

Since every loop has the same number of segments, the first loop (index 0) has edges bm.edges[0:num_segments], the second loop (index 1) has bm.edges[num_segments:2*num_segments], and so on. Therefore, the line

```
loop_ref_edges = [bm.edges[i*num_segments] for i in ↵
    range(num_loops)]
```

grabs the first edge of every loop and accumulates them in a list (loop_ref_edges), which are then fed to bridge_loops_bmesh as reference for which loops to bridge (in this case, all the loops).

Notice that bridge_loops_bmesh creates the faces and edges in the same order the loops are given (in this case, from the bottom up). You can tell this by the way the indices increase since the indices reflect the order of which the faces and edges are created (smaller indices are created first).

If you don't need access to the faces and edges created by the bridging process, you can use bpy.ops.mesh.bridge_edge_loops to perform the bridging as shown in Listing 4-16, which is equivalent to selecting the edge loops with Alt-click followed by *Edge* ➤ *Bridge Edge Loops.*

Listing 4-16. Bridging edge loops by calling bpy.ops.mesh.bridge_
edge_loops

```
def bridge_loops_bpy(bm, ref_edges):
    select_edge_loops(bm, ref_edges)
    bpy.ops.mesh.bridge_edge_loops()
```

To test Listing 4-16, you can simply replace the line

```
resulted_faces, resulted_edges = bridge_loops_bmesh(bm, ↩
    loop_ref_edges)
```

in Listing 4-15 with

```
bridge_loops_bpy(bm, loop_ref_edges)
```

The result of running Listing 4-15 is shown on the left of Figure 4-6. The result of replacing the call to bridge_loops_bmesh in Listing 4-15 with bridge_loops_bpy is shown on the right. You can see that the two are identical.

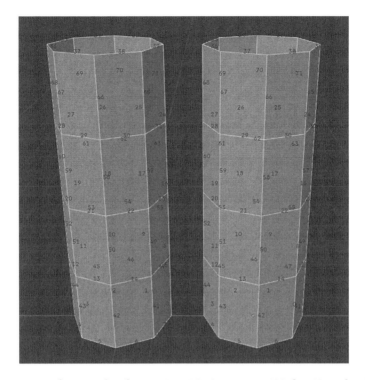

Figure 4-6. *Left: Result of running Listing 4-15. Right: Result of replacing the call to* bridge_loops_bmesh *in Listing 4-15 with* bridge_loops_bpy. *You can see the two are identical*

Extruding Edge Loops

Extrusion is a great way to "grow" meshes with cross-sections similar in shape throughout their length, such as those that are roughly cylindrical or tubular, like a fire hydrant or a horn. In this section, I'll show you how to approach extrusion in Python by utilizing two built-in operators and apply the concepts in action by generating a fun zigzag hornlike mesh using extrusion. If you're following along with the extension version of the examples, you can press the "Test Extrusion" button to call Listing 4-18 and 4-20 in this section.

Extrusion Using bpy.ops.mesh Operator

If you're just looking to extrude an edge loop once along a given direction without scaling or rotation, the simplest way is to use the built-in operator bpy.ops.mesh.extrude_region_move, as shown in Listing 4-17.

Listing 4-17. How to extrude with bpy.ops.mesh.extrude_region_move

```
def loop_extrude_region_move(bm, ref_edge, direction):
    select_edge_loops(bm, [ref_edge], select_rings=False)
    bpy.ops.mesh.extrude_region_move( ↩
        TRANSFORM_OT_translate={"value": direction})
```

The function uses select_edge_loops from Listing 4-8 to select the edge loop that ref_edge belongs to, then uses bpy.ops.mesh.extrude_region_move to extrude the loop along the given direction (a Vector). As with our convention so far, bm is the BMesh instance for the object you intend to edit.

Listing 4-18 shows how you can use loop_extrude_region_move to extrude a circle into a cylinder.

Listing 4-18. How to use loop_extrude_region_move to extrude a circle into a cylinder

```
def test_loop_extrude_region_move(context):
    bm, obj = create_circle_bmesh(context, ↩
        name="test_loop_extrude_region_move", ↩
        location=(0, 0, 0), radius=1, segments=8)
    loop_extrude_region_move(bm, ref_edge=bm.edges[0], ↩
        direction=Vector((1, 1, 2)))
    bmesh.update_edit_mesh(obj.data)
```

A circle is created (as described in the section "Using bmesh.ops Operators to Create Primitives") then extruded along the direction of the Vector((1, 1, 2)), which takes the circle upward two units and displaces it laterally one unit in both the X and Y directions. Note that an edge of the circle—in this case, the first edge bm.edges[0] (but can be any other)—is used to identify the circle as the loop we wish to extrude. You can see the results of running Listing 4-18 in Figure 4-7.

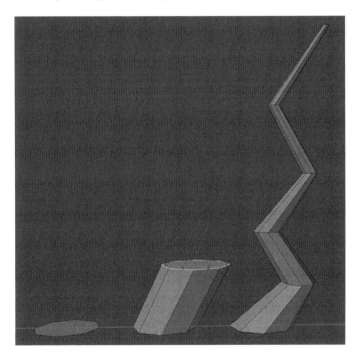

Figure 4-7. *Left: Circle created with* create_circle_bmesh *before extrusion. Middle: Results of calling* loop_extrude_region_move *to extrude the circle along a given Vector (Listing 4-18). Right: Results of extrusion by repeatedly moving copies of the circle, scaling, and bridging loops (Listing 4-20)*

Extrusion by Moving a Copy of the Loop and Bridging to It

If you're looking to have finer control over the course of an extrusion, such as having the option to scale each extruded segment, you can write a function like extrude_edge_loop_copy_move shown in Listing 4-19, which breaks up the process into several steps—copying the loop, performing the desired transformations to the copy, then bridging the original loop to the copy.

Listing 4-19. Extruding by moving a copy of the edge loop, scaling, and bridging the copy to the original loop

```
def extrude_edge_loop_copy_move(bm, ref_edge, direction,↩
    scale_factor):
    select_edge_loops(bm, [ref_edge], select_rings=False)
    bpy.ops.mesh.duplicate()
    bpy.ops.transform.translate(value=direction)
    bpy.ops.transform.resize(value=scale_factor)

    new_edge_loop = []
    for e in bm.edges:
        if e.select:
            new_edge_loop.append(e)

    bridge_loops_bpy(bm, [new_edge_loop[0], ref_edge])
    for e in new_edge_loop:
        e.select = False
    return new_edge_loop
```

The function uses select_edge_loops from Listing 4-8 to select the loop intended for extrusion, makes a copy of the loop via bpy.ops. mesh.duplicate() (same as Shift-D), then moves the copy along the given direction (bpy.ops.transform.translate(value=direction)), and scales it based on the given scale_factor (bpy.ops.transform. resize(value=scale_factor)).

At this point, the loop copy is the only thing selected; therefore, you can find the loop's edges by iterating through all edges and looking for the ones selected.

The extrusion is formed by bridging the original loop to the copy using the function bridge_loops_bpy from Listing 4-16.

You can generate some interesting shapes by repeatedly calling Listing 4-19 with different directions and scales. An example of this is shown in Listing 4-20, where a zigzag, hornlike shape is formed by repeatedly extruding new sections in alternating directions and decreasing scale.

Listing 4-20. Repeatedly extruding and editing the new loop formed at the top of the previous extrusion

```python
def test_extrude_edge_loop_copy_move(context):
    bm, obj = create_circle_bmesh(context, ↵
        name="test_extrude_copy_move", ↵
        location=(0, 3, 0), radius=1, segments=8)
    ref_edge = bm.edges[0]
    num_extrusions = 5

    for i in range(num_extrusions):
        direction = Vector((1,1,1.5)) if i%2 == 0 ↵
            else Vector((1,-1,1.5))
        scale = Vector((0.75,0.5,1)) if i%2 == 0 ↵
            else Vector((0.5,0.75,1))
        new_loop = extrude_edge_loop_copy_move(bm, ↵
            ref_edge,direction,scale)
        ref_edge = new_loop[0]

    bmesh.update_edit_mesh(obj.data)
```

A circle is created (as described in the section "Using bmesh.ops Operators to Create Primitives") and used as the initial cross-section to extrude from.

Each time we want to extrude a new section, we grab one edge from the topmost loop of the previous extrusion (in this case the first edge but can be any other) to indicate where we want to extrude from next. For the first extrusion, the loop to extrude from is the initial circle.

To make the extruded segments look zigzag, we alternate the direction between positive and negative Y every other extrusion. To make them hornlike, we use a scale factor < 1.0 so with each extrusion the cross-section gets smaller. You can see the results of running Listing 4-20 on the right of Figure 4-7.

Moving, Adding, and Sliding Loops

Loop cut-and-slides are great for adding detail and adjusting the contours of a mesh. Each edge loop or ring is like a control point or joint between the neighboring parts of a mesh. You can rotate or scale loops and rings to adjust the curvature of the underlying mesh. If there's no edge to work with where you need to make an edit, you can add more loops by making loop cuts in between neighboring loops or slide loops up and down to where you need them. In this section, I'll show you how to do loop cuts and slides from script functions by utilizing two of the built-in operators. If you're following along with the extension version of the examples, press the "Test Offset Cut Loop Slide" button to run Listings 4-22 and 4-24.

Offset Loop Slide

You can write a function like offset_loop_slide shown in Listing 4-21 to offset and slide from an existing loop.

Listing 4-21. Performing an offset loop slide using bpy.ops.mesh. offset_edge_loops_slide

```
def offset_loop_slide(context, bm, ref_edge, slide_distance):
    select_edge_loops(bm, [ref_edge], select_rings=False)
```

```
context_override = get_context_override(context, ↵
    'VIEW_3D', 'WINDOW')
with bpy.context.temp_override(**context_override):
    bpy.ops.mesh.offset_edge_loops_slide( ↵
        TRANSFORM_OT_edge_slide={"value": slide_distance})
```

select_edge_loops from Listing 4-8 is used to select the edge loops intended for sliding, and the built-in operator bpy.ops.mesh.offset_edge_loops_slide is used to slide the loops based on the given slide_distance. Note that bpy.ops.mesh.offset_edge_loops_slide's poll method requires a context override to make it seem as if the operator is called from the 3D Viewport when run from the Text Editor and other areas of Blender (we'll look at get_context_override in more detail shortly in Listing 4-23).

Listing 4-22 shows an example of creating a cylinder by bridging a vertical stack of edge loops using the functions create_loop_stack (Listing 4-12) and bridge_loops_bmesh (Listing 4-14), then calling offset_loop_slide (Listing 4-21) to slide 0.2 Blender units from the first edge loop relative to the bottom of the cylinder. You can visualize the results of running Listing 4-22 in Figure 4-8.

Listing 4-22. Performing an offset loop slide on the first loop from the bottom of a cylinder

```
def test_offset_loop_slide(context):
    num_loops = 5
    num_segments = 8
    bm, stack_obj = create_loop_stack(context, ↵
        name="test_offset_loop_slide", location=(0, 0, 0), ↵
        radius=1.5, num_loops=num_loops, ↵
        loop_segments=num_segments, level_height=2)
    loop_ref_edges = [bm.edges[i*num_segments] for i in ↵
        range(num_loops)]
```

```
    resulted_faces, resulted_edges = bridge_loops_bmesh( ↵
        bm, loop_ref_edges)
    bmesh.update_edit_mesh(stack_obj.data)
    offset_loop_slide(context, bm, ↵
        ref_edge=loop_ref_edges[1], slide_distance=0.2)
    bmesh.update_edit_mesh(stack_obj.data)
```

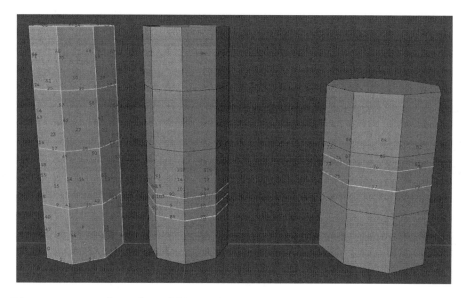

Figure 4-8. *Left and middle: Cylinder before and after the offset loop slide in Listing 4-22. Right: Cylinder after the loop cut-and-slide in Listing 4-25*

Overriding Context

Some of the bpy.ops.mesh and bpy.ops.transform operators have poll methods that require the context passed in to satisfy certain criteria, such as the current screen area type is the 3D Viewport, or the active object is in Edit mode, etc. Normally, this isn't an issue when you model by hand, since you'd only have access to these operators in Edit mode while inside the 3D Viewport; therefore, the context will always be what the operators will expect. However, when you try to use the same operators in script to automate mesh editing tasks, you could be calling them from anywhere, such as from a script open in the Text Editor, from code typed in the Python Console, or from an add-on in the UV Editor. Without the proper context, you'll run into errors.

To get around this issue, we'll write the helper function get_context_ override shown in Listing 4-23 to create a modified version of the context to pass into bpy.ops.mesh and bpy.ops.transform operators to meet their poll methods' expectations.

Listing 4-23. Helper function for creating a context override

```
def get_context_override(context, area_type, region_type):
    override = context.copy()
    for area in override['screen'].areas:
        if area.type == area_type:
            override['area'] = area
            break
    for region in override['area'].regions:
        if region.type == region_type:
            override['region'] = region
            break
    return override
```

get_context_override makes a copy of the context passed in as the basis for creating an override, then sets the override's active area to the given area type and the override's active region to the given region type. For example, the following call to get_context_override creates a context override with the 3D Viewport as the active screen area:

```
get_context_override(context, 'VIEW_3D', 'WINDOW')
```

You can then use the altered context to call an operator to satisfy the requirement of its `poll` method. For example, as you've seen in Listing 4-21 (partially reproduced below), to invoke the `bpy.ops.mesh.offset_edge_loops_slide` operator from a Blender area other than the 3D Viewport, you have to create a context override with the 3D Viewport as the active area, like this:

```
context_override = get_context_override(context, ↵
    'VIEW_3D', 'WINDOW')
with bpy.context.temp_override(**context_override):
    bpy.ops.mesh.offset_edge_loops_slide( ↵
        TRANSFORM_OT_edge_slide={"value": slide_distance})
```

Loop Cut-and-Slide

To make loop cuts and slide the newly cut loops for a given distance, you can write a function like `loop_cut_slide` shown in Listing 4-24.

Listing 4-24. Perform a given number of loop cuts and slide the cuts a specified distance

```
def loop_cut_slide(context, ref_edge, num_cuts, ↵
slide_distance):
    context_override = get_context_override(context, ↵
        'VIEW_3D', 'WINDOW')
    with bpy.context.temp_override(**context_override):
        bpy.ops.mesh.loopcut_slide(MESH_OT_loopcut={ ↵
            "number_cuts":num_cuts, "object_index":0, ↵
            "edge_index":ref_edge.index, ↵
            "mesh_select_mode_init":(False, True, False)}, ↵
            TRANSFORM_OT_edge_slide={"value":slide_distance})
```

The built-in operator bpy.ops.mesh.loopcut_slide (equivalent to Ctrl-R in Edit mode) is used to both make the cut(s) and slide the new loop(s) afterward for the given slide_distance. Note that bpy.ops.mesh. loopcut_slide also has a poll method which requires a context override to make it seem as if it's called from the 3D Viewport when run from the Text Editor and other areas of Blender (see get_context_override in Listing 4-23). num_cuts is the number of loop cuts to perform, and ref_edge is the edge that is closest and *perpendicular* to where the loop cut should be made. slide_distance is the distance to slide the new loops from the cut.

Listing 4-25 shows an example of performing loop cuts-and-slides with loop_cut_slide (Listing 4-24) on an extruded cylinder mesh. You can visualize the results of Listing 4-25 on the right of Figure 4-8.

Listing 4-25. Perform loop cuts-and-slides on an extruded cylinder mesh by calling loop_cut_slide (Listing 4-24)

```
def test_loop_cut_slide(context):
    num_segments = 8
    bm, obj, loops = create_cylinder_by_extrusion(context, ↩
        name= "test_loop_cut_slide", location=(0, -7, 0), ↩
        radius=2, segments=num_segments, num_levels=3)
    bpy.ops.mesh.select_all(action='DESELECT')

    ref_edge_index = loops[1][-1].index + 1
    loop_cut_slide(context, ref_edge=bm.edges[ref_edge_index], ↩
        num_cuts=2, slide_distance=0.3)
    bmesh.update_edit_mesh(obj.data)
```

We first create a cylinder mesh in a similar manner as Listing 4-20— where we repeatedly copy the base circle, move it up, then bridge it to the circle just before it. Instead of doing the scaling and directional change per "level" of extrusion, this time, we just extrude upward with no scaling to create a basic cylinder. We'll look at `create_cylinder_by_extrusion` more closely in the next section. For now, just know that we want to extrude a cylinder this way so we can keep track of the cross-section edge loops and therefore easily determine where to make the loop cuts.

When you perform a loop cut, the `ref_edge` needs to be the closest edge *perpendicular* to the intended cut; therefore, to add a horizontal cut between two cross-section loops, you need the `ref_edge` to be a vertical edge between those two loops, which is what `loops[1][-1].index + 1` is doing—since `loops[1]` is the second loop from the bottom and `loops[1][-1]` is the last edge of that loop, when you offset its index by one, you get a vertical edge that's between two loops.

With a `ref_edge` in hand, to perform the loop cut-and-slide, you'd then simply call `loop_cut_slide` (Listing 4-24) with the desired `num_cuts` and `slide_distance`.

Generating a Cylinder Mesh by Repeatedly Extruding a Circle Using extrude_edge_loop_copy_move

We'll take a closer look at the function `create_cylinder_by_extrusion` in Listing 4-26, which we used in the previous section to create a cylindrical mesh to experiment loop cuts with.

We start by creating a circle (as described in the section "Using `bmesh.ops` Operators to Create Primitives") and use it as the first cross-section loop to extrude from. In each step, we copy the top loop of the previous extrusion, move the copy along a directional `Vector`, scale the copy if necessary, then bridge the copy to the previous extrusion to form a new section.

In this example, the directional `Vector((0, 0, level_height))` points in the positive Z direction, and scale is uniformly 1 (`Vector((1, 1, 1))`), so for each new section, we're just copying the circle as is, moving it upward a fixed distance (`level_height`) then bridging it to the previous circle, therefore creating a basic cylinder.

Listing 4-26. Create a basic cylinder mesh by repeatedly copying and moving a circle along +Z at regular intervals and bridging edge loops

```
def create_cylinder_by_extrusion(context, ↵
name="cylinder_extruded_bmesh", location=(0, 0, 0), ↵
radius=1, segments=8, num_levels=2, level_height=2):
    bm, obj = create_circle_bmesh(bpy.context, name=name, ↵
        location=location, radius=radius, segments=segments)
    bm.verts.ensure_lookup_table()
    seed_edge = bm.edges[0]
    direction = Vector((0, 0, level_height))
    scale = Vector((1, 1, 1))
    loops = []
    for i in range(num_levels):
        new_loop = extrude_edge_loop_copy_move(bm, ↵
            seed_edge,direction,scale)
        seed_edge = new_loop[0]
        loops.append(new_loop)
    bm.edges.ensure_lookup_table()
    return bm, obj, loops
```

As discussed earlier, generating a mesh by extrusion gives you the ability to keep track of where the cross-section loops are, for example, the loops forming a character's arms; therefore, you'll know where to perform loop cuts and slides later to contour that part of the mesh.

Merging and Splitting Mesh Elements

Sometimes you might need to create an opening in a mesh by ripping some vertices in order to connect another piece to it or get rid of redundant vertices by merging them together. Faces can also be strategically joined or split to redirect edge flow for a cleaner topology.

Merging Vertices

In this section, I'll show you how to merge vertices in Python using BMesh and bpy operators. If you're following along with the extension version of the examples, you can press the "Test Merge Verts" button to run all the examples in this section.

Merging Vertices Using bmesh.ops.weld_verts

The first built-in operator we'll look at for merging vertices is bmesh.ops. weld_verts, which has two parameters, a BMesh instance bm for the object whose vertices you intend to merge and a Python dictionary targetmap which dictates which vertex is to be merged into which, as shown in Listing 4-27.

Listing 4-27. Merging vertices with bmesh.ops.weld_verts

```
def test_merge_verts_bmesh(context):
    bm, obj = create_grid_bmesh(context, ↩
        name="test_merge_verts_bmesh", ↩
        location=(-5, 0, 0), x_segments=5, ↩
        y_segments=6, size=3)

    context.tool_settings.mesh_select_mode = [True, False, False]
    bm.verts.ensure_lookup_table()
    from_list = [bm.verts[i] for i in range(1, 4, 1)]
    to_list = [bm.verts[i] for i in range(6, 9, 1)]
    target_map = {from_list[i]: to_list[i] for i in range(3)}
    bmesh.ops.weld_verts(bm, targetmap=target_map)
    bmesh.update_edit_mesh(obj.data)
```

We first make a grid (by using a variation of `create_cylinder_bmesh` from Listing 4-6 but calling `bmesh.ops.create_grid` instead) so there are some vertices to work with. The mesh Select Mode is changed to vertex so we can see the vert indices after the merge. Since we'll be referencing the vertices for the first time after their creation, `bm.verts.ensure_lookup_table()` is called to ensure that the vert lookup table `bm.verts` is initialized and ready to be indexed.

Next, we'll form the dictionary `target_map` to dictate which verts will be merged into which—in this case, vertex 1 to vertex 6, 2 to 7, and 3 to 8. In other words, the *keys* of the dictionary are the verts we're merging from and the *values* the verts we're merging into. Then, all that's left to do is call `bmesh.ops.weld_verts` with `target_map` to perform the merge. You can see the results of running Listing 4-27 in Figure 4-9.

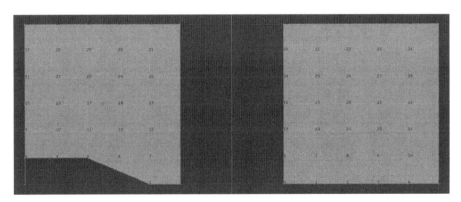

Figure 4-9. *Merging vertices 1, 2, and 3 into vertices 6, 7, and 8. The grid before merging is shown on the right, and the result after merging is shown on the left*

Notice in Figure 4-9 that the indices of vertices are **not** preserved after the merge (in other words, indices of vertices changed after the merge, whether a vertex is involved in the merge or not). In general, be mindful that many mesh operations which remove or introduce new geometry can cause such change in indices. Therefore, rather than storing the index of a vertex in a variable to refer to later, you should look up a vertex, store the vertex itself in a variable, and refer to the variable later, like the following hypothetical example:

```
v0 = bm.verts[0]
# Do some edits through bm here…
v0.co[2] += 5
```

We look up the vertex at index 0 and store it in a variable v0 so we can refer to that vertex later using v0 instead of referring to that vertex as bm.verts[0] since its index may no longer be 0.

Merging Vertices Using bpy.ops.mesh.merge

You can also use the bpy operator bpy.ops.mesh.merge to write a function for merging vertices, like merge_verts_bpy shown in Listing 4-28.

Listing 4-28. Merging vertices with bpy.ops.mesh.merge

```
def merge_verts_bpy(target_map, merge_type='CENTER'):
    for v_from, v_to in target_map.items():
        bpy.ops.mesh.select_all(action='DESELECT')
        v_from.select = True
        v_to.select = True
        bpy.ops.mesh.merge(type=merge_type)
```

Similar to Listing 4-27, merge_verts_bpy borrows the concept of using a dictionary (target_map) to describe pairs of vertices to be merged. Like many bpy.ops operators, bpy.ops.mesh.merge performs its actions on whatever part of a mesh is currently selected. Therefore, for each pair of vertices to be merged, we first deselect all, then select v_from and v_to (the vertices to merge) to ensure they are the only thing selected. We then call bpy.ops.mesh.merge with the given merge_type.

The `merge_type` `'CENTER'` is equivalent to selecting the vertices to merge with Shift-clicks followed by *Merge* (M key) ➤ *At Center*. You can look up other possible merge types, such as `'CURSOR'` or `'COLLAPSE'` in the Blender Python API documentation.

One issue with using `bpy.ops.mesh.merge` is that it's less predictable which vertex is being merged into which—based on my experimentation, it seems to *merge the vertex with the larger index into the vertex with the smaller index*, regardless of the ordering you specify. For example, if `v_from` has index 2 while `v_to` has index 5, it will opt to merge `v_to` into `v_from` and remove `v_to`.

To test `merge_verts_bpy`, you can replace the call to `bmesh.ops.weld_verts` in `test_merge_verts_bmesh` (Listing 4-27) with

```
merge_verts_bpy(target_map, merge_type='CENTER')
```

Since nothing else in Listing 4-27 is changed, `merge_verts_bpy` will merge the same pairs of vertices (1 and 6, 2 and 7, and 3 and 8), but instead of merging the first vertex of each pair into the second like `bmesh.ops.weld_verts` in Figure 4-9, `merge_verts_bpy` merges each pair of vertices at their center, as shown in Figure 4-10.

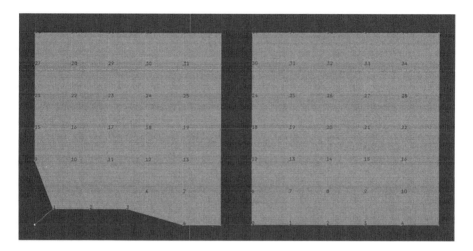

Figure 4-10. *Left: Results of replacing the call to* bmesh.ops.weld_ *verts in* test_merge_verts_bmesh *(Listing 4-27) with* merge_verts_ *bpy(* target_map, merge_type='CENTER' *). Vertices 6, 7, and 8 are merged with vertices 1, 2, 3 at their centers. Right: Grid before the merge for comparison*

Ripping Vertices

You can write a function like rip_verts_bmesh shown in Listing 4-29 to rip away a corner vertex of a face and get a reference to the newly created vertex at the loose corner to connect to another mesh, to use as the starting point for creating more detail through extrusion, and so on.

Listing 4-29. For each given face, rip a specified vertex away

```
def rip_verts_bmesh(rip_map, offset):
    ripped_verts = []
    for f, rip_corner_index in rip_map.items():
        v = bmesh.utils.face_vert_separate( ↩
            f, f.verts[rip_corner_index])
```

```
        v.co += offset
        ripped_verts.append(v)
    return ripped_verts
```

Since each face has at least three corners, the function expects a mapping in the form of a Python dictionary (rip_map) that describes for each face (*key*) which corner (*value*) should be ripped. For each face and corner–index pairing, the built-in operator bmesh.utils.face_vert_ separate performs the rip and returns the vertex v at the loose corner of the face. The corner is moved by adding the given offset (a Vector) to v's coordinates. All the loose corners are accumulated in a list ripped_verts to be returned.

You can test the effects of rip_verts_bmesh with the function test_ rip_verts_bmesh shown in Listing 4-30. If you're following along with the extension version of the examples, you can press the button "Test Rip Verts" to run Listing 4-30.

Listing 4-30. For each given face, rip a specified vertex away

```
def test_rip_verts_bmesh(context):
    bm, obj = create_grid_bmesh(context, name="test_rip_verts_
                                bmesh", ↩
        location=(-7, 0, 0), x_segments=10, y_segments=4, size=6)

    context.tool_settings.mesh_select_mode = [False, False, True]
    bm.faces.ensure_lookup_table()
    offset = Vector((1, 0.75, 1.25))
    rip_map = {bm.faces[10]: 0, bm.faces[12]: 1, bm.faces[14]:
            2, ↩
        bm.faces[16]: 3}
    rip_verts_bmesh(rip_map, offset)
    bmesh.update_edit_mesh(obj.data)
```

We first make a grid (by using a variation of create_cylinder_bmesh from Listing 4-6 but calling bmesh.ops.create_grid instead) so there are some vertices to work with. We then set the mesh Select Mode to face so after the rip we can see the indices of selected faces to verify rip_verts_ bmesh has worked as intended. bm.faces.ensure_lookup_table() is called to ensure the face lookup table bm.faces is initialized and ready to be indexed. An offset to be applied to the ripped verts is specified through offset (a Vector), and a dictionary indicating which corner is to be ripped for each face is created (rip_map), in this case: corner 0 for face #10, corner 1 for face #12, and so on. Finally, rip_verts_bmesh is called to rip and move the face corners. You can see the results of running Listing 4-30 in Figure 4-11.

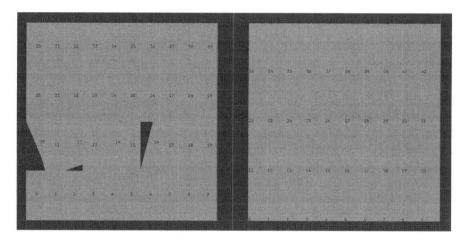

Figure 4-11. *Left: Results of running Listing 4-30, ripping corner 0 of face #10, corner 1 of face #12, corner 2 of face #14, and corner 3 of face #16. Each ripped-away corner is offsetted by (1, 0.75, 1.25). Right: The grid before ripping*

Splitting and Joining Faces

In the process of cleaning up or simplifying a mesh, sometimes it's helpful to join certain neighboring faces together to reduce geometry. In other situations, you might strategically split some faces to redirect edge flows, introduce new edge loops, or eliminate poles to improve the topology of your mesh.

The BMesh module provides the built-in functions bmesh.utils.face_join for joining a list of faces and bmesh.utils.face_split for splitting a given face across two of the face's vertices. An example of how to use these two functions is illustrated in Listing 4-31. If you're following along with the extension version of the examples, you can press the "Test Join Split Faces" button to run Listing 4-31.

Listing 4-31. Joining and splitting faces

```
def test_join_split_faces_bmesh(context):
    bm, obj = create_grid_bmesh(context, ↵
        name="test_join_faces_bmesh", ↵
        location=(-7, 0, 0), x_segments=10, ↵
        y_segments=4, size=6)

    context.tool_settings.mesh_select_mode = [True, False, True]
    bm.faces.ensure_lookup_table()
    faces_to_join = bm.faces[0:9]
    face_to_split = bm.faces[13]
    joined_face = bmesh.utils.face_join(faces_to_join)
    split_face = bmesh.utils.face_split(face_to_split, ↵
        face_to_split.verts[0], face_to_split.verts[2])
    joined_face.select = True
    split_face[0].select = True
    bmesh.update_edit_mesh(obj.data)
```

The same grid used for testing face-corner ripping from Listing 4-30 is used here to set up the example. This time, we set the Select Mode to both vertex and face, which will help us make sense of the new geometry resulting from the joining and splitting. We set up a list of faces to be joined, in this case, across the bottom row of the grid, faces #0 ~ #8 (faces_to_join), and store a reference to face #13 (face_to_split) which will be split after the joining operation. The reason we store face #13 in a variable to refer to later is because the joining operation will cause the indices of faces to change, rendering index 13 out-of-date.

bmesh.utils.face_join is used to join the list of faces (faces_to_join) and return the resulting joined_face. Then, bmesh.utils.face_split is used to split the face face_to_split across the two given corners—in this case, the first vertex (index 0) and third (index 2). The results of the joins and split are shown in Figure 4-12.

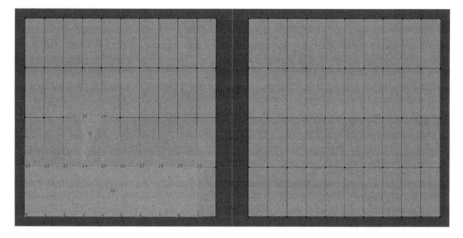

Figure 4-12. *Left: Results of running Listing 4-31, joining the faces across the bottom row and splitting the face in the center across its first (index 0) and third (index 2) vertices. Right: The grid before for comparison*

Notice that after the joining, the row of vertices at the bottom of the grid is left behind. Another thing to note is that `bmesh.utils.face_split` returns a list of two values—the new face created by the split (`split_face[0]`) and a `BMLoop` object (`split_faces[1]`) that describes a corner of the new face. You can see these along with the joined face illustrated in Figure 4-13.

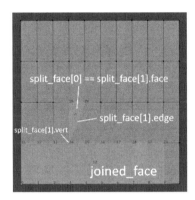

Figure 4-13. *Returned values of bmesh_utils.face_join and bmesh_utils.face_split*

Rotating and Scaling Mesh Objects (Object Mode)

In this section, we'll look at how to rotate and scale mesh objects in Python, just as you would using the R and S keys in the 3D Viewport. To get started, open the default startup `*.blend` file, make sure the cube is active and in Object mode, and head on over to the Python Console.

The cube's current rotation in Euler format is stored in its `rotation_euler` variable, which can be accessed like this:

```
>>> cube = bpy.context.scene.objects["Cube"]
>>> cube.rotation_euler
Euler((0.0, 0.0, 0.0), 'XYZ')
```

You can change cube's rotation through cube.rotation_euler. For example, try entering the following code at the prompt to set cube's rotation to 30 degrees around the X axis, 60 degrees around the Y axis, and 180 degrees around the Z axis.

```
>>> cube.rotation_euler = Euler((radians(30), radians(60), ↩
    radians(180)), 'XYZ')
```

The result of the rotation is shown in Figure 4-14. If you bring up the *Properties* shelf (N key) ➤ *Item* tab in the 3D Viewport, you'll see that *Transform* ➤ *Rotation* has been updated to reflect these changes.

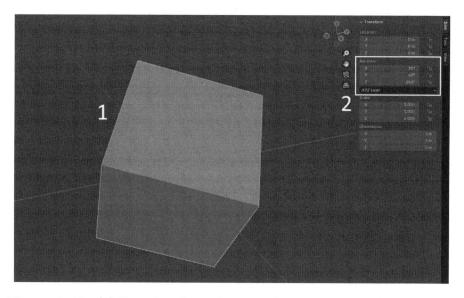

Figure 4-14. *(1) Rotating the cube to 30 degrees around the X axis, 60 degrees around the Y axis, and 180 degrees around the Z axis, using Euler rotation. (2) These rotations have been reflected under Properties shelf (N key) ➤ Item tab ➤ Transform ➤ Rotation*

Note   Recall that the built-in Python Console imports `math` and `mathutils` for you. If you are writing a script, you'll have to import `radians` and `Euler` yourself, via `from math import radians` and `from mathutils import Euler`.

You can apply cube's rotation with the following operator call (equivalent to Ctrl-A ➤ Rotation), which will zero out the numbers listed under *Properties* shelf (N key) ➤ *Item* tab ➤ *Transform* ➤ *Rotation* and reestablish the cube's "baseline" orientation. This is like when you want to weigh an item in a container but don't want to account for the container's weight—you can put the container on the scale first to tare (zero out) the reading. Note that you can only apply the transformation to an object while it's in Object mode.

```
>>> bpy.ops.object.transform_apply(location=False, ↩
        rotation=True, scale=False)
{'FINISHED'}
```

To change cube's scale, you can assign the scale factor on a per-axis basis. The following example changes the X scale factor to 1, the Y scale factor to 2, and the Z scale factor to 0.5, as shown in Figure 4-15:

```
>>> cube.scale[0] = 1
>>> cube.scale[1] = 2
>>> cube.scale[2] = 0.5
```

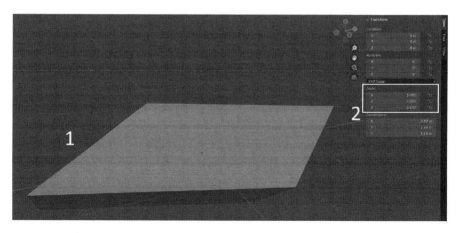

Figure 4-15. *(1) Scaling the cube to scale factor 1 along the X axis, 2 along the Y axis, and 0.5 along the Z axis. (2) The scaling has been reflected under Properties shelf (N key)* ➤ *Item tab* ➤ *Transform* ➤ *Scale*

Equivalently, you can use a Vector to scale along all three axes at once, like the following:

```
>>> cube.scale = Vector((1, 2, 0.5))
```

You can apply the scale to cube using the next operator call, which will return scale to 1 for all axes under *Properties* shelf (N key) ➤ *Item* tab ➤ *Transform* ➤ *Scale*.

```
>>> bpy.ops.object.transform_apply(location=False, ↵
        rotation=False, scale=True)
{'FINISHED'}
```

Rotating and Scaling Mesh Objects (Edit Mode)

Sometimes, during a modeling session, you need to rotate or scale a part of a mesh in order to adjust its contour or align its opening to another mesh so you can stitch them together. In this section, I'll show you how to rotate individual edges as well as a selection on a mesh using Python.

Rotating Individual Edges

In Object mode, add a grid primitive with Add (A key) ➤ Mesh ➤ Grid. Then, switch to Edit mode so we have some edges to work with. Head over to the Python Console, create a bmesh instance bm for modifying the grid object, and call bm.edges.ensure_lookup_table() since we'll be retrieving edges by indices.

```
>>> import bmesh
>>> grid = bpy.context.scene.objects["Grid"]
>>> bm = bmesh.from_edit_mesh(grid.data)
>>> bm.edges.ensure_lookup_table()
```

We'll call bmesh.utils.edge_rotate to rotate a single edge on the grid (in this example, edge #103) counterclockwise, like this:

```
>>> e = bm.edges[103]
>>> rotated_edge = bmesh.utils.edge_rotate(e, True)
>>> bm.edges.ensure_lookup_table()
>>> bmesh.update_edit_mesh(grid.data)
```

The second argument to bmesh.utils.edge_rotate is a boolean value that when True rotates the given edge *counterclockwise* (and when False, clockwise). Note that bmesh.utils.edge_rotate will return the new edge created by the rotation process.

207

The result of the edge rotation is shown in Figure 4-16. You can see that it looks as if the original edge has been disconnected from its neighboring geometry, rotated in the given direction, then reattached to the nearest neighbors. In reality, what happens is that the edge intended for rotation is deleted and replaced by a new edge.

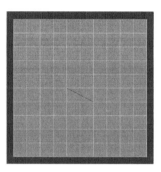

Figure 4-16. *Result of rotating a single edge in the middle of the grid primitive counterclockwise*

If you have a list of edges that all need to be rotated in the same direction, such as all clockwise or all counterclockwise, you can use bmesh. ops.rotate_edges instead, like this:

```
>>> edges_to_rotate = [bm.edges[162], bm.edges[166]]
>>> bmesh.ops.rotate_edges(bm, edges=edges_to_rotate, ↵
        use_ccw=False)
{'edges': [<BMEdge(0x000001EE31B52F80), index=103, ↵
verts=(0x000001EE31AC4528/101, 0x000001EE31AC4090/80)>, ↵
  <BMEdge(0x000001EE31B54240), index=163, ↵
verts=(0x000001EE31AC4598/103, 0x000001EE31AC4100/82)>]} ↵

>>> bmesh.update_edit_mesh(grid.data)
>>> bm.edges.ensure_lookup_table()
```

In the above example, bm is a BMesh instance for the object you want to edit, edges_to_rotate is the list of edges to be rotated through bm, and use_ccw when True rotates the edges counterclockwise, and when False clockwise.

Rotating and Scaling a Selection on a Mesh

It is also possible to emulate the effect of pressing the R key to rotate a selection on a mesh in Python. First, select the parts of the mesh that you want to rotate, then use the operator bpy.ops.transform.rotate to perform the desired rotation. For instance, you can rotate the current selection by 30 degrees around the global X axis like this:

```
bpy.ops.transform.rotate(value=radians(30), orient_axis='X', ↵
    orient_type='GLOBAL')
```

Similarly, you can scale the current selection to 60% uniformly along all three global axes like this:

```
bpy.ops.transform.resize(value=(0.6, 0.6, 0.6), ↵
    orient_type='GLOBAL')
```

Beveling Edges and Vertices

Beveling is a convenient way to round off edges and corners of objects like architectural elements. If you only need the corners or edges smoothed, it's more economical to only bevel these areas rather than subdividing the whole mesh. Limiting additional geometry to only where you need it also helps maintain the overall silhouette of a model, especially one with lots of straight lines, such as a table.

You can write a function like bevel_bpy (shown in Listing 4-32) which calls bpy.ops.mesh.bevel to bevel a list of edges or vertices.

Listing 4-32. Bevel a given list of edges or vertices using bpy.ops.
mesh.bevel

```
def bevel_bpy(edge_list, offset=0.15, segments=2, ↵
    loop_slide=True, vertex_only=False):
    bpy.ops.mesh.select_all(action='DESELECT')
    for e in edge_list:
        e.select = True
    bpy.ops.mesh.bevel(offset=offset, segments=segments, ↵
        loop_slide=loop_slide, ↵
        affect='VERTICES' if vertex_only else 'EDGES')
```

Since bpy.ops.mesh.bevel bases its actions on whatever part of a
mesh is selected, we first deselect all before selecting the list of edges
intended for beveling, to make sure they're the only thing selected.

Here is a description of bpy.ops.mesh.bevel's parameters: offset
is a number that indicates how much an edge should be beveled—you
can think of it as how wide the edge will be after it's rounded. segments is
how many times the rounded edge is divided. When loop_slide is True,
Blender will slide the segments up and down to even them out. If you want
the two end vertices of an edge beveled rather than the edge itself, you can
set vertex_only to True.

The example in Listing 4-33 shows how you can use bevel_bpy
(Listing 4-32) to bevel a given list of edges on a primitive cube mesh. If
you're following along with the extension version of the examples, you can
press the "Test Bevel" button to run Listing 4-33.

Listing 4 33. Example of using bevel_bpy (Listing 4-32) to bevel a
given list of edges on a cube primitive

```
def test_bevel_bpy_edges(context):
    bm, obj = create_cube_bmesh(context, ↵
```

```
    name="test_bevel_bpy_edges", ↵
    location=(0, 6, 3), size=5.0)
bm.edges.ensure_lookup_table()
bevel_bpy(edge_list=bm.edges[0:4], offset=1.0, segments=5, ↵
    loop_slide=True, vertex_only=False)
bmesh.update_edit_mesh(obj.data)
```

We first make a cube (by using a variation of create_cylinder_bmesh from Listing 4-6 but calling bmesh.ops.create_cube instead) so there are some edges to work with. Edges #0 ~ #3 are beveled using bevel_bpy, with each rounded side of the cube spanning a width of one divided into five segments. loop_slide is enabled to even out the segments, and vertex_only is set to False so the given edges of the cube instead of the corners are beveled. You can see the results of running Listing 4-33 in Figure 4-17. I've included results of setting loop_slide to False, as well as beveling the corners of the cube by setting vertex_only to True in the same figure for comparison.

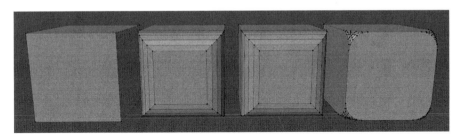

Figure 4-17. *From left to right: (1) Cube before edits; (2) Listing 4-33; (3) Listing 4-33, with* loop_slide *as* False; *and (4) Listing 4-33, with* vertex_only *as* True

Insetting Faces

Insetting and outsetting faces are convenient ways of creating detail on a mesh surface that involve indentation and protrusion. When done by hand, you'd select a face or a group of faces, hit the I key, then move the cursor to resize the insetted face(s), and left-click to confirm. You can then move (G key) the insetted face inward or outward to the desired depth or elevation.

The BMesh module provides two built-in functions for insetting or outsetting faces—bmesh.ops.inset_individual insets a list of faces such that each face is insetted individually and independently from each other, whereas bmesh.ops.inset_region insets a list of faces such that adjacent faces are grouped together and insetted as a whole.

I put together a function named test_inset_bmesh (shown in Listing 4-34) to show you how to use these two functions to inset and outset faces that are part of a grid. If you're following along with the extension version of the examples, you can press the "Test Inset" button to run Listing 4-34.

Listing 4-34. Example of using bmesh operators to inset/outset individual and groups of faces

```
def test_inset_bmesh(context):
    bm, obj = create_grid_bmesh(context, ↩
        name="test_inset_indv", location=(-7, 0, 2), ↩
        x_segments=10, y_segments=4, size=6)
    context.tool_settings.mesh_select_mode = [False, False, True]

    bm.faces.ensure_lookup_table()
    faces_indv_out = bm.faces[0:4]
    faces_indv_in = bm.faces[6:10]
    faces_region_out = bm.faces[20:24]
    faces_region_in = bm.faces[26:30]
```

```
bmesh.ops.inset_individual(bm, faces=faces_indv_out, ↵
    thickness=0.3, depth=0.5)
bmesh.ops.inset_individual(bm, faces=faces_indv_in, ↵
    thickness=0.5, depth=-0.2)
bmesh.ops.inset_region(bm, faces=faces_region_out, ↵
    thickness=0.3, depth=0.5)
bmesh.ops.inset_region(bm, faces=faces_region_in, ↵
    thickness=0.5, depth=-0.2)
bmesh.update_edit_mesh(obj.data)
```

We first make a grid (by using a variation of create_cylinder_bmesh from Listing 4-6 but calling bmesh.ops.create_grid instead) so there are some faces to work with. We then set up several lists of faces to be used as the input to the operator calls coming up next.

The first call to bmesh.ops.inset_individual *outsets* four faces in the lower left corner of the grid, with the outsetted faces at a distance of 0.3 unit (thickness) from their enclosing borders in each direction and lifted up by 0.5 unit (depth).

Note that when depth is greater than zero, the inner face is made to stick out (outsetted). If depth is less than zero, the inner face is made to sink in (insetted). If depth is zero, the inner face is flush with the outer face.

The second call to bmesh.ops.inset_individual *insets* four faces in the lower right corner of the grid.

The next two calls to bmesh.ops.inset_region outset and inset lists of faces, respectively, such that adjacent faces are automatically grouped together and outsetted or insetted as a whole.

You can see the results of running Listing 4-34 in Figure 4-18. bmesh. ops.inset_individual outsets the four faces on the lower left and insets the four faces on the lower right. On the second row of faces from the top, bmesh.ops.inset_region outsets the four faces *together* on the left and insets the four faces together on the right.

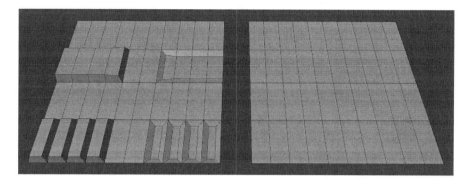

Figure 4-18. *Left: Results of running* test_inset_bmesh *in
Listing 4-34. Right: The grid before edits for comparison*

Editing Normals

Face normals are vectors that are perpendicular to and point away from a
face. Vertex normals point outward from a vertex, along the ray shooting
from the mesh's center of mass. Normals are not only important for
lighting and shading models but also useful in a variety of other scenarios.
For example, you can calculate the average normal of a group of faces
and use it as a guide for smoothing them or for aligning two meshes to be
stitched together. You can also add detail to a part of a mesh by extruding
or scaling along the average normal of the surrounding geometry. In this
section, I'll show you how to access and edit normals using Python.

Configuring Viewport Settings for Debugging

To help us visualize normals better, we'll start by writing a helper function
config_viewport_debug_settings (Listing 4-35) to configure several
viewport settings useful for debugging in one shot.

Listing 4-35. Configuring viewport settings useful for debugging in Python

```
def config_viewport_debug_settings(context, show_indices, ↵
    show_vn, show_fn, normals_length, shading_type):
    for a in context.window.screen.areas:
        if a.type == 'VIEW_3D':
            for s in a.spaces:
                if s.type == 'VIEW_3D':
                    s.shading.type = shading_type
                    s.overlay.show_extra_indices = show_indices
                    s.overlay.show_vertex_normals = show_vn
                    s.overlay.show_face_normals = show_fn
                    s.overlay.normals_length = normals_length
                    return
```

Similar to the function `display_mesh_element_indices` we wrote for Chapter 3, we search for the 3D Viewport within the nested screen spaces under the passed-in `context`. Once we locate the viewport space (`s`), we can set shading with `s.shading.type`, which is `'WIREFRAME'`, `'SOLID'`, etc.

We've already seen in Chapter 3 that the option for displaying mesh element indices (`show_extra_indices`) is part of the viewport space's `overlay`. Similarly, the options to display vertex (`show_vertex_normals`) and face normals (`show_face_normals`) and adjust normal lengths (`normals_length`) are under `overlay`.

For example, you can turn on the display of mesh element indices, vertex normals, and face normals, plus set normal length to 1.0, and viewport shading to `'WIREFRAME'`, by making the following call (if you are following along by running the extension version of the examples, you can press the button "Config Viewport Debug Settings"):

```
config_viewport_debug_settings(bpy.context, True, True, True, ↵
    1.0, 'WIREFRAME')
```

The effects of this call on the default cube is shown in Figure 4-19.

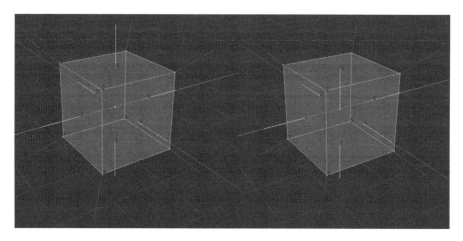

Figure 4-19. *Left: Default cube with vertex and face indices shown, along with face and vertex normals displayed. Right: After calling* bm. faces[0].normal_flip()*. You can see that the normal of face #0 (at the top of the cube) now points inward*

Accessing and Flipping Normals

The following examples are based on the cube object from the default startup blend file. Make sure the cube is active, tab into Edit mode, and head over to the built-in Python Console. We'll start by setting the mesh Select Mode to Vertex and Face and creating a BMesh instance bm to edit the cube with, by entering the following code in the Python Console:

```
>>> bpy.context.tool_settings.mesh_select_mode = [True,
False, True]
>>> cube = bpy.context.scene.objects["Cube"]
>>> import bmesh
>>> bm = bmesh.from_edit_mesh(cube.data)
>>> bm.verts.ensure_lookup_table()
>>> bm.faces.ensure_lookup_table()
```

You can access a vertex's normal, which is of type Vector, like this:

```
>>> bm.verts[0].normal
Vector((0.5773503184318542, 0.5773503184318542,
0.5773503184318542))
```

You can access a face's normal in a similar way:

```
>>> bm.faces[0].normal
Vector((0.0, -0.0, 1.0))
```

Blender automatically recalculates normals as you continuously make edits to a mesh. Since normals need to stick out of a face or vertex, Blender makes assumptions about which side of a mesh is considered the outside. Sometimes, it makes a mistake and points a normal inward instead of outward. If a face normal is in the wrong direction, you can flip it using normal_flip(), like this (here, we purposely flip one inward, as shown in Figure 4-19):

```
>>> bm.faces[0].normal_flip()
>>> bmesh.update_edit_mesh(cube.data)
```

You can also use the operator bpy.ops.mesh.normals_make_consistent() to recalculate normals on any selected parts of a mesh to correct them. For example, you can select the cube in its entirety and recalculate all of its normals like this:

```
>>> bpy.ops.mesh.select_all(action='SELECT')
{'FINISHED'}
```

```
>>> bpy.ops.mesh.normals_make_consistent()
{'FINISHED'}
```

Now, face #0's normal is flipped outward again.

Removing Doubles

A common cleanup task at the end of a modeling session is to remove duplicate vertices—vertices whose distances apart are smaller than a given threshold and therefore considered redundant since they're too close together. These vertices are nicknamed "doubles." If you have a mesh in Edit mode in the viewport, you can enter the following code in the built-in Python Console to remove doubles from the mesh.

```
>>> bpy.ops.mesh.select_all(action='SELECT')
{'FINISHED'}

>>> bpy.ops.mesh.remove_doubles(threshold=0.02)
Info: Removed 0 vertices
{'FINISHED'}
```

If you want more control over what to do with doubles, you can use the BMesh operator bmesh.ops.find_doubles to get a mapping of vertices that are closer together than a given threshold without committing to removing or merging them. You can enter the following code in the Python Console or a script to try it out. obj is any mesh object in Edit mode in the viewport.

```
>>> import bmesh
>>> bm = bmesh.from_edit_mesh(obj.data)
>>> bm.verts.ensure_lookup_table()
>>> doubles = bmesh.ops.find_doubles(bm, verts=bm.verts, ↵
        keep_verts=[], dist=0.2)
>>> doubles
['targetmap': {<BMVert(0x000001EDF2A67390), index=8>: ↵
    <BMVert(0x000001EDF2A673C8), index=9>}}
```

verts is the list of verts you want to check doubles for, keep_verts is the verts you want to keep from being absorbed in a merge, and dist is the threshold under which vertices are considered doubles.

You can also pass the returned value of bmesh.ops.find_doubles from above directly to the operator bmesh.ops.weld_verts, like this:

```
>>> bmesh.ops.weld_verts(bm, targetmap=doubles['targetmap'])
>>> bmesh.update_edit_mesh(obj.data)
```

where bm is the BMesh instance through which you're editing obj with.

Removing Loose Vertices

Sometimes, you might delete bits and pieces of geometry while editing a mesh and accidentally leave behind some vertices that aren't connected to anything. You can write a function like remove_loose_verts shown in Listing 4-36 to remove these loose vertices.

remove_loose_verts takes a single parameter—a BMesh instance bm for editing the object that will undergo the loose vert removal. For each vertex, the function checks if the number of edges connected to it is zero (len(v.link_edges) == 0). If so, it's a loose vertex, which gets appended to the list of verts to be removed later (verts_to_remove). Note that the reason the vertex is not removed right away inside the loop is because doing so would modify the sequence bm.verts while it is being iterated and cause errors. The function finishes by iterating through the list of verts to be removed to remove them one by one.

Listing 4-36. Cleaning up loose vertices

```
def remove_loose_verts(bm):
    verts_to_remove = []
    for v in bm.verts:
        if len(v.link_edges) == 0:
            verts_to_remove.append(v)
    for v in verts_to_remove:
        bm.verts.remove(v)
```

> **Tip**   You can create loose vertices by Ctrl-Right-click in Edit mode (ensure that no other vertices are selected, otherwise the newly created vertex will automatically connect to them).

Summary

In this chapter, you continued to build on your mesh editing skills from Chapter 3. You learned the pros and cons of using bpy and bmesh operators and when to use which. Manipulating edge loops is an important aspect of contouring organic models, as they allow the modeler to deform the mesh cleanly and naturally. You learned how to use bmesh to create edge loops as cross-sections, then extruding and shaping them (through rotation and scaling) into different silhouettes. After that, you learned how to refine an extruded piece by cutting and sliding loops on isolated portions of the mesh.

In addition to loops, you discovered how to merge and split vertices and faces in Python, which are important techniques for redirecting topological flows and stitching mesh pieces together. Then, you tried your hand at rotating and scaling meshes from the Python Console, which are useful for things like adjusting proportions of appendages on a model or aligning neighboring geometry.

To add extra details to a generated mesh, you learned how to programmatically bevel edges and vertices as well as insetting (and outsetting) faces in various ways. To wrap up a modeling session, you learned general techniques for correcting normals and removing doubles and loose verts using Python, which can be used to clean up a procedurally generated piece, as well as turned into helper tools for hand modelers.

Along the way, you learned how to import and reuse functions from other scripts, both for running in the Text Editor and for structuring an extension. You also learned how to turn a Python function you've been developing into an operator that can be integrated into part of an add-on.

CHAPTER 5

Procedurally Generating Stylized Fire Hydrants

In this chapter, I'll show you how to combine the techniques you've learned so far to develop an algorithm for generating stylized fire hydrant meshes. You'll use your knowledge of working with edge loops to form the silhouette of the fire hydrant, then inset and bevel various parts of the model to add detail. You'll also learn how to use the same technique for generating the horn mesh from Chapter 4 to add whimsical zigzags to stylize the models.

Running This Chapter's Examples

The source code for this book is available on GitHub via the book's product page, located at www.apress.com/979-8-8688-1126-5). I've prepared this chapter's examples in two versions. The first version is meant to run in the Text Editor and the second version installed as an extension add-on. Both versions contain the same Python examples. I will go over how the user input is implemented in the extension at the end of the chapter.

© Isabel Lupiani 2025
I. Lupiani, *Blender Scripting with Python*, https://doi.org/10.1007/979-8-8688-1127-2_5

Setting Up/Running the Script Version

Go to the Scripting workspace and open /Ch5/text_editor/fire_
hydrant_generator.py in the Text Editor. There is a block already set up
at the bottom of that file which invokes test_gen_fire_hydrant(bpy.
context) when you click the Run button and calls the generation routine
gen_stylized_fire_hydrant 12 times with different parameter values to
produce the 12 models shown in Figures 5-16 and 5-17. We will discuss
gen_stylized_fire_hydrant in great detail throughout the chapter.

```
if __name__ == "__main__":
    test_gen_fire_hydrant(bpy.context)
```

Installing/Running the Extension Add-On Version

Go to Edit ➤ Preferences... ➤ Get Extensions, click the blue downward
"v" at the upper right to expand the menu, and click *Install from
Disk....* Navigate to the Ch5/extension/fire_hydrant_generator/
folder in the downloaded source, and choose the file fire_hydrant_
generator-2.0.0.zip. The add-on, "Fire Hydrant Generator," which
contains this chapter's examples will be installed and automatically
enabled. Once installed, you can access the add-on in the 3D Viewport
Properties shelf (N key) ➤ *Tool* tab.

The inputs in the add-on panel correspond to arguments to the
function gen_stylized_fire_hydrant, which we'll discuss in great detail
throughout the chapter. To generate a model, move the 3D cursor to where
you want the model to appear, adjust the various generation parameters
via the sliders and check boxes, and click the "Generate" button.

The "Generate With Presets" button at the bottom of the panel invokes
test_gen_fire_hydrant(bpy.context), which calls the generation
routine gen_stylized_fire_hydrant 12 times with different parameter

values to produce the 12 models shown in Figures 5-16 and 5-17. Clicking "Generate With Presets" has the same effect as running the Text Editor version out of the box.

Imports from Chapters 3 and 4

This chapter's code imports the scripts `creating_and_editing_mesh_objs.py` from Chapter 3 and `mesh_editing_ops.py` from Chapter 4. These imports have been set up for you in both versions of the examples. For detail on how imports are handled for both scripts run in the Text Editor and for packaged extensions, please refer to Chapter 4.

Designing the Generation Algorithm

Before delving into code, let's go over how I came up with this chapter's generation algorithm at a high level. Just like modeling by hand, the first step is to find one or more reference photos of the subject, preferably depicting it from different angles, like the fire hydrant photo I found on Wikipedia shown in Figure 5-1. After studying the photos, it's time to deliberate which details to keep and which to abstract away to formulate a design. For example, I decided that the base, pole, dome, and cap are enough to capture the impression of a fire hydrant, whereas the rivets and the connectors on the side can be omitted to simplify the design.

Figure 5-1. *Example of a reference photo for fire hydrant modeling. From Wikipedia:* https://commons.wikimedia.org/wiki/ File:Downtown_Charlottesville_fire_hydrant.jpg. *Fire hydrant on the Downtown Mall in Charlottesville, Virginia. (Photo by Ben Schumin on December 25, 2006)*

Breaking the Generation into Stages

Once I formulated a general design for the fire hydrant, I tried modeling it by hand and discovered I could break down the generation process into the following stages:

1. Create the cylindrical base.

2. Extrude upward to add the pole and the top band while shaping them by extruding the cross-sections (E key then Esc) and scaling them along normals (Alt-S).

3. Continue to extrude upward while shaping to form the dome and the basis for the cap.

4. Finish contouring the cap and close the top of the model.

5. Add detail such as insets on the dome and the bottom of the pole. Close the bottom of the base and clean up (e.g., by correcting normals).

While test-modeling the design, I kept an eye on the Info Editor so I can see which operators get executed and how their parameters change as I perform edits in the viewport. By the time I'm done, I have accumulated a list of operators I can use to implement the algorithm.

To make the algorithm more versatile, I had the idea of putting in an option for stylizing the fire hydrants by adding zigzags to the pole, top band, and dome, a trick borrowed from the horn generation example you've seen in Chapter 4. The zigzag is achieved by adding a X/Y offset to each extrusion alternating between positive and negative while forming the pole, top band, and the dome. A scale factor < 1 is also added to each extrusion so that each extruded segment gets a little smaller over time, adding to the quirkiness of the model. An example of this is shown in Figure 5-2.

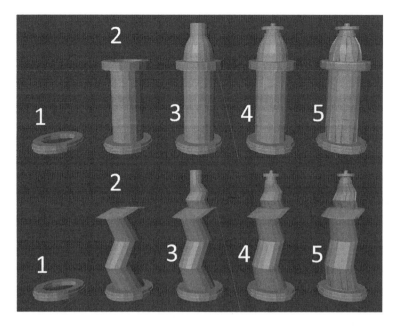

Figure 5-2. *Stages of the fire hydrant model generation, progressing from (1) to (5). The bottom row is the stylized counterparts of the top row*

Deciding Which Parameters Should Be Adjustable

With the generation algorithm in place, the next step is to decide which parameters should be made adjustable so they can be used to alter the appearance of the generated models. For the rest of this section, the names quoted in parentheses are the parameters from the implementation of the fire hydrant generation algorithm that we'll look at in the next few sections.

Using Figure 5-2 as a guide, let's think about what parameters are at our disposal. The base, pole, top band, dome, and cap each have three parameters: a radius, a height, and a number of segments. However, since these components are vertically connected, they need to play off each other so that the overall proportion of the model is aesthetically pleasing and stays relatively fire-hydrant-like. If you look at the reference photo in Figure 5-1, the pole and the dome have roughly the same radius, while the base and the top band stick out roughly the same amount from the pole. Therefore, you can make the pole radius (pole_radius) adjustable then derive the radius of the base and the top band, as shown in Figure 5-3. Dialing the pole radius up and down will then make the fire hydrant wider or skinnier as a whole and maintain its overall proportion.

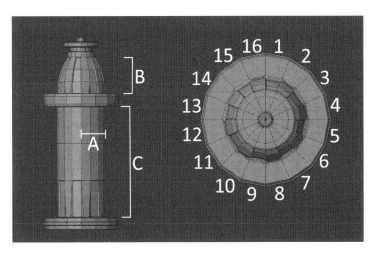

Figure 5-3. *How adjustable parameters influence the appearance of the generated models. Left: Front view. Right: Top view. Left: A, pole_radius; B, num_dome_levels; and C, num_pole_levels. Right: Result when num_cir_segments is 16. The parameter names are from the function gen_stylized_fire_hydrant in Listings 5-1 to 5-5*

Changing the number of times the base is extruded upward (num_pole_levels) to form the pole is an intuitive way to control the height of the pole. Similarly, the number of extruded loops in the dome (num_dome_levels) correlates naturally to the height of the dome. As you'll see shortly when we go over the code, I've made the height of each "level" (i.e., extrusion) of the pole and the dome to be derived from pole_radius, which reduces the total number of parameters needed and helps us maintain the proportion of the model as a whole.

A simple way to control the polycount of the generated model is to adjust the number of segments (num_cir_segments) used to approximate the circular cross-sections. To simplify the design, I tied the inset details on the dome and on the bottom of the pole to every other segment, as opposed to making the interval of the insets adjustable or maintaining a certain number of insets despite the total number of segments. You can see the effects of this in Figure 5-4. Once the cylindrical base is generated with num_cir_segments segments, as you extrude upward from the base continuously to form the pole, top band, dome, and cap, all these components will share the same number of segments, which keeps the topology clean with uninterrupted edge loops down the side of the fire hydrant.

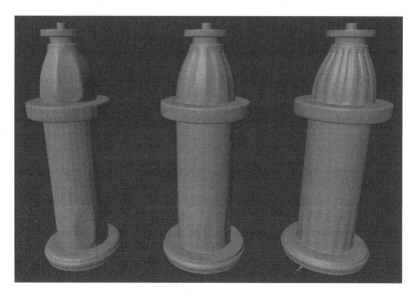

Figure 5-4. *Fire hydrants generated with different numbers of circular segments. From left to right: 8, 16, and 32 segments. Notice that since the inset detail is added every other segment, when the number of segments is odd, one pair of adjacent segments are insetted*

To make the zigzags for stylizing the model more intuitive to control, I added two parameters, pole_bent_factor and dome_bent_factor, that when dialed up (down) will increase (decrease) how much the pole, top band, and dome are zigzagged, respectively, as shown in Figure 5-5. These parameters are simply floats that get multiplied with the X/Y offsets and scale factors applied to the extrusions that create the zigzagged portions, as explained in the previous section. To make the algorithm capable of generating both regular and stylized models, I added a parameter stylize which when set to False zeroes out the X/Y offsets and returns the scale factors to 1, causing the extrusion to go straight up instead of zigzagging.

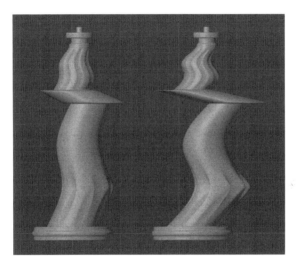

Figure 5-5. *Making the zigzags in the pole and dome adjustable. Left: pole_bent_factor = 1 and dome_bent_factor = 1. Right pole_bent_factor = 2 and dome_bent_factor = 2*

For added convenience, I also added a subsurf parameter to control whether a subsurf modifier gets added to the generated model and subsurf_level for specifying the level of subdivision (I used the same level for both preview and render. You could of course use two inputs in your own design—one for controlling the preview level, the other the render level).

Since we're generating fire hydrants, which are hard surface models, we want the option to prevent the subsurf modifier from rounding sharp edges too much such that the model no longer appears rigid. One way to achieve this is to cut an edge loop on either side of a sharp edge and push the extra loops right up against it. For example, to keep the base of the fire hydrant looking like a hockey puck (short closed cylinder), you want to cut extra edge loops around both the cylinder's top and bottom end cap loops.

Whether to preserve the sharp edges really comes down to how you plan to use the generated models. There is no single right answer. If you're going for a more realistic look, you'll likely want to keep hard surface models looking rigid. However, if you are going for a whimsical look, you may actually prefer the rounded look. For this reason, I've made the extra loop cuts controllable via a boolean parameter add_geo_for_sharp_loops, so you can experiment with both and compare for yourself.

Generating the Base

With the generation algorithm formulated, let's delve into the Python implementation. Following the breakdown in Figure 5-2, we'll go over one stage of generation at a time over the next few sections, for a total of five generation stages (shown from Listings 5-1 to 5-5). Listing 5-1 shows the beginning of the function gen_stylized_fire_hydrant, which generates the base of the fire hydrant.

Listing 5-1. Function gen_stylized_fire_hydrant, part 1 of 5, generating the fire hydrant base

```
def gen_stylized_fire_hydrant(context, name, location=(0, 0, 0),
    num_cir_segments=16, pole_radius=3, num_pole_levels=3,
    num_dome_levels=3, stylize=False, pole_bent_factor=1,
    dome_bent_factor=1, subsurf=False, subsurf_level=2,
    add_geo_for_sharp_loops=True):
```

```python
bm, fh_obj = get_placeholder_mesh_obj_and_bm(context, ↵
    name=name, location=location)
if subsurf:
    fh_subsurf_mod = fh_obj.modifiers.new( ↵
        "subsurf_mod", 'SUBSURF')
    fh_subsurf_mod.levels = subsurf_level
    fh_subsurf_mod.subdivision_type = 'CATMULL_CLARK'

ratio_base_to_pole = 1.5
base_radius = pole_radius*ratio_base_to_pole
base_height = pole_radius*0.5
loops_to_add_geo = []

bmesh.ops.create_cone(bm, cap_ends=False, cap_tris=False, ↵
    segments=num_cir_segments, radius1=base_radius, ↵
    radius2=base_radius, depth=base_height)

bm.edges.ensure_lookup_table()
bm.faces.ensure_lookup_table()
base_ref_edges = []
loop_cut_ref_edge = None
for e in bm.faces[0].edges:
    if e.verts[0].co[2] == e.verts[1].co[2]:
        base_ref_edges.append(e)
    else:
        loop_cut_ref_edge = e

base_loops = get_edge_loops(bm, base_ref_edges, ↵
    select_rings=False)
loops_to_add_geo.extend(base_loops)
loop_cut_slide(context, loop_cut_ref_edge, ↵
    num_cuts=2, slide_distance=0)
bm.edges.ensure_lookup_table()
```

```
for f in bm.faces:
    num_edges_selected = sum([1 if f.edges[i].select ↩
        else 0 for i in range(4)])
    if num_edges_selected >= 2:
        f.select = True
context.tool_settings.mesh_select_mode = [False, False, True]

bpy.ops.mesh.extrude_region_move( ↩
    TRANSFORM_OT_translate={"value": Vector((0,0,0))})
bpy.ops.transform.resize(value=(1.05, 1.05, 1.0), ↩
    orient_type='GLOBAL')
bm.faces.ensure_lookup_table()

if add_geo_for_sharp_loops:
    base_ridge_loop_ref_edges = []
    for f in bm.faces:
        if f.select:
            for e in f.edges:
                if e.verts[0].co[2] == e.verts[1].co[2]:
                    base_ridge_loop_ref_edges.append(e)
            break
    bpy.ops.mesh.select_all(action='DESELECT')
    select_edge_loops(bm, base_ridge_loop_ref_edges, ↩
        select_rings=False)
    bpy.ops.mesh.bevel(offset=0.1, segments= 2, ↩
        loop_slide=False)
    bpy.ops.mesh.select_all(action='DESELECT')

context.tool_settings.mesh_select_mode = [False, True, False]
bm.edges.ensure_lookup_table()
top_loop_edge = base_ref_edges[0] if ↩
    base_ref_edges[0].verts[0].co[2] > ↩
        base_ref_edges[1].verts[0].co[2] else base_ref_edges[1]
```

```
select_edge_loops(bm, [top_loop_edge], select_rings=False)

bpy.ops.mesh.extrude_region_move( ↵
    TRANSFORM_OT_translate={"value": Vector((0, 0, 0))})
ratio_pole_to_base = 1 / ratio_base_to_pole
bpy.ops.transform.resize(value=(ratio_pole_to_base, ↵
    ratio_pole_to_base, 1), orient_type='GLOBAL')
```

We start generating the base by creating a placeholder mesh object fh_obj with blank mesh data and a BMesh instance bm for editing it, using get_placeholder_mesh_obj_and_bm from Chapter 3 (Listing 3-9). If the subsurf argument is True, a subsurf modifier is optionally added next with the specified number of subdivisions (subsurf_level) and the subdivision type set to Catmull Clark.

Next, we establish some internal parameters for maintaining the proportions between various parts of the fire hydrant. Since not every generation parameter is exposed to the user (there would be too many), we'll calculate the parameters not directly specified by the user from the ones that are. Since the radius of the pole is entered by the user (but not the base) and the base should be larger than the pole (for maintaining the overall proportion and aesthetic of the model), we use a ratio of 1.5 (so the radius of the base is 1.5 times the radius of the pole). Similarly, we make the height of the base half the radius of the pole. We also create a list named loops_to_add_geo to keep track of which loops we want to preserve sharpness by cutting extra loops around later.

With the proportion of the base and the pole decided, we call bmesh.ops.create_cone to add an open-ended cylinder to fh_obj via bm with the given number of segments (num_cir_segments), a radius 50% larger than pole_radius, and a height 50% of pole_radius, which is shown as (1) in Figure 5-6.

Next, we want to retrieve the edge loops at the two ends of the cylinder so we can add them to the list of edges to preserve sharpness (loops_to_add_geo). To do this, we call get_edge_loops from Chapter 4 (Listing 4-10) with two reference edges, one belonging to each edge loop. Since the cylinder is open-ended at this stage, with all of its quad faces facing outward from its side, we can take face #0 (or any other face) and look at its four edges—one edge will be part of the cylinder's top edge loop, and one edge will be part of the bottom (while the other two edges will connect the top and the bottom). An edge that is part of either the top or bottom loop will lay horizontal, with its two end vertices having the same Z coordinate (`e.verts[0].co[2] == e.verts[1].co[2]`). We find two such edges (`base_ref_edges`) to call `get_edge_loops` with and save the loops returned (`base_loops`) to the list of loops to cut extra loops around later for sharpness (`loops_to_add_geo`).

We also require (any) one vertical edge connecting the cylinder's top loop to the bottom, so we can use it as reference to make loop cuts for creating the bumped out ridge detail in the base. Notice that we already found this while examining face#0 above—any of its two edges with one end vertex sitting above the other (in Z) will fit the criteria. We take the one with the highest index (`loop_cut_ref_edge`) as reference and call `loop_cut_slide` to cut two loops without sliding, with the results shown as (2) in Figure 5-6.

Next, we want to extrude the face loop between the cuts outward along the cylinder's normals to create the bumped out detail in the base. Since `loop_cut_slide` does not return the cut edge loops but only leaves them selected, we have to find the face loop ourselves. We iterate through the cylinder's faces and select those that have two edges selected (which would indicate they belong to the loop cuts since they are the only thing selected postcuts). We call `bpy.ops.mesh.extrude_region_move` to extrude the face loop and resize the extrusion with `bpy.ops.transform.resize` so it sticks outward from the cylinder's sides (the result of which is shown as (3) in Figure 5-6).

After the extrusion, the front face loop of the ridge remains selected, which we can take advantage of and iterate through to find the ridge's top and bottom edge loops (via a similar process as the top and bottom loops of the base's cylinder, by locating the edges that have two end vertices with the same Z). We bevel these loops to create the same effects as cutting extra loops from either side and sliding them close (shown as (4) in Figure 5-6).

Next, we want to close the top of the base partially, so it's ready to extrude to form the pole in the second generation stage. We reuse the two reference edges we derived earlier for selecting the top and bottom loops of the cylinder (base_ref_edges) and compare the Z coordinates of their first end vertex (base_ref_edges[0].verts[0].co[2] and base_ref_edges[1].verts[0].co[2])—the edge in the top loop (top_loop_edge) will have the end vertex with the larger Z, which we use as reference to select the top edge loop (shown as (5) in Figure 5-6).

With the top loop of the cylinder selected, we extrude it (by calling bpy.ops.mesh.extrude_region_move) and scale the extrusion along the XY plane based on the ratio of the pole and base. Recall that we established this earlier with ratio_base_to_pole = 1.5, which makes the base radius 1.5 times of the pole radius. Since we are extruding from the top of the base toward the pole, we need to go from larger to smaller—therefore scaling by 1/ratio_base_to_pole). You can see the result of this step as (6) in Figure 5-6.

Figure 5-6. *Generating the base of the fire hydrant. (1) Adding a cylinder to fh_obj via bm by calling bmesh.ops.create_cone. (2) Cut two edge loops with* loop_cut_slide. *(3) Select the faces between the newly cut edge loops, then extrude and scale them along XY to form the bumped out ridge detail in the base. (4) Bevel the edges of the bumped out ridge to create extra loops to preserve sharpness under subsurf. (5) Select the edge loop at the top of the cylinder. (6) Extrude and scale the edge loop at the top of the cylinder to form the partial cap of the base*

Adding the Pole and Top Band

We continue the generation by extruding upward from the base to form the pole and the top band with the second part of gen_stylized_fire_hydrant, as shown in Listing 5-2.

Listing 5-2. Function gen_stylized_fire_hydrant, part 2 of 5, adding pole and top band

```
bm.edges.ensure_lookup_table()
pole_bottom_loop = []
for e in bm.edges:
    if e.select:
```

```
        pole_bottom_loop.append(e)
ref_edge = pole_bottom_loop[0]
loops_to_add_geo.append(pole_bottom_loop)

context.tool_settings.mesh_select_mode = [False, False, True]
edge_loops_pole_cross_sections = []
pole_level_height = pole_radius*1.5
face_loop_pole_bottom = []

for i in range(num_pole_levels+1):
    z_offset = pole_level_height if i < num_pole_levels ↵
        else top_band_height
    if stylize:
        skew = pole_radius*0.5*pole_bent_factor
        direction = Vector((skew, skew, z_offset)) if ↵
            i%2 == 0 else Vector((-skew, -skew, z_offset))
        scale = Vector((0.85,1,1)) if i%2 == 0 else ↵
            Vector((1,0.85,1))
    else:
        direction = Vector((0, 0, z_offset))
        scale = Vector((1, 1, 1))
    extrusion = extrude_edge_loop_copy_move(bm, ref_edge, ↵
        direction, scale)
    edge_loops_pole_cross_sections.append(extrusion)
    ref_edge = extrusion[0]

    if i == 0:
        face_idx = 0
        for f in bm.faces:
            if f.select:
                if face_idx%2 == 0:
                    face_loop_pole_bottom.append(f)
                face_idx += 1
```

```
    if i >= num_pole_levels-1:
        loops_to_add_geo.append(extrusion)

bpy.ops.mesh.extrude_region_move( ↩
    TRANSFORM_OT_translate={"value": Vector((0,0,0))})
bpy.ops.transform.resize(value=(ratio_base_to_pole, ↩
    ratio_base_to_pole, 1), orient_type='GLOBAL')
```

At the end of the last section, we extruded and scaled the top edge loop of the base cylinder. Since this loop is still selected, to find it, we simply iterate through bm.edges and queue up the selected edges (pole_bottom_loop). We append this loop to the list of loops to cut extra loops around later to preserve sharpness (loops_to_add_geo). We also grab the first edge of this loop (pole_bottom_loop[0]) to use as reference for extruding the first (bottom) level of the pole.

Since the height per pole level is not a user-editable parameter, we calculate it from 1.5 times the pole radius (pole_level_height = pole_radius*1.5). We also create a list to keep track of the bottom face loop of the pole (face_loop_pole_bottom) so we can inset them later.

Next, we extrude the pole upward num_pole_levels plus one times, with the last extrusion purposed for forming the top band (the "hat rim" at the bottom of the dome), as shown in steps (1) and (2) and (4) and (5) of Figure 5-7. Notice that the direction of each pole level's extrusion is controlled by stylize, which when True skews the extrusion by adding a pole_radius*0.5*pole_bent_factor displacement in both the X and Y directions, alternating between +X+Y and -X-Y, creating a zigzag shape, similar to the example we've seen in Chapter 4 (Listing 4-20). We also add a scaling factor of 0.85 alternating between X and Y. If stylize is False (turned off), then the extrusion per pole level simply goes upward without scaling, forming a cylindrical shape.

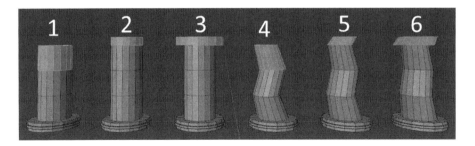

Figure 5-7. *Extruding upward from the base to create the pole and the top band. (1) Extrude num_pole_levels times to form the pole. (2) Extrude an extra time upward with which to create the top band. (3) Extrude the extra level along its normals and scale it larger. (4), (5), and (6) show the same three steps in a stylized generation*

Each level of the pole is extruded by calling extrude_edge_loop_copy_ move (Listing 4-19), which creates a copy of the topmost edge loop of the previous extrusion, moves it and scales it according to the given direction and scale, then bridges it to the previous extrusion. Each extrusion is able to look up the topmost loop of the previous extrusion via a reference edge—which is any edge of that loop, but we use the first edge (edge #0) for convenience.

At the end of the first extrusion, which forms the bottom level of the pole, we queue up every other face of that level in a list (face_loop_pole_ bottom), so we can inset these faces later to create detail. At the "bonus" level (i.e., the "plus" one level beyond the top of the pole that we extrude on purpose to make the top band), we also add the top edge loop to the list to cur extra loops around to preserve sharpness (loops_to_add_geo).

After the pole is fully formed, we extrude and scale the face loop of the bonus level to form the top band, which matches the fire hydrant's base in dimension (shown as steps (3) and (6) in Figure 5-7).

Adding the Dome and the Basis for the Cap

Moving onto part 3 of gen_stylized_fire_hydrant, as shown in Listing 5-3, we continue extruding upward from the top band to form the dome and the basis for the cap.

Listing 5-3. Function gen_stylized_fire_hydrant, part 3 of 5, generating the dome and the basis for the cap

```
bm.faces.ensure_lookup_table()
face_loop_pole_top = []
for f in bm.faces:
    if f.select:
        face_loop_pole_top.append(f)

face_loops_dome = []
face_loops_dome_cap = []
dome_radius = pole_radius
dome_height = pole_level_height
dome_level_height = dome_height/num_dome_levels
pcrt_of_sphere_for_dome = 0.75
r_prev_level = pole_radius

for i in range(num_dome_levels+4):
    if i < num_dome_levels:
        z_offset = (dome_radius/num_dome_levels)*(i+1)* ↵
            pcrt_of_sphere_for_dome
        theta = asin(z_offset/pole_radius)
        r_at_level = polc_radius*cos(theta)

        level_scale_factor = r_at_level/r_prev_level
        scale = Vector((level_scale_factor, ↵
            level_scale_factor, 1))
```

```
        skew = dome_radius*0.2*dome_bent_factor if ↵
            stylize else 0
        direction = Vector((skew, skew, dome_level_height)) ↵
            if i%2 == 0 else ↵
            Vector((-skew, -skew, dome_level_height))
    else:
        z_offset = pole_radius*0.2
        direction = Vector((0, 0, z_offset))
        scale = Vector((1, 1, 1))
    extrusion = extrude_edge_loop_copy_move(bm, ref_edge, ↵
        direction, scale)
    edge_loops_pole_cross_sections.append(extrusion)
    ref_edge = extrusion[0]
    r_prev_level = r_at_level
    bm.faces.ensure_lookup_table()

    if i < num_dome_levels:
        face_idx = 0
        for f in bm.faces:
            if f.select:
                if face_idx%2 == 0:
                    face_loops_dome.append(f)
                face_idx += 1
    else:
        cur_loop = []
        for f in bm.faces:
            if f.select:
                cur_loop.append(f)
        face_loops_dome_cap.append(cur_loop)
```

Here, our strategy for generation is similar to Listing 5-2—we perform num_dome_levels extrusions upward to build the dome, optionally adding X/Y offsets (skew by dome_bent_factor) and scaling for stylization along the way. After that, we extrude up four more times to form the basis for the cap, using a fixed z_offset per extrusion without stylization (which is by design, since the base and cap are not stylized). You can see the results of Listing 5-3 in Figure 5-9.

While building the dome, we keep track of every other face of each extruded level in the list face_loops_dome so we can apply inset to them later. We also queue up the faces of each extruded cap loop in a list (cur_loop) and append that list to a master list face_loops_dome_cap so we are able to edit each cap loop independently at a later time.

We will now look at the dome extrusion process in more detail. The dome is generated as an incomplete hemisphere (with the percentage pcrt_of_sphere_for_dome set to 75%). I've made it so the overall height of the dome matches the height of one pole level (dome_height = pole_level_height) since this produces a nice proportion. The height of each dome level is then just the dome height divided by the number of dome levels:

dome_level_height = dome_height/num_dome_levels

Figure 5-8 shows a visualization of how the XY scale factor of each dome level level_scale_factor is calculated based on the aforementioned parameters. Intuitively, as you travel upward a hemisphere, the horizontal cross-sections get smaller as you ascend the levels. Since we are extruding up from the bottom of the dome, we have to scale the cross-section smaller each level.

Note that we're not restricting the dome_height to be equal to the dome_radius at the bottom of the dome; therefore, the generated dome may not necessarily be a hemisphere but possibly a squashed or elongated hemisphere. We'll start with the simplest case, where dome_height is equal to dome_radius. The height h of a level measuring from the bottom of the dome (in Figure 5-8) is then

$$h = (\text{level number}) * (\text{dome\_radius} / \text{num\_dome\_levels})$$

For example, if the dome radius is 15, and there are 3 dome levels, then adjacent levels are 15/3 = 5 units apart, and the second level will measure 5*2 units from the bottom of the dome.

Let's call the angle opposite h in Figure 5-8 θ (theta). It follows that $\sin(\theta) = h/r$, where r is the dome radius. We're then able to calculate θ:

$$\theta = \arcsin(h/r)$$

Therefore, r', the radius of the level cross-section, can be calculated as

$$r' = r * \cos(\text{theta})$$

We can now calculate r' at each level of the dome and compare the current level's r' to the previous level's r'.

Let's revisit Listing 5-3 and see which step of our derivation above corresponds to which line of code. In Listing 5-3, h is calculated as z_offset at this line:

```
z_offset = (dome_radius/num_dome_levels)*(i+1)* ↩
    pcrt_of_sphere_for_dome
```

θ is calculated as theta at this line:

```
theta = asin(z_offset/pole_radius)
```

r' at each level is calculated as r_at_level, at this line:

```
r_at_level = pole_radius*cos(theta)
```

Recall that our extrusion process is

1. Make a copy of the topmost loop of the previous extrusion.

2. Calculate the XY scale factor and use it to scale the copy to match the current level's cross-section size.

3. Move the scaled copy to the right position (updated level height, plus any horizontal skew).

4. Bridge the current level cross-section to the previous level.

In other words, each level is copied and scaled from the level just before it, which is why in the code, we calculate and save each level's cross-section radius (r_prev_level = r_at_level), so we can use it to calculate the next level's XY scale factor.

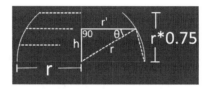

Figure 5-8. *Calculating the per-level XY scale factor for the dome extrusion*

Remember that we simplified the math by making the dome_height equal the dome_radius. But even if they are different, the same process still gives you a very good estimate of the scale factor level_scale_factor. Therefore, we calculate level_scale_factor the same way regardless of the ratio between dome_height and dome_radius and simply move each level based on dome_level_height (which is based on dome_height).

The XY skew for the dome is applied the same way as the pole; for more detail, refer to Listing 5-2 in the section "Adding the Pole and Top Band."

In the for loop in Listing 5-3 we extrude a total of num_dome_levels plus four times, with the last four times forming the basis for the cap. For the cap extrusion portion, we simply extrude upward a fixed amount (pole_radius*0.2) each time with no scaling, for a total of four times. We will modify these four face loops in the next section to form the cap of the fire hydrant.

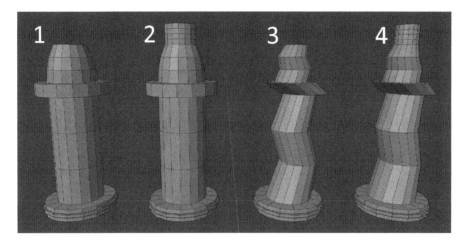

Figure 5-9. *Generating the dome and the basis for the cap. (1) Three dome levels generated. (2) Four additional cap levels generated on top of the dome that will be modified into the fire hydrant cap. (3) and (4) show the same two steps as (1) and (2) but with* stylize = True

Shaping the Cap

At the end of Listing 5-3, we started building the cap with a four-tiered open-top cylinder. In this section, we'll finish the cap by giving it contour and closing its top, in the fourth part of gen_stylized_fire_hydrant, as shown in Listing 5-4.

Listing 5-4. Function gen_stylized_fire_hydrant, part 4 of 5, shaping the cap and closing the top

```
new_face_loops_dome_cap = []
dome_cap_scale_factors = {1:0.8, 2:1.3, 3:0.3}
for i in range(1, 4, 1):
    bpy.ops.mesh.select_all(action='DESELECT')
    for f in face_loops_dome_cap[i]:
        f.select = True
```

```
    bpy.ops.mesh.extrude_region_move( ↵
        TRANSFORM_OT_translate={"value": Vector((0,0,0))})
    scale_factor = dome_cap_scale_factors[i]
    bpy.ops.transform.resize(value=(scale_factor, ↵
        scale_factor, 1), orient_type='GLOBAL')

    new_face_loop_this_level = []
    bm.faces.ensure_lookup_table()
    for f in bm.faces:
        if f.select:
            new_face_loop_this_level.append(f)
    new_face_loops_dome_cap.append(new_face_loop_this_level)

bpy.ops.mesh.select_all(action='DESELECT')
select_edge_loops(bm, [ref_edge], select_rings=False)
bpy.ops.mesh.edge_collapse()
```

Recall that at the end of Listing 5-3, we recorded the four horizontal face loops reserved for the cap in a list (face_loops_dome_cap). In this part of the code, we'll edit the second, third, and fourth face loops (counting from the bottom of the cap) to give the cap contour, before closing the cap's top, as shown in Figure 5-10.

From bottom to top, the cap will recess, bump out, then recess again into a bolt. To achieve these effects, I used scale factors 0.8, 1.3, and 0.3, respectively, and stored them in a dictionary for lookup for when we iterate the cap levels (dome_cap_scale_factors = {1:0.8, 2:1.3, 3:0.3}). These are just values that I happen to find aesthetically pleasing. I encourage you to experiment by changing these values or setting them up as user inputs to the extension.

We iterate the cap face loops from bottom to top. For each iteration of the for loop, we select one face loop, call bpy.ops.mesh.extrude_region_move to extrude it in place, then call bpy.ops.transform.resize to resize the extrusion with the scale factor for that level (dome_cap_scale_ factors[i]). The three iterations of the for loop are visualized as (2), (3), and (4) in Figure 5-10, which extrude and scale cap levels at indices #1, #2, and #3.

Recall that we've been saving edges that we want to cut extra loops around to preserve sharpness in the list loops_to_add_geo (see Listing 5-1 and Listing 5-2 and their associated sections). We want the different levels of the cap to stay sharp as well, so we want to save a list of the newly extruded edge loops from the cap shaping.

At the end of each for loop iteration, since the selection remains post scaling, we can queue up faces that are selected to find the new face loop for that level, new_face_loop_this_level. The loops from all levels are saved in the master list, new_face_loops_dome_cap.

After shaping all the cap levels, we select the topmost edge loop of the cap with select_edge_loops (Listing 4-8) and collapse its edges by calling bpy.ops.mesh.edge_collapse() to close the hole. The result is shown as (5) in Figure 5-10. Since no stylization is applied to the cap by design, the caps on a regular and stylized model are of the same proportions, as shown in Figure 5-11.

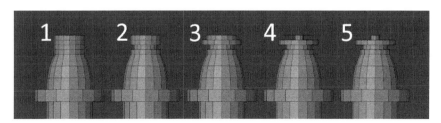

Figure 5-10. *Shaping the cap and closing its top in Listing 5-4. (1) The mesh at the end of Listing 5-3. (2) Extruding and scaling the second cap loop from the bottom so it recesses inward. (3) Extruding and scaling the third cap loop from the bottom so it sticks out. (4) Extruding and scaling the top cap loop so it recesses inward. (5) Collapsing the edges at the top to close the cap*

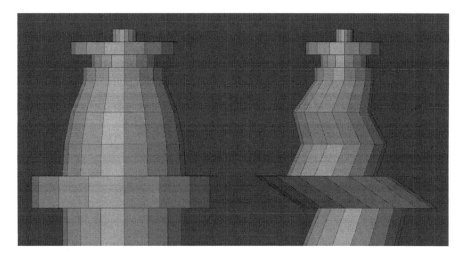

Figure 5-11. *Examples of fire hydrant meshes after their caps have been shaped*

Adding Details and Finishing Up

As we continue into the fifth and final part of gen_stylized_fire_ hydrant, as shown in Listing 5-5, our goals are to add finishing touches to the model with inset details, close the bottom of the base, cut extra loops around edges that we want to preserve sharpness under subsurf, and correct normals.

Listing 5-5. Function gen_stylized_fire_hydrant, part 5 of 5, insetting details, closing the bottom, cutting extra loops to preserve sharpness, and correcting normals

```
bmesh.ops.inset_region(bm, faces=face_loop_pole_top, ↵
    thickness=0.3, depth=0.1)
bmesh.ops.inset_individual(bm, ↵
    faces=face_loop_pole_bottom, thickness=0.1, depth=-0.15)
bmesh.ops.inset_region(bm, faces=face_loops_dome, ↵
    thickness=0.1, depth=-0.15)
```

```
bpy.ops.mesh.select_all(action='DESELECT')
bot_base_loop = base_loops[0] ↵
    if base_loops[0][0].verts[0].co[2] < ↵
    base_loops[1][0].verts[0].co[2] ↵
    else base_loops[1]
for e in bot_base_loop:
    e.select = True
bpy.ops.mesh.edge_face_add()
bpy.ops.mesh.select_all(action='DESELECT')

if add_geo_for_sharp_loops:
    for l in loops_to_add_geo:
        for e in l:
            e.select = True
    bpy.ops.mesh.bevel(offset=0.1, segments=2, ↵
        loop_slide=False)
    bpy.ops.mesh.select_all(action='DESELECT')

    for nfldc in new_face_loops_dome_cap:
        bpy.ops.mesh.select_all(action='DESELECT')
        f0 = nfldc[0]
        nfldc_loop_ref_edges = []
        for e in f0.edges:
            if e.verts[0].co[2] == e.verts[1].co[2]:
                nfldc_loop_ref_edges.append(e)
        select_edge_loops(bm, nfldc_loop_ref_edges, ↵
            select_rings=False)
        bpy.ops.mesh.bevel(offset=0.1, segments=2, ↵
            loop_slide=False)

    bpy.ops.mesh.select_all(action='DESELECT')
```

```
bmesh.ops.recalc_face_normals(bm, faces=bm.faces)
bmesh.update_edit_mesh(fh_obj.data)
bpy.ops.object.mode_set(mode='OBJECT')
```

We'll start by adding details to the top band, dome, and pole, as shown in Figure 5-12. First, we add an outset (with a depth > 0) to the top band to give it a rounded look (recall that we recorded the list of faces face_loop_ pole_top in Listing 5-2). Then, we add an inset to every other segment of the pole's bottom face loop (see face_loop_pole_bottom in Listing 5-2). Finally, we add insets to every other segment of the dome (see face_ loops_dome in Listing 5-3). Notice that bmesh.ops.inset_region is used for insetting the dome so the faces that belong to the same segment of the dome across the different horizontal face loops are automatically grouped together for the inset.

Next, we'll close the bottom of the base, as shown in Figure 5-13. Recall we saved the base's top and bottom edge loops in the list base_loops (Listing 5-1). Since we're unsure which loop is the bottom, we compare the two loops by the Z coordinate of the first end vert of the first edge (base_loops[0][0].verts[0].co[2] and base_loops[1][0].verts[0]. co[2])— whichever has the smaller Z is the bottom. We select this loop (by iterating and selecting every edge), and call bpy.ops.mesh.edge_face_ add() to fill it with an n-gon.

Remember the list of edges we've been tracking (loops_to_add_geo) that we want to cut extra edge loops around to keep sharp under subsurf? If the argument add_geo_for_sharp_loops is True, we do that here, by selecting one loop in loops_to_add_geo at a time and calling bpy.ops. mesh.bevel with two segments. Figure 5-14 shows a visualization of all the extra loops that are cut, which include the top and bottom of the base (base_loops from Listing 5-1), the loop at the pole's bottom connecting to the base (pole_bottom_loop from Listing 5-2), and the loops at the top and bottom of the top band (the last two iterations of the pole extrusion for loop, at i >= num_pole_levels - 1, in Listing 5-2).

In addition, we want to keep the cap sharp. Recall that we saved the cap's face loops in the list new_face_loops_dome_cap from Listing 5-4. Since we saved face loops, we have to get the top/bottom edge loops from each face loop first before we can bevel them. To do this, we grab the first face of each face loop, and find the edges that have end vertices with the same Z, and use them as references to call select_edge_loops (Listing 4-8). We then bevel them using bpy.ops.mesh.bevel with two segments, as shown in Figure 5-15.

We wrap up the generation by calling bmesh.ops.recalc_face_ normals to recompute normals to ensure they're all facing outward. We then call bmesh.update_edit_mesh to flush all the bmesh edits to fh_obj's mesh data and switch fh_obj to Object mode.

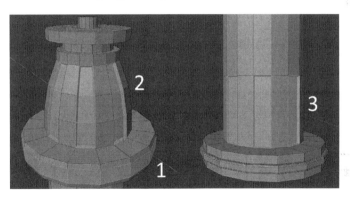

Figure 5-12. *Creating detail by outsetting and insetting. (1) Outsetting (insetting with a positive depth) the top band. (2) Insetting every other face of the dome. (3) Insetting every other face of the bottom level of the pole*

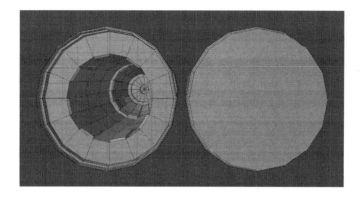

Figure 5-13. *Closing the bottom of the base by selecting the bottom edge loop and calling* bpy.ops.mesh.edge_face_add() *to fill it with an n-gon*

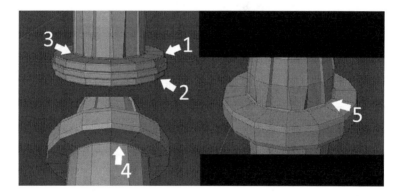

Figure 5-14. *Cutting extra edge loops around loops that we want to keep sharp under subsurf. (1) and (2): Top and bottom edge loops of the base (*base_loops*). (3) Loop at the bottom of the pole, connecting to the base (*pole_bottom_loop*). (4) Loop at the bottom of the top band (at i == num_pole_levels-1 of pole extrusion* for *loop). (5) Loop at the top of the top band (at i == num_pole_levels of pole extrusion* for *loop)*

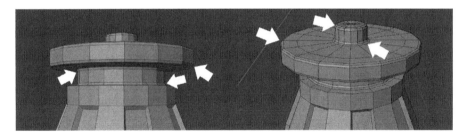

Figure 5-15. *Cutting extra edge loops around loops that we want to keep sharp under subsurf. The white arrows point out the top and bottom edge loops of the top three cap levels where extra loops are cut*

Generating a Variety of Fire Hydrants by Changing Parameters

In this section, we'll look at how changing input values for gen_stylized_ fire_hydrant (Listings 5-1 to 5-5) impacts the generated meshes, to get an idea of the types of variations we can achieve. Figures 5-16 and 5-17 show the meshes generated by calling test_gen_fire_hydrant in the Text Editor version of the chapter examples (or by pressing the "Generate with Presets" button in the extension version). These function calls are too verbose to list and difficult to read in the text, so I'll leave it to you to review them in the downloaded source and encourage you to experiment further.

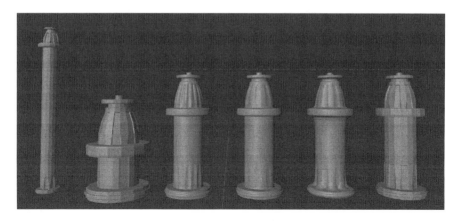

Figure 5-16. *Various nonstylized fire hydrants generated by calling* `test_gen_fire_hydrant` *in the Text Editor version of the chapter examples or by pressing the "Generate with Presets" button in the extension version*

Notice in Figure 5-16, the first four models from right to left are generated with

1. Default parameters (16 segments, no subsurf)

2. Defaults with subsurf but *without* keeping sharp edges (`subsurf=True, add_geo_for_sharp_loops=False`)

3. Defaults with subsurf *with* sharp edges (`subsurf=True, add_geo_for_sharp_loops=True`)

4. Thirty-two segments with three levels of subsurf and sharp edges (`num_cir_segments=32, subsurf=True, subsurf_level=3, add_geo_for_sharp_loops=True`)

You can see that cutting extra edge loops is very effective at keeping edges sharp, even at three levels of subsurf (fourth model from the right in Figure 5-16).

Figure 5-17. *Various stylized fire hydrants generated by calling* test_gen_fire_hydrant *in the Text Editor version of the chapter examples or by pressing the "Generate with Presets" button in the extension version*

Figure 5-17 shows six stylized models with different numbers of pole and dome levels as well as pole and dome bent factors. The third model from the left has 2.5 times the pole and dome bent factors than default, while the fifth model from the left has 1.5 times the pole bent factor and 1.25 times the dome bent factor.

You can see with the higher bent factors, not only are the bends more noticeable but the domes appear to shift away from the poles toward the opposite side of the top bands. Without subsurf (the first, fourth, fifth, and sixth models from the left), the models look more mechanical, whereas with subsurf (the second and third models from the left), the models look more organic and whimsical.

Turning the Generation Algorithm into an Extension

In this section, I'll briefly go over how I adapted the Text Editor version of the chapter source (`fire_hydrant_generator.py`) into an extension. We'll look at how the arguments to `gen_stylized_fire_hydrant` (Listings 5-1 to 5-5) are set up as input widgets, how the operator is created to call the generation routine with the widget values, and how the operators are exposed to the users in the UI panel.

Exposing Generation Parameters as User Inputs

The purpose of the extension is to provide an interface for users to enter parameter values and kick off the generation. Now that you're familiar with `gen_stylized_fire_hydrant`, you'll be able to plan this out quite easily by finding the corresponding `bpy.props` type to each of its arguments (e.g., `num_cir_segments` as an `IntProperty` instance). We'll go over this together in this section.

Using the 3D Cursor As Input to Specify Location

The users will likely want to generate multiple models in the same scene, so it makes sense that they are able to specify the `location` for each mesh. Several possible ways come to mind for getting a location `Vector` from the user. One is to enter it as a string (via a `StringProperty` with `subtype='NONE'` as we've seen in Chapter 2). This is not great since it's ambiguous what format the user is expected to enter the vector (with or without parentheses? Commas to separate the numbers?). In addition, you would have to convert the string into numbers. A better option is to let users enter three numbers separately, in three `FloatProperty` (or `IntProperty`) instances (we've seen these in Chapter 2). This is still not ideal, since it's a lot of separate fields to manage for one quantity.

An intuitive way to specify a location is by positioning the 3D cursor in the viewport—which is what I used to get the input for where to place the model when the "Generate" button is clicked in the extension.

Let's head over to the built-in Python Console and enter the following line to access the 3D cursor's current location:

```
>>> bpy.context.scene.cursor.location
Vector((0.0, 0.0, 0.0))
```

You can try moving the 3D cursor around in the viewport and access this value again in the Console to see it change.

You'll be able to get a valid Vector for the 3D Cursor's location this way even when the 3D Cursor is hidden in the viewport (to hide the 3D Cursor, uncheck the *3D Cursor* box under *Viewport Overlays* ➤ *Guides*).

Creating Input Widgets for Generation Parameters

With location out of the way, the rest of gen_stylized_fire_hydrant's arguments are string, integers, decimal numbers, and booleans, which correspond to StringProperty, IntProperty, FloatProperty, and BoolProperty instances, respectively, as summarized in Table 5-1.

Table 5-1. Mapping gen_stylized_fire_hydrant's arguments to bpy.props types

StringProperty	IntProperty	FloatProperty	BoolProperty
name	num_cir_segments	pole_radius	stylize
	num_pole_levels	pole_bent_factor	subsurf
	num_dome_levels	dome_bent_factor	add_geo_for_sharp_loops
	subsurf_level		

We can now implement each argument as a scene variable of its corresponding bpy.props type, in an init_scene_vars() function, which we'll call in register(). Since we've already learned about the bpy.props types from Table 5-1 in Chapter 2, we'll only look at one example of each type in Listing 5-6. You can revisit Chapter 2 for more detail on the purpose of init_scene_vars() and register() in an add-on.

Listing 5-6. Implementation of arguments to gen_stylized_fire_ hydrant as scene variables (except)

```
def init_scene_vars():
    bpy.types.Scene.fh_object_name = StringProperty(
        name="Object Name",
        description="Name for the fire hydrant object",
        default="fire_hydrant",
        subtype="NONE")

    bpy.types.Scene.num_cir_segments = bpy.props.IntProperty(
        name="Num Segments",
        description="Number of segments for the cross section",
        default=16,
        max=64,
        min=8)

    bpy.types.Scene.pole_radius= bpy.props.FloatProperty(
        name="Pole Radius",
        description="Radius of fire hydrant pole",
        default=3.0,
        max=50.0,
        min=1.0)
<  -------------------- SNIP --------------------- >
    bpy.types.Scene.subsurf = bpy.props.BoolProperty(
        name="Subsurf",
```

```
description="Whether to add a subsurf modifier to ↵
    the generated mesh",
default=True)
```

You'll notice that I've used the same default values from gen_ stylized_fire_hydrant's keyword arguments in the property definitions in Listing 5-6. For example, num_cir_segments=16 and bpy.types. Scene.num_cir_segments has default=16. Note that bpy.types.Scene. fh_object_name has a default value of "fire_hydrant", which is what will appear in the text input field when the extension is loaded; however, this does not prevent the user from deleting the string and leaving the text field empty, in which case, Blender will throw out the empty string and default the generated object's name to "Object".

While gen_stylized_fire_hydrant's arguments have no limits, I've imposed max and min values for the IntProperty and FloatProperty instances in Listing 5-6, since it's generally a good idea to do so in a user interface so the user cannot accidentally enter an invalid or unreasonable value (e.g., one that will cause a crash or make a mesh too expensive to edit interactively in the viewport). For example, for bpy.types.Scene. num_cir_segments, I've set a min value of 8 so the user cannot enter too few segments for the fire hydrant's cross-section (you need an absolute minimum of 3 to produce a valid polygon, while 8 is a reasonable minimum for a circle).

Recall that description is the string that will show up in the tool tip when you hover the mouse cursor over a UI widget. I suggest that you always enter a value for description since it helps the user understand what aspect of the mesh generation the parameter controls and therefore how its value might influence the generated model.

Creating an Operator to Call the Generation Routine with Widget Values

The next step is to create an operator GenerateFireHydrantOperator that will call gen_stylized_fire_hydrant with the values from the scene variables (UI widgets), as shown in Listing 5-7.

Listing 5-7. Implementing an operator to invoke the generation routine with values from the UI widgets

```
class GenerateFireHydrantOperator(Operator):
    bl_idname = "mesh.generate_fire_hydrant"
    bl_label = "Generate"
    """Generate Fire Hydrant Meshes With User Input Values"""
    def execute(self, context):
        gen_stylized_fire_hydrant(context, ↵
            context.scene.fh_object_name, ↵
            location=context.scene.cursor.location, ↵
            num_cir_segments=context.scene.num_cir_segments, ↵
            pole_radius=context.scene.pole_radius, ↵
            num_pole_levels=context.scene.num_pole_levels, ↵
            num_dome_levels=context.scene.num_dome_levels, ↵
            stylize=context.scene.stylize, ↵
            pole_bent_factor=context.scene.pole_bent_factor, ↵
            dome_bent_factor=context.scene.dome_bent_factor, ↵
            subsurf=context.scene.subsurf, ↵
            subsurf_level=context.scene.subsurf_level, ↵
            add_geo_for_sharp_loops= ↵
                context.scene.add_geo_for_sharp_loops)

        self.report({'INFO'}, "Generate Fire Hydrant Meshes With ↵
            User Input Values.")
        return {'FINISHED'}
```

Recall from Chapter 2 that to access the value of the scene variable bpy.types.Scene.<variable>, you'll use context.scene.<variable>. For example, to access the value of bpy.types.Scene.num_cir_segments in your operator, you'll use context.scene.num_cir_segments.

As mentioned earlier in the section "Using the 3D Cursor As Input to Specify Location," we access the 3D Cursor's current location via context.scene.cursor.location and use that as the value for the location argument.

Exposing the Input Widgets and the Operator in the UI Panel

We'll now add the input widgets and the operator for invoking the generation routine to the add-on's UI panel. Listing 5-8 shows an excerpt of the implementation for the extension's UI panel FIRE_HYDRANT_GENERATOR_PT_ToolPanel, which sets up the panel's layout and adds bpy.types.Scene.fh_object_name (Listing 5-6) as a text input widget and the operator GenerateFireHydrantOperator (Listing 5-7) as a button.

Listing 5-8. Excerpt of the Fire Hydrant Generator extension's UI panel

```
class FIRE_HYDRANT_GENERATOR_PT_ToolPanel(bpy.types.Panel):
    bl_idname = "FIRE_HYDRANT_GENERATOR_PT_ToolPanel"
    bl_label = "FIRE_HYDRANT_GENERATOR"
    bl_space_type = 'VIEW_3D'
    bl_region_type = 'UI'
    bl_category = 'Tool'
    """Fire Hydrant Generator Tool"""
    def draw(self, context):
        layout = self.layout
        col0 = layout.column()
```

```
box0 = col0.box()
box0.label(text="Generation Params:", icon='TEXT')
r = box0.row(align=True)
r.prop(context.scene, "fh_object_name")
```

‹ ----------------------SNIP---------------------- ›

```
box0.operator("mesh.generate_fire_hydrant", ↵
    icon='MESH_DATA')
```

To add a scene variable bpy.types.Scene.<variable> as a UI widget, you'll create a row in a box under the panel's layout, like this:

```
r = box0.row(align=True)
```

Then, add the scene variable as a widget to the row, like this:

```
r.prop(context.scene, "<variable>")
```

For example, you can add bpy.types.Scene.fh_object_name to the row like this:

```
r.prop(context.scene, "fh_object_name")
```

To add an operator as a button to the panel, you'll use the operator's bl_idname. For example, to add the operator GenerateFireHydrantOperator (Listing 5-7) which invokes our generation routine, you'll use the value of its bl_idname, which is mesh.generate_ fire_hydrant, like this:

```
box0.operator("mesh.generate_fire_hydrant", icon='MESH_DATA')
```

The text that will show up on the button is the operator's bl_label, which for GenerateFireHydrantOperator is "Generate". You can see the finished UI panel for the extension in Figure 5-18.

Figure 5-18. *UI panel for the Fire Hydrant Generator extension. (1) The scene variable* bpy.types.Scene.fh_object_name *is added as a text input widget. (2) The operator* GenerateFireHydrantOperator *is added as a button*

Wrapping Up the Extension Implementation

Recall from Chapter 2 that to finish implementing the extension, you'll need to create a del_scene_vars() function which deletes every scene variable defined by init_scene_vars() (in this case, the UI widgets we created one-to-one for the arguments of gen_stylized_fire_hydrant), as shown in Listing 5-9.

You'll also need to create a register() function, which calls init_scene_vars() to initialize scene variables, as well as bpy.utils.register_class to register every operator class you implement for the add-on. An unregister() function is also needed to undo everything that register() does, by calling del_scene_vars() and bpy.utils.unregister_class, respectively. When a user installs (uninstalls) your extension, Blender calls the register() (unregister()) function in your add-on's __init__.py file.

Lastly, as a reminder, you'll also need to create a "blender_manifest.toml" file which contains metadata for your extension placed alongside __init__.py in a folder named after the extension package. You can revisit Chapter 2 for a refresher.

Listing 5-9. Wrapping up the extension's implementation by defining del_scene_vars(), register(), and unregister() functions

```
def del_scene_vars():
    del bpy.types.Scene.fh_object_name
    del bpy.types.Scene.num_cir_segments
    del bpy.types.Scene.pole_radius
    del bpy.types.Scene.num_pole_levels
    del bpy.types.Scene.stylize
    del bpy.types.Scene.subsurf_level
    del bpy.types.Scene.add_geo_for_sharp_loops
    del bpy.types.Scene.pole_bent_factor
    del bpy.types.Scene.dome_bent_factor
```

```
classes = [GenerateFireHydrantOperator,
           GenerateFireHydrantsWithPresetsOperator,
           FIRE_HYDRANT_GENERATOR_PT_ToolPanel]
def register():
    for c in classes:
        bpy.utils.register_class(c)
    init_scene_vars()

def unregister():
    for c in classes:
        bpy.utils.unregister_class(c)
    del_scene_vars()
```

Summary

In this chapter, you built on the skills you learned in Chapters 3 and 4 and developed your first procedural generation algorithm to generate stylized fire hydrant meshes. Starting with a placeholder object with empty mesh data and a bmesh instance for modifying it, you first added a cylinder primitive to form the base, then grew your fire hydrant upward by continuously extruding and shaping.

You also learned to take advantage of the selection left over on a mesh from a previous call to a bpy.ops.mesh operator (such as from extruding a face loop on the fire hydrant cap), to chain up another edit, or to save the new geometry in a list to modify later.

In addition, you learned several ways to identify edge loops based on the relative positioning of their constituent edges. For example, you discovered that you can tell which of two loops is at the top by grabbing the first edge of each loop and comparing the Z coordinates of their end vertices. You also learned to extract the edge loops framing a face loop by dissecting one of its faces and finding the edges of that face with end verts that have equal Z.

Adding a subsurf modifier is a great way to quickly refine a generated mesh; however, it also tends to round off a hard surface model too much and make it lose its sharp edges. Utilizing the techniques you learned for identifying and selecting loops, you were able to save edges you intend to keep sharp in a list and cut extra loops around them at the end of the generation process.

To wrap up the model, you created detail on the fire hydrant pole and dome by insetting and outsetting faces and cleaned up by correcting normals. You also explored how changing parameter settings influence the outcomes of the generation.

Last but not least, you learned how to turn a procedural generation routine you've developed into an extension, by creating UI widgets that allow users to enter generation parameters and buttons to invoke operators which call the generation routine under the hood with the widget values.

## CHAPTER 6

Sculpting and Retopology

Digital sculpting is a technique which lets you create a model as if you're working with clay. Using the various brushes in Blender Sculpt mode, you can grab, pinch, and scrape a mesh to shape its silhouette while adding more geometry on the fly with Dyntopo (dynamic topology). To use a sculpted model in applications like games, however, that require high frame rates and deformation-based animations, you'll have to recreate a lower-poly version of the same mesh with cleaner edge flows to closely approximate the shape of its high-res counterpart—we call this process retopology.

In this chapter, you'll learn how to develop Python tools that automate some of the steps in sculpting and retopology to make both processes easier. You'll start by writing Python tools to set up reference photos as image empties in several different ways. Then, you'll develop tools that let users draw on a sculpted mesh with the Grease Pencil (GP) to mark areas to carve, inset, and outset. After that, taking inspiration from the popular "RetopoFlow" add-on, you'll learn how to build your own simplified version that lets users mark with the GP on a mesh for an area to automatically retopologize. Along the way, you'll learn how to use BMesh connectivity data to analyze topology, like finding poles and isolating faces with sharp or dull corners. By the end of the chapter, you'll have assembled a selection of the tools you've written into a Sculpt Retopo Toolkit extension.

© Isabel Lupiani 2025
I. Lupiani, *Blender Scripting with Python*, https://doi.org/10.1007/979-8-8688-1127-2_6

Running This Chapter's Examples

The source code for this book is available on GitHub via the book's product page, located at www.apress.com/979-8-8688-1126-5). This chapter's examples come in two parts—the first part consists of two Python scripts that are meant to run in the Text Editor, and the second part is an extension to be installed from disk. We will go over how to set these up next.

Setting Up/Running the Scripts

In the downloaded source, navigate to the folder /Ch6/text_editor, where you'll find two scripts: reference_image.py and mesh_connectivity.py. As you follow along the chapter, open the file indicated by the text in the built-in Text Editor. At the bottom of each script, there is a block already set up which invokes the code listings with sample arguments.

Installing/Running the Sculpt Retopo Toolkit Extension

Go to Edit ➤ Preferences... ➤ Get Extensions, click the blue downward "v" at the upper right to expand the menu, and click *Install from Disk....* Navigate to the Ch6/extension/sculpt_retopo_toolkit_4.2(4.3)/ folder in the downloaded source if you are running Blender 4.2 (4.3), and choose the file sculpt_retopo_toolkit-2.0.0.zip. The extension "Sculpt Retopo Toolkit" will be installed and automatically enabled. Once installed, you can access the extension in the 3D Viewport *Properties* shelf (N key) ➤ *Tool* tab.

Imports from Chapters 3 and 4

This chapter's code imports the scripts `creating_and_editing_mesh_`
`objs.py` from Chapter 3 and `mesh_editing_ops.py` from Chapter 4. These
imports have been set up for you in the downloaded source. For detail
on how to handle imports in scripts run in the Text Editor as well as in
packaged extensions, please refer to Chapter 4.

Automating the Setup of Reference Images

Open `/Ch6/text_editor/reference_image.py` in the Text Editor to follow
this section's code examples.

Before delving into sculpting, let's think about a tool that's commonly
used across all styles of modeling—reference images. Many artists find it
helpful to display reference images that depict a subject in the viewport
from different angles while creating a model. Setting up these images one
by one is tedious. Luckily, you can write Python scripts to automate this
process.

In Blender, reference images can be set up a few different ways—as
reference images, background images, or image empties. Let's go ahead
and try this. Head over to the 3D Viewport, and add a reference image via
Add (Shift-A) ➤ Image ➤ Reference. You should see a new image empty
with the name "Empty" appear in the viewport centered at the 3D cursor
and the following line logged in the Info Editor:

```
bpy.ops.object.empty_image_add(filepath=<filepath to your
image>, align='VIEW', location=(0, 0, 0), rotation=(1.26932,
-1.13991e-06, 1.48998), scale=(1, 1, 1), background=False)
```

Go back to the viewport, move the 3D Cursor and add a background
image this time, via Add (Shift-A) ➤ Image ➤ Background, which creates
another image empty, named "Empty.001".

269

```
bpy.ops.object.empty_image_add(filepath=<filepath to your
image>, align='VIEW', location=(0, -6, 0), rotation=(1.26932,
-1.13991e-06, 1.48998), scale=(1, 1, 1), background=True)
```

Note that the same operator bpy.ops.object.empty_image_add is called to create both the reference (**background=False**) and background image empties (**background=True**). If you compare both empties under the Properties editor ➤ Object tab, as shown in Figure 6-1, you'll see that the two are identical, except for two settings: Depth, which controls which other object(s) will occlude the image, and Side, which controls on which side of the empty the image will show.

The reference image has Depth=Default, meaning it will occlude (block) other objects behind it, and Side=Both, meaning the image will show on both sides (with the reverse side image mirrored).

On the other hand, the background image has Depth=Back, so it will always go "behind" other objects (in other words, its visibility is below others in priority—like a view layer sent to the back), and Side=Front, so the image will only show on the front side but not the back, as shown in Figure 6-2.

Tip   In the Info Editor, you can left-click a line then Ctrl-C (or Right-click ➤ Copy) to copy it to the clipboard.

Figure 6-1. *Background and reference image empties are identical except for their Depth and Side settings. Left: Background image. Right: Reference image*

The gotcha is you can't control the name of the empty created by bpy. ops.object.empty_image_add—Blender defaults it to "Empty" (and for subsequent calls, "Empty.001", "Empty.002", etc. if the previous instances are not renamed). You can work around this by writing a function like rename_empty shown in Listing 6-1, to rename the empty created by bpy. ops.object.empty_image_add immediately after its creation.

Listing 6-1. Rename a given empty object (see /Ch6/text_editor/ reference_image.py)

```
def rename_empty(context, name):
    active_obj = context.view_layer.objects.active
    if active_obj and active_obj.type == 'EMPTY':
        active_obj.name = name
```

```
    else:
        num_objs = len(context.view_layer.objects)
        for i in range(num_objs - 1, -1, -1):
            obj = context.view_layer.objects[i]
            if obj.type == 'EMPTY':
                obj.name = name
                context.view_layer.objects.active = obj
                break
```

rename_empty starts by checking if there is an active object of type 'EMPTY'—if so, it's renamed. Otherwise, it iterates through objects in the view layer in reverse order of their creation (from indices num_objs - 1 to 0) and renames the first empty found (which would be the last empty created).

Putting it all together, you can write a function like load_reference_or_background_image in Listing 6-2 which calls bpy.ops.object.empty_image_add with a context override to create either a reference or background empty, then rename_empty (Listing 6-1) immediately after to rename the empty.

Listing 6-2. Creating a reference or background image empty with the given name, location, and rotation (see /Ch6/text_editor/reference_image.py)

```
def load_reference_or_background_image(context, filepath, ↵
    name, location, rotation_degrees=(90,0,0), ↵
    is_background=False):
    rotation_rads = [radians(d) for d in rotation_degrees]
    context_override = get_context_override(context, 'VIEW_3D', ↵
        'WINDOW')
```

```
with bpy.context.temp_override(**context_override):
    bpy.ops.object.empty_image_add(filepath=filepath, ↵
        relative_path=False, align='VIEW', ↵
        location=location, ↵
        rotation=rotation_rads, scale=(1,1,1), ↵
        background=is_background)

    rename_empty(context, name)
```

I set up the rotation argument in degrees (since it's more human friendly) then convert it to radians at the line `rotation_rads = [radians(d) for d in rotation_degrees]`, using the function `radians` from Python's math module, which is imported at the top of `reference_image.py`.

`load_reference_or_background_image` calls `get_context_override` from Chapter 4 so it can pretend it's calling `bpy.ops.object.empty_image_add` from the viewport. The argument `is_background` when `True` will create a background image (and when `False` a reference image). `rename_empty` is called immediately after to rename the newly created empty.

Figure 6-2. *Effects of the Depth and Side settings on image empties.
Top and bottom show the same pair of image empties. Left:
Background. Right: Reference. A cube mesh is physically behind each
empty. The background image appears behind the cube, whereas the
reference image occludes the cube. A mirrored version of the image is
shown on the back of the reference empty, whereas nothing is on the
back of the background empty*

Instead of reference and background images, you could create an
empty object of display type 'Image' and set up its image data post
creation. You'd do this in the viewport with Add (Shift-A) ➤ Empty ➤
Image in Object mode (under the hood, this calls the operator bpy.ops.
object.empty_add(type='IMAGE', align='WORLD', location=<3D
Cursor location>, scale=(1, 1, 1)) and creates a new empty named
"Empty").

With the empty selected, you'd then go to the Properties editor ➤ Data
tab to set up its image. For our purpose of setting up modeling reference
photos in Python, this is not a better solution, since it involves more steps
than our previous attempt with bpy.ops.object.empty_image_add.

Calling bpy.ops operators to create empties then renaming them is obviously not ideal. Listing 6-3 shows an improved solution where we forgo the bpy.ops operators and instead create an empty object directly with the name we want, set up its image data, and configure its options within a single function.

Listing 6-3. Create a new empty object of type 'IMAGE', load its image data, and configure its options (see /Ch6/text_editor/ reference_image.py)

```
def load_image_empty(context, name, image_file_path, ↵
    location, rotation_degrees, depth, side, transparency):
    empty = bpy.data.objects.new(name, None)
    empty.empty_display_type = 'IMAGE'
    empty.data = bpy.data.images.load(image_file_path)
    empty.location = location
    empty.rotation_euler = Euler((radians(d) for d in ↵
        rotation_degrees), 'XYZ')
    empty.empty_image_depth = depth
    empty.empty_image_side = side
    empty.color[3] = transparency
    empty.empty_display_size = 5
    context.collection.objects.link(empty)
```

To create an empty object, you'd call bpy.data.objects.new with the argument object_data as None. You'd then set the empty's empty_display_type to 'IMAGE' to make it an image empty and call bpy.data.images.load to load an image from disk as the empty's data. The empty's rotation is set up via an Euler instance (from the module mathutils) created using a list of angles in radians around X, Y, and Z.

To make the empty a background image, you'd set its Depth and Side options as follows (which recreates the left side of Figure 6-1):

```
empty.empty_image_depth = 'BACK'
empty.empty_image_side = 'FRONT'
```

To make the empty a reference image instead, you'd set its Depth and Side options as follows (which recreates the right side of Figure 6-1):

```
empty.empty_image_depth = 'DEFAULT'
empty.empty_image_side = 'DOUBLE_SIDED'
```

You can optionally make the image semitransparent by setting the empty's alpha to a value less than 1, for example:

```
empty.color[3] = 0.75
```

Recall that the empty's color is specified as a list of four values (RGBA), with alpha at the last index.

I've found that the default value for `empty.empty_display_size` at 1 makes the image too small—through experimentation, 5 seems to be a good value. Lastly, after configuring the empty object's settings, you'd add it to the scene collection via `context.collection.objects.link(empty)`.

Note that regardless of how an image empty is created, whether through `bpy.ops` operators or from scratch like in Listing 6-3, the image is centered at the empty's `location` by default—this is due to the empty's `empty_image_offset` variable having default values of [-0.5, -0.5]. You could change `empty_image_offset` to make the image align with the empty's location differently. For example, you can add the following lines to Listing 6 3 to make the image's bottom left corner align with the empty's location:

```
empty.empty_image_offset[0] = 0
empty.empty_image_offset[1] = 0
```

Note   It's also possible to create a reference image by adding an
Image Mesh plane (in Object mode, Add (Shift-A) ➤ Image ➤ Mesh
Plane), unwrap its UVs (UV (or U key) ➤ Unwrap in Edit mode), then
set it up with a material node that uses an texture with the reference
photo as its image. Since we've not discussed unwrapping UVs in
Python up to this point, I've not included it here. Besides, it's more
convenient to use image empties anyway.

Implementing the Sculpt Retopo Toolkit Extension

Drawing on a mesh with the Grease Pencil is an intuitive way to make a
selection. On a complex mesh, it's also easier than selecting individual
edges. For the remainder of this chapter, I'll show you how to create
an extension called Sculpt Retopo Toolkit which encompasses a suite
of sculpting- and retopology-related tools using Grease Pencil inputs,
for example, a Carve tool that lets users draw on a mesh for a shape
to cut out. You can open the script /Ch6/extension/sculpt_retopo_
toolkit_4.2(4.3)/__init__.py in any IDE to follow along (though
it won't be runnable in the built-in Text Editor due to how imports are
set up). You can also install the Blender 4.2 (or 4.3) packaged version
of the extension from the file /Ch6/extension/sculpt_retopo_
toolkit_4.2(4.3)/sculpt_retopo_toolkit-2.0.0.zip and try out the
various operators from the toolkit.

Using the Sculpt Retopo Toolkit

Let's go over how to use the tools in the Sculpt Retopo Toolkit in more detail. After installing the extension, head over to the 3D Viewport ➤ Properties shelf (N key) ➤ Tool tab, where you'll find the SCULPT RETOPO Toolkit, as shown in Figure 6-3. Click on the eyedropper at the right of the Edit Mesh drop-down to select a mesh object in the viewport to edit (or click to expand the drop-down and select a mesh from the list).

To carve a hole on the mesh, click "Draw with GP" to summon the GP, draw the desired shape on the mesh (check the "Cut Through" box if you want the shape to cut through to the back side), and click "Carve" to cut. Similarly, to in/outset a selection, draw a shape on the mesh with the GP, use the "In/Outset Amount" slider to specify the amount (a positive value outsets (bumps out), while a negative value insets) and click the In/Outset button. Checking the Cut Through box will in/outset the back side of the mesh as well. You can see examples of editing meshes with the *Carve* and *In/Outset* tools in Figure 6-4.

The toolkit also comes with a retopo tool, which generates a grid mesh conforming to the mesh surface based on the current selection. To use the retopo tool, select a mesh to edit with the dropper tool, summon the GP by clicking "Draw with GP", and draw a series of vertical lines on the mesh to mark the area to retopologize. Use the "Grid Lines" slider to specify the number of horizontal lines with which to generate the grid mesh, and click "Draw Grid". You can see an example of using the "Draw Grid" tool in Figure 6-4.

Figure 6-3. *UI panel for the SCULPT RETOPO Toolkit extension, located in the Properties shelf (N key) ➤ Tool tab*

Now you're familiar with the various tools that are part of the extension, in the next few sections, we'll go behind the scenes and see how these tools are implemented in Python as operators and assembled into an extension.

279

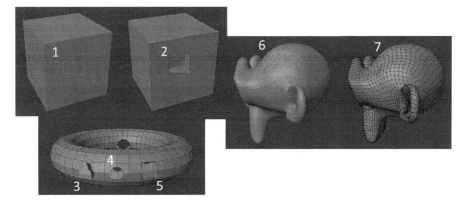

Figure 6-4. *Editing meshes with the Sculpt Retopo Toolkit. (1) Drawing on the mesh with the GP to select the portion of the mesh for editing. (2) Carve with Cut Through unchecked. (3) Outset with an amount of 0.10 (4) Carve with Cut Through checked. (5) Inset with an amount of -0.05. (6) Drawing vertical lines on the mesh with the GP to select the portion of the mesh to retopologize. (7) Draw Grid based on (6) with Grid Lines = 5*

Creating User Input Widgets As Scene Variables

In this section, we'll take a quick look at how the input widgets are created for the Sculpt Retopo Toolkit extension. Listing 6-4 shows the implementation for the extension's init_scene_vars() function, where all of its scene variables are defined.

Listing 6-4. Initialize scene variables for the Sculpt Retopo Toolkit (see /Ch6/extension/sculpt_retopo_toolkit_4.2(4.3)/__init__.py)

```
def init_scene_vars():
    bpy.types.Scene.select_mesh_dropdown = ↵
        bpy.props.PointerProperty(
        name="Edit Mesh",
```

```
    type=bpy.types.Object,
    poll=poll_select_mesh_dropdown_filter)

bpy.types.Scene.cut_thru_checkbox = BoolProperty(
    name="Cut Through",
    description="Whether to cut thru the mesh to the other ↩
        side with Carve and In/Outset.",
    default=False)

bpy.types.Scene.inoutset_amount = FloatProperty(
    name="In/Outset Amount",
    description="Amount to inset(+) or outset(-).",
    default=0.1)

bpy.types.Scene.num_grid_lines = IntProperty(
    name="Grid Lines",
    description="Number of horizontal grid lines ↩
        to make from GP strokes.",
    default=5,
    min=2)
```

Creating Input for Selecting a Mesh Object in the 3D Viewport

Since there may be many objects in the scene, it can be ambiguous which mesh the user intends to draw on with the Grease Pencil. We can address this by making the user explicitly select a mesh for editing using an instance of bpy.props.PointerProperty, which gives the user the option to either pick the object in the viewport with an eyedropper tool or select it from a drop-down, as shown in Figure 6-3. We initialize an instance of PointerProperty and assign it to a scene variable at the top of init_scene_vars() in Listing 6-4, which is reproduced here:

```
bpy.types.Scene.select_mesh_dropdown = ↵
    bpy.props.PointerProperty(
    name="Edit Mesh",
    type=bpy.types.Object,
    poll=poll_select_mesh_dropdown_filter)
```

Setting `type=bpy.types.Object` will populate the `PointerProperty` drop-down with objects. Since the toolkit only operates on meshes, we want to filter the list further to only contain mesh objects. To do this, we pass a custom poll function `poll_select_mesh_dropdown_filter` (Listing 6-5) to the `poll` argument of `bpy.types.Scene.select_mesh_dropdown`. The custom `poll` function simply checks whether a given object's type is `'MESH'`.

Listing 6-5. Writing a custom `poll` function for a `PointerProperty` instance to filter the type of objects in the drop-down

```
def poll_select_mesh_dropdown_filter(self, object):
    return object.type=='MESH'
```

Tip   You can modify Listing 6-5 to check for a different `object.type` (e.g., 'CURVE', 'SURFACE', 'LIGHT', etc.) to create filters that narrow down different object types. You can find the complete list of object types in the Blender Python online documentation at `https://docs.blender.org/api/current/bpy_types_enum_items/object_type_items.html#object-type-items`.

Implementing the Cut Through Check Box, In/Outset Amount Slider, and Grid Lines Slider

The second widget bpy.types.Scene.cut_thru_checkbox in Listing 6-4 is a check box implemented using a BoolProperty instance, which gives user control over whether the *Carve* operator cuts through the mesh to the other side. The same Cut Through box is used to control the *In/Outset* operator, as you'll see shortly. The default argument of bpy.types.Scene. cut_thru_checkbox is False, which means the box will be unchecked when first loaded.

The third widget bpy.types.Scene.inoutset_amount in Listing 6-4 is a decimal slider created using a FloatProperty instance for specifying the amount to inset or outset for the *In/Outset* operator (a positive value will outset (bump out), whereas a negative value will inset).

The fourth widget bpy.types.Scene.num_grid_lines in Listing 6-4 is a whole number slider created using an IntProperty instance for inputting the number of horizontal grid lines to use when generating the retopologized version of the mesh selection.

Accessing and Configuring Grease Pencil in Python

Next, we'll look at how to access and configure the Grease Pencil in Python. The function reset_gp (Listing 6-6) creates a Grease Pencil object (GP for short) with a designated layer and frame where the extension expects input strokes—this simplifies things since the extension would only need to process strokes in this particular layer and frame and users are free to use the remaining layers as they'd like outside this add-on. In addition, reset_gp configures the settings needed for GP strokes to automatically project ("stick") on the surface of the mesh.

Note that the Blender Python Grease Pencil implementation has undergone notable changes from Blender 4.2 to 4.3 and will continue to evolve in future 4.X versions. In 4.3, the GP we've known up to 4.2 has become the legacy GP (bpy.types.GreasePencil), and a new GP type bpy.types.GreasePencilv3 is introduced. Since most add-ons at the time of writing still use the legacy GP and the new GP will likely continue to change, for this chapter, I included implementation for 4.2 using the legacy GP in the code listings, with extra sections explaining how to adapt the code from 4.2 to 4.3 as needed. All remaining chapter code is identical between 4.2 and 4.3. As mentioned earlier in the section "Installing/Running the Sculpt Retopo Toolkit Extension," in the downloaded source for the book, I've included both 4.2 and 4.3 versions of the code for the Sculpt Retopo Toolkit, along with packaged versions of the extension that you can install and compare.

Listing 6-6 shows the Blender 4.2 version of reset_gp. We'll go over how to adapt the underlined portion of the code in Listing 6-6 to Blender 4.3 in the section immediately after.

Listing 6-6. Setting up a GP object with a designated layer and frame for receiving input strokes in Blender 4.2 (see /Ch6/extension/sculpt_retopo_toolkit_4.2/__init__.py)

```
srtk_gp_obj_name = "Sculpt_Retopo_Toolkit_GP"
def reset_gp(context, clear_strokes=False):
    if bpy.data.grease_pencils.find("srtk_gp_data") < 0:
        gp_data = bpy.data.grease_pencils.new("srtk_gp_data")
    else:
        gp_data = bpy.data.grease_pencils["srtk_gp_data"]

    if gp_data.layers.find("srtk_gp_data_layer") < 0:
        gp_data.layers.active = ↵
            gp_data.layers.new("srtk_gp_data_layer")
```

```
else:
    gp_data.layers.active = ↵
        gp_data.layers["srtk_gp_data_layer"]

frame0_found = False
for f in gp_data.layers.active.frames:
    if f.frame_number == 0:
        if clear_strokes:
            f.clear()
        frame0_found = True
        break
if not frame0_found:
    gp_data.layers.active.frames.new(0)

context.scene.frame_set(0)
gp_data.layers.active.show_points = False
gp_data.layers.active.color = (0, 0.5, 0.5)

context.scene.tool_settings. ↵
    gpencil_stroke_placement_view3d = 'SURFACE'
context.scene.grease_pencil = gp_data
gp_data.zdepth_offset = 0

existing_gp_obj_index = ↵
    context.collection.objects.find( ↵
        srtk_gp_obj_name)
if existing_gp_obj_index < 0:
    gp_obj = bpy.data.objects.new( ↵
        srtk_gp_obj_name, gp_data)
    context.collection.objects.link(gp_obj)
else:
    gp_obj = context.collection.objects[ ↵
        existing_gp_obj_index]
    gp_obj.data = gp_data
```

We start by looking up a GP data block named "srtk_gp_data" (or creating it if one doesn't yet exist) and setting it as the scene's GP. Next, we find (or create) a layer named "srtk_gp_data_layer" and set it as the GP block's active layer. Within this layer, we then locate (or create) frame #0 as the active frame and optionally clear its strokes. The current display frame for the scene is also set to #0 so we can see it in the viewport. The choice to use frame #0 here is arbitrary.

Next, we configure the GP data block's display options. We disable the drawing of individual points in strokes (gp_data.layers.active.show_points = False) so they appear as smooth lines and make the stroke color teal with (0, 0.5, 0.5) (default is black). Notice that the color here is specified as a triple of RGB values with each value ranging from 0 to 1. To make GP strokes stick to the nearest mesh surface, we set the variable context.scene.tool_settings.gpencil_stroke_placement_view3d to 'SURFACE'.

With gp_data configured, next we look up whether a GP object gp_obj with the name srtk_gp_obj_name exists; if not, we create it and link it to the scene (since this name is referred a few times throughout the extension code, I stored it in a global variable srtk_gp_obj_name = "Sculpt_Retopo_Toolkit_GP"). We set gp_data as gp_obj's data.

Adapting reset_gp to Blender 4.3

In Listing 6-7, we'll go over how to adapt reset_gp from Listing 6-6 to Blender 4.3. In 4.3, the clear() method for the legacy GP frame (bpy.types.GPencilFrame) is removed. As a workaround, when we need to clear GP strokes (clear_strokes is True), we simply remove the legacy GP layer and recreate the layer in the subsequent block of code.

Another change in 4.3 is that the `active` field of the legacy GP layer collection (`bpy.types.GreasePencilLayers`) is removed; therefore, the line `gp_data.layers.active` from Listing 6-6 no longer works. As a workaround, we set the layer collection's `active_index` instead:

```
gp_data.layers.active_index = ↩
    gp_data.layers.find("srtk_gp_data_layer")
```

And use the `active_index` to retrieve a reference to the active layer and store the reference in the variable `active_layer`, like this:

```
active_layer = gp_data.layers[gp_data.layers.active_index]
```

We then replace all occurrences of `gp_data.layers.active` in Listing 6-6 with `active_layer`.

Next, since the `show_points` field is removed from the legacy GP layer (`bpy.types.GPencilLayer`) in 4.3, the line of code `gp_data.layers.active.show_points = False` is removed.

The next 4.3 change is that `context.scene.tool_settings.`**`gpencil`**`_stroke_placement_view3d` is renamed to `context.scene.tool_settings.`**`annotation`**`_stroke_placement_view3d`. Therefore, the line to set the GP strokes to stick to the nearest mesh surface becomes

```
context.scene.tool_settings. ↩
    annotation_stroke_placement_view3d = 'SURFACE'
```

Lastly, in Blender 4.3, the `zdepth_offset` setting is removed from the legacy GP (`bpy.types.GreasePencil`). In Listing 6-6, `gp_data` is of type `bpy.types.GreasePencil`, therefore, the line `gp_data.zdepth_offset = 0` no longer works in 4.3 and is removed. You can find the most recent change log to the Blender Python API at `https://docs.blender.org/api/current/change_log.html`.

Listing 6-7. Adapting the reset_gp function (Listing 6-6) to
Blender 4.3 (see /Ch6/extension/sculpt_retopo_toolkit_4.3/__
init__.py)

```
if clear_strokes:
    if gp_data.layers.find("srtk_gp_data_layer") >= 0:
        gp_data.layers.remove( ↵
            gp_data.layers["srtk_gp_data_layer"])
    if gp_data.layers.find("srtk_gp_data_layer") < 0:
        new_layer = gp_data.layers.new("srtk_gp_data_layer")

gp_data.layers.active_index = ↵
    gp_data.layers.find("srtk_gp_data_layer")
active_layer = gp_data.layers[gp_data.layers.active_index]

frame0_found = False
for f in active_layer.frames:
    if f.frame_number == 0:
        frame0_found = True
        break
if not frame0_found:
    active_layer.frames.new(0)

context.scene.frame_set(0)
active_layer.color = (0, 0.5, 0.5)
context.scene.tool_settings. ↵
    annotation_stroke_placement_view3d = 'SURFACE'
context.scene.grease_pencil = gp_data
```

Creating an Operator for Accessing reset_gp

To make reset_gp accessible to the extension's users, we'll create an operator class BUTTON_OT_reset_gp as shown in Listing 6-8, which simply calls reset_gp when it's run.

Listing 6-8. Creating an operator class for accessing reset_gp (see /Ch6/extension/sculpt_retopo_toolkit_4.2(4.3)/__init__.py)

```
class BUTTON_OT_reset_gp(Operator):
    bl_idname = "button.reset_gp"
    bl_label = "Reset GP"
    '''Reset GP'''

    def execute(self, context):
        reset_gp(context, clear_strokes=True)
        self.report({'INFO'}, ↵
            "Sculpt & Retopo Toolkit: Reset GP.")
        return {'FINISHED'}
```

Later, we'll hook this operator up to a button in the draw code for the extension's UI panel so the users can use the operator to erase strokes or reconfigure the GP's settings. Recall that an operator's bl_idname is what we'll use to insert it into the UI panel, and its bl_label is the text that will display on the button.

As you'll see shortly, reset_gp is also used internally by the extension's other operators to erase strokes after they've been processed or to switch to the right GP, layer, and frame to look for input.

Creating an Operator to Summon the GP for Drawing (Draw with GP)

Next, we'll look at how to implement the "Draw with GP" operator (Listing 6-9) for Blender 4.2, which resets (or initializes) the GP and switches it to Draw mode. We'll go over how to adapt Listing 6-9 to Blender 4.3 right after.

Listing 6-9. Implementing the "Draw with GP" operator (see /Ch6/ extension/sculpt_retopo_toolkit_4.2/__init__.py)

```python
class BUTTON_OT_draw_with_GP(Operator):
    bl_idname = 'button.draw_with_gp'
    bl_label = 'Draw with GP'
    '''Draw with GP'''

    def execute(self, context):
        reset_gp(context, clear_strokes=False)
        existing_gp_obj_index = ↵
            context.collection.objects.find( ↵
                srtk_gp_obj_name)
        gp_obj = context.collection.objects[ ↵
            existing_gp_obj_index]

        for obj in context.view_layer.objects:
            obj.select_set(False)

        gp_obj.select_set(True)
        context.view_layer.objects.active = gp_obj
        context_override = ↵
            mesh_editing_ops.get_context_override( ↵
                context, 'VIEW_3D', 'WINDOW')
```

```
with bpy.context.temp override(**context override):
    bpy.ops.object.mode set(mode='PAINT GPENCIL')

self.report({'INFO'}, ↵
    'Sculpt & Retopo Toolkit: Draw with GP.')
return {'FINISHED'}
```

In execute, the first thing the operator does is calling reset_gp() from Listing 6-6 (6-7), which initializes (or resets) the GP's settings, but without erasing the GP's strokes (clear_strokes=False). Remember that the purpose of this operator is to afford the user the convenience of summoning the GP (making it active and putting it in the right mode for drawing)—it should not erase the strokes already made so the users can pick up where they are left off. The user should use the "Reset GP" button we implemented in Listing 6-8 instead to erase the strokes.

Next, the operator gets a reference to the GP object, deselects all and selects the GP and makes it the active object, then switches it to Draw mode (mode='PAINT_GPENCIL') with a context override, pretending to call bpy.ops.object.mode_set from the viewport.

Adapting the "Draw with GP" Operator to Blender 4.3

Listing 6-10 shows an excerpt of BUTTON_OT_draw_with_GP, with the code change for 4.3 marked in **bold**. Instead of switching the GP to Draw Mode with a context override (as the portion of code underlined in Listing 6-9), in Blender 4.3, we press the Annotate button in the Tool shelf instead, with the line bpy.ops.wm.tool_set_by_id(name="builtin.annotate") (shown in **bold** in Listing 6-10).

Listing 6-10. Adapting the "Draw with GP" operator to Blender 4.3
(see /Ch6/extension/sculpt_retopo_toolkit_4.3/__init__.py)

```
class BUTTON_OT_draw_with_GP(Operator):
    bl_idname = "button.draw_with_gp"
    bl_label = "Draw with GP"
    '''Draw with GP'''

    def execute(self, context):
        # ---- SNIPPED ----
        gp_obj.select_set(True)
        context.view_layer.objects.active = gp_obj
        bpy.ops.wm.tool_set_by_id(name="builtin.annotate")
        # ---- SNIPPED ----
```

Implementing the Carve and In/Outset Functionalities for the Toolkit

It's often difficult to make a precise selection on a sculpted (high-poly) mesh since you can't select individual verts and edges like you do on a low-poly mesh. The ability to draw your selection with a GP allows you to make a relatively accurate selection very quickly and easily. The *Carve* operator lets you draw an arbitrarily shaped hole on a sculpted model with a GP to define the portion of the mesh you want to cut out. We'll peek under the hood how *Carve* accomplishes this over the next few sections.

Using Grease Pencil Strokes to Knife Project

After the user draws a shape on the selected mesh with the GP to outline a cut to be made, the first step is to create edges on the mesh based on the GP strokes which will eventually become the border of the hole. To do this, we convert the GP strokes into a curve object, then use the curve as the "cookie cutter" object for Knife Project (3D Viewport in Edit mode, Mesh ➤ Knife Project), which works like projecting the curve onto the mesh surface then tracing it with the Knife tool. This process is implemented in the gp_knife_project function shown in Listing 6-11.

Listing 6-11. Knife project using a curve created based on GP strokes (see /Ch6/extension/sculpt_retopo_toolkit_4.2/__init__.py)

```
def gp_knife_project(context, mesh_obj_to_edit):
    existing_gp_obj_index = ↵
        context.collection.objects.find(srtk_gp_obj_name)
    gp_obj = context.collection.objects[existing_gp_obj_index]
    curve_data = bpy.data.curves.new(name="curve_data", ↵
        type='CURVE')
    curve_data.dimensions = '3D'
    curve_obj = bpy.data.objects.new(name="curve_obj", ↵
        object_data=curve_data)
    context.collection.objects.link(curve_obj)

    num_pts = 0
    layer = gp_obj.data.layers.active
    for f in layer.frames:
        for s in f.strokes:
            s_spline_data = ↵
                curve_obj.data.splines.new( ↵
                    type='POLY')
            s_num_pts = len(s.points)
            if s_num_pts < 1:
                continue

            num_pts += s_num_pts
```

```
            s_spline_data.points.add(s_num_pts - 1)
            for i in range(s_num_pts):
                pi = s.points[i].co
                s_spline_data.points[i].co = ↵
                    [pi[0], pi[1], pi[2], 1]

            s_spline_data.points.add(1)
            p0 = s.points[0].co
            s_spline_data.points[-1].co = ↵
                [p0[0], p0[1], p0[2], 1]

    if num_pts < 3:
        return False, None, num_pts

    for obj in context.view_layer.objects:
        obj.select_set(False)
    context.view_layer.objects.active = mesh_obj_to_edit
    mesh_obj_to_edit.select_set(True)
    curve_obj.select_set(True)
    context_override = ↵
        mesh_editing_ops.get_context_override( ↵
            context, 'VIEW_3D', 'WINDOW')
    with bpy.context.temp_override(**context_override):
        bpy.ops.object.mode_set(mode='EDIT')

    context.scene.tool_settings.mesh_select_mode[1] = True
    context_override = ↵
        mesh_editing_ops.get_context_override( ↵
            context, 'VIEW_3D', 'WINDOW')
    with bpy.context.temp_override(**context_override):
        bpy.ops.mesh.knife_project( ↵
            cut_through=context.scene.cut_thru_checkbox)

    reset_gp(context, clear_strokes=True)
    return True, curve_obj, num_pts
```

We start by looking up the extension's GP. Next, we create a blank curve data block `curve_data` by calling `bpy.data.curves.new` with `type='CURVE'` and set its dimension to `'3D'`. We then use `curve_data` to create a new curve object `curve_obj` and link it to the scene.

In the next code block, we iterate through the frames under the GP's active layer and convert each stroke `s` into a new poly spline block under `curve_obj.data` (`s_spline_data = curve_obj.data.splines.new(type='POLY')`). A poly spline block starts with 1 point at creation, so to make it the same length as the stroke, we add (`s_num_pts - 1`) points to the spline, where `s_num_pts` is the number of points in the stroke s. We then iterate through the points in s and copy the coordinates of each point in s to its counterpart in the poly spline block. Note that the coordinates of a point in the poly spline has four numbers—we copy the first three (which are X, Y, and Z) over from the coordinates of the corresponding point in the stroke and use 1 for the last number (`[pi[0], pi[1], pi[2], 1]`). After we finish copying the coordinates of all of a stroke's points to the spline, we add an extra point to the end of the spline and copy over the stroke's first point's coordinates—this is to make the spline a closed loop, so Knife Project cuts better.

While converting the GP strokes to splines, we kept count of how many points total are from all the splines in `num_pts`. If `num_pts` is less than 3 (therefore does not make a valid polygon), we know that we can't cut with it and we can fail the operation and return early.

With the strokes converted to splines, we're now ready to perform the Knife Project. We deselect all objects, set the object to perform the Knife Project on (`mesh_obj_to_edit`) as active, then select both `mesh_obj_to_edit` and `curve_obj`. Then, we call `bpy.ops.mesh.knife_project` with a context override (as if from the viewport), using the Cut Through check box's value (see Listing 6-4) for its `cut_through` argument (`cut_through=context.scene.cut_thru_checkbox`).

Finally, we wrap up by erasing the GP strokes using `reset_gp` (Listing 6-6 (6-7)) with `clear_strokes` as True and return a bool to indicate whether the Knife Project operation was successful, along with the curve object converted from the GP strokes and the number of points in the curve.

Adapting gp_knife_project to Blender 4.3

There is only a one line change to adapt `gp_knife_project` to 4.3, which is to replace the line `layer = gp_obj.data.layers.active` in Listing 6-11 with `layer = gp_obj.data.layers[gp_obj.data.layers.active_index]`. Recall from the section "Adapting reset_gp to Blender 4.3" that in 4.3 the `active` field of the legacy GP layer collection (`bpy.types.GreasePencilLayers`) is removed; therefore, as a workaround, we use the layer collection's `active_index` to look up the active layer.

Implementing the Carve Operator

We are ready to implement the Carve operator, which performs Knife Project based on GP strokes, then uses a boolean modifier to do a Difference operation with the curve object to cut the shape away.

Since Carve requires that a mesh object is selected for edits and that the user has drawn the shape to cut away with the GP, we write a helper function `gp_strokes_mesh_selection_check` (Listing 6-12) that checks for each of these conditions and reports warning messages if they are not met. Since we defaulted the frame number to 0 in `reset_gp()`, we check for the number of strokes there.

Listing 6-12. Helper function that checks a mesh object is selected for edits and the user has made GP strokes (see /Ch6/extension/ sculpt_retopo_toolkit_4.2/__init__.py)

```
def gp_strokes_mesh_selection_check(self, context, ↵
    mesh_obj_to_edit):
    if len(context.scene.grease_pencil.layers.active. ↵
        frames[0].strokes)==0:
        self.report({'WARNING'}, ↵
            'Sculpt & Retopo Toolkit: No GP strokes.')
        return False

    if not mesh_obj_to_edit:
        self.report({'WARNING'}, ↵
            'Sculpt & Retopo Toolkit: No mesh object ↵
                selected to edit.')
        return False
    return True
```

Adapting gp_strokes_mesh_selection_check to Blender 4.3

To adapt gp_strokes_mesh_selection_check to Blender 4.3, in the first if statement in Listing 6-12, we replace

```
context.scene.grease_pencil.layers.active
```

with

```
context.scene.grease_pencil.layers[↵
    context.scene.grease_pencil.layers.active_index]
```

Essentially looking up the GP active layer using active_index instead of accessing it directly.

Implementing the Carve Operator

We're now ready to dig into the Carve operator's implementation, which is shown in Listing 6-13. We start by calling reset_gp() from Listing 6-6 (6-7), which ensures the GP is valid and sets the GP to the correct layer and frame, before calling gp_strokes_mesh_selection_check (Listing 6-12) to check whether the user has made strokes and selected a mesh object to edit. If so, we call gp_knife_project (Listing 6-11) to convert the GP strokes to a curve object and use it to Knife Project on the selected mesh.

If Knife Project fails, we report a warning to the user; otherwise, we try and separate the selected portion on the mesh (which are the edges created by Knife Project) by calling bpy.ops.mesh.separate—if it can't be done, Knife Project must have not used a closed loop to do the projection; therefore, there is no point to proceed further, since we won't be able to cut a hole successfully.

We're now ready to cut the shape away. We add a boolean modifier to the mesh to edit (obj_to_be_carved) and set 'DIFFERENCE' as the type of operation and the curve (hole_template_obj) as the object to do the difference with. Then, under a context override (as if from the viewport), we switch obj_to_be_carved to Object mode where we apply the boolean modifier.

With the cut complete, we can clean up by removing the curve (hole_template_obj) as well as the mesh portion that is cut away (the result of the boolean modifier difference), which is the last object created (context.scene.objects[-1]). We also reset the Edit Mesh drop-down via context.scene.select_mesh_dropdown = None.

Listing 6-13. Implementing the Carve operator (see /Ch6/ extension/sculpt_retopo_toolkit_4.2(4.3)/__init__.py)

```
class BUTTON_OT_carve(Operator):
    bl_idname = "button.carve"
    bl_label = "Carve"
    '''Carve'''
```

```
def execute(self, context):
    reset_gp(context, clear_strokes=False)
    obj_to_be_carved = context.scene.select_mesh_dropdown

    if not gp_strokes_mesh_selection_check(self, ↵
        context, obj_to_be_carved):
        return {'FINISHED'}

    knife_project_success, hole_template_obj, num_pts = ↵
        gp_knife_project(context, obj_to_be_carved)

    if not knife_project_success:
        if num_pts < 3:
            self.report({'WARNING'},  ↵
                'Sculpt & Retopo Toolkit: ↵
                    Carve - GP stroke does not ↵
                        define a polygon.')
        else:
            self.report({'WARNING'}, 'Sculpt & Retopo ↵
                Toolkit: Carve - Knife project from ↵
                    GP strokes failed.')
        return {'FINISHED'}

    try:
        bpy.ops.mesh.separate(type='SELECTED')
    except:
        self.report({'WARNING'}, 'Sculpt & Retopo ↵
            Toolkit: Carve - Draw a hole to carve with ↵
                a closed loop.')
        return {'FINISHED'}
```

```
        hole_template_obj.select_set(True)
        if hole_template_obj != obj_to_be_carved and ↵
            hole_template_obj.type == 'MESH':
            boolean_mod = obj_to_be_carved.modifiers.new( ↵
                "boolean_mod", 'BOOLEAN')
            boolean_mod.object = hole_template_obj
            boolean_mod.operation = 'DIFFERENCE'

            context.scene.tool_settings. ↵
                mesh_select_mode[1] = True
            context_override = ↵
                mesh_editing_ops.get_context_override( ↵
                    context, 'VIEW_3D', 'WINDOW')
            with bpy.context.temp_override(**context_override):
                bpy.ops.object.mode_set(mode='OBJECT')
                bpy.ops.object.modifier_apply( ↵
                    modifier=boolean_mod.name)

    bpy.data.objects.remove(hole_template_obj)
    bpy.data.objects.remove(context.scene.objects[-1])
    context.scene.select_mesh_dropdown = None
    self.report({'INFO'}, 'Sculpt & Retopo Toolkit: ↵
        Carve.')
    return {'FINISHED'}
```

You can see examples of cutting GP-drawn shapes on meshes using the Carve operator in Figures 6-5 and 6-6, where the Cut Through check box is unchecked (cut front side only) and checked (cut through to the back side), respectively.

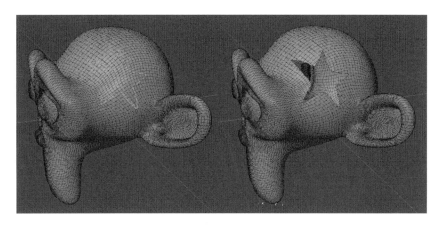

Figure 6-5. *GP strokes drawn on the mesh (left) are converted to a curve then used as the "cookie cutter" object for Knife Project to cut into the mesh (right). cut_through is set to False so only the near side of the mesh (where the strokes are drawn) is cut*

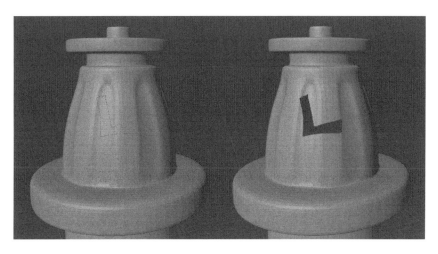

Figure 6-6. *When the Cut Through box is checked, Carve cuts through the mesh to the back side as shown on the right*

You might have noticed that instead of writing a helper function like gp_strokes_mesh_selection_check (Listing 6-12) and calling it inside the Carve operator's execute method, you could've implemented Carve's poll method and do the same checks there, like in Listing 6-14.

Listing 6-14. Performing the GP strokes and mesh selection check in Carve's poll method instead

```
@classmethod
def poll(cls, context):
    return context.scene.select_mesh_dropdown and ↩
        len(context.scene.grease_pencil.layers. ↩
            active.frames[0].strokes)>0
```

The reason that I opted for Listing 6-12 is because you can call self. report to display the appropriate warning messages if either criteria is not met. If you go the poll method route as in Listing 6-14, the Carve button is grayed out if poll returns False (which is the case if either condition fails); however, the user has no way of knowing why since it's *not* possible to call self.report in poll.

Implementing the In/Outset Operator

The In/Outset operator in Listing 6-15 takes a GP-drawn shape and uses it to in or outset a mesh based on the amounts from the In/Outset Amount slider. The operator starts out the same way as Carve: first, call reset_gp() (Listing 6-6 (6-7)) to ensure the GP is valid and set to the correct active layer and frame, then call gp_strokes_mesh_selection_check (Listing 6-12) to check that there's a mesh selected for edits and the user has made GP strokes, after which call gp_knife_project (Listing 6-11) to convert the GP strokes to a curve object and perform Knife Project with it.

If Knife Project is successful, In/Outset then extrudes the projected shape and calls bpy.ops.transform.shrink_fatten to create the inset or outset effects via Shrink/Fatten (in Edit mode, Tool bar (T key) ➤ Shrink/Fatten or Mesh ➤ Transform ➤ Shrink/Fatten (Alt-S)), based on the In/Outset slider value (context.scene.inoutset_amount). Finally, bpy.data.objects.remove is called to rid of the curve object outlining the in/outset (hole_template_obj), and the Edit Mesh drop-down is reset via context.scene.select_mesh_dropdown = None.

Listing 6-15. Implementing the In/Outset operator (see /Ch6/ extension/sculpt_retopo_toolkit_4.2(4.3)/__init__.py)

```python
class BUTTON_OT_inset(Operator):
    bl_idname = "button.inset"
    bl_label = "Inset"
    '''Inset'''

    def execute(self, context):
        reset_gp(context, clear_strokes=False)
        obj_to_inset = context.scene.select_mesh_dropdown
        if not gp_strokes_mesh_selection_check(self, ↵
            context, obj_to_inset):
            return {'FINISHED'}

        knife_project_success, hole_template_obj, _ = ↵
            gp_knife_project(context, obj_to_inset)
        if knife_project_success:
            bpy.ops.mesh.extrude_region_move( ↵
                TRANSFORM_OT_translate={ ↵
                    'value': Vector((0, 0, 0))})
            bpy.ops.transform.shrink_fatten( ↵
                value=context.scene.inoutset_amount)
            bpy.data.objects.remove(hole_template_obj)
```

```
context.scene.select_mesh_dropdown = None
self.report({'INFO'}, ↵
    'Sculpt & Retopo Toolkit: In/Outset.')
return {'FINISHED'}
```

You can see examples of using Listing 6-15 to inset or outset a GP-drawn selection on a mesh, with or without the Cut Through check box checked, in Figure 6-7.

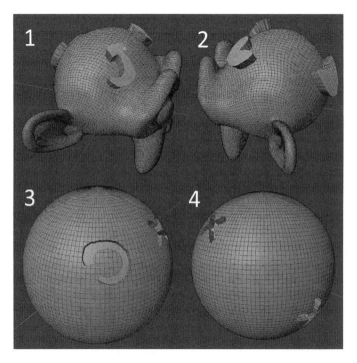

Figure 6-7. *Editing meshes with the In/Outset operator. (1) Outsetting with 0.1 and Cut Through unchecked. (2) Outsetting with 0.13 and Cut Through checked. Notice the heart-shaped protrusion on both the front and back sides of Suzanne's head. (3) Insetting with -0.05 and Cut Through unchecked. (4) Inset with -0.08 and Cut Through checked. Notice the X-shaped indent on two sides of the sphere*

Retopology

Topology refers to the organization of vertices, edges, and faces on the surface of a mesh. It's often possible to define the same mesh surface with more than one topological configuration. For meshes that are intended for static scenes, such as inanimate objects or ones to be rendered in a still image, their underlying topologies often don't affect rendering results much, other than perhaps artifacts introduced by textures stretched over uneven or problematic triangulation of faces.

For meshes that're purposed to be animated by deformation, however, the impact of their underlying topologies is much greater. For example, when a person opens his mouth, his lips and surrounding muscles expand radially outward like an enlarging set of concentric circles. If the edge flow were to defy this trend of deformation, the resulting animation would look awkward and unnatural. Therefore, it's important to plan ahead for purposeful edge flows that conform to the natural contours and muscle contractions of the subject.

In Chapter 4, you learned how to build and edit meshes using edge loops to produce models with purposeful edge flows that deform and animate cleanly. You did this by directly manipulating the vertices, edges, and faces of a small section of a mesh at a time and gradually building up a model by adding loops. Building a model this way allows you to have direct control over its underlying topology. However, many people prefer sculpting since you can focus on creating the silhouette of the model without being bogged down by its underlying structure, while others find sculpting a more intuitive and organic way to model since you can tap into what you already know about working with real clay. Sculpting allows you to create high-resolution meshes with intricate detail; however, these meshes usually have messy topologies that prevent them from deforming and animating cleanly, with polycounts too high to be rendered and animated in real time. To address these issues, retopology is born. *Retopology* refers to the process of recreating a lower-poly version of a sculpted model, with edge flows following its subject's natural trend of deformation, making the lower-poly model suitable for animation and for use in real-time applications like games that require high frame rates (e.g., 60+ fps) with a high level of responsiveness.

Making a "Draw Grid" Retopo Helper Tool

My next inspiration comes from the RetopoFlow add-on sold on Blender Market (`https://blendermarket.com/products/retopoflow`), which is a suite of retopo tools that give you controls ranging from fine (down to the vertex level) to coarse (laying out whole face loops at a time). I admire how effortlessly and intuitively users seem to be able to layout the simplified geometry over the surface of the high-res model with their mouse cursors. I also like the fact that when you add new geometry to the retopologized mesh with RetopoFlow, it automatically adheres to the surface of the high-poly original.

Since we already implemented GP functionality for our Sculpting and Retopo Toolkit extension earlier in the chapter for drawing strokes on the surface of meshes, we can utilize it to create a very basic Draw Grid tool inspired by RetopoFlow in the form of an operator that automatically creates a grid which conforms to the surface of a mesh based on the vertical GP strokes you draw on that mesh—if you imagine the GP strokes as the fret lines on a guitar, the operator will automatically add the "strings" that cut across to form a grid.

Note that Draw Grid is somewhat similar in behavior as RetopoFlow's Contours tool; the difference is Draw Grid only allows you to draw the strokes in a single directional sequence and creates only a single layer of grid on the side of the original mesh visible from the current view, whereas Contours allows you to draw strokes from any direction, out-of-order, and add more strokes in between existing ones while creating new geometry that wraps around the original mesh. Another difference is that Draw Grid is designed to work with meshes of any shape, whereas Contours is designed to work with meshes that are roughly cylindrical in shape. The input scheme of Draw Grid and Contours are similar in the sense that they both allow users to gesture in a drawing-like, fluid motion to indicate where to add new edges; however, Draw Grid uses GP strokes explicitly, whereas Contours use the mouse cursor. You also have to draw all the spots where you want to add more edges ahead of time with Draw Grid.

We add Draw Grid as an operator class to the Sculpting and Retopo Toolkit extension that we've been working on throughout the chapter, as shown in Listing 6-16.

Listing 6-16. Implementing the Draw Grid operator (see /Ch6/ extension/sculpt_retopo_toolkit_4.2/__init__.py)

```
class BUTTON_OT_draw_grid(Operator):
    bl_idname = "button.draw_grid"
    bl_label = "Draw Grid"
    '''Draw Grid'''

    def execute(self, context):
        reset_gp(context, clear_strokes=False)
        obj_to_add_grid = context.scene.select_mesh_dropdown
        if not gp_strokes_mesh_selection_check( ↵
            self, context, obj_to_add_grid):
            return {'FINISHED'}

        existing_gp_obj_index = context.collection. ↵
            objects.find(srtk_gp_obj_name)
        gp_obj = context.collection.objects[ ↵
            existing_gp_obj_index]
        for obj in context.view_layer.objects:
            obj.select_set(False)
```

```
context.view_layer.objects.active = obj_to_add_grid
obj_to_add_grid.select_set(True)

context_override = ↵
    mesh_editing_ops.get_context_override( ↵
        context, 'VIEW_3D', 'WINDOW')
with bpy.context.temp_override(**context_override):
    bpy.ops.object.mode_set(mode = 'OBJECT')

context_override = ↵
    mesh_editing_ops.get_context_override( ↵
        context, 'VIEW_3D', 'WINDOW')
with bpy.context.temp_override(**context_override):
    bpy.ops.object.transform_apply( ↵
        location=True, rotation=True, scale=True)
    bpy.ops.object.mode_set(mode = 'EDIT')

context_override = ↵
    mesh_editing_ops.get_context_override( ↵
        context, 'VIEW_3D', 'WINDOW')
with bpy.context.temp_override(**context_override):
    bpy.ops.mesh.select_all(action='DESELECT')

context.scene.tool_settings.use_snap = True
context.scene.tool_settings.snap_elements = {'FACE'}
context.scene.tool_settings.snap_target = 'CLOSEST'
context.scene.tool_settings.use_snap_self = True
bm = bmesh.from_edit_mesh(obj_to_add_grid.data)
verts_prev_stroke = []
for s in gp_obj.data.layers.active.frames[0].strokes:
    num_pts = len(s.points)
    if num_pts < context.scene.num_grid_lines:
        continue
```

```
    num_pts_per_cell = ↵
        floor(num_pts/context.scene.num_grid_lines)

    v_prev = None
    verts_cur_stroke = []
    num_gls_left = context.scene.num_grid_lines
    for i in range(0, num_pts, num_pts_per_cell):
        if num_gls_left == 0:
            break
        v = bm.verts.new( ↵
            s.points[i].co - obj_to_add_grid.location)
        v.select = True
        if v_prev:
            e = bm.edges.new([v_prev, v])
            e.select = True

        v_prev = v
        verts_cur_stroke.append(v)
        num_gls_left -= 1

    if len(verts_prev_stroke) > 0:
        num_verts_to_bridge = min( ↵
            len(verts_prev_stroke), ↵
                len(verts_cur_stroke))
        for j in range(num_verts_to_bridge):
            e = bm.edges.new([verts_prev_stroke[j], ↵
                verts_cur_stroke[j]])
            e.select = True
    verts_prev_stroke = verts_cur_stroke
bpy.ops.mesh.edge_face_add()
bmesh.update_edit_mesh(obj_to_add_grid.data)
context.view_layer.update()
```

```
self.report({'INFO'}, ↵
    'Sculpt & Retopo Toolkit: Draw Grid.')
context.scene.select_mesh_dropdown = None
reset_gp(context, clear_strokes=True)
return {'FINISHED'}
```

First, we call reset_gp() (Listing 6-6 (6-7)) to ensure the GP is valid and set to the correct active layer and frame, followed by gp_strokes_ mesh_selection_check (Listing 6-12) to check that there's a mesh selected for edits (obj_to_add_grid) and the user has made GP strokes. If so, we prepare obj_to_add_grid for the addition of new geometry, by deselecting all objects in the scene, setting obj_to_add_grid as the active object and selecting it, then changing it to Object mode and applying all transforms (therefore any subsequent snapping will work as expected). We then switch obj_to_add_grid to Edit mode and deselect all again.

Note that you need to use one context override to switch to Object mode, then create another context override to call bpy.ops.object. transform_apply with (instead of calling it under the same override). This is because bpy.ops.object.transform_apply only works in Object mode, so we need to create a new override based on the context post mode-switching. Similarly, you need to switch to Edit mode under one context override, then create another override to call bpy.ops.mesh.select_ all(action='DESELECT') (which only works in Edit mode).

Next, we enable snapping to the closest face (onto the object itself) so new geometry adheres to the surface of the active object. We then create a BMesh instance bm from obj_to_add_grid.data so we can start adding geometry to it.

We enter a loop where each iteration we convert one GP stroke into a grid line. We use an IntProperty (context.scene.num_grid_lines) to let users enter the number of grid lines that should cut across the GP strokes perpendicularly to control the grid's polycount. If a stroke contains less points than the number of perpendicular grid lines, that stroke is skipped.

We compute the interval of points between each pair of adjacent perpendicular grid lines by dividing the number of points in a stroke by the number of perpendicular grid lines, rounding down to the nearest integer using floor (from the Python module math). For example, if a stroke has 16 points and we want 5 grid lines to cut across, then you'd create a vertex at points #0, #3, #6, etc., and connect each vertex to the one created before it with an edge.

Notice that when you create a vertex based on a point from a GP stroke, you need to subtract the location of the object the vertex is being added to from the coordinates of that point—this is because the point's frame of reference is the global coordinate system (relative to the origin of the viewport), whereas the vertex's frame of reference is the object's local coordinate system (relative to the object's location). For example, if a stroke point is at (3, 4, 5) and the object you're adding the vertex to has location (0, 1, 2), then you need to create the vertex at (3-0, 4-1, 5-2), which is (3, 3, 3).

We select each vertex and edge as it's created so when we're done with the grid, the whole grid is selected, and we just need to call bpy.ops.mesh. edge_face_add() (F key) once to fill in all the grid faces. We also record the vertices created from each stroke so we can connect vertices stroke-wise. Notice that since the number of points in each stroke varies, we only connect as many vertices as the shorter stroke would allow. For example, if we were connecting a grid line with six vertices to one with four vertices, we would only connect four pairs of vertices between them.

To finish up, the operator clears the selected mesh under Edit Mesh via context.scene.select_mesh_dropdown = None and clears the GP strokes via reset_gp(context, clear_strokes=True) to return the extension back to a state ready for the next edit.

You can see examples of using the Draw Grid operator with different numbers of Grid Lines in Figure 6-8.

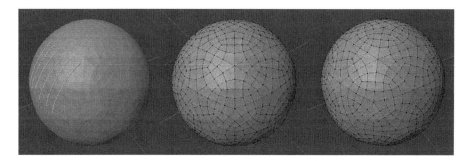

Figure 6-8. *Examples of using the Draw Grid operator with five (middle) and ten (right) grid lines on a subdivided icosphere (left). You can see that the generated grid conforms to the surface of the icosphere*

Adapting the Draw Grid Operator to Blender 4.3

We only need to change one line of code to adapt the Draw Grid operator to Blender 4.3. We replace the following line in Listing 6-16:

```
for s in gp_obj.data.layers.active.frames[0].strokes:
```

with

```
for s in gp_obj.data.layers[gp_obj.data.layers.active_index].
frames[0].strokes:,
```

where we again use the `active_index` to look up the active GP layer instead of accessing it directly.

Analyzing Mesh Topology Using BMesh Connectivity Data

In this section, I'll show you how to use a mesh's connectivity data to assess the quality of its topology. You'll learn how to start at any vertex and find the edges connected to it, then use the concept to quickly find problem areas on a mesh such as poles or faces with corner angles that are too sharp (or too dull).

Accessing a Vertex's Connected Edges Through BMesh

Let's learn how to access a vertex's connected edges using BMesh through an example. Head over to the Scripting workspace and ensure the 3D Viewport is in Object mode. Enter the following commands in the Python Console to add a primitive cube object to the scene (if there isn't one already), set it as active, switch it to Edit mode, deselect all, and create a BMesh instance bm for editing it.

```
>>> bpy.ops.mesh.primitive_cube_add(location=(0, 0, 0))
{'FINISHED'}

>>> cube = bpy.context.scene.objects["Cube"]
>>> bpy.context.view_layer.objects.active = cube
>>> bpy.ops.object.mode_set(mode='EDIT')
{'FINISHED'}

>>> bpy.ops.mesh.select_all(action='DESELECT')
{'FINISHED'}

>>> import bmesh
>>> bm = bmesh.from_edit_mesh(cube.data)
```

We'll also switch to vertex and edge select:

```
>>> bpy.context.tool_settings.mesh_select_mode = [True,
True, False]
```

And enable mesh element indices display so later when we select a vertex and its connected edges on the cube, we can see their indices.

313

Tip   Recall from Chapter 4, to enable the display of selected mesh
element indices (e.g., indices of selected edges), you need to enable
Edit ➤ Preferences… ➤ Interface ➤ Display ➤ Developer Extras,
then in the 3D Viewport in Edit mode, go to the Mesh Edit Overlays
Menu (top right corner, fourth button from the left), and check the
Developer ➤ Indices check box.

You can access the edges connected to a vertex through its link_edges
variable like this:

```
>>> bm.verts.ensure_lookup_table()
>>> bm.verts[5].link_edges
<BMElemSeq object at 0x000001E5EC967240>

>>> bm.verts[5].link_edges[0]
<BMEdge(0x000001E5E32613D0), index=8, ↩
    verts=(0x000001E5E272D298/7, 0x000001E5E272D228/5)>
```

which reveals that the first edge connected to vertex #5 is edge #8, with end
vertices #7 and #5. To verify this, select all of vertex #5's connected edges in
a for loop to display them in the viewport with the following commands
(hit Enter after typing each line of the for loop and an extra time after the
last line of the loop to mark its end).

```
>>> for e in bm.verts[5].link_edges:
...      e.select = True
...      bmesh.update_edit_mesh(cube.data)
...
```

You should see the three edges connected to vertex #5 selected on the
cube in the viewport, which in Blender 4.2 at the time of writing are edges #8,
#9, and #11. Python's built-in len function can also be used on link_edges to
find its length, which tells us how many edges are connected to that vertex:

```
>>> len(bm.verts[5].link_edges)
3
```

Analogously, you could access the faces connected to a vertex via link_faces like this:

```
>>> bm.verts[5].link_faces
<BMElemSeq object at 0x000001E5EC967240>

>>> len(bm.verts[5].link_faces)
3

>>> for f in bm.verts[5].link_faces:
...     print(f)
...
<BMFace(0x000001E5E2C272E8), index=5, totverts=4>
<BMFace(0x000001E5E2C27240), index=2, totverts=4>
<BMFace(0x000001E5E2C27278), index=3, totverts=4>
```

which tells us that vertex #5 is connected to three quads (face with four vertices, totverts=4): face #5, face #2, and face #3.

Finding Poles Through a Vertex's Link Edges

Putting it altogether, let's look at an example which utilizes link_edges for analyzing topology. Recall that poles are vertices with either three, or five, or more connected edges. Poles are generally considered undesirable since they terminate edge loops. However, since it's often not possible to completely avoid poles, they should be used sparingly and strategically placed on a mesh to redirect edge loops. It's therefore helpful during a retopology session to keep track of where the poles are and how they're distributed on a mesh.

You can write a function like select_poles shown in Listing 6-17 to automatically select all the poles on the active mesh object so you can quickly locate them. Open /Ch6/text_editor/mesh_connectivity.py from the downloaded source in the built-in Text Editor to follow along.

Listing 6-17. Selecting poles (verts with 3 or >=5 connected edges) on the active mesh object (see /Ch6/text_editor/mesh_connectivity.py)

```
def select_poles(context):
    obj = context.view_layer.objects.active
    if obj is not None and obj.type=='MESH':
        bpy.ops.object.mode_set(mode='EDIT')
        bpy.ops.mesh.select_all(action='DESELECT')
        context.tool_settings.mesh_select_mode = ↵
            [True, False, False]
        bm = bmesh.from_edit_mesh(obj.data)
        for v in bm.verts:
            valence = len(v.link_edges)
            if valence == 3 or valence > 4:
                v.select = True
        bmesh.update_edit_mesh(obj.data)
        context.view_layer.update()
```

First, we'll create a variable obj for storing a reference to the active object in the current scene (of the passed-in context) so there's less typing to do. Before proceeding, we'll check that obj is a valid mesh object, then switch to Edit mode, deselect all, set the selection mode to vertex, and create a BMesh instance bm for accessing obj's mesh data (obj.data).

We then enter a for loop to iterate through obj's vertices. For each vertex, we check the number of edges connected to it (len(v.link_edges)). If it's either 3 or 5 or more, then by definition, the vertex is a pole so we select it. Figure 6-9 shows an example of calling `select_poles` to select all the poles on Suzanne (the built-in primitive monkey mesh).

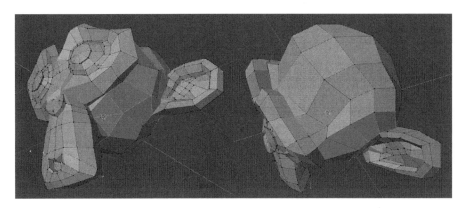

Figure 6-9. *Using the* `select_poles` *function from Listing 6-17 to select the poles on Suzanne*

Finding Sharp (or Dull) Face Corners

While retopologizing a mesh, we're often looking to even out the faces as uniformly as possible to reduce stretching or distortion when a texture is applied. To help with this process, we can write a function to identify faces with unusually sharp (or dull) corners by analyzing each face vertex's connected edges.

Finding Angle Between Two Edges

The first step is to write a function like get_angle_between_edges (Listing 6-18) to compute the angle between two given edges that share a vertex (which we can then use to get the angle at each corner of a face later).

Listing 6-18. Getting the angle in degrees between a pair of edges that share a vertex (see `/Ch6/text_editor/mesh_connectivity.py`)

```
def get_angle_between_edges(e1, e2):
    if e1.verts[0] in e2.verts:
        vert_shared = e1.verts[0]
    else:
        vert_shared = e1.verts[1]

    e1_end_v = e1.other_vert(vert_shared)
    e2_end_v = e2.other_vert(vert_shared)
    vector1 = e1_end_v.co - vert_shared.co
    vector2 = e2_end_v.co - vert_shared.co
    return get_angle_between_vectors(vector1, vector2)
```

To keep things simple, we skip the input validation and assume the caller of the function has verified that the two passed-in BMesh edges e1 and e2 share one end vertex. Our first order of business is to find this shared vertex. To do this, we check if e1's first vertex is also among e2's vertices (if `e1.verts[0] in e2.verts`); if so, then that's our shared vertex. Otherwise, e1's other (second) vertex must be the shared vertex.

As shown in Figure 6-10, the angle theta between e1 and e2 can be derived from the dot product of vector1 and vector2 that point away from vert_shared toward the far ends of e1 and e2, respectively. Since we already know that vert_shared is one of e1's end vertices, we can use the BMEdge built-in method other_vert to find e1's other vertex e1_end_v (`e1.other_vert(vert_shared)`) and similarly e2's other vertex e2_end_v.

We then find vector1 by subtracting the coordinates of the shared vertex from the coordinates of the other (far) end of e1. We can find vector2 in a similar fashion. With vector1 and vector2 derived, we'll delegate the calculation of the angle between vector1 and vector2 to the function get_angle_between_vectors as we'll see next in Listing 6-19.

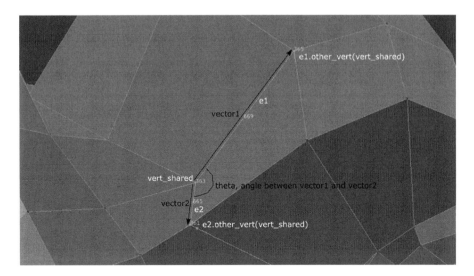

Figure 6-10. *Deriving the angle between two edges that share a vertex*

Finding Angle Between Two Vectors

The function get_angle_between_vectors in Listing 6-19 calculates the angle (in degrees) between two given Vector instances vector1 and vector2.

Listing 6-19. Computing the angle in degrees between two Vector instances (see /Ch6/text_editor/mesh_connectivity.py)

```
def get_angle_between_vectors(vector1, vector2):
    theta = math.acos( ↵
        vector1.dot(vector2)/(vector1.length*vector2.length))
    return math.degrees(theta)
```

We derive the angle between vector1 and vector2 from their dot product. Let's look at this step by step. We calculate the dot product of vector1 and vector2 by

$$dot(vector1, vector2) = |vector1| * |vector2| * cos(theta)$$

319

which reads "The dot product between vectors *vector1* and *vector2* is equal to the product of the two vector's lengths times the cosine of the angle *theta* between them." Therefore, after manipulating this equation, the angle *theta* between the two vectors becomes

$$theta = arccos(\ dot(vector1,\ vector2)\ /\ (|vector1|^*|vector2|)\ )$$

Translating this formula into Python, we compute the dot product of vector1 and vector2 with vector1.dot(vector2); divide it by the product of their lengths, vector1.length * vector2.length; then call math.acos to compute the arc cosine to get the angle theta between vector1 and vector2. Before returning theta, we convert it from radians to degrees with math.degrees (conversion to degrees is optional, but I personally find 90 degrees easier to grasp than 1.57 radians!).

Filtering Faces with Sharp (or Dull) Corners

With the ability to calculate the angle between any pair of edges with a shared vertex, we can now put together a function for filtering face corners that are smaller than a given threshold, like select_face_corners_less_than_angle shown in Listing 6-20.

Listing 6-20. Selecting face corners with angles less than or equal to a given threshold (see /Ch6/text_editor/mesh_connectivity.py)

```
def select_face_corners_less_than_angle(context, ↩
    angle_in_degrees):
    obj = context.view_layer.objects.active
    if obj is not None and obj.type=='MESH':
        bpy.ops.object.mode_set(mode='EDIT')
        bpy.ops.mesh.select_all(action='DESELECT')
        context.tool_settings.mesh_select_mode = ↩
            [False, True, False]
```

```
bm = bmesh.from_edit_mesh(obj.data)
for v in bm.verts:
    num_edges = len(v.link_edges)
    for i in range(num_edges):
        e1 = v.link_edges[i]
        e2 = v.link_edges[0] if i == num_edges-1 ↵
            else v.link_edges[i+1]

        if get_angle_between_edges(e1, e2) ↵
            <= angle_in_degrees:
            e1.select = True
            e2.select = True
bmesh.update_edit_mesh(obj.data)
context.view_layer.update()
```

To keep things simple, we again make the object to be operated on (obj) the active object of the passed-in context. If obj is a valid mesh object, we go on to switch it to Edit mode, deselect all, choose edge select, then create a BMesh instance bm for accessing obj.data.

Next, we enter a for loop to iterate through obj's vertices (bm.verts). For each vertex, we want to calculate the angle between each adjacent pair of its connected edges using get_angle_between_edges (Listing 6-18). For each connected edge at index i, its immediate neighboring edge is at index i+1, except for the last edge (at index num_edges-1) whose neighbor is edge 0. For example, if a vertex has three connected edges (with indices 0, 1, and 2), then you'd calculate the angle between edges #0 and #1, #1 and #2, and between edges #2 and #0. If the angle between a pair of edges is less than or equal to the passed-in threshold, then we select both edges in that pair.

Note that you can replace the <= by a > to make it select angles *greater* than the threshold, therefore selecting dull instead of narrow corners. You can see the results of running Listing 6-20 to select face corners <= 60 degrees on a built-in monkey primitive in Figure 6-11.

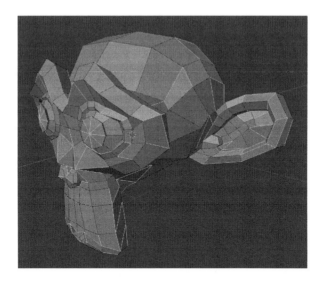

Figure 6-11. *Selecting face corners <= 60 degrees on Suzanne with* `select_face_corners_less_than_angle` *from Listing 6-20*

Wrapping Up the Extension Implementation

In this section, we'll wrap up the Sculpt Retopo Toolkit's implementation by creating a UI panel and assembling all the input widgets and operators under it. We'll also go over creating the elements required by Blender for creating an extension.

Creating a UI Panel and Adding Input Widgets and Operators to It

We'll create a UI panel class named SCULPTRETOPO_PT_ToolShelfPanel (Listing 6-21). To place the panel in the Properties shelf (N key) ➤ Tool tab, we'll set bl_space_type as 'VIEW_3D', bl_region_type as 'UI', and bl_category as 'Tool'. Blender requires that the name of the panel class contain the shorthand corresponding to its location. For example, since we're placing the panel in **P**roperties shelf (N key) ➤ **T**ool tab, the panel class needs to have "_PT_" in its name; therefore, we name our class SCULPTRETOPO_**PT**_ToolShelfPanel.

Listing 6-21. Implementing the Draw Grid operator (see /Ch6/ extension/sculpt_retopo_toolkit_4.2(4.3)/__init__.py)

```
class SCULPTRETOPO_PT_ToolShelfPanel(bpy.types.Panel):
    bl_idname = "SCULPT_RETOPO_PT_ToolShelfPanel"
    bl_label = "SCULPT RETOPO Toolkit"
    bl_space_type = 'VIEW_3D'
    bl_region_type = 'UI'
    bl_category = 'Tool'
    '''A collection of grease pencil driven sculpt and retopo
    tools'''

    def draw(self, context):
        layout = self.layout
        col0 = layout.column()
        col0.operator("button.reset_gp")
        col0.operator("button.draw_with_gp")
        col0.prop(context.scene, "select_mesh_dropdown")

        box0 = col0.box()
        box0.label(text="Sculpt Tools", icon='SCULPTMODE_HLT')
        box0_row0 = box0.row(align=True)
        box0_row0.prop(context.scene, "cut_thru_checkbox")
        box0.operator("button.carve")
        box0_row1 = box0.row(align=True)
        box0_row1.prop(context.scene, "inoutset_amount")
        box0.operator("button.inset", text="In/Outset")
```

```
box1 = col0.box()
box1.label(text="Retopo Tools", icon='MESH_GRID')
box1_row0 = box1.row(align=True)
box1_row0.prop(context.scene, "num_grid_lines")
box1.operator("button.draw_grid")
```

To add an operator or a scene variable bpy.types.Scene.<variable> as a UI widget, you'll create a column, row, or box under the panel's layout, like the following lines from Listing 6-21:

```
col0 = layout.column()
box0 = col0.box()
box0_row0 = box0.row(align=True)
```

Recall that box, column, and row are nested UI elements under layout which stack items within them differently. You can add an operator or a scene variable to any of these UI elements the same way.

To add an operator as a button, you'll call a column, row, or box's operator method with the bl_idname of the operator to be added. For example, to add the Carve operator (BUTTON_OT_carve from Listing 6-13) to box0, you'll use its bl_idname, which is "button.carve", like this:

```
box0.operator("button.carve")
```

The text that will show up on the button is the operator's bl_label, which for the Carve operator (BUTTON_OT_carve from Listing 6-13) is "Carve". You can see the finished UI panel for the extension in Figure 6-3.

To add a scene variable to a column, row, box, etc., you'd call that UI element's prop method with the variable's name, like this:

```
<row, col, box...>.prop(context.scene, "<variable>")
```

For example, in Listing 6-21, the scene variable bpy.types.Scene.select_mesh_dropdown is added to the column col0 with the following line of code, which creates the "Edit Mesh" drop-down:

```
col0.prop(context.scene, "select_mesh_dropdown")
```

Adding del_scene_vars(), register(), and unregister()

Recall from Chapter 2, to finish implementing an extension, you'll need to create a del_scene_vars() function to undo all the scene variables defined in init_scene_vars(), a register() function to register all the operator classes that are part of the extension (which Blender will call during the extension's installation), and a unregister() function that reverses everything register() does (which Blender will call during the extension's uninstallation). The implementation of these functions for the Sculpt Retopo Toolkit is shown in Listing 6-22.

Lastly, remember that Blender requires a "blender_manifest.toml" file (which contains the extension's metadata) placed alongside __init__.py in a folder named after the extension package. See Chapter 2 for a refresher on how to create a "blender_manifest.toml" file.

Listing 6-22. Add del_scene_vars(), register(), and unregister() to wrap up the extension (see /Ch6/extension/sculpt_retopo_ toolkit_4.2(4.3)/__init__.py)

```
def del_scene_vars():
    del bpy.types.Scene.select_mesh_dropdown
    del bpy.types.Scene.cut_thru_checkbox
    del bpy.types.Scene.inoutset_amount
    del bpy.types.Scene.num_grid_lines

classes = [BUTTON_OT_reset_gp, BUTTON_OT_draw_with_GP, ↵
    BUTTON_OT_carve, BUTTON_OT_inset, ↵
    SCULPTRETOPO_PT_ToolShelfPanel, BUTTON_OT_draw_grid]
```

```
def register():
    for c in classes:
        bpy.utils.register_class(c)
    init_scene_vars()

def unregister():
    for c in classes:
        bpy.utils.unregister_class(c)
    del_scene_vars()
```

Summary

After learning all about editing and generating meshes in Chapters 3, 4, and 5, we shifted our focus in this chapter to making helper tools that cater to our day-to-day workflow. You familiarized yourself with the basics of setting up reference photos in Python, using reference images, background images, and image empties. You then learned to make a Carve operator that let users draw arbitrary shapes with a Grease Pencil on a sculpted mesh to be cut out. You also implemented an In/Outset operator that lets users draw shapes on a mesh with a GP to indent or protrude.

In the second half of the chapter, you switched gears to developing retopology tools, starting with a "Draw Grid" operator that lets you quickly populate a grid adhering to the surface of a high-poly object by drawing parallel GP strokes in sequence. You also learned to write Python functions for analyzing bmesh connectivity data, which you subsequently used to detect poles and filter face angles with sharp (or dull) corners.

By the end of the chapter, you've assembled the three operators (Carve, In/Outset, and Draw Grid) you've developed throughout the chapter into a Sculpting and Retopo Toolkit extension, complete with a UI panel in the viewport Properties shelf ➤ Tool tab.

CHAPTER 7

UV Mapping

UV mapping (or "unwrapping UV coordinates" or simply "unwrapping") is the process of establishing how a 2D image texture is projected onto the surface of a 3D model. UV mapping sets up the relationship between which faces on your mesh correspond to where you are painting on a 2D texture and tells the renderer how to shade a model by applying contents of normal maps, ambient occlusion maps, and the like to the appropriate spots on the model. Unwrapping is therefore a fundamental step in a modeling pipeline as it prepares the mesh for texturing and shading. As you get more acquainted with modeling, you'll likely find that UV mapping is both a bit of an art and a science. Although there are often no hard and fast rules on how to seam and unwrap a model, there are general guidelines for approaching different categories of models to achieve clean results.

In this chapter, I'll show you how to write Python functions to expedite and simplify your UV mapping workflow. I'll start by discussing an important preparatory step for unwrapping: seam placement—how they work, how seams affect the quality of your UVs, and best practices for seaming several commonly used types of meshes. Next, I'll go over the process of unwrapping a model by hand in Blender, followed by automating the same steps in Python. I'll show you how to split Blender screen areas to open a UV/Image editor, how to configure commonly used UV settings, and how to mark seams on and unwrap a model in script. You'll also learn how to use script functions to create and apply a basic UV grid texture to your model in the 3D Viewport to visualize the quality

© Isabel Lupiani 2025
I. Lupiani, *Blender Scripting with Python*, https://doi.org/10.1007/979-8-8688-1127-2_7

of the unwrapped UVs. I'll wrap up the chapter by showing you how to write scripts to automate the tasks of saving image data blocks to disk and exporting UV layouts to file to be used as templates for painting textures with external image editing software.

Running This Chapter's Examples

The source code for this book is available on GitHub via the book's product page, located at www.apress.com/979-8-8688-1126-5).

Setting Up/Running the Scripts

Navigate to the folder /Ch7 in the downloaded source. As you follow along the chapter, open the *.py file indicated by the text in the built-in Text Editor. At the bottom of each script, there is a block already set up which invokes the code listings with sample arguments.

Handling Imports Between Scripts

This chapter's scripts import functions from one another. The imports have been set up for you in the downloaded source.

(Optional) Make Your Own Scripts Available As Python Modules in Blender

There is an alternative way of handling imports when running in the Text Editor. Rather than having to include Listing 4-2 at the top of every script to make Blender scan the current directory, you can copy the scripts you want to import from to the /scripts/modules/ directory under your Blender installation, at

```
<your Blender installation directory>/Blender <version>/ ↵
    <version>/scripts/modules/
```

Note   Recall in Chapter 4 you learned that when running in the Text Editor, Blender's built-in Python does *not* automatically look in the directory your active *.py is for imports. You have to derive the directory's path and add it to the list of paths Blender's Python will scan, as shown in Listing 4-2.

For example, for Blender 4.2 installed to the default directory on Windows, if you copy the /Ch7 folder from the downloaded source to /scripts/modules, you would end up with a folder hierarchy similar to the following:

```
C:/Program Files/Blender Foundation/Blender 4.2/ ↩
    4.2/scripts/modules/Ch7
```

All scripts in /Ch7 will then become available as Python modules when you work inside the Text Editor. For example, you can import the function apply_all_modifiers from /Ch7/apply_modifiers.py to use in your script with the following line of code:

```
from Ch7.apply_modifiers import apply_all_modifiers
```

You can then call apply_all_modifiers as if that function is defined in the same script.

Since this method of setting up imports relies on modifying your Blender installation, it's not suitable for the purpose of sharing scripts with others; however, it is a convenient way to set up imports for your own Blender Python experimentation.

Before Unwrapping: Marking Seams

While Blender does not strictly require you to mark seams on a mesh before unwrapping it, it's usually a good idea to do so since it almost always produces a better quality textured appearance by minimizing distortion and stretching of the texture over the surface of the model.

How Do Seams Work?

I like to think about the process of marking seams on a 3D model using two metaphors. The first is taking apart a piece of clothing by separating it at the seams, like reverse engineering a finished garment back down to its pattern. Figure 7-1 shows a couple common ways to pattern a T-shirt.

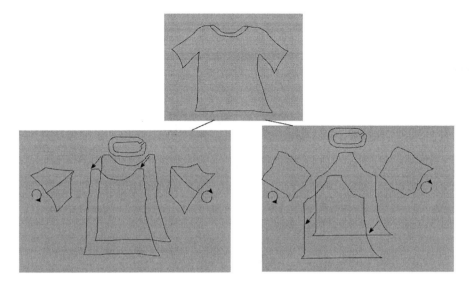

Figure 7-1. *The same T-shirt sewn from two different patterns*

Impact of Seams on the Quality of UVs

If you imagine trying on each of these T-shirts, you can see how they might stretch differently on your body since the locations of the seams are different. Even though the overall shapes of the shirts are the same, some seam placements will make more sense than others. For example, you'll usually want to put seams somewhere less noticeable, since a seam that runs across the front of the shirt will call for attention and look unattractive. If you think of this in terms of marking seams on a model, it would be the equivalent of placing seams on a head mesh along the hairline or in the back of the head where they would be less obvious.

Although seams introduce discontinuity that can be undesirable, they also tend to relieve pressure. The portion of a garment made of one seamless piece of fabric would need to stretch more to fit over the contour of a body, distorting the graphic printed on the fabric. Similarly, the portion of a 2D texture that has to stretch over a larger or curved surface area on a 3D mesh will produce more distortion.

The second metaphor I like to use is flattening a cardboard box back down into its cutout template. Imagine you are an industrial designer trying to come up with the best way to cut out a printed cardstock that will be folded into a box for product packaging (we'll forgo a bit of the realism here and pretend we don't need the extra "lips" to glue adjoining sides of the box together). Structural integrity aside, there are multiple ways you can cut the cardstock that will fold into the same box. For example, the four cutout patterns in Figure 7-2 ultimately fold into the same box shape, but each one produces a slightly different look since different parts of the printed cardstock are mapped to different faces on the box.

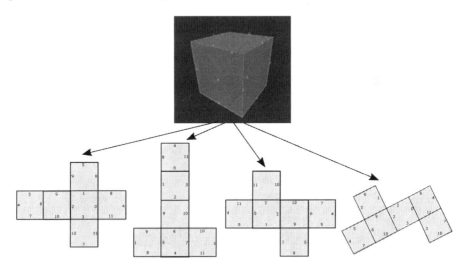

Figure 7-2. *Four cutout patterns that fold into the same box shape*

UV Mapping in Blender by Hand

Before diving into scripts, let's think about how you'd usually approach unwrapping UVs for a model by hand. This will give you a good idea on how to translate the steps into script functions and automate the process.

To unwrap a mesh object in Blender, you'd first inspect the object's modifier stack to see if there are any modifiers that may affect its geometry and therefore need to be applied before unwrapping. Then, you'd select the object and switch it to Edit mode and mark seams on the mesh in a repeated process of selecting edges and Ctrl-E ➤ Mark Seam. Often you'd select continuous flows of edges while marking seams, perhaps with the help of edge loops (Alt-click) or shortest paths (Select one edge, hold down Ctrl, then select the other end of the intended path of edges).

Once the seams have been marked, you'd toggle-select the whole mesh by pressing the A key (Blender will only unwrap the portion of the mesh that has been selected), followed by U key ➤ Unwrap. The unwrapped UVs will appear in the UV Editor (e.g., under the UV Editing workspace). You'd then manually adjust the UVs to minimize stretching, rearrange and pack the UV islands to optimize texel density, and so on.

Automating the UV Mapping Process in Python

Here's a quick recap of the main stages of the UV mapping process in Blender:

1. In Object mode, prep the model by applying modifiers that may affect its geometry and therefore impact its UVs.

2. In Edit mode, mark seams and select parts of the mesh to be unwrapped.

3. Unwrap the model.

4. Open a UV Editor to inspect and edit the UVs.

5. Create a material node and set it up with an image texture (if applicable) and apply it to the model.

6. Export the UV layout to file to be painted in an external image editing program, if applicable.

In the remainder of this section, I'll show you how to automate each of these stages using the Blender Python API, so you can start thinking about how to put together your own extension for automating parts of the UV workflow.

Applying Modifiers in Python

If you used modifiers such as Mirror or Solidify which affect the geometry of a model, it might make sense to apply them before unwrapping. For instance, if you unwrap a model with a Mirror modifier without applying it first, Blender will automatically mirror the UVs and prevent you from independently tweaking parts of the UVs without affecting each other— this may not be desirable if you want to introduce asymmetries in the mapped texture for increased realism.

You can write a function like `apply_all_modifiers` in Listing 7-1 to apply all modifiers on an object's modifier stack. Open the file `/Ch7/apply_modifiers.py` from the downloaded source in the Text Editor to follow along.

Listing 7-1. Apply all modifiers on a given object's modifier stack

```
def apply_all_modifiers(context, obj_to_apply_modifier):
    for obj in context.view_layer.objects:
        obj.select_set(False)
    context.view_layer.objects.active = obj_to_apply_modifier
```

```
obj_to_apply_modifier.select_set(True)

context_override, override_succesful = ↵
    get_context_override(context, 'VIEW_3D', 'WINDOW')
if override_succesful:
    with bpy.context.temp_override(**context_override):
        bpy.ops.object.mode_set(mode='OBJECT')

context_override, override_succesful = ↵
    get_context_override(context, 'VIEW_3D', 'WINDOW')
if override_succesful:
    with bpy.context.temp_override(**context_override):
        for m in obj_to_apply_modifier.modifiers:
            bpy.ops.object.modifier_apply( ↵
                modifier=m.name)
```

apply_all_modifiers starts by switching the current active object
in the given context to Object mode, then sets obj_to_apply_modifier
as the new active object to make subsequent calls to bpy.ops operators
interacting with it.

Since modifiers can only be applied in Object mode, we switch obj_
to_apply_modifier to Object mode with a context override (as if from
the viewport); if that's successful, we iterate through its modifiers and
apply them one by one by calling bpy.ops.object.modifier_apply, again
with a context override (as if from the viewport). Note that here we use an
updated version of get_context_override (which can be found in
/Ch7/view_fit.py) that returns a bool flag to indicate whether the context
override is created successfully. We'll look at this function in more detail
later in this chapter.

Note that <modifier>.name is the name of a modifier—this is the
string customizable through the text field at the top of a modifier box.
For example, the name of the modifier shown in Figure 7-3 is "subsurf_1",
which is a modifier of type 'SUBSURF'.

Figure 7-3. *You can edit a modifier's name by going to (1) the Properties editor ➤ Modifier tab and clicking the (2) text field at the top of a modifier's box*

Tip   You can find the string denoting a modifier's type in Python from the tool tip that pops up when you hover over its entry in the Properties editor ➤ Modifier tab ➤ Add Modifier menu (you must have both check boxes checked under Edit ➤ Preferences... ➤ Interface ➤ Display ➤ Tooltips to enable this feature).

Instead of applying an object's entire modifier stack at once, you can modify `apply_all_modifiers` (Listing 7-1) to selectively apply only the modifier that matches a given type and name, as the function `apply_given_modifier` shown in Listing 7-2.

Listing 7-2. Applying a modifier of a given name and type on an object

```
def apply_given_modifier(context, obj_to_apply_modifier, ↵
    modifier_type, modifier_name):
    for obj in context.view_layer.objects:
        obj.select_set(False)
    context.view_layer.objects.active = obj_to_apply_modifier
    obj_to_apply_modifier.select_set(True)

    context_override, override_succesful = ↵
        get_context_override(context, 'VIEW_3D', 'WINDOW')
    if override_succesful:
        with bpy.context.temp_override(**context_override):
            bpy.ops.object.mode_set(mode='OBJECT')

        context_override, override_succesful = ↵
            get_context_override(context, 'VIEW_3D', 'WINDOW')
        if override_succesful:
            with bpy.context.temp_override(**context_override):
                for m in obj_to_apply_modifier.modifiers:
                    if m.type==modifier_type and ↵
                        m.name==modifier_name:
                        bpy.ops.object.modifier_apply( ↵
                            modifier=m.name)
                        return
```

`apply_given_modifier` is largely the same as `apply_all_modifiers`, except that during the iteration of `obj_to_apply_modifier`'s modifier stack, `apply_given_modifier` checks for two things: if a modifier m's type (`m.type`) and name (`m.name`) match the given type and name; if so, it is applied and the function returns since its job is done.

Note that certain modifiers can have different effects when applied out of order. So it's always a good idea to double-check the order in which an object's modifiers are meant to be applied when designing extensions.

Marking Seams from Script Functions

Seam placements is both a bit of an art and a science: there are often no hard and fast rules and where you'd put the seams tend to be highly dependent upon the nature of your subject. For example, it might be acceptable (or even preferable) to have visible seams that introduce noticeable discontinuities in textures projected on a clothing mesh to match sewing seams seen on a real garment. On the other hand, you'll want to hide the seams as much as possible on a human mesh or other organic forms (animals don't have seams!). Put another way, what makes sense for one category of models might be the opposite of what you'd want to do with a different category. Therefore, it's difficult, if not impossible, to come up with an extension that could automate the seaming process for all types of models. The good news is if you know the category of the models you (or your add-on) are expected to work with, there are general rules of thumb you can follow.

For rigid or inanimate objects, a good rule of thumb is to approach them as the closest resembling primitive shapes. For example, for architectural models that are roughly rectangular, you'd place the seams as if you were unwrapping boxes. For clothing models, you can place seams in similar spots as the seams on real garments.

Due to the increased amount of curvature, organic forms usually require more strategic seam cuts to relieve pressure and prevent stretching while at the same time hide seams in places that are less noticeable. For example, to unwrap a human head, a popular strategy is to place one seam across the hairline and a second seam starting at the midpoint of the hairline up the top of the skull continuing down the center back of the head. This placement generally reduces stretching while hiding the seams under the hair. You can see an example of this in Figure 7-4 (I traced over the seams with some grease pencil strokes to make them easier to see).

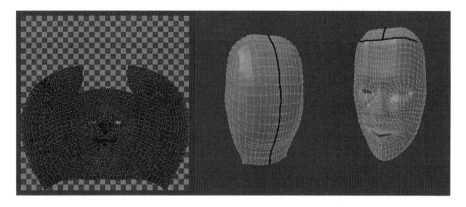

Figure 7-4. *Good seam placements on a head mesh minimize stretching*

Notice the unwrapped UVs on the left side of Figure 7-4 are blue in the UV Stretch color view, which indicates none to very little stretching. To enable Stretch color view, expand the overlays menu in the UV Editor and check the UV Stretch box, as shown in Figure 7-5. You will see the faces of unwrapped UVs displayed in colors ranging from blue (little distortion or stretching), to green, yellow, orange, and red (most stretching). I will show you how to enable this feature from Python later in this chapter.

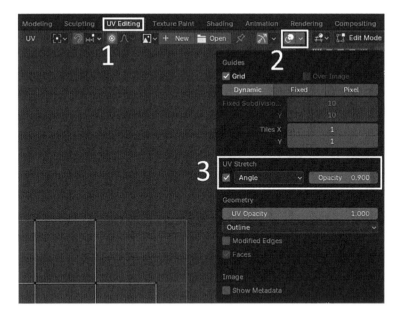

Figure 7-5. *Enabling the UV Stretch color view. (1) In a UV Editor window (such as under the UV Editing workspace as shown), (2) click the overlay icon in the upper right corner to expand the overlay menu, and (3) check the UV Stretch check box*

Example: Marking Seams on a Cube

The function generate_and_seam_cube in Listing 7-3 demonstrates how you can use the bmesh module and bpy operators to generate a cube mesh then mark its seams. Open the script /Ch7/unwrap_model.py from the downloaded source in the Text Editor to follow along.

Listing 7-3. Generate a cube mesh via bmesh, mark its seams, and unwrap its UVs

```
def generate_and_seam_cube(context, obj_name="cube_obj", ↩
    side_length=1, center=(0, 0, 0)):
    if bpy.data.meshes.find("cube_mesh") >= 0:
        bpy.data.meshes.remove(bpy.data.meshes["cube_mesh"])
    cube_mesh = bpy.data.meshes.new(name="cube_mesh")
    if bpy.data.objects.find(obj_name) < 0:
        cube_obj = bpy.data.objects.new(name=obj_name, ↩
            object_data=cube_mesh)
        context.collection.objects.link(cube_obj)
    else:
        cube_obj = bpy.data.objects[obj_name]
        cube_obj.data = cube_mesh
        if context.collection.objects.find(cube_obj) < 0:
            context.collection.objects.link(cube_obj)

    for o in context.view_layer.objects:
        o.select_set(False)
    context.view_layer.objects.active=cube_obj
    cube_obj.select_set(True)

    viewport_context_override, override_successful = ↩
        get_context_override(context, 'VIEW_3D', 'WINDOW')
    if override_successful:
        with bpy.context.temp_override( ↩
            **viewport_context_override):
            bpy.ops.object.mode_set(mode='EDIT')
    else:
        return
```

```
bm = bmesh.from_edit_mesh(cube_mesh)
half_side_len = side_length/2
bottom_z = center[2] - half_side_len
top_z = center[2] + half_side_len
verts = []
verts.append(bm.verts.new((center[0]+half_side_len, ↵
    center[1]-half_side_len, bottom_z)))
verts.append(bm.verts.new((center[0]+half_side_len, ↵
    center[1]+half_side_len, bottom_z)))
verts.append(bm.verts.new((center[0]-half_side_len, ↵
    center[1]+half_side_len, bottom_z)))
verts.append(bm.verts.new((center[0]-half_side_len, ↵
    center[1]-half_side_len, bottom_z)))
bottom_face = verts[0:4]
verts.append(bm.verts.new((center[0]+half_side_len, ↵
    center[1]-half_side_len, top_z)))
verts.append(bm.verts.new((center[0]+half_side_len, ↵
    center[1]+half_side_len, top_z)))
verts.append(bm.verts.new((center[0]-half_side_len, ↵
    center[1]+half_side_len, top_z)))
verts.append(bm.verts.new((center[0]-half_side_len, ↵
    center[1]-half_side_len, top_z)))
top_face = verts[4:]

bm.faces.new(verts[0:4])
bm.faces.new(verts[4:])
for i in range(3):
    bm.faces.new([verts[i], verts[i+1], ↵
        verts[i+1+4], verts[i+4]])
bm.faces.new([verts[3], verts[0], verts[4], verts[7]])
bm.edges.ensure_lookup_table()
```

```
edge_indices_to_select = [1, 3, 5, 6, 7, 9, 10]
for idx in edge_indices_to_select:
    bm.edges[idx].select = True
bpy.ops.mesh.mark_seam(clear=False)

viewport_context_override, override_successful = ↵
    get_context_override(context, 'VIEW_3D', 'WINDOW')
if override_successful:
    with bpy.context.temp_override( ↵
        **viewport_context_override):
        bpy.ops.mesh.select_all(action='SELECT')
        bpy.ops.mesh.normals_make_consistent(inside=False)

bpy.ops.mesh.select_all(action='DESELECT')
```

We start by creating a mesh data block cube_mesh which we'll be adding geometry to shortly. cube_mesh is hooked up as the data block for the mesh object cube_obj, which has its name specified by the user (obj_name). We deselect all objects in the scene, set cube_obj as the new active object and select it, then switch it to Edit mode using a context override (as if from the viewport) so we can create a bmesh instance bm to add geometry to it.

Next, we compute the distance between the center of the cube and any one of its six faces (to be created shortly), which is equal to half of the side_length passed in. We then create the four corner vertices of the bottom face in counterclockwise order when viewed from top-down, followed by the four corner vertices of the top face in the same order. At this point, all eight corner vertices of the cube have been created, we proceed to fill in the faces: first the bottom face, then the top face, followed by the four vertical faces in counterclockwise direction when viewed from the top. bm.edges.ensure_lookup_table() is called next, which validates the internal lookup indices of the cube's edges since the edges were automatically constructed on the fly as the cube's faces were filled in.

(Blender will likely complain the edge indices are out of date if you omit this call.) At this point, the construction of the cube mesh is complete. After selecting the appropriate edges on the cube, we call the operator `bpy.ops.mesh.mark_seam(clear=False)` to mark the seams (which is equivalent to Ctrl-E ➤ Mark Seams when done by hand).

The final block of code calls `bpy.ops.mesh.normals_make_consistent(inside=False)` to ensure the normals on the generated mesh are consistent and facing outward.

You might be wondering how I came up with the list of edge indices to be marked as seams —the internal indices of mesh elements (verts, edges, faces) increase sequentially in the order they are created—for example, the corners of the bottom face are verts #0, 1, 2, 3 counterclockwise, and the corners of the top face are verts #4, 5, 6, 7. The indices of the faces and edges can be derived in a similar manner.

Generating and Seaming Box-Shaped Objects

You can easily adapt `generate_and_seam_cube` (Listing 7-3) to generate and seam a variety of box-shaped objects (cuboids), such as rectangular prisms, trapezoid prisms, parallelogram prisms, and so on. All of these shapes have one thing in common—having a fixed boxlike cross-section along a length. As a result, they can all be generated in a similar way to `generate_and_seam_cube`, where the top and bottom faces are created first, then the vertical faces filled in to connect the two. The box-shaped variations can then be thought of as a cube with two corners of its top/bottom faces offsetted apart or toward each other. The seams can then be placed in the same pattern on any of the box-shaped variations as the cube.

Another way you could go about this is create one face first (either the top or bottom), then extrude it along the length of the shape. Yet another way is to generate a cube first, then scale the cube to create the variation. For example, stretch the cube along one of the face normal directions to create a rectangular prism, or select one face on the cube and scale it up or down to make a trapezoid. Select one face of the cube and grab it horizontally then you get a parallelogram (see Chapter 3 for a refresher on how to extrude and scale objects in Python).

Box-shaped objects by themselves may not be very exciting. However, the good news is they can be used as the basis for creating many useful models for your project, such as crates, containers, buildings, furniture items, and so on. So, take some time and experiment and see what you can come up with!

Opening a UV or Image Editor Using Python

Once you've marked the seams on a model, you are ready to unwrap it. Before doing that, you'll need to open a UV Editor so the unwrapped UVs have somewhere to go. Usually, it's best to have both a 3D Viewport and a UV Editor open at the same time while working with UVs, so as you make adjustment to the UVs you can see the effects on the model, and as you tweak the seams on the mesh you can unwrap again right away and see how it's changed the UVs.

The UV Editing workspace gives you the combination of a 3D Viewport and a UV Editor out of the box; however, sometimes you want the option to work from a different workspace but with the convenience of splitting the screen area to add on editors of your choice—for example, when you are debugging a UV mapping script from the Scripting workspace but want access to the UV Editor.

The function split_screen_area in Listing 7-4 will split the screen under the passed-in context in the direction split_dir ('VERTICAL' or 'HORIZONTAL') by split_ratio (0.5 means split in half) and set the new area to type_of_new_area (e.g., 'IMAGE_EDITOR' for Image Editor). The optional flag check_existing specifies whether an existing area matching the desired type should be returned if found (when check_existing=False, a new area is always split). Open /Ch7/split_screen_area.py from the downloaded source in the Text Editor to follow along.

Listing 7-4. Split the screen under the passed-in context into a given type of editor, in the specified direction and ratio

```
def split_screen_area(context, split_dir, split_ratio, ↩
    type_of_new_area, ui_type_of_new_area, ↩
    check_existing=False):
    existing_areas = list(context.screen.areas)

    if check_existing:
        for area in existing_areas:
            if area.type == type_of_new_area and ↩
                area.ui_type == ui_type_of_new_area:
                return area

    bpy.ops.screen.area_split(direction=split_dir, ↩
        factor=split_ratio)

    for area in context.screen.areas:
        if area not in existing_areas:
            area.type = type_of_new_area
            area.ui_type = ui_type_of_new_area
            return area
```

split_screen_area first makes a copy of the existing areas (to be checked against later for identifying the new area, if one is created). If check_existing is True, it iterates through the existing areas to see if any matches the desired type. If so, its job is done and the existing area is returned. Otherwise, it proceeds to split the active area by calling the built-in operator bpy.ops.screen.area_split with the given split direction and ratio. Since bpy.ops.screen.area_split does not return a reference to the newly created area, we have to iterate through all the areas and check each one to see if it is one of the areas before the split (if not, it's the new area!). The new area is set to the specified type, and a copy of the new area is returned.

Using Listing 7-4, you can split the screen vertically in half to create a UV editor like this:

```
new_uv_editor_vertical = split_screen_area(bpy.context, ↩
    'VERTICAL', 0.5, 'IMAGE_EDITOR', 'UV')
```

You can split the screen horizontally in half to create an Image editor like this:

```
new_image_editor_horizontal = split_screen_area(bpy.context, ↩
    'HORIZONTAL', 0.5, 'IMAGE_EDITOR', 'IMAGE_EDITOR')
```

Note that a UV Editor and an Image Editor have the same area *type* (`'IMAGE_EDITOR'`) but different area *ui type* (UV Editor has ui type `'UV'`, whereas Image Editor has ui type `'IMAGE_EDITOR'`).

Maximizing a Screen Area

The function `maximize_screen_area` in Listing 7-5 shows how you can look up a screen area of a given type and call `bpy.ops.screen.screen_full_area()` to maximize it. Open `/Ch7/maximize_screen_area.py` from the downloaded source in the Text Editor to follow along.

Listing 7-5. Maximize a given type of screen area under the passed-in context

```
def maximize_screen_area(context, type_of_area_to_maximize):
    for window in context.window_manager.windows:
        for area in window.screen.areas:
            if area.type == type_of_area_to_maximize:
                for region in area.regions:
                    if region.type == 'WINDOW':
                        override = {'window': window, ↩
                            'screen': window.screen, ↩
                            'area': area,'region': region}
```

```
with bpy.context.temp_override( ↵
    **override):
    bpy.ops.screen.screen_full_area()
break
```

Recall that in Blender, the screen is organized into a hierarchy of nested UI elements from outside in—window, screen, area—`maximize_screen_area` iterates through this hierarchy until it finds an area that matches the given type (for instance, `'VIEW_3D'` for viewport). Each area in Blender is further divided into at least two regions: one of type `'HEADER'`, which is the menu bar, and one of type `'WINDOW'`, which is the main editor area where you perform the edits. For instance, the 3D Viewport (area of type `'VIEW_3D'`) contains a menu bar at the top (region of type `'HEADER'`) and the actual 3D view area where you edit your models (region of type `'WINDOW'`).

Once `maximize_screen_area` locates the `'WINDOW'` region of the target area, it puts together a context override consisting of the UI hierarchy and uses it to call `bpy.ops.screen.screen_full_area()` to maximize the area.

Recall from Chapter 4, when Blender operators are called, they are by default supplied with an implicit context (in the form of a Python dictionary) which tells the operator where in Blender the operator is called from (e.g., the 3D Viewport), what the current active object is, and so on, so the operator knows what object or screen area to perform its action upon.

In this case, `bpy.ops.screen.screen_full_area()` will *by default maximize whichever area it's called from*. For instance, if your add-on is located somewhere inside the UV Editor, and it calls `bpy.ops.screen.screen_full_area()`, the UV Editor will get maximized. However, if you want to change this behavior and force the operator to maximize a different area (e.g., the 3D Viewport), you can construct a context override that contains the 3D Viewport and use it to call `bpy.ops.screen.screen_full_area()`, so it can infer the alternative screen area to maximize.

Configuring Commonly Used Settings for UV Mapping

In this section, I'll show you how to configure some commonly used settings for UV mapping in Python, which is useful for developing a variety of add-ons, for example, if you have certain "presets" that you always use for mapping UVs in your workflow, like a set of options for unwrapping game assets, and a different set for unwrapping models for static indoor scenes. You can make an add-on that loads these presets automatically. Another example might be when you want to automate parts of a UV mapping workflow and need certain options turned on or off without user input.

Getting a Reference to the UV Editor

Many settings in the UV Editor are configured in Python through the SpaceUVEditor instance of the currently open UV Editor's screen area. get_uv_editor in Listing 7-6 shows how you can retrieve a reference to the first open UV Editor found under the given context's screen. Open the script /Ch7/uv_settings.py from the downloaded source in the Text Editor to follow along.

Listing 7-6. Retrieve a reference to the first UV Editor found under the given context's screen

```
def get_uv_editor(context, image_name=''):
    for area in context.screen.areas:
        if area.type=='IMAGE_EDITOR' and area.ui_type=='UV':
            for space in area.spaces:
                if space.type=='IMAGE_EDITOR':
                    if len(image_name) == 0:
                        return area, space, space.uv_editor
                    else:
```

```
    if space.image and ↩
        space.image.name== ↩
            image_name:
        return area, space, space.uv_editor

return [None, None, None]
```

Recall that Blender organizes its UI elements in a nested hierarchy (from outside in) of screen, areas, and spaces. `get_uv_editor` iterates through this nested hierarchy under the given context, until it finds the first area of type `'IMAGE_EDITOR'` with `area.ui_type=='UV'`. The first area found is usually the "oldest" area (one that's been open the longest), since whenever you open a new area in Blender, it gets added to the end of the list of open areas. Although a user can have any number of UV Editors open simultaneously, to simplify things, `get_uv_editor` just stops at the first area it finds.

`get_uv_editor` continues to search for a *space* under this area of type `'IMAGE_EDITOR'` (which is a `bpy.types.SpaceImageEditor` object instance). The UV Editor (`bpy.types.SpaceUVEditor` instance) is stored under this space and can be accessed via `space.uv_editor`.

`get_uv_editor` returns the area, space, and `SpaceUVEditor` instance it finds or a triple of `None` if nothing is found. You'll see why these return values are useful when we look at how to set UV Editor settings in Python later in this chapter.

Getting a Reference to the Image Editor

Note that you can adapt Listing 7-6 to search for an Image Editor instead of a UV Editor, by searching for `area.ui_type=='IMAGE_EDITOR'`, as shown in Listing 7-7.

> **Note**   UV Editor and Image Editor both have `area.type=='IMAGE_EDITOR'` and `space.type=='IMAGE_EDITOR'`. The only difference between the two is that UV Editor has `area.ui_type=='UV'`, whereas Image Editor has `area.ui_type=='IMAGE_EDITOR'`.

Listing 7-7.   Retrieve a reference to the first Image Editor found under the given context's screen

```
def get_image_editor(context, image_name = ''):
    for area in context.screen.areas:
        if area.type=='IMAGE_EDITOR' and ↵
            area.ui_type=='IMAGE_EDITOR':
            for space in area.spaces:
                if space.type=='IMAGE_EDITOR':
                    if len(image_name) == 0:
                        return [area, space]
                    else:
                        if space.image and ↵
                            space.image.name==image_name:
                            return [area, space]
    return [None, None]
```

Distinguishing Between Multiple Open UV Editors

If there are multiple UV Editors open and you need to locate a specific one, you can modify get_uv_editor (Listing 7-6) to check for additional constraints, such as whether the area is located within a certain part of the screen, as shown in the following snippet:

```
if area.type=='IMAGE_EDITOR' and area.ui_type=='UV':
    if 100 <= area.x <= 250 and 0 <= area.y <= 200:
```

(area.x, area.y) is the 2D screen location of the *lower left* corner of area. Recall that in Blender, the origin of the screen is at the lower left corner, with x increasing horizontally to the right and y increasing vertically upward. The line

```
if 100 <= area.x <= 250 and 0 <= area.y <= 200
```

checks if the x coordinate of the lower left corner of area is between 100 and 250 pixels and if the y coordinate is between 0 and 200 pixels.

Another thing you might use to identify a particular UV Editor area is the image currently open inside it, which is a data block of type bpy. types.Image and can be accessed with space.image. The name of the image is a string stored in space.image.name (like "face.jpg"). If there are multiple UV Editors open, you might distinguish between them based on the name of the image that is open in each one.

Enabling the UV Stretch Color View in Python

You can call get_uv_editor from Listing 7-6 to get a reference to (the first) UV Editor open under the passed-in context and use it to enable the UV Stretch color view as shown in the following snippet:

```
uv_editor = get_uv_editor(bpy.context)[-1]

if uv_editor:
    uv_editor.show_stretch = True
```

which will show the amount of stretch in the UV map with colors ranging from blue to red like the example shown on the left side of Figure 7-4. Note that get_uv_editor returns the hierarchy of area, space, and SpaceUVEditor instance of the first UV Editor found under the given context as a sequence of three values; therefore, you have to use the last of these values (at index -1, the SpaceUVEditor instance) to access the show_ stretch setting.

Note   Remember that get_uv_editor will only return a UV Editor that is open under the passed-in context, so if you are running the above snippet from the Text Editor inside the Scripting workspace, you'd need to split the screen and open a UV Editor under the same workspace to see the effect of running the snippet.

Enabling Live Unwrap

Another handy option is Live Unwrap (UV ➤ Live Unwrap in the UV Editor), which as its name suggests automatically updates the UVs in the UV Editor in real time as you make changes to the corresponding mesh in the viewport. This is particularly helpful when you are trying to figure out where to place seams on a mesh, since you can move the seams around or cut additional seams and observe the effects as you go.

You can enable Live Unwrap via the SpaceUVEditor instance returned by Listing 7-6 like this:

```
uv_editor = get_uv_editor(bpy.context)[-1]

if uv_editor:
    uv_editor.use_live_unwrap = True
```

Keeping UV and Edit Mode Mesh Selection in Sync

"UV Sync Selection" is a button located at the upper left corner of the UV Editor as shown in Figure 7-6. As its name suggests, when you select vertices (or edges/faces) on the mesh you've unwrapped in the viewport, Blender will automatically select the corresponding vertices (or edges/faces) on that mesh's UVs in the UV Editor. What's better is that anything you select on the UVs will also get selected on the mesh. This lets you quickly identify and isolate a problem area on the UVs. For example, if you see a spot with a lot of stretching using the UV Stretch color view, you can select only that area and see where on the mesh it corresponds to, adjust the seams, then check right away if the stretching has improved with Live Unwrap.

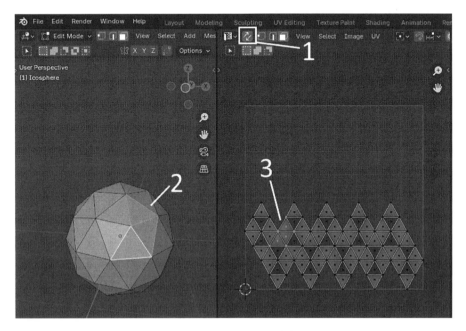

Figure 7-6. *Enabling UV Sync Selection. (1) Click the UV Sync Selection button at the upper left corner of the UV Editor to toggle the option. (2) and (3) show faces selected on the mesh in the viewport and their corresponding UVs in the UV Editor*

Instead of going through the SpaceUVEditor instance, you have to enable UV Sync Selection via scene.tool_settings under the current context, like this:

```
bpy.context.scene.tool_settings.use_uv_select_sync = True
```

Fitting UV Image to View

Another feature I'd like to point out is View Fit (which can be accessed inside the UV Editor via View ➤ Zoom ➤ Zoom to Fit, or Shift Home). View Fit automatically zooms the image or UVs displayed in the UV Editor to fill out the view, whatever the size the editor happens to be at the time, as the example shown in Figure 7-7.

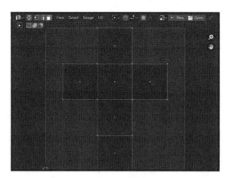

Figure 7-7. *View Fit in the UV Editor, which zooms the UV map or image displayed to fill out the UV Editor as much as possible, however big the UV Editor happens to be at the moment*

The function make_image_editor_fit_view in Listing 7-8 shows how you can call bpy.ops.image.view_all with a context override to make the image or UV map currently on display inside a UV or Image Editor zoom to fit. You can find the function in the script /Ch7/view_fit.py from the downloaded source.

Listing 7-8. Zoom the image or UV map currently on display inside a UV or Image Editor to fill out the view

```
def make_image_editor_fit_view(context, editor_area_x=-1):
    image_editor_context_override, found_area_and_region = ↵
        get_context_override(context, 'IMAGE_EDITOR', ↵
        'WINDOW', editor_area_x)
```

```
if found_area_and_region:
    with bpy.context.temp_override( ↵
        **image_editor_context_override):
        bpy.ops.image.view_all(fit_view=True)
```

get_context_override with UV/Image Editor Options

For this chapter, I've adapted the function get_context_override from Chapter 4 (Listing 4-23 in section "Overriding Context") to allow optional matching of the area's X coordinate and the name of the image displayed in the area, as shown in Listing 7-9. This is useful for identifying a particular UV Editor among multiple ones that are open simultaneously within a workspace.

Listing 7-9. Revised get_context_override that allows optional matching of area x and the name of the image displayed within the area

```
def get_context_override(context, area_type, region_type, ↵
    area_x=-1, image_name=''):
    override = context.copy()
    found_area_and_region = False
    image_matched = True
    area_x_matched = True
    for area in override['screen'].areas:
        if area.type == area_type:
            override['area'] = area

            if len(image_name)>0 and area.type=='IMAGE_EDITOR':
                image_matched = False
                for space in area.spaces:
                    if space.type=='IMAGE_EDITOR':
```

```
                    if space.image and ↵
                        space.image.name==image_name:
                        image_matched = True
            if area_x >= 0:
                area_x_matched = (area.x==area_x)

            if image_matched and area_x_matched:
                for region in override['area'].regions:
                    if region.type==region_type:
                        override['region'] = region
                        found_area_and_region = True
                        break

            if found_area_and_region:
                break

    return override, found_area_and_region
```

As with the Chapter 4 version of get_context_override, we iterate through the nested screen, area, and spaces/regions to find ones of the matching types, except for this time, if space.type=='IMAGE_EDITOR' (which means it's either a UV Editor or Image Editor), we also check if it has an image displayed (space.image is not None) and whether its name matches the given image_name (space.image.name==image_name). If applicable, we also check if the X coordinate of the area (area.x) matches the given value.

The matching of area X coordinate is skipped when -1 is given as axis_x, while the matching of the image displayed is skipped when an cmpty string is given as image_name.

Configuring UV Settings in General

At this point, you might wonder, there are so many UV-related settings, wouldn't it take forever to figure out how to set each one individually in Python? Luckily, there's a simple pattern for mapping these settings, which I'll show you in this section.

When you hover over an item in one of the menus in the UV Editor, you'll notice that its tool tip will contain a line that reads one of three ways:

1. Python: SpaceImageEditor.<setting>

2. Python: SpaceUVEditor.<setting>

3. Python: ToolSettings.<setting>

This tells you exactly how to configure the setting in Python. I'll show you an example from each category next.

Tool Tip Type #1: Python: SpaceImageEditor.<setting>

When you see a tool tip that reads *Python: SpaceImageEditor.<setting>*, such as the tool tip for View ➤ Update Automatically in Figure 7-8, which reads

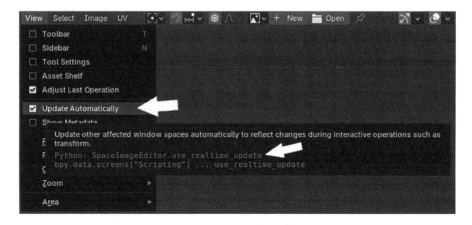

Figure 7-8. *In the UV Editor, the Python tool tip for View ➤ Update Automatically shows Python: SpaceImageEditor.use_realtime_update*

*Python: SpaceImageEditor.**use_realtime_update**, you'll use the *screen space* (which is a SpaceImageEditor instance) that encloses the UV Editor to access that setting.

Using get_uv_editor from Listing 7-6, you can configure the setting this way:

```
area, image_editor, uv_editor = get_uv_editor(bpy.context)
if image_editor:
    image_editor.use_realtime_update = True
```

Tool Tip Type #2: Python: SpaceUVEditor.<setting>

When you see a tool tip that reads *Python: SpaceUVEditor.<setting>*, such as the tool tip for View ➤ Show Metadata in Figure 7-9, which reads

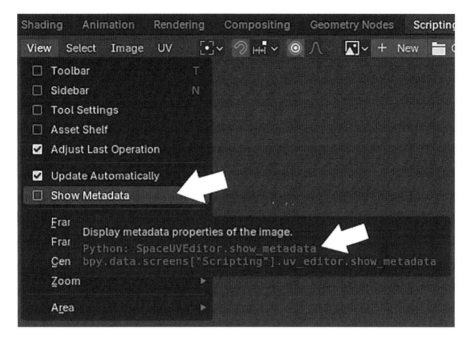

Figure 7-9. *In the UV Editor, the Python tool tip for View ➤ Show Metadata reads Python: SpaceUVEditor.show_metadata*

Python: SpaceUVEditor.__show_metadata__, you'll use the UV Editor (which is a SpaceUVEditor instance) to access the setting.

Using `get_uv_editor` from Listing 7-6, you can configure the setting like this:

```
area, image_editor, uv_editor = get_uv_editor(bpy.context)
if uv_editor:
    uv_editor.show_metadata = True
```

As we've seen previously, the UV Stretch option in the overlays menu and UV ➤ Live Unwrap are two other examples that are accessed the same way:

```
area, image_editor, uv_editor = get_uv_editor(bpy.context)

if uv_editor:
    uv_editor.show_stretch = True
    uv_editor.use_live_unwrap = True
```

Tool Tip Type #3: Python: ToolSettings.<setting>

When you see a tool tip that reads *Python: ToolSettings.<setting>*, such as the tool tip for Sticky Selection Mode in Figure 7-10, which reads

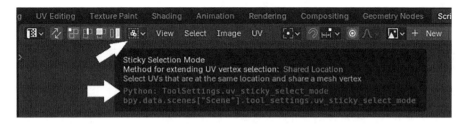

Figure 7-10. *In the UV Editor, the Python tool tip for Sticky Selection Mode reads Python: ToolSettings.uv_sticky_select_mode*

*Python: ToolSettings.**uv_sticky_select_mode***, you could access that setting via scene.tool_settings under the current context, like this:

```
bpy.context.scene.tool_settings.uv_sticky_select_mode = ↩
    'SHARED_VERTEX'
```

As we've seen previously, the UV Sync Selection (Figure 7-6) can be accessed the same way:

```
bpy.context.scene.tool_settings.use_uv_select_sync = True
```

Visualizing Unwrapped UVs on the Model

In this section, we'll look at how to create a material node in Python with an image texture and configure viewport settings for previewing it on the unwrapped model.

Creating a New Image Data Block

When you press the +*New* button at the top of the UV or Image Editor, it creates a new image data block. Data blocks are the basic units of data in Blender and primary building blocks of *.blend files. They come in many different types, such as images, meshes, materials, etc. The image data blocks are stored at the *.blend file level in bpy.data.images, and you can look up an image by name like this:

```
bpy.data.images[<name>]
```

Listing 7-10 shows how you can write a function create_image_data_block to create an image data block, either by loading an image file from disk or generating a UV or color grid. Open the script /Ch7/create_and_save_images.py from the downloaded source in the Text Editor to follow along.

Listing 7-10. Function to create a new image data block by loading an image file from disk or generating a UV or color grid

```
def create_image_data_block(context, name, ↵
    image_type='UV_GRID', color=(0, 0, 0, 1), ↵
    image_filepath='', display_image=True, ↵
    area_ui_type='IMAGE_EDITOR'):
    image_block = None
    if bpy.data.images.find(name) < 0 or ↵
        not bpy.data.images[name].has_data:
        if os.path.isfile(image_filepath):
            image_block = bpy.data.images.load(image_filepath)
            image_block.name = name
        else:
            bpy.data.images.new(name=name, width=1024, ↵
                height=1024, alpha=True, ↵
                float_buffer=False, stereo3d=False)
```

```
            image_block = bpy.data.images[name]
    else:
        image_block = bpy.data.images[name]

    image_block.generated_color = color
    image_block.generated_type = image_type

    if not display_image:
        return image_block, None

    [image_editor_area, image_editor_space, uv_editor] = ↵
        [None, None, None]
    if area_ui_type=='IMAGE_EDITOR':
        [image_editor_area, image_editor_space] = ↵
            get_image_editor(context, name)
    else:
        [image_editor_area, image_editor_space, uv_editor] = ↵
            get_uv_editor(context, name)

    if image_editor_space:
        image_editor_space.image = image_block
    else:
        image_editor_area = split_screen_area(context, ↵
            'VERTICAL', 0.5, 'IMAGE_EDITOR', area_ui_type, ↵
                False)
        for s in image_editor_area.spaces:
            if s.type == 'IMAGE_EDITOR':
                image_editor_space = s
                image_editor_space.image = image_block
                if area_ui_type == 'UV':
                    uv_editor = s.uv_editor
                break
```

```
image_editor_context_override, override_successful = ↵
    get_context_override(context, 'IMAGE_EDITOR', ↵
        'WINDOW', image_editor_area.x, name)
if override_successful:
    with bpy.context.temp_override( ↵
        **image_editor_context_override):
        bpy.ops.image.view_all(fit_view=True)

return image_block, uv_editor
```

The function checks if an image with the given name already exists, and if not (find returns -1), it calls bpy.data.images.load(image_ filepath) to load the image from disk at image_filepath and create a new image block from it, before assigning it the given name. If there is no valid image_filepath, the function calls bpy.data.images.new to create a blank image data block using the given name.

image_block.generated_color is configured through a four-tuple of RGB-Alpha values, for example, red with opacity at 50% is (1, 0, 0, 0.5). image_block.generated_type can be either 'BLANK' (for image loaded from disk), 'UV_GRID' (black and white grid), or 'COLOR_GRID' (colored grid). Since the image block creation is complete, if the caller has specified not to display the image in an Image Editor (not display_image), we can return at this point.

Next, depending on the passed-in area_ui_type, the function looks for either a UV or Image Editor already open with an image loaded with the matching name. If found, that editor's image is set to image_block. If not, it calls split_screen_area from Listing 7-4 to split the screen vertically half way into the appropriate editor type. Then, image_block is set as the new editor's image (image_editor_space.image = image_block). Lastly, the function calls bpy.ops.image.view_all with a context override to zoom image_block so it fills the editor.

Creating a Material Node with Image Texture

In the last section, we learned how to create an image data block by either loading a file from disk or generating one with a UV (or color) grid. We'll now write a function create_matieral (Listing 7-11) to create a material node, set it up with an image texture, and apply it to a given model. Open the script /Ch7/unwrap_model.py from the downloaded source in the Text Editor to follow along.

Listing 7-11. Create a new material node with the given image as texture and apply it to the given object

```
def create_material(obj, material_name, image):
    if bpy.data.materials.find(material_name) < 0:
        bpy.data.materials.new(material_name)
    material = bpy.data.materials[material_name]
    obj.data.materials.append(material)
    obj.active_material_index = ↵
        obj.data.materials.find(material.name)
    material.use_nodes = True

    tcm_nodes = material.node_tree.nodes
    bsdf_index = tcm_nodes.find('Principled BSDF')
    node_bsdf = tcm_nodes.new( ↵
        type='ShaderNodeBsdfPrincipled') if ↵
        bsdf_index < 0 else tcm_nodes[bsdf_index]

    node_texture = tcm_nodes.new('ShaderNodeTexImage')
    nodc_tcxture.image = image
    node_output = tcm_nodes.new( ↵
        type='ShaderNodeOutputMaterial')

    tcm_links = material.node_tree.links
    tcm_links.new(node_texture.outputs['Color'], ↵
```

```
    node_bsdf.inputs['Base Color'])
  tcm_links.new(node_bsdf.outputs['BSDF'], ↵
    node_output.inputs['Surface'])
```

We start by looking up the material with the given `material_name` (or create one if it doesn't exist yet), add it to the given `obj`'s material stack with `obj.data.materials.append(material)`, and set it as `obj`'s active material (`obj.active_material_index = obj.data.materials.find(material.name)`). We also set `material.use_nodes` to True to enable shader nodes for rendering the `material`.

Next, we'll edit the shader nodes under `material`'s node tree (`material.node_tree.nodes`). We look up the existing Principled BSDF node in the tree (or create one if it doesn't exist), then create an Image Texture node and hook up the passed-in `image` as the Image Texture node's image. We also create a Material Output node.

With the nodes created, we'll link them together next. The links between nodes in `material`'s node tree are stored under `material.node_tree.links`. When we create new links, we add them to this list. We create a new link from the Image Texture node's Color output to the Principled BSDF node's Base Color input. We also link the Principled BSDF node's BSDF output to the Material Output node's Surface input. Figure 7-11 shows an example of running Listing 7-11 to apply a grid texture to a cube mesh. Figure 7-12 shows the same material from Figure 7-11 shown in the Properties editor ➤ Material tab.

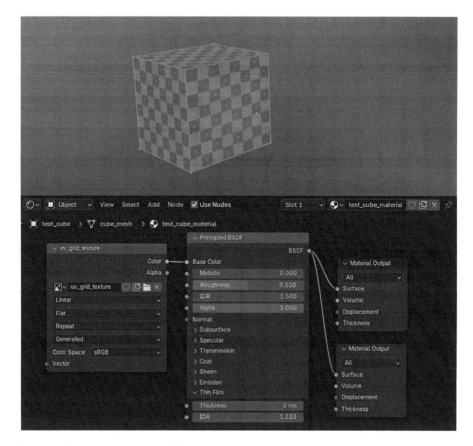

Figure 7-11. *Example of a material node with grid image texture generated by running Listing 7-11, shown under the Shading workspace*

Figure 7-12. *The material generated by Listing 7-11 shown in the Properties editor ➤ Material tab*

Configure Viewport Settings for Previewing Texture on a Model

With the material and image texture set up on the model, we're now ready to preview it in the viewport. Listing 7-12 shows how you can write a function `config_viewport_materials` to set viewport shading to Material Preview and enable backface culling. You can find the function in /Ch7/ unwrap_model.py in the downloaded source.

Listing 7-12. Configure viewport shading to Material Preview and enable backface culling

```
def config_viewport_materials(context):
    for a in context.window.screen.areas:
        if a.type == 'VIEW_3D':
            for s in a.spaces:
                if s.type == 'VIEW_3D':
                    s.shading.show_backface_culling = True
                    s.shading.type = 'MATERIAL'
```

Putting It Altogether: Automating UV Unwrapping of a Given Mesh

After seaming the mesh and configuring UV settings, the next steps are to select the portion of the mesh that you want to unwrap and choose the appropriate type of projection algorithm to perform the mapping (in the 3D Viewport in Edit mode, U key ➤ UV Mapping). For most intents and purposes, you'd select a mesh in its entirety (A key in 3D Viewport) then use U key ➤ Unwrap to do the mapping for the whole model.

The function `unwrap_model` in Listing 7-13 takes an already seamed mesh, unwraps it, and applies a UV grid image texture to it for previewing it in both the UV Editor and viewport. Open the file `/Ch7/unwrap_model.py` from the downloaded source in the Text Editor to follow along.

Listing 7-13. Unwrap a given mesh and apply a material with an image texture for previews

```
def unwrap_model(context, model_name, ↵
    num_min_stretch_iterations, ↵
    uv_map_name="uv_map", ↵
    image_block_name="uv_grid_texture"):
    if context.scene.objects.find(model_name) < 0:
        return
    obj = context.scene.objects[model_name]
    if obj.type != 'MESH':
        return

    obj_mesh = obj.data
    if not obj_mesh:
        return False

    if len(uv_map_name) < 1:
        uv_map_name = "uv_map"
```

```
uv_map_index = obj_mesh.uv_layers.find(uv_map_name)
if uv_map_index < 0:
    obj_mesh.uv_layers.new(name=uv_map_name)
    uv_map_index = obj_mesh.uv_layers.find(uv_map_name)

uv_map = obj_mesh.uv_layers[uv_map_name]
obj_mesh.uv_layers.active_index = uv_map_index

for o in context.view_layer.objects:
    o.select_set(False)
context.view_layer.objects.active = obj
obj.select_set(True)

viewport_context_override, override_successful = ↵
    get_context_override(context, 'VIEW_3D', 'WINDOW')
if override_successful:
    with bpy.context.temp_override( ↵
        **viewport_context_override):
        bpy.ops.object.mode_set(mode='EDIT')
else:
    return

viewport_context_override, override_successful = ↵
    get_context_override(context, 'VIEW_3D', 'WINDOW')
if override_successful:
    with bpy.context.temp_override( ↵
        **viewport_context_override):
        bpy.ops.mesh.select_all(action='SELECT')
        bpy.ops.uv.unwrap(method='ANGLE_BASED', ↵
            margin=0.001)
        bpy.ops.uv.minimize_stretch( ↵
            iterations=num_min_stretch_iterations)
else:
    return
```

```
uv_grid = None
if bpy.data.images.find(image_block_name) < 0 or ↵
    not bpy.data.images[image_block_name].has_data:
    uv_grid, uv_editor = ↵
        create_image_data_block( ↵
            context, image_block_name, ↵
            image_type='UV_GRID', ↵
            color=(0, 0, 0, 1), ↵
            image_filepath='', ↵
            display_image=True, ↵
            area_ui_type='UV')
    uv_editor.use_live_unwrap = True
    uv_editor.show_stretch = True
else:
    uv_grid = bpy.data.images[image_block_name]

create_material(obj, model_name + "_material", uv_grid)
bpy.ops.object.material_slot_assign()
config_viewport_materials(context)
```

First, the function looks up the object by the given model_name and checks that it is a mesh object (of type 'MESH') with valid data. Then, it checks whether a UV map slot (under Properties editor ➤ Data tab ➤ UV Maps) with the given uv_map_name exists—if not, it's created, and we set the active UV index to the index of this slot so when we unwrap next, the UVs are saved to this slot (obj_mesh.uv_layers.active_index = uv_map_index)

Then, to get the object (obj) ready to unwrap, we deselect all, set obj as the active object and select it, then switch it to Edit mode with a context override (as if from the viewport).

We'll now unwrap obj. We select obj in its entirety with bpy.ops.mesh. select_all(action='SELECT'), then call bpy.ops.uv.unwrap to unwrap and bpy.ops.uv.minimize_stretch to minimize stretch with the desired number of iterations.

Next, we'll call `create_image_data_block` (Listing 7-10) to create a UV grid image block `uv_grid` if one does not yet exist and display it in a UV Editor, with Live Unwrap and UV Stretch color view enabled. We then call `create_material` (Listing 7-11) to create a material node with `uv_grid` as the image texture and assign it to `obj` and call `config_viewport_materials` (Listing 7-12) to set viewport shading to Material Preview and enable backface culling. Figure 7-13 shows the results of running Listing 7-13 on a cube mesh.

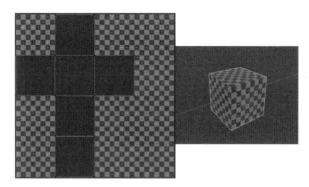

Figure 7-13. *Result of running Listing 7-13 on a cube mesh*

Saving to File

In this section, you'll learn how to export UVs you've already unwrapped as image files and how to write image data blocks to disk in general.

Exporting UV Layout

If you need to paint a texture using external image editing software, Blender has a handy feature that lets you export UV layouts to file to be used as "guided" canvases, so as you paint you can see which parts of the image would be mapped to which parts on the model. To do this, you can write a simple function like `export_uv_layout` shown in Listing 7-14. Open /Ch7/unwrap_model.py from the downloaded source to follow along.

Listing 7-14. Export a UV layout to file

```
def export_uv_layout(context, name, dirpath):
    image_editor_context_override, override_successful = ↵
        get_context_override(context, 'IMAGE_EDITOR', 'WINDOW')
    if override_successful:
        image_filepath = dirpath + '\\' + name + '.png'
        with bpy.context.temp_override( ↵
            **image_editor_context_override):
            bpy.ops.uv.export_layout( ↵
                filepath=image_filepath, ↵
                check_existing=True, ↵
                export_all=False, modified=False, ↵
                mode='PNG', size=(1024, 1024), ↵
                opacity=0.25)
```

The function forms a filepath to write the image out to (image_
filepath) using the given file name (name) and directory path (dirpath). It
then calls the operator bpy.ops.uv.export_layout with a context override
(as if from the UV Editor) to perform the export.

Let's go over the arguments for bpy.ops.uv.export_layout and see
what they do. When check_existing is True, a warning will be triggered
on an attempt to overwrite an existing file. The rest of the argument values
are the same as the default values shown on the right side of the file open
dialog when you click UV ➤ Export UV Layout in the UV Editor, as shown
in Figure 7-14.

Figure 7-14. *The file open dialog when you click UV ➤ Export UV Layout in the UV Editor. The file name as well as the options in the box on the right correspond to the arguments for the operator* bpy. ops.uv.export_layout

export_all=False (which corresponds to the All UVs box unchecked) will export only the visible portions of the UVs. modified=False (which corresponds to the Modified box unchecked) means not to export from the modified mesh. mode='PNG' (which corresponds to Format: PNG Image (.png) selected from the drop-down) creates a file in *.png format. size=(1024, 1024) (the two Size sliders) makes the size of the exported image 1024 by 2014, and lastly opacity=0.25 (the Opacity slider) will set the opacity of the exported layout at 25%. Figure 7-15 shows an example of a set of UVs exported to a PNG file by calling Listing 7-14.

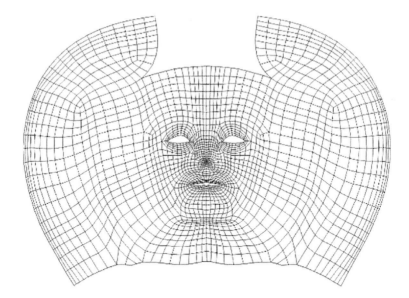

Figure 7-15. *Example of a set of UVs exported to a PNG file by calling Listing 7-14 using default argument values for* `bpy.ops.uv.export_layout`

Saving Image Data Block to File

When you press the +New button at the top of the UV or Image Editor, it creates a new image data block that only lives in memory. It's a good idea to save the data block out to a stand-alone image file on disk, which you'll also have access to outside of Blender. You can write a function like `save_image_to_file` shown in Listing 7-15 which writes an image data block with the given name to the given path in PNG format. Open /Ch7/ `create_and_save_images.py` from the downloaded source in the Text Editor to follow along.

Listing 7-15. Saving an image data block to file

```
def save_image_to_file(context, name, dirpath):
    if bpy.data.images.find(name) < 0:
        print("No image by the name " + name + " exists.")
        return

    image = bpy.data.images[name]
    image.filepath_raw = dirpath + '\\' + name + '.png'
    image.file_format = 'PNG'
    image.save()
```

Calling save_image_to_file has the same effect as Image ➤ Save As… in the UV or Image Editor. The function starts by checking that an image data block (image) with the given name exists; if so, it sets image.filepath_raw to a filepath formed by concatenating the given directory path (dirpath) with the name of the image file to write to (in .png extension). image.file_format is set to 'PNG', and the image is written out with image.save().

Summary

In this chapter, you visited every stage of the UV mapping workflow and learned how to automate its related tasks in Python. Before unwrapping a model, it's generally a good idea to strategically cut seams to minimize distortion in UVs—you reviewed the effects of seam placements on UV quality, learned to write a Python function to procedurally generate a cube mesh and cut its seams, then explored how it could potentially be generalized to generate and unwrap buildings, furniture, and other cuboid shaped models.

Users working with UVs often prefer multiple UV editors open alongside other areas so they can review how changes to a mesh affect its UVs and vice versa. You learned how to write scripts to split screen areas under the current context to open UV or Image editors and adjust their settings. You also learned how to differentiate between multiple open editors, how to zoom the UVs or images to the extent of an editor, and how to maximize a screen area.

In the second half of the chapter, you learned how to write functions to unwrap a model, create a material using shader nodes with an image texture hooked up and applied to the model, and configure viewport shading to preview it.

Lastly, you learned how to export UV layouts to file so they can be painted outside of Blender and wrote functions to create image data blocks by loading them from image files or generating UV/colored grids then writing them to disk.

CHAPTER 8

Texture Painting

In this chapter, I'll show you a cool but perhaps lesser-known feature in Blender: projection painting textures for a mesh by sampling from the same reference photos used to model it. I'll start by going over how the procedure works, then walk you through the steps to perform it by hand. Once you're familiar with the manual process, I'll show you how to automate its key stages with Blender Python. To wrap up the chapter, I'll discuss the pros and cons of using projection-painted textures over hand-painted ones and the types of scenarios suitable for each.

Running This Chapter's Examples

The source code for this book is available on GitHub via the book's product page, located at www.apress.com/979-8-8688-1126-5. This chapter's examples come in two versions. The first version is designed to run in the Text Editor and the second version installed as an extension add-on. Both versions contain the same implementation of the Projection Painting Helper extension we'll discuss throughout the chapter.

Setting Up/Running the Text Editor Version

Navigate to the /Ch8/text_editor folder in the downloaded source for the book, then the /4.2 subfolder if you are using Blender 4.2, or the /4.3 subfolder if you are using Blender 4.3. As you follow along the chapter, open the *.py file indicated by the text in the built-in Text Editor. At the

© Isabel Lupiani 2025
I. Lupiani, *Blender Scripting with Python*, https://doi.org/10.1007/979-8-8688-1127-2_8

bottom of each script, there is an `if __name__ == "__main__"` block already set up which invokes the code listings with sample arguments. You can easily experiment by changing these arguments.

Installing/Running the Extension Add-On Version

Go to Edit ➤ Preferences... ➤ Get Extensions, click the blue downward "v" at the upper right to expand the menu, and click *Install from Disk....* Navigate to the `Ch8/extension/projection_painting_helper_4.2(4.3)/` folder in the downloaded source if you're using Blender 4.2 (4.3), and choose the file `projection_painting_helper-2.0.0.zip`. The add-on "Projection Painting Helper" will be installed and automatically enabled. Once installed, you can access the add-on in the 3D Viewport *Properties* shelf (N key) ➤ *Tool* tab.

Handling Imports from Chapters 6 and 7

This chapter's scripts import functions from Chapters 6 and 7. These imports have been set up for you in the downloaded source. You can revisit Chapter 4 for detailed explanations on how to structure imports for both scripts run from the Text Editor and for packaged extensions. Chapter 7 describes an alternative for setting up imports to run in the Text Editor by copying scripts to your Blender installation to make them available as modules.

Utilizing Reference Images for Texture Painting

As you're probably already aware, in Texture Paint mode, you can use the Clone brush to sample from a source image to paint a texture with. Depending on the type of brush mapping used, the source image is sampled in different ways during the painting process. Projection painting works by using each reference photo as a source image and a corresponding UV mapping as the custom brush mapping for the Clone brush. As you move the Clone brush over the surface of the 3D model, Blender uses the designated UV mapping to determine where on the 2D reference photo (source image) to sample and copy pixels from.

For example, let's say you are creating a texture for a head mesh that you previously modeled from two reference photos (of the front and side views), and you'd like to use the Clone brush to sample from the same two photos to paint the texture with. You'd create two custom brush mappings to establish which parts of the photos correspond to which parts of the mesh surface—by unwrapping the mesh via projection from the same angle each reference photo is taken—once from the front and once from the side. If you've modeled a mesh using more than two photos, separate brush mappings can be created for any number of photos taken from different views.

In addition to creating UV maps by projecting from view, you'll need to seam and unwrap the model the usual way, irrespective of view. The UVs projected from view provide mappings between where the Clone brush would sample from the reference photos in relation to the surface of the 3D mesh. The UVs unwrapped irrespective of view create a mapping between where you are painting on the 3D mesh and the 2D texture you are painting onto.

Projection Painting Workflow by Hand

Now that you're familiar with how projection painting works at a conceptual level, let's dive into the nitty-gritty of Blender menu options for performing the process by hand. To summarize, the projection painting workflow consists of the following three steps:

1. Seam and unwrap the mesh to create a UV map, which describes how the 2D image texture you'll be painting will be applied to the surface of the 3D mesh.

2. Create a separate UV map for each reference photo by unwrapping the mesh with "Project From View" at the angle each photo is taken.

3. In Texture Paint mode, paint the 2D texture with the Clone brush using each reference photo as a source image and its corresponding UV map as the brush mapping, which tells Blender where on the reference photo to sample pixels from as you move the Clone brush over the surface of the 3D mesh.

Let's look at each of these steps in more detail in the next few sections. You can follow along using a mesh of your own that you also have the modeling reference photos for, or use the tortoise shell model (`/Ch8/sample_model/tortoise_shell.blend`) from the downloaded source and its corresponding reference photos `tortoise_front.jpg` and `tortoise_side.jpg`.

Note   The tortoise in the sample model and photos is Tiddles, the author's pet tortoise. Tiddles asks that you please not post her photos online without her permission.

You might be tempted to skip ahead to the next section to see how the workflow is automated—however, if you're seeing projection painting for the first time or haven't done it for a while, make sure to go through this section in its entirety at least once before diving into code, as this can be a difficult process to grasp. Load up a mesh and play with the various menu options as you follow along—it will really help drive the concept home.

We'll start by heading over to the UV Editing workspace, which will give you a nice side-by-side view of the texture, UVs, and the mesh as you go through the unwrapping process.

Step #1: Seam and Unwrap Your Model

The first step is to mark seams on your model and unwrap it. In Edit mode, ensure Edge select is on, select edges to be marked as seams, and use Mesh ➤ Edges (or Ctrl-E) ➤ Mark Seam to mark them. Toggle the A key to select the mesh in its entirety, and use U key ➤ Unwrap to unwrap. Create and name a new image overall_uv_texture in the UV Editor to sit under the unwrapped UVs—you'll use this image to texture the mesh later. Go to Properties editor ➤ Data tab ➤ UV Maps, and double left-click to rename the corresponding UV map slot from the default name UVMap to overall_uv. Figure 8-1 shows an example of the tortoise shell mesh from the downloaded source seamed and unwrapped with its UVs renamed to overall_uv.

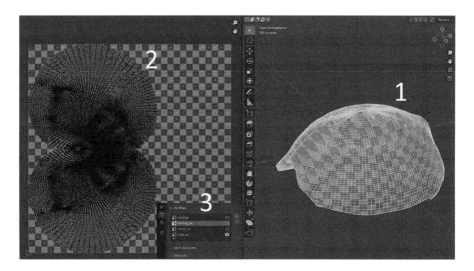

Figure 8-1. *(1) The tortoise shell mesh from the downloaded source (2) seamed and unwrapped, with (3) its UV map renamed to overall_ uv (screenshot of Properties editor ➤ Data tab ➤ UV maps is cropped and collaged here to show the UV slots)*

Tip   Since you'll be using multiple UV maps during projection painting, try and give the images' and UV maps' descriptive names, so it's easier to keep track and tell them apart during the painting process.

Step #2: Unwrap by "Project From View" to Create a Separate UV Map for Each Reference Photo

The second step is to create a separate UV map for each reference photo you want to projection paint the texture with, so Blender knows where on the photo to sample pixels from when you move the Clone brush over the model.

Tab into Edit mode in the 3D Viewport. For each reference photo, you'll create a new UV map slot, then unwrap the mesh into the slot by projecting from the same view the photo was taken at. Go to Properties editor ➤ Data tab ➤ UV Maps, and add a new UV map slot by clicking the "+" button on the right. Double left-click the slot to rename it to something descriptive of the view so it's easier to identify later—for example, front_uv for the frontal profile photo. Make sure the slot is selected—whichever slot is selected is where the next set of UVs will unwrap to (it'll be highlighted if it's selected, otherwise left-click to select it). Open the reference photo in the UV Editor. Change the view of the mesh in the viewport to match the view angle of the photo (e.g., 1 for Front to match a frontal profile photo) while using the +/- key to zoom in/out as necessary. Toggle the A key to select the mesh in its entirety and U key ➤ Project From View to unwrap—you should see a new set of UVs appear over the reference photo in the UV Editor that look like a snapshot of the mesh in its current view in wireframe.

Since Blender will use the UVs unwrapped from view for mapping the reference photo to the mesh surface, it's important to edit the UVs so they line up well with the subject in the photo. With the cursor inside the UV Editor, tab A to select the UVs in full then G to grab, move the UVs until they center on the subject, and left-click to confirm. Edit the UVs as if you're editing a mesh object, with operations such as scale (S) and rotate (R). Repeat the same steps for every reference photo that you used to model the mesh with and intend to sample from during projection painting. Figure 8-2 shows an example of unwrapping the tortoise shell model (/Ch8/sample_model/tortoise_shell.blend) from the left view (Ctrl-Numpad 3) and editing the corresponding UVs to match the reference photo /Ch8/sample_model/tortoise_side.jpg.

Figure 8-2. *(1) The tortoise shell mesh from the downloaded source unwrapped in the left view (Ctrl-Numpad 3) via U key ➤ Project From View. (2) The unedited side UVs immediately after unwrapping. (3) The side UVs edited to match the reference photo*

Step #3: Projection Paint with Clone Brush Using Each <Reference Photo, UV Map> Pairing

The final step is to paint the image overall_uv_texture from step #1 using the Clone brush, with each reference photo as a source image, and the UVs unwrapped from that photo's view as the brush mapping. Recall that overall_uv_texture is the image that'll be used to texture the mesh.

First, switch the image in the UV editor to overall_uv_texture, and switch the mesh object in the viewport to Texture Paint mode (alternatively, you can switch from the UV Editing workspace to the Texture Paint workspace). We'll now configure options for the Clone brush's "painting target." In the viewport, click the Clone brush button in the Tool shelf (T key) to select it. Click the image menu at the top to expand it, as shown in Figure 8-3; in the Mode drop-down, choose Single Image. In the image-open dialog, open overall_uv_texture as the image (this is the canvas that will be painted on). In the next drop-down, select overall_uv, then Closest for the interpolation method. Recall that overall_uv is the set of UVs we unwrapped from the whole model irrespective of view and overall_uv_texture is the image we'll use to texture the model.

Next, we'll configure the Clone brush's sampling source. Under Properties shelf (N key) ➤ Tool tab, locate the settings for the Clone brush, then check the "Clone from Paint Slot" check box, which will expand the submenu to reveal two more options: Source Clone Image and Source Clone UV Map. This is where the reference photo and the UV projected from the corresponding view get paired up: the front reference photo is matched with UVs projected from the front view, and so on. For the sample tortoise shell model, you'll use the pairing <tortoise_front.jpg, front_uv>, and <tortoise_side.jpg, side_uv>.

To preview the texture on the model in the viewport as you paint, you'll need to create a material with overall_uv_texture as the image texture and apply it to the mesh. You can do so by selecting the mesh, going to the Properties editor ➤ Material tab, and creating a new material, as shown in Figure 8-4. Under the new material, set Surface to Principled BSDF, click Base Color to expand the menu and click Image Texture, then open overall_uv_texture as the image.

I find that a starting brush radius of 100 px with strength 1.000 and the stroke set to Airbrush with rate 1.000 (as shown in Figure 8-5) work well for projection painting—since we're not doing detailed work but rather transferring pixels from the reference images in broad strokes. Feel free to play around with these settings and see what works best for your particular images.

With all the settings in place for the Clone brush, you are now ready to try painting. Move the brush over the 3D mesh and use LMB to paint—you should see strokes appear that look like pixels from the reference photo being spray painted onto the surface of the mesh, as if blobs of the reference photo are stretched and smoothed over the mesh. Figure 8-6 shows an example of a texture projection painted using the tortoise shell mesh (tortoise.blend) and its two reference photos (tortoise_front.jpg and tortoise_side.jpg), using UVs unwrapped from their corresponding views (front and left).

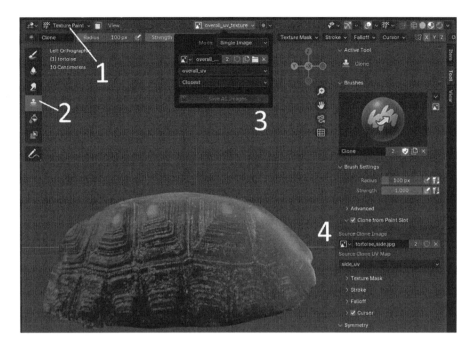

Figure 8-3. *Configure the Clone brush mapping for projection painting (1) Switch to Texture Paint mode in the viewport. (2) Click the Clone brush button in the Tool shelf to select it. (3) Click the image menu at the top to expand it; in the Mode drop-down, choose Single Image, and open overall_uv_texture as the image (this is the canvas that will be painted onto). In the next drop-down, select overall_uv, then Closest for interpolation. (4) Under the Properties shelf (N key) ➤ Tool tab, check the "Clone from Paint Slot" check box; then, for Source Clone Image and Source Clone UV Map, select a reference photo paired with the UV projected from its matching view*

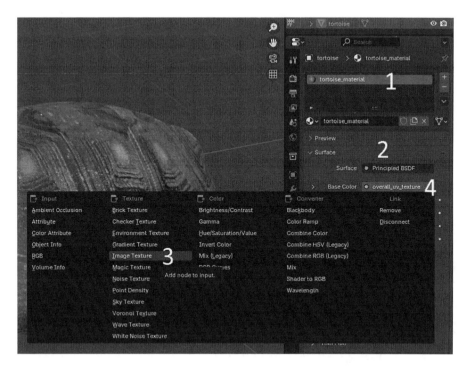

Figure 8-4. *Creating a material with overall_uv_texture as image texture and applying it to the mesh. (1) Go to Properties editor ➤ Material tab, and create a new material. (2) Set Surface to Principled BSDF. (3) Click Base Color to expand the menu, and select Image Texture. (4) Open overall_uv_texture as the image for the texture*

388

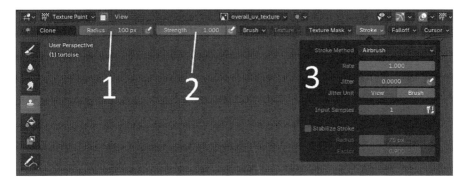

Figure 8-5. *Configuring Clone brush size and stroke settings for projection painting. (1) Brush radius = 100 px. (2) Strength = 1.000. (3) Under the Stroke menu, set Stroke Method to Airbrush and Rate to 1.000*

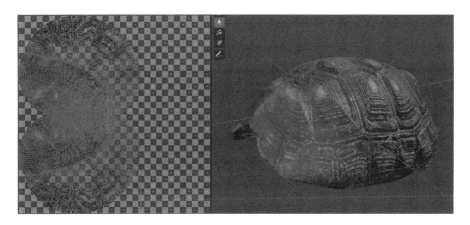

Figure 8-6. *overall_uv_texture projection painted for the sample tortoise mesh using its two reference photos, tortoise_front.jpg and tortoise_side.jpg*

Designing a Projection Painting Helper Extension

Now that you've familiarized yourself with projection painting by either experimenting with a mesh of your own or the sample tortoise mesh, it's time to switch gears and think about how to design an extension that will streamline this process using the Blender Python API.

Extension Structural Design

Instead of diving headfirst into code, I'd like to pause for a moment and show you how I approached the add-on design—by analyzing the manual workflow to isolate tasks that are suitable for automation, turning those tasks into operators, then assembling the operators into an add-on.

Dividing Tasks into Logical Groupings

Recall that the manual workflow consists of the following steps—mark seams and unwrap the mesh, unwrap by projecting from each photo's view, edit the UVs to match, and projection paint from each view. We'll assume that the user will mark the seams themselves and focus on the unwrapping and painting portions of the process. As we group the remaining tasks that are similar in nature—such as all the painting tasks in one group, potential operators will start to take shape. With this strategy, we end up with the following three groups:

1. The group with the UV mapping tasks: unwrap overall, unwrap from the front, and unwrap from side view.

2. The UV editing group: edit front UVs to match the front photo and side UVs to match the side photo.

3. The painting group: projection paint from the front view and the side view.

Assessing Which Groups of Tasks Are Suitable for Automation

You've already mastered the automation of UV Mapping tasks from Chapter 7, so we're well on our way to implementing the first group. The "unwrap from view" tasks are similar, except that the viewport view needs to be adjusted prior to unwrapping, which I'll show you how later in this chapter.

Since the UV editing tasks require computer vision techniques to recognize features and their locations and boundaries in the photos, they're difficult to automate, and we likely won't get the UVs and photos aligned to the level of precision we're after, we'll have the users manually edit the UVs. However, as a compromise, we can add some helpful features such as automatically display the reference photo corresponding to the view we're unwrapping in the UV Editor, as shown in Figure 8-2, so users can start aligning the UVs to the photos right away after the add-on unwraps them.

As you've seen in previous sections, a lot of settings need to be configured before you can start projection painting, like setting up material and texture on the mesh, setting the target texture to paint on, selecting the clone source image and UVs, and so on—it'll be convenient if the add-on can take care of these so all you have to do is press a couple buttons to start painting. Therefore, we'll focus on implementing the painting tasks as helper tools that will configure all the required settings for you before painting can start.

Formulating Tasks into Operators

Since it makes sense to unwrap and edit one set of UVs at a time, each of the three unwrap tasks should be implemented as its own operator. Structuring the operators this way also allows users to independently reset a set of UVs by calling one of the operators without affecting other UVs that have already been edited.

Since there's almost always some overlap between the views covered by different reference photos—for example, the forehead is seen in both the frontal and side profile views of a face—it's natural for a user to do a few strokes at a time, switch back and forth between the views, and blend the results. The user will need to check from time to time what strokes laid down in one view look like when seen from the other view as well. Therefore, it makes sense to implement painting from each view as its own operator. Since many models have lateral symmetry, using Suzanne's orientation (the built-in monkey mesh), we assume that the mesh would be mirrored across the left and right views. With this in mind, it would be convenient to have an operator that flips the view from one side of the model to the other. With this division of responsibility, we end up with the design of five operators, as shown in Figure 8-7.

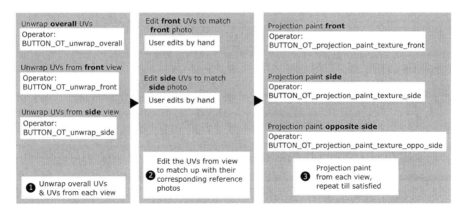

Figure 8-7. *Formulating projection painting tasks as operators*

Using an Operator's `poll` Method to Enforce Prerequisites

You can think of the work done by each group of operators in Figure 8-7 as the prerequisite of the group after it. For example, you can only paint from a view after the mesh has been unwrapped from that view. You can check for these prerequisites in an operator's poll method and disable it if they're not fulfilled. For example, you can check in the BUTTON_OT_unwrap_ overall operator's poll method whether there's a valid mesh selected and if not return False to inform Blender to disable the operator and gray out its button. This strategy will prevent errors such as an operator trying to unwrap a mesh that isn't there and communicate to users that something is preventing an operator from running, which needs to be addressed before it can be used.

Extension User Interface Design

With the add-on's operators planned out, let's take a moment and think about how to lay out the UI components for accessing them. We'll need one menu entry or button for each of the five operators and various bpy. props Property type instances for user input. We'll also need a dropper tool for selecting a mesh in the viewport to unwrap. We'll make some decisions on which operator parameters should be user-configurable, and go over the code for adding input widgets and operators to the UI panel as buttons.

Deciding Which Parameter to Let Users Customize

Since there are numerous options available with each of the tasks we're trying to automate and they can't all fit into the UI panel, we need to decide which ones stay and which ones go—too many options make the add-on tedious or difficult to use, and too few options restrict the type of scenarios the add-on is useful for. For unwrapping, I decided to let users specify the number of iterations to minimize stretch (UVs ➤ Minimize Stretch or Ctrl-V in the UV Editor), the direction (LEFT or RIGHT) for the side view, and the names for the three sets of UVs to be unwrapped, as shown in Figure 8-8.

Letting users specify names for the UV maps is certainly optional, and you can get away with a simpler design; however, it does offer some advantages—for example, users can prevent default names from clashing with names of other UV maps they're already editing and ensure that the names are consistent with the convention they're using. By specifying default names as default values for the `StringProperty` instances, they're displayed in the text boxes as shown in Figure 8-8 when the add-on is loaded up, which also communicates to the users what the default names are.

Assuming that "front" aligns with Front view (Numpad 1) in Blender, then "side" could mean either Left (Ctrl-Numpad 3) or Right (Numpad 3). Since it is not clear which, we'll ask the user to explicitly select a direction through the Side Dir drop-down in Figure 8-8, which is implemented as a `bpy.props.EnumProperty` instance, which we've seen in Chapter 2.

Figure 8-8. *User interface for the Projection Painting Helper extension. Note that the three unwrap buttons are grayed out due to their* poll *methods detecting that no mesh is selected. The three projection painting buttons are grayed out since no UVs have been unwrapped*

Creating a Dropper Tool for Selecting a Mesh in the 3D Viewport

To create a widget for selecting a mesh object in the viewport, we'll use a
bpy.props.PointerProperty instance (Listing 8-1) to create a dropper
tool with a drop-down populated with objects in the scene (like we've seen
in Chapter 6).

Listing 8-1. Using a PointerProperty instance with a custom poll
function to create a mesh selection dropper tool that also provides a
drop-down (see /Ch8/extension/projection_painting_helpe_4.2(4.3)
r/__init__.py)

```
def init_scene_vars():
    bpy.types.Scene.select_mesh = bpy.props.PointerProperty(
        name="Mesh to Unwrap",
        type=bpy.types.Object,
        poll=poll_select_mesh_filter)
```

The PointerProperty instance by default lets you select *objects of any
type*. Since we want the user to select a mesh for unwrapping, we want
to allow only meshes—we can do so by creating a custom poll function
(Listing 8-2) and assigning it to the PointerProperty instance's poll
argument.

Listing 8-2. Custom poll function that checks whether the passed-in
object is a mesh (see /Ch8/extension/projection_painting_
helpe_4.2(4.3)r/__init__.py)

```
def poll_select_mesh_filter(self, object):
    return object.type == 'MESH'
```

Adding Input Widgets to the UI Panel

In addition to PointerProperty, we use three `bpy.props` types to gather inputs for Projection Painting Helper's UI panel: an `EnumProperty` for the side direction (Side Dir) drop-down, an `IntProperty` for the Minimize Stretch Iterations slider, and three `StringProperty` instances for entering UV map names. Please revisit Chapters 2, 5, and 6 for detailed explanations on how to create widgets with these `bpy.props` types.

Adding Operators to the UI Panel As Buttons

You can add any operators as buttons to a `bpy.types.Panel` using the following syntax:.

```
<sub-layout>.operator(<operator's bl_idname>, ↵
    text=<(optional) text to display instead of bl_idname>, ↵
    icon=<(optional) Enum value to identify icon>)
```

`<sub-layout>` is any UI element of type `bpy.types.UILayout`, like the box, row, and column you used to put together the UI panel in Chapter 2. By default, an operator's `bl_idname` is displayed on the button, which can be optionally replaced by the argument `text`. You can add an icon to the button through the optional `icon` argument—to see a list of all `Enum` values for specifying `icon` types, see Chapter 2.

For example, I used the following line of code to add the `BUTTON_OT_unwrap_overall` operator to the Projection Painting Helper extension's UI panel `PROJECTION_PAINTING_HELPER_PT_PANEL`, with the UV icon and the text 'Unwrap Overall UV', as shown in Figure 8-8.

```
box0.operator("button.unwrap_overall", ↵
    text="Unwrap Overall UV", icon='UV')
```

All other buttons shown in Figure 8-8 are added to the panel in a similar fashion.

Making an Operator to Unwrap the Selected Mesh

Recall in Chapter 7, we implemented the function `unwrap_model` (Listing 7-13) to unwrap a given mesh and apply a UV grid texture to it for previewing in the viewport. We will reuse this function to implement the `BUTTON_OT_unwrap_overall` (Listing 8-6) operator, with some modifications to how we set the images to display in UV Editors.

Setting the Image to Display in (All Open) UV Editors

When a mesh has multiple unwrapped UVs under Properties editor ➤ Data tab ➤ UV Maps, there are two "active" selections you have to make: the first is the Active UV Map Index, which is the UV map highlighted in the list, and the second is the Active Render, which is the UV Map with the "camera" icon toggled on, as shown in Figure 8-9. The two selections are independent of one another, meaning you can set them to two different UV maps.

The Active UV Map Index tells Blender which UV map to display in any open UV Editor (if there are multiple UV Editors open, the same UV map is displayed across all of them). The Active Render controls which UV map is used for Material Preview on the object in the 3D Viewport.

With our purpose to projection paint, once we set the Active UV Map Index to the UVs of the associated view, we want the corresponding reference photo to show under the UVs in any UV Editor. While we're painting, we want to set the Active UV Map Index to `overall_uv` and the image in the UV Editor to the `overall_uv_texture` (the texture we're painting).

The function `set_image_in_uv_editors` in Listing 8-3 takes a given image data block and sets it as the image displayed in all open UV Editors. If there is no UV Editor open, `set_image_in_uv_editors` splits the screen to open one and sets the given image as the newly opened UV Editor's image.

Listing 8-3. Setting a given image as the display image in all open UV Editors (or split the screen to open one if none is yet open) (see /Ch8/extension/projection_painting_helper_4.2(4.3)/unwrap_model.py)

```
def set_image_in_uv_editors(context, image):
    override = context.copy()
    found_uv_editor = False
    for area in context.screen.areas:
        if area.type=='IMAGE_EDITOR' and area.ui_type=='UV':
            for space in area.spaces:
                if space.type=='IMAGE_EDITOR':
                    space.image = image
                    space.uv_editor.use_live_unwrap = True
                    space.uv_editor.show_stretch = True
                    found_uv_editor = True

                    override['area'] = area
                    for region in override['area'].regions:
                        if region.type=='WINDOW':
                            override['region'] = region
                            break
                    with bpy.context.temp_override(**override):
                        bpy.ops.image.view_all(fit_view=True)

    if not found_uv_editor:
        uv_editor_area = split_screen_area(context, ↵
            'VERTICAL', 0.5, 'IMAGE EDITOR', 'UV', False)
        override['area'] = uv_editor_area
        for s in uv_editor_area.spaces:
            if s.type=='IMAGE_EDITOR':
                s.image = image
```

```
            s.uv_editor.use_live_unwrap = True
            s.uv_editor.show_stretch = True
            break

    for region in override['area'].regions:
        if region.type=='WINDOW':
            override['region'] = region
            break
    with bpy.context.temp_override(**override):
        bpy.ops.image.view_all(fit_view=True)
```

Recall from Chapter 7, we can identify UV Editors under the passed-in context by area.type=='IMAGE_EDITOR' and area.ui_type=='UV'. The space s of type 'IMAGE_EDITOR' under that area is then the space containing the UV Editor (s.uv_editor). We can change the image that UV Editor displays via s.image (note that the image is stored under the space s itself, not s.uv_editor). We can also set certain UV Editor options through s.uv_editor, such as UV ➤ Live Unwrap (s.uv_editor.use_live_unwrap) and Overlays ➤ UV Stretch (s.uv_editor.show_stretch).

Since we want to afford users the convenience of editing UVs to match the underlying reference photo straight away, it would be nice that once we set which image to display in the UV Editors, the images also zoom automatically to fit the extent of each Editor. For this reason, each time we find a UV Editor and set its image, we also edit a copy of the passed-in context based on that Editor so we can use it to call bpy.ops.image.view_all(fit_view=True) and zoom the image to fit that Editor.

Figure 8-9. *Setting the Active UV Map Index and Active Render under Properties editor ➤ Data tab ➤ UV Maps. In this example, the (1) Active UV Map Index is set to side_uv, whereas the (2) Active Render is set to front_uv*

Modifying How `unwrap_model` Sets Images in UV Editors

With set_image_in_uv_editors (Listing 8-3) implemented, we will now use it to customize unwrap_model from Chapter 7 so we can reuse it to create an operator. The final block of unwrap_model from Listing 7-13 is reproduced in Listing 8-4, with the modifications marked in bold.

Listing 8-4. Excerpt of unwrap_model where we modify how images are displayed in UV Editors and adjust the view of the selected mesh in the viewport (see /Ch8/extension/projection_painting_ helper_4.2(4.3)/unwrap_model.py)

```
uv_grid = None
if bpy.data.images.find(image_block_name) < 0 or ↩
    not bpy.data.images[image_block_name].has_data:
    uv_grid, _ = create_image_data_block(context, ↩
        image_block_name, image_type='UV_GRID', ↩
        color=(0, 0, 0, 1), image_filepath='', ↩
        display_image=False)
else:
    uv_grid = bpy.data.images[image_block_name]
```

```
set_image_in_uv_editors(context, uv_grid)
create_material(obj, model_name + "_material", uv_grid)
bpy.ops.object.material_slot_assign()
config_viewport_materials(context)

viewport_context_override, override_successful = ↵
    get_context_override(context, 'VIEW_3D', 'WINDOW')
if override_successful:
    with bpy.context.temp_override( ↵
        **viewport_context_override):
        bpy.ops.view3d.view_selected(use_all_regions=False)
```

We pass display_image=False in the call to create_image_data_
block (Listing 7-10) so it no longer handles image display in UV Editors.
Instead, we call set_image_in_uv_editors (Listing 8-3) to do so. At the
end of unwrap_model, we call bpy.ops.view3d.view_selected with a
context override (as if from the viewport) so it frames the view on the
currently selected object in the viewport (in this case, the object that's just
been unwrapped).

Adding Runtime Exception Handling to `apply_all_` `modifiers`

Recall from Chapter 7 that in general, we should apply any modifiers that
alter geometry before unwrapping UVs. For this purpose, we implemented
the function apply_all_modifiers (Listing 7-1), which worked well
except in the case when a modifier cannot be applied (such as a Sub surf
modifier that has levels set to 0). Calling bpy.ops.object.modifier_apply
in such a case will cause a RuntimeError. In Listing 8-5, we make a simple
improvement where we catch the RuntimeError in a try/except block,
then skip the modifier and continue.

Listing 8-5. Excerpt of `apply_all_modifiers` (Listing 7-1) where we add runtime exception handling for modifiers that cannot be applied (see /Ch8/extension/projection_painting_helper_4.2(4.3)/ apply_modifiers.py)

```
for m in obj_to_apply_modifier.modifiers:
    try:
        bpy.ops.object.modifier_apply(modifier=m.name)
    except RuntimeError:
        continue
```

> **Note**   Some modifiers alter an object at the geometry level. If not applied before unwrapping, the resulting UVs may not accurately reflect the changes to the mesh introduced by the modifiers. For example, if a Solidify modifier is not applied before unwrapping, the UVs might not account for the extra thickness it adds to the mesh.

Implementing the BUTTON_OT_unwrap_overall Operator

With the modifications to `apply_all_modifiers` and `unwrap_model` ready, we can compose those two functions to create an operator to unwrap UVs, as shown in Listing 8-6.

Listing 8-6. Implementing an operator to unwrap overall UVs (see / Ch8/extension/projection_painting_helper_4.2(4.3)/__init__.py)

```
class BUTTON_OT_unwrap_overall(Operator):
    bl_idname = "button.unwrap_overall"
    bl_label = "Unwrap Overall UV"
    """Unwrap Overall UV for the Selected Mesh"""
```

```
def execute(self, context):
    apply_all_modifiers(context, context.scene.select_mesh)
    unwrap_model(context, ↵
        context.scene.select_mesh.name, ↵
        context.scene.uv_min_stretch_iterations, ↵
        context.scene.uv_name_overall, ↵
        context.scene.uv_name_overall+"_texture")
    self.report({'INFO'}, ↵
        "Projection Painting Helper: Mesh ↵
            overall UV unwrapped.")
    return {'FINISHED'}

@classmethod
def poll(cls, context):
    return True if context.scene.select_mesh else False
```

First, we call apply_all_modifiers (Listing 8-5) on the mesh selected
with the dropper tool context.scene.select_mesh so all modifiers on
its stack are applied. Then, we call unwrap_model (Listing 8-4) with the
selected mesh's name, the number of UV stretch iterations from the int
slider, and the name for the overall UV typed in by the user. Note that we
overrode BUTTON_OT_unwrap_overall's poll method so it returns True if
the dropper tool selected mesh is valid and False otherwise.

The @classmethod line above the poll method is required as it tells
Python to call classmethod(poll) under the hood—this turns poll into
a method that is associated with the class itself instead of individual
instances. The class type is passed as a first argument instead of self.

Tip   The @<function> mechanism in Listing 8-6 is called
a *decorator* in Python. When you place it above another
function's definition (let's call it function1), it tells Python to
call <function>(function1) instead of function1, when
function1 is called.

Making Operators to Unwrap the Selected Mesh via "Project From View"

Next, you'll implement two operators for unwrapping the selected mesh by projecting from the front and the side (left or right) view, respectively.

Implementing the Core Functionality of the Unwrap from View Operators in a Function

Since the two unwrap from view operators will have almost identical functionalities, you'll delegate the unwrapping to the function unwrap_by_ projecting_from_view (Listing 8-7), then call this function from each of the two operators with its respective view as an argument.

Listing 8-7. Unwrapping a given mesh via Project From View (see /Ch8/extension/projection_painting_helper_4.2(4.3)/unwrap_ by_project_from_view.py)

```
def unwrap_by_projecting_from_view(context, ↩
    obj_to_unwrap_name, view, uv_map_name, ↩
    image_block_name):
    if bpy.data.objects.find(obj_to_unwrap_name) < 0:
        return False
```

```python
obj_to_unwrap = bpy.data.objects[obj_to_unwrap_name]

if obj_to_unwrap.type != 'MESH':
    return False

obj_mesh = obj_to_unwrap.data
if not obj_mesh:
    return False

if len(uv_map_name) < 1:
    uv_map_name = "uv_map"

uv_map_index = obj_mesh.uv_layers.find(uv_map_name)
if uv_map_index < 0:
    obj_mesh.uv_layers.new(name=uv_map_name)
    uv_map_index = obj_mesh.uv_layers.find(uv_map_name)

uv_map = obj_mesh.uv_layers[uv_map_name]
uv_map.active_render = True
obj_mesh.uv_layers.active_index = uv_map_index

apply_all_modifiers(context, obj_to_unwrap)

override, co_successful = get_context_override( ↵
    context, 'VIEW_3D', 'WINDOW')
if co_successful:
    with bpy.context.temp_override(**override):
        bpy.ops.object.mode_set(mode='EDIT')

override, co_successful = get_context_override( ↵
    context, 'VIEW_3D', 'WINDOW')
```

```
if co_successful:
    with bpy.context.temp_override(**override):
        bpy.ops.mesh.select_all(action='SELECT')
        bpy.ops.view3d.view_selected(use_all_regions=False)

override, co_successful = get_context_override( ↵
    context, 'VIEW_3D', 'WINDOW')
if co_successful:
    with bpy.context.temp_override(**override):
        bpy.ops.view3d.view_axis(type=view, ↵
            align_active=False)

for a in context.window.screen.areas:
    if a.type=='VIEW_3D':
        for s in a.spaces:
            if s.type=='VIEW_3D':
                s.region_3d.update()

override, co_successful = get_context_override( ↵
    context, 'VIEW_3D', 'WINDOW')
if co_successful:
    with bpy.context.temp_override(**override):
        bpy.ops.uv.project_from_view( ↵
            (camera_bounds=False, correct_aspect=True, ↵
                scale_to_bounds=False)

override, co_successful = get_context_override( ↵
    context, 'VIEW_3D', 'WINDOW')
if co_successful:
    with bpy.context.temp_override(**override):
        bpy.ops.uv.select_all(action='SELECT')
```

```
uv_grid = None
if bpy.data.images.find(image_block_name) < 0 or ↩
    not bpy.data.images[image_block_name].has_data:
    uv_grid, _ = create_image_data_block(context, ↩
        image_block_name, image_type='UV_GRID', ↩
        color=(0, 0, 0, 1), image_filepath='', ↩
        display_image=False)
else:
    uv_grid = bpy.data.images[image_block_name]

set_image_in_uv_editors(context, uv_grid)
bpy.ops.object.material_slot_assign()
config_viewport_materials(context)

return True
```

unwrap_by_projecting_from_view has five arguments—context, name of the object to unwrap, the view, name of the UV map to unwrap to, and the name of the image block to display in the UV Editors under the unwrapped UVs.

The function starts by checking that the object to unwrap exists and is a mesh object with valid data. If so, it proceeds to look up the UV map index based on the given UV map name, which is the UV slot we'll be unwrapping into. If not found, a new slot is created with that name. Recall the UV map index is the index into the list under Properties editor ➤ Data tab ➤ UV Maps. Note that if the given UV map name is an empty string, the function defaults it to "uv_map".

Next, you'll get a reference to the UV map itself instead of its slot index via obj_mesh.uv_layers[uv_map_name], through which you'll set the map's Active Render to True (this is equivalent to toggling on its "camera" icon under Properties editor ➤ Data tab ➤ UV Maps). You'll also select this UV map as the current active via obj_mesh.uv_layers.active_index = uv_map_index so it will be the slot the next unwrapping goes to (this is the same as highlighting it under Properties editor ➤ Data tab ➤ UV Maps). You'll then call `apply_all_modifiers` (Listings 7-1 and 8-5) to apply the modifiers on `obj_to_unwrap`'s stack.

With the UV slot configured, switch the object to Edit mode with a context override as if from the viewport; then, after the mode switching is complete, select all and adjust view to frame selected (`bpy.ops.view3d.view_selected`) with a separate override. After that, you'll set the viewport to the correct view to get ready for unwrapping, by calling `bpy.ops.view3d.view_axis(type=view, align_active=False)`. For our purpose to projection paint, `view` will be either `'FRONT'`, or `'LEFT'`, or `'RIGHT'`. Note that you have to force a viewport update for the view change to take effect via the following block of code, where you iterate through the nested screen hierarchy under the passed-in context, locate the space `s` under the viewport, and call `s.region_3d.update()`.

You can now unwrap via Project From View, by calling `bpy.ops.uv.project_from_view` with a context override (as if from the viewport). You then call `bpy.ops.uv.select_all(action='SELECT')` so the UVs are selected and ready to be edited.

Following the unwrapping, you'll look up the image block passed in and call `set_image_in_uv_editors` (Listing 8-3) to display it in the UV Editors. From the two unwrap from view operators that you'll create shortly, the image block will be the reference photo that corresponds to the view you project to unwrap from. If the reference photo doesn't exist, a UV grid image is created as a fallback. You'll ensure the material is assigned and the viewport configured to Material Preview (`config_viewport_materials`, Listing 7-12) before returning.

Implementing the Unwrap from View Operators

With the core functionality to unwrap from a given view implemented in `unwrap_by_projecting_from_view` (Listing 8-7), you can now create two operators to unwrap from the front and side views simply by calling

Listing 8-7 with the respective view. We'll look at how to create the operator for unwrapping from the front, BUTTON_OT_unwrap_front, in Listing 8-8, then modify it to create the other operator.

Listing 8-8. Creating an operator to unwrap from the front view (see /Ch8/extension/projection_painting_helper_4.2(4.3)/__init__.py)

```
class BUTTON_OT_unwrap_front(Operator):
    bl_idname = "button.unwrap_front"
    bl_label = "Unwrap Front UV"
    """Unwrap UV for the Selected Mesh from the Front View"""

    def execute(self, context):
        if len(context.scene.uv_name_front) < 1:
            context.scene.uv_name_front = "front_uv"

        front_empty = context.scene.image_empties[ ↵
            front_empty_name]
        front_image_name = front_empty.data.name if ↵
            front_empty and front_empty.data else ↵
            context.scene.uv_name_front+"_texture"
        unwrap_by_projecting_from_view(context, ↵
            context.scene.select_mesh.name, 'FRONT', ↵
            context.scene.uv_name_front, front_image_name)

        self.report({'INFO'}, ↵ "Projection Painting
        Helper: Face
            mesh front UV unwrapped.")
        return {'FINISHED'}

    @classmethod
    def poll(cls, context):
        return True if context.scene.select_mesh else False
```

Coming up in the next section, we'll call load_image_empty (Listing 6-3) to implement operators for users to load reference photos, then use a scene variable to keep track of them, allowing us to simply look up the front view image empty (which holds the front reference photo), and call unwrap_by_projecting_from_view (Listing 8-7) with it. We also override the poll method here so BUTTON_OT_unwrap_front is only enabled if the user selected mesh is valid. Figure 8-10 shows an example of calling BUTTON_OT_unwrap_front to unwrap the sample tortoise shell mesh from the front view.

To create the BUTTON_OT_unwrap_side operator, you'll modify Listing 8-8 to look up the side image empty instead. For the view argument you pass the value the user selects via the "Side Dir" drop-down context. scene.uv_name_side.

```
side_empty = context.scene.image_empties[side_empty_name]
side_image_name = side_empty.data.name if side_empty and ↵
    side_empty.data else context.scene.uv_name_side+"_texture"
unwrap_by_projecting_from_view(context, ↵
    context.scene.select_mesh.name, context.scene.side_dir, ↵
    context.scene.uv_name_side, side_image_name)
```

Figure 8-10. *(1) The tortoise shell mesh from the downloaded source (2) unwrapped in the front view (Ctrl-Numpad 1) via U key ➤ Project From View. (3) The front UVs edited to match the reference photo*

Making Operators to Open Reference Photos

To provide users the means of importing reference photos, you'll use load_
image_empty (Listing 6-3) to implement two operators—one for creating
the front image empty (IMPORT_OT_open_front_ref in Listing 8-9) and one
for creating the side empty (IMPORT_OT_open_side_ref).

411

Listing 8-9. Creating a front view reference photo empty (see /Ch8/
extension/projection_painting_helper_4.2(4.3)/__init__.py)

```
class IMPORT_OT_open_front_ref(Operator, ImportHelper):
    bl_idname = "import.open_front_ref"
    bl_label = "Open front ref image"
    """Load front reference image file."""

    def execute(self, context):
        empty_loc = context.scene.select_mesh.location if ↵
            context.scene.select_mesh else (0,0,0)
        if bpy.data.objects.find(front_empty_name) >= 0:
            bpy.data.objects.remove( ↵
                bpy.data.objects[front_empty_name])
        load_image_empty(context, front_empty_name, ↵
            self.filepath, empty_loc, [90,0,0], ↵
            'DEFAULT', 'DOUBLE_SIDED', 1.0)
        context.scene.image_empties[front_empty_name] = ↵
            bpy.data.objects[front_empty_name]
        context.scene.image_empties[front_empty_name]. ↵
            hide_set(True)

        self.report({'INFO'}, "Projection Painting ↵
            Helper loaded frontal ref: " +
            self.filepath)
        return {'FINISHED'}
```

Note that in addition to Operator, IMPORT_OT_open_front_ref inherits
from ImportHelper, which provides the file open dialog when the operator
is invoked. The operator defaults the empty's location to the selected
mesh's origin if available, otherwise the world origin. If you look in /Ch8/
extension/projection_painting_helper_4.2(4.3)/__init__.py, you'll
notice that I've defined the empties' names as global variables:

```
front_empty_name = "front_empty"
side_empty_name = "side_empty"
```

If there is already an object named front_empty_name (or side_empty_name), it is removed before the operator calls load_image_empty with the empty's name, location, and filepath (self.filepath—which is a member inherited from ImportHelper). We store a reference to the newly created empty in the scene variable context.scene.image_empties (a dictionary) so we can refer to the empty's image block easily when the user invokes the operator. Note that we hide the empty by default after its creation (.hide_set(True)) so it doesn't clutter the scene. Figure 8-11 shows the front and side image empties created by calling IMPORT_OT_open_front_ref and IMPORT_OT_open_side_ref with the sample tortoise shell's reference photos.

Figure 8-11. *Front and side image empties for the sample tortoise shell reference photos, created by invoking IMPORT_OT_open_front_ref and IMPORT_OT_open_side_ref, respectively. Note that the subject is not centered in the front view photo, so the front image empty has been moved manually to line up with the side empty*

Making Operators to Projection Paint

With operators for unwrapping and loading reference photos completed, you're ready to implement operators for projection painting. Over the next few sections, you'll create a function for checking whether the prerequisites for projection painting are met. Then, you'll write a function to configure all the settings necessary for projection painting, which you'll in turn use to create the projection paint operators.

Checking Prerequisites for Projection Painting

First, you'll write a function, ready_for_projection_painting (Listing 8-10), to check for conditions that must be met before you can projection paint.

Listing 8-10. Checking that the conditions to projection paint are met (see /Ch8/extension/projection_painting_helper_4.2(4.3)/__init__.py)

```
def ready_for_projection_painting(context, view):
    selected_mesh = context.scene.select_mesh
    if not selected_mesh or not selected_mesh.data:
        return False

    if selected_mesh.data.uv_layers.find( ↵
        context.scene.uv_name_overall) < 0:
        return False

    if view == 'FRONT':
        if not context.scene.image_empties[ ↵
            front_empty_name] or not ↵
            context.scene.image_empties[ ↵
            front_empty_name].data:
            return False
```

```
    if selected_mesh.data.uv_layers.find( ↵
        context.scene.uv_name_front) < 0:
        return False
else:
    if not context.scene.image_empties[ ↵
        side_empty_name] or not ↵
        context.scene.image_empties[ ↵
        side_empty_name].data:
        return False
    if selected_mesh.data.uv_layers.find( ↵
        context.scene.uv_name_side) < 0:
        return False
return True
```

The function starts by checking that the user has selected a mesh with mesh data. Recall that context.scene.select_mesh is a PointerProperty instance with a custom poll function to filter mesh objects for selection; therefore, you don't need to check the object's type here since it's prefiltered.

Regardless of which view you'd be projection painting from, the overall UVs need to already have been unwrapped, which the function verifies. For each view the user wishes to projection paint from, the function also checks that the corresponding image empty is loaded and UVs are projected.

Each time any condition fails, the function skips the rest of the checks by returning False early. If all conditions are met, True is returned at last. When you call this function in the poll method of any projection paint operators, it will disable the operator if any of these conditions fails.

Helper Functions for Configuring Projection Paint Settings

Next, you'll write two helper functions to facilitate the configuration of projection paint settings. The first is make_mesh_active_selected (Listing 8-11), which deselects all objects in the scene, before setting the dropper-tool-selected mesh the active object and selecting it.

Listing 8-11. Making the mesh picked by the dropper tool the active selected mesh (see /Ch8/extension/projection_painting_ helper_4.2(4.3)/__init__.py)

```
def make_mesh_active_selected(context):
    selected_mesh = context.scene.select_mesh
    if selected_mesh:
        for obj in context.scene.objects:
            obj.select_set(False)
        context.view_layer.objects.active = selected_mesh
        context.view_layer.objects.active.select_set(True)
```

The second helper function get_uv_map_index (Listing 8-12) iterates through a given object's UV maps and returns the index of the UV map matching the given name (uv_name). If none is found, -1 is returned to mimic the find function's behavior for containers.

Listing 8-12. Getting the index of the UV map with the given name (see /Ch8/extension/projection_painting_helper_4.2(4.3)/__ init .py)

```
def get_uv_map_index(obj, uv_name):
    if obj and obj.data:
        for i in range(len(obj.data.uv_layers)):
            uv_map = obj.data.uv_layers[i]
```

```
    if uv_map.name == uv_name:
        return i
return -1
```

Configuring Projection Paint Settings

You're now ready to write the function setup_for_projection_painting (Listing 8-13) to automatically configure everything needed for projection painting—viewport view, interaction mode, clone brush mappings, and other brush settings.

Listing 8-13. Configuring all settings required for projection painting (see /Ch8/extension/projection_painting_helper_4.2(4.3)/__init__.py)

```
def setup_for_projection_painting(context, view):
    context.scene.render.engine = 'CYCLES'
    make_mesh_active_selected(context)
    override, co_successful = get_context_override( ↵
        context, 'VIEW_3D', 'WINDOW')
    if co__successful:
        with bpy.context.temp_override(**_override):
            bpy.ops.view3d.view_axis( ↵
                type=view, align_active=False)

    uv_overall_index = get_uv_map_index( ↵
        context.scene.select_mesh, ↵
        context.scene.uv_name_overall)
    context.scene.select_mesh.data.uv_layers.active_index = ↵
        uv_overall_index

    for uv in context.scene.select_mesh.data.uv_layers:
        uv.active_render = False
```

```
context.scene.select_mesh.data.uv_layers[ ↵
    context.scene.uv_name_overall].active_render = True

bpy.ops.object.mode_set(mode='TEXTURE_PAINT')
context.scene.tool_settings.image_paint.mode = 'IMAGE'
context.scene.tool_settings.image_paint. ↵
    use_clone_layer = True
context.scene.tool_settings.image_paint.interpolation = ↵
    'CLOSEST'

overall_texture = bpy.data.images[ ↵
    context.scene.uv_name_overall+"_texture"]
context.scene.tool_settings.image_paint.canvas = ↵
    overall_texture
set_image_in_uv_editors(context, overall_texture)

bpy.ops.paint.brush_select(image_tool='CLONE')

empty_name = front_empty_name if view=='FRONT' ↵
    else side_empty_name
context.scene.tool_settings.image_paint.clone_image = ↵
    context.scene.image_empties[empty_name].data
context.scene.tool_settings.image_paint.use_symmetry_y = ↵
    False if view=='FRONT' else True
context.scene.tool_settings.image_paint.use_symmetry_x = ↵
    False
context.scene.tool_settings.image_paint.use_symmetry_z = ↵
    False

uv_proj_name = context.scene.uv_name_front if ↵
    view=='FRONT' else context.scene.uv_name_side
uv_proj_index = get_uv_map_index( ↵
    context.scene.select_mesh, uv_proj_name)
```

```
bpy.ops.wm.context_set_int(data_path= ↵
    "active_object.data.uv_layer_clone_index", ↵
    value=uv_proj_index)
```

```
context.scene.tool_settings.unified_paint_settings. ↵
    size = 100
bpy.data.brushes["Clone"].strength = 1.0
bpy.data.brushes['Clone'].blend = 'MIX'
bpy.data.brushes["Clone"].use_accumulate = False
bpy.data.brushes["Clone"].use_alpha = False
bpy.data.brushes["Clone"].stroke_method = 'AIRBRUSH'
bpy.data.brushes["Clone"].rate = 1.0
```

We start by calling make_mesh_active_selected (Listing 8-11) to deselect all and make the user-selected mesh active and selected. We then call bpy.ops.view3d.view_axis with a context override (as if from the viewport) to orient the viewport to the given view, before calling get_uv_map_index (Listing 8-12) to look up the index of the passed in UV map by name and setting it as the selected mesh's Active UV Map Index (the highlighted slot under Properties editor ➤ Data tab ➤ UV Maps). The same UV slot also gets its Active Render toggled on.

Next, we switch the selected mesh to Texture Paint mode and set the painting target to Single Image mode, the interpolation method to Closest, and the texture to paint the overall texture (these steps are equivalent to configuring the settings in Figure 8-3 (3)). We also call set_image_in_uv_ editors (Listing 8-3) to set the overall_texture to display in all open UV Editors and zoom the image to fit the extent of each editor.

We'll now select the Clone brush. In Blender 4.2, this is done via the line:

```
bpy.ops.paint.brush_select(image_tool='CLONE')
```

In Blender 4.3, the above call to bpy.ops.paint.brush_select is replaced by the following snippet, where we call bpy.ops.wm.tool_set_by_id and bpy.ops.wm.tool_set_by_brush_type with a context override (as if from the viewport):

```
override, co_successful = get_context_override( ↵
    context, 'VIEW_3D', 'WINDOW')
if co_successful:
    with bpy.context.temp_override(**override):
        bpy.ops.wm.tool_set_by_id(name="builtin_brush.Clone")
        bpy.ops.wm.tool_set_by_brush_type( ↵
            brush_type="CLONE", space_type='VIEW_3D')
```

In the next block of code, we set up the Clone brush's source mapping, by setting the clone_image to the reference photo based on the given view, enabling symmetry across the Y axis if we're painting from the side, and setting the clone UV map index to the set of UVs unwrapped for the corresponding view via the line:

```
bpy.ops.wm.context_set_int(data_path= ↵
    "active_object.data.uv_layer_clone_index", ↵
    value=uv_proj_index)
```

In the final block of code, we set the brush radius (unified_paint_settings.size) to 100 and strength to 1.0. We also set the strokes to blend ('MIX') and to not accumulate nor use alpha. The stroke method is set to Airbrush with a rate of 1.0. Effectively, here, we configure the same settings shown in Figure 8-5 in Python.

Operators to Projection Paint from Different Views

You can implement all three operators for projection painting (front, side, opposite side) now by calling setup_for_projection_painting (Listing 8-13) with different view arguments. You can also call ready_for_ projection_painting (Listing 8-10) in all three operators' poll methods to check whether the prerequisites to paint have been satisfied. In Listing 8-14, we'll look at how the front projection paint operator BUTTON_OT_ projection_paint_texture_front is implemented.

Listing 8-14. Creating an operator to projection paint with the front UV and front reference photo (see /Ch8/extension/projection_ painting_helper_4.2(4.3)/__init__.py)

```python
class BUTTON_OT_projection_paint_texture_front(Operator):
    bl_idname = "button.projection_paint_texture_front"
    bl_label = "Projection Paint Texture - Front"
    """Projection Paint Texture using the Front UV and
    Reference Photo"""

    def execute(self, context):
        self.report({'INFO'}, "Projection Painting Helper: ↵
            Texture projection painted from frontal ↵
            reference photo.")
        return {'FINISHED'}

    @classmethod
    def poll(cls, context):
        return ready_for_projection_painting(context, 'FRONT')

    def invoke(self, context, event):
        setup_for_projection_painting(context, 'FRONT')
        return self.execute(context)
```

To implement BUTTON_OT_projection_paint_texture_side you
would simply pass context.scene.side_dir in place of 'FRONT', which
is what the user selects in the "Side Dir" drop-down. For BUTTON_OT_
projection_paint_texture_oppo_side, you'll also use context.scene.
side_dir for its poll method, since it requires the same set of UVs.
However, you'll use the view opposite to context.scene.side_dir (e.g.,
'LEFT' for 'RIGHT') when calling setup_for_projection_painting so the
painting view is correct, as shown in Listing 8-15.

Listing 8-15. Excerpt of BUTTON_OT_projection_paint_
texture_oppo_side (see /Ch8/extension/projection_painting_
helper_4.2(4.3)/__init__.py)

```
@classmethod
def poll(cls, context):
    return ready_for_projection_painting(context, ↵
        context.scene.side_dir)

def invoke(self, context, event):
    oppo_dir = 'LEFT' if context.scene.side_dir=='RIGHT' ↵
        else 'RIGHT'
    setup_for_projection_painting(context, oppo_dir)
    return self.execute(context)
```

Wrapping Up Implementation for The Projection Painting Helper Extension

With all the operators and UI widgets created, all that's left to wrap up
the extension is to finish implementing the UI panel class (PROJECTION_
PAINTING_HELPER_PT_PANEL) and create the init_scene_vars() function
to group the scene variables definitions in one place, the del_scene_
vars() to undo everything init_scene_vars() does, and the mandatory

`register()` and `unregister()` functions required by Blender during the extension's installation and uninstallation, respectively. Please refer to Chapters 2, 4, 5, and 6 for more detail on how to implement these classes and functions.

Advantages of Projection Painting and Texture Generation and When to Use It

While projection-painted textures don't always measure up in quality compared to hand-painted ones, there are some scenarios where you could use them to your advantage to speed up production or lower cost by reducing artist involvement—for example, in cases where you could get away with lower levels of detail, such as texturing low-poly models for background crowds that appear only briefly or don't attract much attention. For performance-critical applications like games, generated textures of lower resolution can be used for less noticeable items like those in the background or below the player's eye level or items not crucial to gameplay like noninteractive props.

Beyond projection painting, procedurally generated textures in general are great for adding replay value to a game as they can be used to create new visual interests for players each time they revisit a level. Postponing texture generation until runtime is a great way to reduce the size of a game when storage space is limited by the target device or distribution platform. You can also utilize generated images to quickly texture a large number of similar models, like the vegetation for background scenery in a game or simulation.

When you want to get a quick feel of how something looks or throw together several renders to see how they compare—like putting together several looks for an interior design visualization or making quick prototypes in the early stages of a new game—generated textures may be a solution.

In addition to applying generated textures to models as they are, you can use them as the bases for hand-painting to simplify your workflow. Think of projection painting as automating the beginning stages of a hand-painting session—with base colors of the major regions of a texture already filled in, you can skip directly to fine-tuning details and adding personal touches.

Summary

In this chapter, you learned how to projection paint textures in Blender using the same reference photos used for modeling the mesh, by creating Clone brush mappings from pairings of reference photos with UVs unwrapped by projecting from the corresponding views. You then learned how to analyze the process and break it down into manageable chunks of related tasks and assess which tasks are suitable for automation—you deduced that setting up reference images, unwrapping from given views, and configuring texture painting settings are great candidates, while aligning UVs with underlying reference photos is not, as that would require computer vision techniques to recognize features in the photos and UVs and transforming both to match, which is too complex and unlikely to produce satisfactory results.

After arriving at an overall design, you implemented the Projection Painting Helper extension by extracting the core functionality of each group into a function and sharing it among several operators, for example, writing a function `unwrap_by_projecting_from_view` (Listing 8-7) to unwrap by projecting from a given view, then implementing both of the operators for unwrapping from the front and side views by calling this function. You also distilled the code for configuring Clone brush mappings into one function (`setup_for_projection_painting` in Listing 8-13) and used it to implement three operators—for projection painting the front, side, and opposite side views.

Last but not least, you learned that projection-painted or procedurally generated textures can be effective for speeding up workflow or lowering production costs when substituted for background objects or objects that are less noticeable. They can also serve as shortcuts to replace beginning stages of texture painting, letting you skip right to customizing details.

CHAPTER 9

Showcasing and Publishing Your Extensions and Scripts

In this chapter, you'll learn how to take your Blender scripts and add-ons from code to products. In the first part of the chapter, you'll learn how to license and package extensions using the Blender command line tool. Then, you'll formulate high-level marketing plans through case studies of similar products, as well as analyze your potential customer base. Once you decide on a publication channel, you'll create a product listing, weigh the pros and cons of different pricing and subscription models, and create a plan for your product for providing support and building a community post release.

With a high-level product strategy in place, in the second part of the chapter, you'll take a closer look at tapping into the user base to promote the add-on and create a personal brand, through showcasing the add-on in videos or tutorials and boosting sales with testimonials. The third and fourth parts of the chapter will show you how to utilize the Blender Python API to create marketing materials. You'll write script functions to customize display options for the viewport, hide distractions, and

© Isabel Lupiani 2025
I. Lupiani, *Blender Scripting with Python*, https://doi.org/10.1007/979-8-8688-1127-2_9

take screenshots. You'll also make time-lapsed demos to show off your procedural generation algorithm using modal operators with 3D text as captions. Finally, you'll produce a variation of the demo where users use the Down Arrow key to advance the mesh generation stages.

Running This Chapter's Examples

The source code for this book is available on GitHub via the book's product page, located at www.apress.com/979-8-8688-1126-5). This chapter's examples come in two versions. The first version is designed to run in the Text Editor and the second version installed as an extension add-on. Both versions contain the same implementation of the *Barrel PCG Demo* extension we'll discuss throughout the chapter.

Setting Up/Running the Text Editor Version

Navigate to the /Ch9/text_editor folder in the downloaded source for the book. As you follow along the chapter, open the *.py file indicated by the text in the built-in Text Editor under the Scripting workspace.

Installing/Running the Extension Add-On Version

Go to Edit ➤ Preferences... ➤ Get Extensions, click the blue downward "v" at the upper right to expand the menu, and click *Install from Disk...*. Navigate to the Ch9/extension/barrel_pcg_demo/ folder in the downloaded source, and choose the file barrel_pcg_demo-1.0.0.zip. The add-on "Barrel PCG Demo" will be installed and automatically enabled. Once installed, you can access the add-on in the 3D Viewport *Properties* shelf (N key) ➤ *Tool* tab.

Handling Imports from Chapters 3

This chapter's scripts import functions from Chapters 3. These imports have been set up for you in the downloaded source. You can revisit Chapter 4 for detailed explanations on how to structure imports for both scripts run from the Text Editor and for packaged extensions. Chapter 7 describes an alternative for setting up imports to run in the Text Editor by copying scripts to your Blender installation to make them available as modules.

From Code to Product

In the first part of the chapter, you'll go through the high-level process of taking an extension from code to product. You'll first prepare for publication by licensing and packaging the extension, then choose a publication channel, and form high-level marketing strategies via case studies of your favorite add-ons and analyzing your customer base. Once you've solidified how to distribute the product, you'll create a product listing, weigh the pros and cons of different pricing models, and formulate a plan for support after the release.

Licensing

Recall that at the end of Chapter 2, you included a GNU GPLv3 license block at the top of the source file to prepare the add-on for publication. The official word of the Blender Foundation is that any Python scripts which make calls to the Blender API must have a license compatible with GNU GPLv3 if shared publicly. This includes whether you're sharing scripts or add-ons for free or selling them commercially. In a nutshell, under the GPL, users are free to modify and distribute your scripts or add-ons as they wish and use them for any purpose royalty free.

If you have *.blend files that embed Python scripts which call the Blender API, the aforementioned licensing terms also apply. Otherwise, since *.blend files contain only data, they're considered program output and therefore by themselves the sole copyright of the Blender users that created them. For more detail on licensing scripts, add-ons, and *.blend files, check out the FAQ section at `https://www.blender.org/support/faq/`.

Package Your Extension

To prepare an extension package, structure the source files of your add-on and create a `blender_manifest.toml` file with metadata as described in Chapter 2, then use the Blender command line tool to build the extension package, by entering the following command in the terminal:

```
blender --command extension build --source-dir <source_dir> ↵
    --output-dir <output_dir>
```

For example, on my Windows system, to build the Chapter 8 extension package, I would open a Command Prompt window and cd to the directory where the Ch8 add-on source files reside, which is

```
C:\blender_scripting_with_python_4.2\Ch8\extension\ ↵
    projection_painting_helper_4.2
```

Inside that directory are `__init__.py`, `blender_manifest.toml`, and other source files used by the extension. To build the extension package and output the zip file to the current directory, I would enter the following command at the prompt:

```
blender --command extension build --source-dir . --output-dir .
```

During the build, the command line tool will check the extension against Blender's requirements, for example, that its `blender_manifest.toml` file is properly filled in and formatted, with a tagline at most 64 characters long.

If all is well, the tool will output a zipped package for the extension. In the above example, the tool will generate a file named `projection_painting_helper-2.0.0.zip` in the current directory and display the following message:

```
building: projection_painting_helper-2.0.0.zip
complete
created: ".\projection_painting_helper-2.0.0.zip", 12450
```

The zip file can then be installed via Edit ➤ Preferences… ➤ Get Extensions ➤ Install From Disk… and tested. You can find more about the Blender command line tool in the online Blender manual at `https://docs.blender.org/manual/en/latest/advanced/command_line/extension_arguments.html#command-line-args-extension-build`.

If `blender` does not come up as a valid command, you may need to add your Blender install directory (the folder where blender.exe resides) to the PATH environment variable on your system. If you have multiple versions of Blender installed, you can control which version of Blender command line tool is invoked by the `blender` command by adding the path to that version of Blender to the PATH variable.

Note that to ensure compatibility of your extension with the intended Blender version, you must build the extension with that Blender version's command line tool. For example, if you need your extension to run in Blender 4.3, you must build the extension's package with Blender 4.3's command line tool, by adding the directory of the Blender 4.3 install to the PATH environment variable. This is because the version of Blender command line tool will determine the version of Blender Python API used to build your extension package. Unless you are sure the part of Blender Python API used by the extension has not changed between Blender versions, it is always better to be safe than sorry.

Submitting to the Blender Extensions Platform

If you decide to submit your extension to the Blender Extensions Platform, log in with your Blender ID and password at `https://extensions.blender.org/submit/` and upload the zip file built with the Blender command line tool as described in the previous section. Your extension will be placed in the Extension Approval Queue to be reviewed.

Deciding on a Publication Outlet

Depending on the outlet, it is possible to publish either Python scripts or Blender extension add-ons. The former are loose Python source files (*.py files) that either provide a handful of functionalities on their own or work as modules with functions or classes importable by other Python code. Extension add-ons, as we've seen throughout the book, are installable applications meant to work as plug-ins in Blender. You can publish both paid and free scripts or add-ons on your own site or commercial sites like Blender Market. The Blender Extensions Platform will only accept packaged extension add-ons, not scripts, that have gone through an official review process. Add-ons and scripts published anywhere have to bear a license compatible with GNU GPLv3.

If you decide to host free scripts or add-ons on your own, a popular choice is to do so directly through a public GitHub repository. The benefits are you can easily provide wikis, documentation, or FAQs in one place. It is also straightforward to continuously release updates, plus users can check out your other projects easily. It's a great way to build up a code portfolio.

Case Studies on the Marketing Strategies of Your Favorite Add-Ons

Before putting together a marketing plan for your add-on, let's take a few moments and conduct some mini-case studies on existing products to get your creative juices flowing and get a general sense of what works and what doesn't. Pick five of your favorite add-ons developed by other members of the Blender community. Review the product page of each add-on, and contemplate the following questions:

1. How did you first hear about the add-on? (Blogs, forums, author's site, browsing Blender Market, social media, etc.).

2. What is your favorite feature of the add-on?

3. Does the add-on's product page or other promotional material convey your favorite feature in a clear and attractive way? Why or why not? If not, can you improve it?

4. Is there anything that made you hesitant to purchase the add-on?

5. What type(s) of media (photos, videos, etc.) were used to describe the add-on? Were certain types of media more effective than others?

6. What influenced your decision to purchase the add-on? (Price, reviews, author(s)' reputation, testimonials, contents and quality of the product listing, tutorials demonstrating the add-on's usage, particular feature(s) not available elsewhere, etc.).

Know Your Audience

The typical audience for Blender extensions that come to mind are game or film devs. In this section, I will attempt to describe as diverse a Blender user base as possible, so you can consider whether there are segments of the market you have yet to tap into.

In addition to game devs, many simulation (a.k.a. serious game) developers also use 3D contents or rely on tools for editing 3D content, for example, vehicle models for driving simulation. Many researchers use Blender as well, both as a visualization tool and for producing scientific or engineering renderings in publications.

DIY hobbyists who want to make their own designs for 3D printing also use Blender for its low cost of entry. Those that do not own 3D printers can take advantage of online 3D printing services like Shapeways and Sculpteo that let you upload your designs and ship the printed models to you. Therefore, any individual or company interested in 3D printing may use Blender to create models for printing, whether they own the hardware to print the models or not.

Many architects, landscape designers, and interior designers utilize Blender for visualization. A notable example is Allan Brito, an architect from Brazil that uses Blender to render designs and communicate his vision. DIYers that want to plan small home remodeling or redecorating projects may also do so in Blender.

College students often choose Blender for its low cost of entry, with the most obvious being art students studying 3D modeling and animation. Both art and computer science students may study procedural content generation and generative art in Blender. Computer science majors may also use Blender to study subjects like graphics and computational geometry. Engineering students may use Blender to model parts for their electronics, robotics, and vehicle projects, whereas math majors may use Blender to create fractals and 3D surfaces. The university faculty teaching these subject areas are equally likely to use Blender for producing course materials. Many K-12 educators nowadays have also integrated Blender into their classroom, particularly for the purpose of teaching 2D and 3D geometry.

Your audience may be one or more of the aforementioned groups. If it's more than one—great! You have more potential customers; however, it also means you need to think about marketing to each group differently if the groups span unique market sectors. Users make purchasing decisions based on how a product is useful particularly to *them*, so you'll need to come up with use cases tailored to each group.

Writing a Product Listing

Sum up in one sentence what your add-on or script does, to use as the tagline for the listing and to remind yourself what the most important selling point of your product is. Then, write an "Elevator Pitch" style summary for the product that is short enough to easily read through in the span of an elevator ride but highlights the uniqueness and major features of your product. Imagine yourself catching a customer on the way out the door, if you only have a few seconds to talk, what would you say to convince someone to buy the product?

Nothing breaks the sense of professionalism and spoils your painstakingly crafted product page like typos and grammatical mistakes. Remember to always spell-check and proofread the text portion of a product listing before making it public. It's always a good idea to check how the product page looks on both desktop and mobile browsers as well.

Still Images and Videos

Prepare a "headline" shot for the product page, with appropriate branding, logos, and watermarks. Research and pay attention to the form factor and layout for the specific outlet of your choice. For example, if a marketplace crops the lower third of the photo on import, make sure you don't put anything there. Since web photos usually have size restrictions, make sure you take your screenshot at a resolution that can survive resizing and compression and still look professional.

When taking screenshots, pay attention to lighting and choose a composition that will minimize distractions and make your product the focal point. The still shots you choose should be self-explanatory or only requiring one-sentence captions. If your add-on has features better explained with videos, consider uploading a video or adding a link to the video on your product page to accompany the still images. Don't be tempted to skip the still images or only use videos. Videos require a higher level of engagement from users so they often don't get played unless the users are already interested and want to find out more. Most videos are not indexed and therefore difficult to skim. In addition, users often don't have the attention span nor time to watch whole videos. As a result, features of your product will likely go unnoticed if they are only highlighted in videos. Still images and videos go hand in hand as images give a birds'-eye view of the add-on and pique the users' curiosity to click the videos to learn more. If a site does not allow videos, you might be able to substitute animated GIFs for short clips, where appropriate.

Keywords or Hashtags

Think of keywords as what your potential customers may use as search terms to look up a product like yours. What are the categories the product belongs to, the key features the product offers, and buzz words or trends the product is associated with? If a keyword has acronyms, think of which one(s) are the most commonly accepted (does it make sense to include multiple?).

Sample Results and Applications

For a product that edits or produces content, like a material editing tool or a procedural generation add-on, it makes sense to include screenshots and videos demonstrating sample results, with descriptions of what they are useful for. Think of your target audience and convey how your add-on will save their time and streamline their workflow. Be sure to highlight any unique features or notable improvements your add-on has over similar products.

Demo Videos

While photos do a decent job conveying the functionalities of some add-ons, like showing sample results of a texture generation tool, some add-ons are much easier explained when they're shown in action. An example of such an add-on is one of my personal favorites, a suite of modeling tools called Loop Tools that help you quickly manipulate edge and face loops.

Demoing add-ons or scripts in videos has the added benefits of showing the add-on's ease of use and responsiveness. It's also a great way to summarize what sort of scenarios the add-on is helpful for. If your add-on uses hotkeys, be sure to get the Screencast Keys extension, available on the official Blender Extensions Platform at: `https://extensions.blender.org/add-ons/screencast-keys/`. Screencast Keys are great for recording tutorials and demo videos as it automatically displays keys and mouse buttons on screen as you press them. The tool can also be customized to show the last operation executed.

Remember that something obvious to you might not be obvious to someone else. So while making demos, always make sure to include a quick walk-through of the user interface and explain each setting (what does this button do?).

Manual, FAQ, and Wiki

If you've produced demos or tutorial videos for an add-on, you may be tempted to do away with a written manual. However, written materials have benefits not provided by videos, such as allowing users to search and locate menu names and shortcut keys easily. Some users prefer written formats over videos since you can quickly skim and skip parts not relevant to them. As a convenience to the users, you could compile some of the most important or commonly asked questions into a FAQ and include that with the manual or the product page.

For a more complex add-on, you could start a Wiki and let users contribute to a knowledge base and share work they've done with the add-on. You could also offer tips and tricks on how to customize or extend the add-on.

Support After Release

As with all software products, another thing to consider is the level of support you'll provide after the sale. Decide ahead of time what method(s) of contact your customers should use—for example, via posts on a forum for the add-on, a dedicated email address, or comments left on the product page? Should there be different means of communication for issues of different nature, like reporting bugs, getting help for setup trouble, and so on?

If you plan on releasing new versions of an add-on in the future, think about whether you'll offer customers who bought an earlier version free or discounted access to newer version(s). If so, for how long a period, and through what channels (download link via email, discount code, etc.)? New versions can mean a number of different things, like new features, improvements or bug fixes over existing features, compatibility with new Blender releases, and so on. If you do decide to offer this perk, remember to mention it in the product listing!

Pricing

Prices for add-ons vary greatly depending on what problems they solve. My motto for this is research, research, research. What do similar products charge? What sets your add-on apart from existing ones? Does it do the same task(s) more efficiently, is it easier to use, or does it offer more features? If so, you can consider setting a higher price for your add-on. However, keep in mind that the higher the price, the more customers will expect. At the end of the day, selling an add-on is no different than selling any other types of commercial software. Pricing is a subtle art—just as you could stay competitive by making an add-on better thus charging more, offering a similar product at a slightly lower price could also attract customers. If you have several related add-ons in your repertoire, you could consider bundling them and offer a discount over buying each add-on individually.

If your add-on solves a problem that's never been solved before or provides functionality not found in any existing add-ons—congratulations! You have a revolutionary product. The upside is you have no competition, and the downside is it's harder to get a sense of what a competitive yet profitable price would be. Think about who your add-on's potential audience is. For example, if the add-on automates an animation task, talk to the animators, and if it solves a modeling problem, chat with some modelers. Remember that commonsense still applies here—the more difficult a problem your add-on solves or more complex a task it automates, the higher the potential price. Any exclusive feature also adds to the appeal. However, supply and demand is a factor too. The more expensive an add-on, the more reluctant people will make the purchase.

Get the Most Out of "Free"

Even if you've decided to make an add-on available for free, you can still use it as an opportunity to build up a following. If you're offering a download for the add-on from a blog or personal site, you can ask users to sign up for a free account or a subscription to a mailing list which you can then use to send out notifications when updates or new versions of the add-on become available. You could utilize the same channels to announce future products and recruit volunteers to test drive an add-on for feedback or testimonials.

In addition to a subscription, you could ask users to fill out a one-time survey before revealing the download link to find out how they heard about your site, what made them interested in your add-on, and what other types of add-ons they'd like to see to gather ideas for future projects. Alternatively, you could implement a pay-as-you-want model or ask for donations to support the development of future projects.

Paid Subscription Models

You can consider using a "Patreon" type model where you provide multitiered paid memberships, and in return, users get benefits based on the level they buy in. This type of model is inspired by the traditional artist-in-residence programs where artists and musicians are supported by a regular income stream funded by donors which free them from the stress of making ends meet and allowing them to create more freely. Patreon is one such platform that lets you set up a modernized version of artist-in-residence so you can collect periodic donations from your followers. In return, the subscribers get content from you—the higher the subscription level, the more benefits. The subscriptions may also include a free tier, where users sign up to receive newsletters and perhaps a small prize just for showing interest. Many subscriptions also offer a "pure donation" tier, where users choose to pay a low monthly fee only for the sake of donation without anything in return.

In addition to providing a stable income stream, having subscribers that expect periodic updates will motivate you to produce more and keep you on a routine. However, the expectation could also interfere with your creative process if you don't work well on a fixed schedule. You may at times feel pressured to push out contents that you don't feel ready, just to have something new for the subscribers.

Subscription models also only work if you already have a reputation, since users are paying in advance without knowing what they'll receive. Unless you have a sizable following, the subscription model alone likely won't bring you enough income, therefore forcing you to juggle between several things at once—whether it be paid contracts, full- or part-time positions, and so on.

On the flip side, the subscription models provide a minimum bottomline to fall back on, if you can maintain a relatively stable subscriber base. Since the subscribers already know and love your work, you could potentially take more risks and show them more experimental products than you would to a general audience.

Multilevel Pricing to Target Different Groups of Customers

In an article titled "The Smart Way for Pricing Your Products" in the Blender Market Blog, Matthew Muldoon suggested that instead of selling your product at a single price, you can create a "Lite" version of a product with a subset of the features and price it lower to reach customers that find the regular version too pricey or only need the basic features. If you have an add-on that includes a suite of related functionalities, this is a strategy you could use to reach a wider audience. For the customers that purchase the Lite version, you could offer them an upgrade discount to buy the full-featured version later.

Promoting Your Add-On

Now that you have an eye-catching product page and a competitive price, the next step is to get the word out to your potential audience. Make announcements through your Blender, 3D art, or programming-related blog, website, YouTube channel, and social media accounts. Ask personal or professional contacts if they'd be willing to tweet it out or write about it. If there are forums you frequent where viewers might be interested in your add-on, start a thread of discussion and invite people to check it out. For example, if your add-on generates meshes or textures, you could post it on the procedural generation sub-reddit (`https://www.reddit.com/r/proceduralgeneration/`) or other popular CG communities like blenderartists.org or CGSociety (`http://forums.cgsociety.org/`).

Using the Add-On in Video or Written Tutorials

Another great way to promote an add-on is to use the add-on in a tutorial video or blog post. For example, you can use an add-on that you've developed for manipulating edge loops in a YouTube video that teaches modeling. You can write up a blog post that discusses vertex painting weight maps for animation using bipedal rigs generated from your add-on. This approach has several benefits—the viewers get to see the add-on in action (seeing is believing!), and you get to go over the add-on's features plus provide sample scenarios in which the add-on is useful.

Remember to enable Screencast Keys so viewers can easily see which shortcut keys are used with your add-on as they're pressed and tag the vidcos or posts with relevant keywords so they come up in searches. (See the section "Demo Videos" earlier in this chapter for more detail on how to get the Screencast Keys extension.)

Boost Sales with Reviews or Testimonials

Much like books, movies, and games, positive reviews or testimonials for your add-ons can make a big difference in the confidence of your customers. If you're new to the game, it can even be one of the determining factors of whether they make the purchase.

Are there any Blender artists that are well respected in their specialties whose work you admire? Try politely messaging them and offering free copies of your add-on to try out. Be sure to take the time to follow up and thank them for their time. If they like your add-on, they may be willing to give you an endorsement or testimonial and, if not, valuable feedback on how you could improve the add-on.

If you're selling add-ons from a personal site, you could let customers post reviews on the add-on's catalog page. You could also ask customers whether they'd like to opt in to receive communications from you when they check out, and follow up with them after the purchase to see how they like the add-on.

Borrowing the idea from games with open betas, you could consider allowing a limited number of users to test drive a beta version of your add-on and solicit feedback and testimonials that way. These can be a select few from your social media or blog followers or fellow members of a forum that you frequent. Soliciting feedback this way allows you to promote an add-on while it's still in development. Like play-testing games with focus groups, beta-testing an add-on also lets you get a sense of what your potential audience likes or dislikes about your product, therefore enabling you to find and fix as many bugs as possible before the add-on's release.

Drive Traffic by Offering Discounts

If you're selling add-ons or scripts from a personal site, you could offer holiday sales or time-sensitive coupon codes and post them on forums or spread the words through social media. If you have a Blender blog or tutorial site, you could also reserve a portion of the contents for registered users and, as a bonus for signing up, give out exclusive coupon codes for purchasing your add-ons. Some CG content shops like Blender Market allow their sellers to optionally participate in occasional site-wide promotions. Since these are usually periods where the site sees high volume traffic, opting in these sales can be an effective way to increase exposure.

Creating a Personal Brand

Building up a reputation takes time. Making Blender tutorial videos, writing blog posts, giving people critique on art work on forums, or answering questions on Blender Stack Exchange and other CG art forums are all great ways to create a personal brand. Come up with a unique logo which you could use as an avatar when posting online or as a watermark on photos. Try and use a consistent handle across different sites so that over time, online users can start to associate your work with your brand. Create a dedicated email address for answering questions about your add-on and responding to support tickets and bug reports post release. Retain customers with a mailing list opt-in to receive updates and info on future releases.

You could also volunteer to give feedback or test other developers' add-ons, for a chance that others may help test yours in the future. Many developers also find it helpful to try and build up a reputation in specific areas of CG, such as materials, rigging, and so on, which helps create impressions that you are the matter expert, particularly if you are releasing a product in that category.

Creating Marketing Materials for Your Add-On

In this section, we'll go over how to gather and create marketing materials for your add-on, starting with decluttering the viewport by hiding distractions and customizing display colors, followed by collecting screenshots automatically using Blender Python. In the second part of the section, you'll learn how to create a time-lapsed demo for your PCG algorithm as a Blender extension, which generates meshes gradually in stages based on user-entered parameters with 3D text captions. You'll also learn how to modify this extension to let users advance generation stages using the Down Arrow key instead of waiting for timed intervals.

Customize Viewport Visuals for Captures

Whether you're setting up the scene for an interactive demo or a render, you'll want to deemphasize objects that are unsightly or distracting so you can accentuate the ones that matter. Some visual guides that are indispensable during modeling can get in the way of screen captures and make the results look messy—in this section, you'll learn how to hide some of these in Python. In addition, I'll show you how to customize vertex and edge colors.

Turning Off 3D Viewport Guides

You can find visibility check boxes for viewport guides under Viewport Overlays, such as Floor, which controls whether the grid is shown in perspective view. To edit these check boxes in Python, you can iterate through the nested screen hierarchy under the passed-in context and locate the area a of type `'VIEW_3D'` and in turn the space s of type `'VIEW_3D'`, as shown in Listing 9-1. The overlay is part of s, and you can set `s.overlay.<guide>` to `True` to show `<guide>` and `False` to hide `<guide>`.

445

Listing 9-1. Setting the visibility of viewport guides (see /Ch9/
extension/barrel_pcg_demo/utils.py)

```
def set_viewport_guides_visibility(context, visibility):
    for a in context.window.screen.areas:
        if a.type == 'VIEW_3D':
            for s in a.spaces:
                if s.type == 'VIEW_3D':
                    s.overlay.show_ortho_grid = visibility
                    s.overlay.show_floor = visibility
                    s.overlay.show_axis_x = visibility
                    s.overlay.show_axis_y = visibility
                    s.overlay.show_axis_z = visibility
                    s.overlay.show_cursor = visibility
```

s.overlay.show_ortho_grid is the "Grid" check box controlling
whether the grid is shown in orthographic view. s.overlay.show_floor is
the "Floor" check box controlling whether the grid is shown in perspective
view. The three "show_axis" variables that dictate whether the X, Y, and Z
axes are on display in the viewport correspond to the "Axes" buttons under
Viewport Overlays. s.overlay.show_cursor sets the visibility of the 3D
Cursor and corresponds to the "3D Cursor" check box.

Turning Off 3D Viewport Overlays

You can use Listing 9-1 to set the visibility of viewport guides individually
or many of them at once. However, if you just want to toggle all guides off
temporarily (e.g., to take a screenshot) then toggle them back on without
losing individual settings you've previously configured, you can hide
Viewport Overlays itself, as the example shown in Listing 9-2.

Listing 9-2. Setting visibility of the Viewport Overlays itself (see /Ch9/extension/barrel_pcg_demo/utils.py)

```
def set_viewport_overlays_visibility(context, visibility):
    for a in context.window.screen.areas:
        if a.type == 'VIEW_3D':
            for s in a.spaces:
                if s.type == 'VIEW_3D':
                    s.overlay.show_overlays = visibility
```

When you set s.overlay.show_overlays to False, the individual guide settings such as s.overlay.show_floor, s.overlay.show_cursor, and so on are retained. All you need to do is set s.overlay.show_overlays to True again to restore them.

Hiding Objects in the Scene

Listing 9-3 shows an example of how you can hide (unhide) all objects regardless of type in the current scene under the passed-in context, which has the equivalent effect of using the A key to select all in the viewport followed by the H (Alt-H) key to hide (reveal) them.

Listing 9-3. Setting visibility of scene objects (see /Ch9/extension/barrel_pcg_demo/utils.py)

```
def hide_scene_objects(context, hide=True):
    for obj in context.scene.objects:
        obj.hide_set(hide)
```

We iterate through the scene objects one by one, calling hide_set(hide) on each. hide as True will hide the object, whereas hide as False will unhide (reveal) it.

Customizing Viewport Display Colors of Vertices and Edges

You might have noticed by now that I customized some of the mesh viewport display colors for better contrast (and for personal enjoyment!). These values are changeable through Edit ➤ Preferences... ➤ Themes ➤ 3D Viewport as shown in Figure 9-1.

You can change the viewport vertex display color to dark blue in Python, like this:

```
bpy.context.preferences.themes[0].view_3d.vertex = ↵
    (0.1, 0.1, 0.8)
```

or change the viewport edge display color to light blue like this:

```
bpy.context.preferences.themes[0].view_3d.wire_edit = ↵
    (0.4, 0.7, 1.0)
```

Notice that the color specification is a triple of three numbers between 0.0 and 1.0, representing each component of a RGB color mapped from the range of 0 to 255 to the range of 0.0 to 1.0. For example, if you have a color (100, 125, 56), you would divide each of its components by 255 to map it to the range 0.0 to 1.0, like this:

```
(100/255, 125/255, 56/255) ➤ (0.39, 0.49, 0.22)
```

Collecting Screenshots

You can take a screenshot in Blender with a call to bpy.ops.screen. screenshot, which captures the entire Blender application window:

```
bpy.ops.screen.screenshot(filepath="C:\\My_Documents\\ss.png")
```

Alt-Prt Sc on Windows takes a screenshot of the current focused program window and therefore has the same effect. Note that filepath is the full path to the image file you are writing to, not the directory path. You can find the other optional keyword arguments to this operator in the Blender Python documentation.

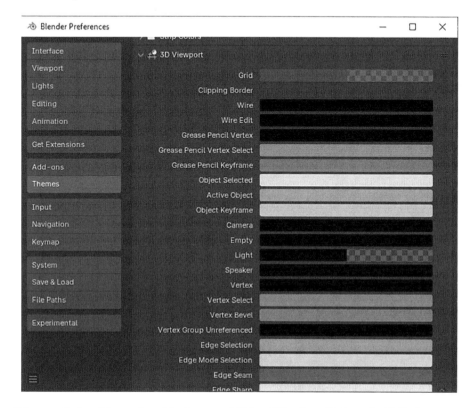

Figure 9-1. *Changing Vertex and Edge Display Colors in Edit* ➤ *Preferences...* ➤ *Themes* ➤ *3D Viewport*

Configuring Viewport Rotation and View Settings

Recall in Chapter 8 you learned that you can emulate the view changes from pressing Numpad 1 to 9 with a call to the following operator with a context override (as if from the viewport):

```
bpy.ops.view3d.view_axis(type=view, align_active=False)
```

where view can be one of the following values: 'FRONT', 'BACK', 'LEFT', 'RIGHT', 'TOP', 'BOTTOM', and 'CAMERA' for camera view.

What if you want to rotate the viewport with an angle that does not align with a global axis? To do so, you can write a function like set_viewport_rotation in Listing 9-4, which rotates the viewport by a given quaternion wxyz, switches view to perspective or orthographic, and sets view distance to view_dist.

Listing 9-4. Rotate the viewport by the given quaternion, switch view (perspective or orthographic), and adjust view distance (see /Ch9/extension/barrel_pcg_demo/utils.py)

```
def set_viewport_rotation(context, wxyz, view_persp, ↵
    view_dist):
    for a in context.window.screen.areas:
        if a.type == 'VIEW_3D':
            for s in a.spaces:
                if s.type == 'VIEW_3D':
                    s.region_3d.lock_rotation = False
                    s.region_3d.view_location = ↵
                        Vector((0, 0, 0))
                    s.region_3d.view_rotation.w = wxyz[0]
                    s.region_3d.view_rotation.x = wxyz[1]
                    s.region_3d.view_rotation.y = wxyz[2]
                    s.region_3d.view_rotation.z = wxyz[3]
                    s.region_3d.view_perspective = view_persp
                    s.region_3d.view_distance = view_dist
                    s.region_3d.update()
```

wxyz is a four-tuple of numbers, for example, (0.716, 0.439, 0.291, 0.459). view_persp is either 'PERSP' (perspective) or 'ORTHO' (orthographic), and view_dist is a number. Quaternion is a method for specifying rotation that avoids gimbal lock, an issue with Euler angles

450

where one degree of freedom is lost when certain axes are aligned. The price you pay with quaternion is the loss of intuitiveness—it is hard to think of a rotation relative to an axis or a plane and translate it to the equivalent quaternion. There is however a simple cheat—you can write a function like get_viewport_rotation in Listing 9-5, where the current viewport rotation quaternion is printed as a string to the System Console.

Listing 9-5. Print the viewport rotation quaternion to the System Console (see /Ch9/text_editor/get_viewport_rotation.py)

```
def get_viewport_rotation(context):
    for a in context.window.screen.areas:
        if a.type == 'VIEW_3D':
            for s in a.spaces:
                if s.type == 'VIEW_3D':
                    print("view_rotation = " + ↵
                        str(s.region_3d.view_rotation))
```

In get_viewport_rotation, you iterate through the nested screen hierarchy under the passed-in context, to locate context ➤ area ('VIEW_3D') ➤ space ('VIEW_3D') ➤ region_3d and print out its view_rotation, which is of type mathutils.Quaternion. Open the script containing this function (/Ch9/text_editor/get_viewport_rotation.py) in the Text Editor, head over to the viewport and drag the mouse while holding down the middle mouse button to rotate the view, then hit the play button in the Text Editor. If you then open the System Console via Window ➤ System Console, you'll see the Quaternion value printed, which resembles something like the following:

```
view_rotation = ↵
    <Quaternion (w=0.7139, x=0.4386, y=0.2857, z=0.4651)>
```

You can experiment by repeating the aforementioned process of rotating the viewport with the mouse and printing out the corresponding Quaternion value, to easily find rotations to call `set_viewport_rotation` (Listing 9-4) with.

Running a Script at Blender Startup or in the Background

If you have a script that does not require user input, such as a noninteractive project demo or tutorial, you might find it convenient to have the script automatically load up and run as soon as Blender starts up. To do this, you can start Blender from a terminal with the following command:

```
blender --python <path to *.py file> ↵
    -- <optional command line arguments for the *.py file>
```

For instance, to run the script C:/my_docs/my_script.py with the arguments 120 and True, you could enter the following line in Command Prompt on Windows:

```
blender --python C:/my_docs/my_script.py -- 120 True
```

If the command `blender` is not recognized on your system, you'll need to either add your Blender install directory to the PATH environment variable (as described in the "Package Your Extension" section) or type out the full path to blender.exe on the command line. For example, with a Blender 4.2 installation to the default directory on Windows, this is

```
C:/Program Files/Blender Foundation/Blender 4.2/blender.exe ↵
    --python C:/my_docs/my_script.py -- 120 True
```

To run the same script with Blender in the background, you can add the --background flag to the command line arguments:

```
blender --background --python C:/my_docs/my_script.py ↵
    -- 120 True
```

You can also pass a *.blend file along as input data for the script to operate on as a command line argument, like this:

```
blender my_data.blend --python C:/my_docs/my_script.py ↵
    -- 120 True
```

You can save the output of a script to a *.blend file by adding the following call to bpy.ops.wm.save_as_mainfile at the end of an operator's execute method or at the end of a Python script:

```
bpy.ops.wm.save_as_mainfile( ↵
    filepath="C:/my_docs/results.blend")
```

You can try this out for yourself, by making a copy of /Ch9/text_editor/utils.py (let's call it utils_copy.py), adding the line import sys at the top of the file, then modifying the last block of code like this:

```
if __name__ == "__main__":
    set_viewport_guides_visibility(bpy.context, ↵
        sys.argv[0].lower()=="true")
    set_viewport_overlays_visibility(bpy.context, ↵
        sys.argv[1].lower()=="true")
    hide_scene_objects(bpy.context, ↵
        sys.argv[2].lower()=="true")

    bpy.ops.wm.save_as_mainfile( ↵
        filepath=<output blend filepath>)
```

sys.argv is the command line arguments as a list of strings. Since there is no straightforward way of converting strings to boolean values in Python, as a simple workaround, we call the Python built-in function lower() to convert each string argument to all lowercase then compare it to "true" (which will make "TRUE", "True", "true", "tRue", and so on all True). We'll also try saving to a *.blend file from a script by adding a call to bpy.ops.wm.save_as_mainfile.

You can now experiment by entering the following command in a Command Prompt window:

```
blender <input blend filepath> --python ↵
    <filepath of utils_copy.py> -- False True True
```

Which will launch Blender, open the input blend file you specify, run utils_copy.py with the three arguments False True True (that are passed to the first three functions calls in the if __name__ == "__main__" block above), and save to the blend filepath you passed to bpy.ops. wm.save_as_mainfile.

If you add the flag --background to the last command, the same sequence of events will take place except with Blender running silently in the background. When done, Blender will automatically quit, and you will see the following output message appear in the Command Prompt window:

```
Blender 4.2.0 (hash a51f293548ad built 2024-07-16 06:29:33)
Read blend: <input blend filepath>
Info: Total files 0 | Changed 0 | Failed 0
Info: Saved <output blend filepath>

Blender quit
```

An added benefit of running scripts from the command line is you can group a series of script execution into a Linux shell script or Windows batch file and not have to type in the individual arguments each time. This can greatly simplify testing, as well as tasks for which you would always run the same sequence of scripts.

Tip   If you are looking to do more command line processing, I encourage you to look into the Python built-in module argparse for parsing arguments (`https://docs.python.org/3/library/argparse.html`).

Making a Time-Lapsed Demo

Upon seeing a procedural content generation (PCG) program, often the first thing anyone asks is *how does it work*? The best way to answer that is to show the generation in action. In this section, we'll look at how to create a Blender extension to demo a PCG algorithm which lets users configure generation parameters then watch the model "grow" in time-lapsed stages in the viewport, with captions explaining what parts of the mesh are added in each stage and how.

In addition to PCG algorithms, you could create similar extensions to demo other types of contents being edited or generated, such as rigs, animations, materials, textures, etc. As you'll see later, you can position the 3D text used for the captions relative to other objects, so they are great for making annotations for tutorials too.

To follow this section's examples, install the extension "Barrel PCG Demo" from the downloaded source as described in the section "Running This Chapter's Examples." Once installed, you'll find the extension under the Properties shelf (N key) ➤ Tool tab in the viewport.

Overview of the Barrel PCG Demo Extension

Before diving into code, let's go over the inputs and operating modes of Barrel PCG Demo and see what they do. Figure 9-2 shows the extension's UI panel in the Properties shelf (N key) ➤ Tool tab. The underlying PCG algorithm of the extension is the barrel generation example generate_ barrel (Listing 3-14) from Chapter 3. You will modify generate_barrel so it can output intermediate stages of the generation. The extension's UI lets users enter a name for the generated model, plus the top/bottom radii, the middle radius, height, and the number of segments for the barrel. These user-entered parameter values take effect across any of the three operating modes: ***Generate Barrel***, which generates a single model (same as Listing 3-14); ***Barrel Demo Interactive***, which shows intermediate stages of the generation, with each stage advanced with the Down Arrow key; and ***Barrel Demo Timelapse***, which shows the same intermediate stages of generation advanced automatically on a timed interval.

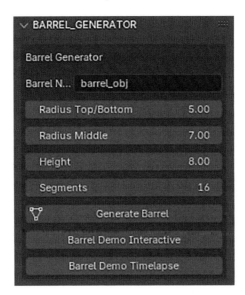

Figure 9-2. *Barrel PCG Demo's UI panel under Properties shelf (N key) ➤ Tool tab*

Implementing the Input Widgets

The text field for entering the Barrel Name in the extension UI panel is implemented as a bpy.props.StringProperty instance. The next three sliders for entering the top/bottom radii, middle radius, and height for the barrel are implemented using bpy.props.FloatProperty instances. You can revisit Chapters 2, 5, 6, and 8 for a refresher on how to implement input widgets with these bpy.props types and adding them to a custom UI panel's draw method.

Implementing the "Generate Barrel" Operator

In this section, you'll modify the generate_barrel function from Listing 3-14 so it's able to output one of four intermediate generation stages as well as the complete model. You'll then use the modified generate_barrel to create a "Generate Barrel" operator, which takes user-entered parameter values through the UI panel and outputs a complete model.

Modifying the generate_barrel Function to Output Intermediate Stages of Generation

To modify generate_barrel to output partially generated models, you'll first define an enum class BarrelGenSteps (Listing 9-6) to outline the intermediate generation stages. BarrelGenSteps derives from the built-in Python type enum.IntEnum so its members are integers and can be used anywhere integers are expected. Figure 9-3 shows the partially generated mesh corresponding to CrossSections, TopBottomFaces, BridgeLoops, and SubdivSmooth in Listing 9-6. Before is before the generation starts (so there is no mesh), whereas Whole means the whole model. SubdivSmooth creates the same mesh as Whole. I'll explain later why we want to distinguish between Whole and SubdivSmooth as separate enum values.

Listing 9-6. `IntEnum` defining barrel generation stages (see /Ch9/ extension/barrel_pcg_demo/__init__.py)

```
@unique
class BarrelGenSteps(IntEnum):
    Before = 0
    CrossSections = 1
    TopBottomFaces = 2
    BridgeLoops = 3
    SubdivSmooth = 4
    Whole = 5
```

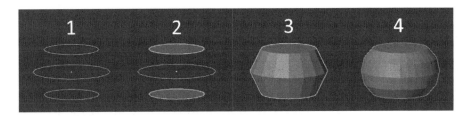

Figure 9-3. *Barrel generation stages. (1) to (4) correspond to CrossSections, TopBottomFaces, BridgeLoops, and SubdivSmooth in Listing 9-6 (see /Ch9/extension/barrel_pcg_demo/__init__.py)*

The `@unique` just above `BarrelGenSteps` in Listing 9-6 is a class decorator specifically for enums. By default, multiple enum entries with the same value are allowed (for example, you could have both `BridgeLoops = 3` and `SubdivSmooth = 3` in Listing 9-6). Since we want to use `BarrelGenSteps`'s values to uniquely identify generation stages, we decorate the class with `@unique`, which will raise a `ValueError` if any of the decorated enum values are duplicates. Note that the generative stages are accumulative—meaning that stage 2 will add to stage 1.

Next, you'll define the caption strings that will be used to create 3D text objects for describing each generation stage in the two demo modes, "Barrel Demo Interactive" and "Barrel Demo Timelapse". You'll simply create a dictionary demo_steps_msgs as shown in Listing 9-7, with BarrelGenSteps (Listing 9-6) values as keys and strings defining the captions for the stages as values.

Listing 9-7. Caption strings corresponding to barrel generation stages (see /Ch9/extension/barrel_pcg_demo/__init__.py)

```
demo_steps_msgs = { ↩
    BarrelGenSteps.Before: "Welcome to the ↩
        Barrel Generation Demo",
    BarrelGenSteps.CrossSections: "Create ↩
        Circular Cross-Sections",
    BarrelGenSteps.TopBottomFaces: "Fill in ↩
        Top and Bottom Faces",
    BarrelGenSteps.BridgeLoops: "Bridge the ↩
        Cross-Sections with Edge Loops",
    BarrelGenSteps.SubdivSmooth: "Subdivide Smooth",
    BarrelGenSteps.Whole: "Complete Model"}
```

With the enum depicting generation stages defined, you're ready to modify generate_barrel to optionally output a partial mesh at the stage specified by a BarrelGenSteps value, as shown in Listing 9-8.

Listing 9-8. Modifying generate_barrel (Listing 3-14) to optionally output intermediate stages of the generation (see /Ch9/extension/barrel_pcg_demo/__init__.py)

```
default_barrel_name = "barrel_obj"
def generate_barrel(context, name, radius_end, ↩
    radius_mid, height, num_segments, center, ↩
    step):
    if len(name) < 1:
        name = default_barrel_name
```

```
bm, barrel_obj = get_placeholder_mesh_obj_and_bm( ↵
    context, name, center)
if step.value < BarrelGenSteps.Whole.value:
    barrel_obj.name += ("_"+str(step.value)+ ↵
        "_"+step.name)

if step.value > BarrelGenSteps.Before.value:
    bottom_cap_verts = add_circle(bm, radius_end, ↵
        num_segments, -height/2)
    add_circle(bm, radius_mid, num_segments, 0)
    top_cap_verts = add_circle(bm, radius_end, ↵
        num_segments, height/2)

if step.value > BarrelGenSteps.CrossSections.value:
    bm.faces.new(top_cap_verts)
    bm.faces.new(bottom_cap_verts)

if step.value > BarrelGenSteps.TopBottomFaces.value:
    bmesh.ops.bridge_loops(bm, edges=bm.edges)
    bmesh.ops.recalc_face_normals(bm, faces=bm.faces)

if step.value > BarrelGenSteps.BridgeLoops.value:
    bpy.ops.mesh.select_all(action='SELECT')
    bpy.ops.mesh.subdivide(smoothness=1)

bmesh.update_edit_mesh(barrel_obj.data)
```

Since name will be entered by the user through the text field, we check if it's an empty string—if so, we substitute it with a default name "barrel_obj". We then call get_placeholder_mesh_obj_and_bm from Chapter 3 (Listing 3-9) to create a new object, barrel_obj, with placeholder mesh data and a bmesh instance bm for modifying it. If the passed-in step is an intermediate stage (step.value < BarrelGenSteps.Whole.value), we want to name the output model with a suffix which includes the step's number (`step.value`) and name (`step.name`). For example, if `name` is the default name and step is `BarrelGenSteps.BridgeLoops`, the output model's name will be "barrel_obj_3_BridgeLoops".

With metadata for the mesh set up, we can now proceed to add geometry to it through `bm`. The barrel generation part of the code is identical to Chapter 3's version of `generate_barrel` (Listing 3-14), except here, we break it down into four blocks—depending on which `step` (`BarrelGenSteps` value) is given, we selectively run one to four out of four of the blocks. For example, if `step` is `BarrelGenSteps.BridgeLoops`, then the generation will conclude just *before* the block that starts with the line `if step.value > BarrelGenSteps.BridgeLoops.value:`, therefore completing three out of the four stages (note that `BarrelGenSteps.BridgeLoops`' value is 3). If `step` is `BarrelGenSteps.Whole`, all four blocks will run. After completing the required number of stages, the function calls `bmesh.update_edit_mesh(barrel_obj.data)` to flush changes queued up on `bm` to `barrel_obj`'s mesh data before returning.

You might have noticed that a `step` value of `BarrelGenSteps.SubdivSmooth` and `BarrelGenSteps.Whole` will both run four out of four blocks of generation code and produce complete models. The reason we distinguish between the two is because when `step` is `BarrelGenSteps.Whole`, we name the output model directly using the `name` entered by the user through the text field, whereas when `step` is `BarrelGenSteps.SubdivSmooth`, we name the model `<name>_obj_4_SubdivSmooth` to indicate its stage of generation. The former is used when the user presses the "Generate Barrel" button outside of demo mode, and the latter is used for both the interactive and time-lapse modes which we'll see shortly.

Creating the GenerateBarrelOperator Class

We'll start simple and implement the GenerateBarrelOperator class first (Listing 9-9), which just calls generate_barrel (Listing 9-8) to generate a whole barrel model. It is added to the UI panel as the "Generate Barrel" button.

Listing 9-9. Operator to generate a complete barrel mesh based on the 3D Cursor position and user-entered parameter values (see /Ch9/extension/barrel_pcg_demo/__init__.py)

```
class GenerateBarrelOperator(Operator):
    bl_idname = "mesh.generate_barrel"
    bl_label = "Generate Barrel"
    """Unwrap Side UV for the Face Mesh from View"""

    def execute(self, context):
        generate_barrel(context, context.scene.barrel_name, ↵
            context.scene.barrel_radius_ends, ↵
            context.scene.barrel_radius_mid, ↵
            context.scene.barrel_height, ↵
            context.scene.barrel_segments, ↵
            context.scene.cursor.location, ↵
            BarrelGenSteps.Whole)
        self.report({'INFO'}, "Barrel generated.")
        return {'FINISHED'}

    def invoke(self, context, event):
        hide_all_meshes(context)
        set_view(context)
        return self.execute(context)
```

To hide the clutter in the viewport, in GenerateBarrelOperator's invoke method, we call hide_all_meshes (Listing 9-10) to hide all mesh objects in the scene, then set_view (Listing 9-11) to set the viewport rotation and view distance. We then call generate_barrel (Listing 9-8) in GenerateBarrelOperator's execute method with user-entered parameter values from the UI panel, plus the current 3D Cursor position, and BarrelGenSteps.Whole to indicate that we want to generate a whole model. Recall that we also used the 3D cursor position (context.scene.cursor.location) as the fire hydrant model's position in Chapter 5.

hide_all_meshes (Listing 9-10) is modified from hide_scene_objects (Listing 9-3), where we add the check for the object's type ('MESH'). set_view (Listing 9-11) is just a convenience function that calls set_viewport_rotation (Listing 9-4) with a fixed set of argument values.

Listing 9-10. Hiding all mesh objects in the scene under the given context (see /Ch9/extension/barrel_pcg_demo/__init__.py)

```
def hide_all_meshes(context):
    for obj in context.scene.objects:
        if obj.type == 'MESH':
            obj.hide_set(True)
```

Listing 9-11. Helper function to set viewport rotation and distance to a fixed view (see /Ch9/extension/barrel_pcg_demo/__init__.py)

```
def set_view(context):
    utils.set_viewport_rotation(context, ↵
        context.scene.cursor.location, ↵
        wxyz=(0.716,0.439,0.291,0.459), ↵
        view_persp='PERSP', view_dist=30.0)
```

Implementing the "Barrel Demo Timelapse" Operator

In this section, we'll look at how to implement the `BarrelDemoTimelapse` operator, which when invoked calls `generate_barrel` (Listing 9-8) in a series of timed events to generate four meshes that correspond to intermediate stages of the barrel generation. The operator will be added to the UI panel as the "Barrel Demo Timelapse" button.

Implementing Timed Events with Modal Operators

In Blender Python, modal operators are operators that run only when a certain type of event is detected, for example, when a timer ticks or when a user presses or releases certain key(s) on the keyboard. Instead of `execute`, a modal operator has a `modal` method which continuously waits for a desired event to happen. The `modal` method performs its task when it sees that the passed-in event is of the correct type and optionally satisfies other required criteria. A modal operator will run continuously and return `{'RUNNING_MODAL'}` from its `modal` method to indicate that it is currently in an event-detection loop or return `{'CANCELLED'}` when it is done.

The operator class `BarrelDemoTimelapse` in Listing 9-12 is implemented as a modal operator. `BarrelDemoTimelaps` creates a timer in its `invoke` method—each time it ticks, it creates an `event.type` of `'TIMER'`. When the operator's `modal` method detects such an event, it calls `generate_barrel` (Listing 9-8) to output a partial mesh, advancing one generation stage with each timer tick, until there is no more stage left, in which case, `modal` stops running and returns `{'FINISHED'}`. While the operator is running, if the user presses the Esc key on the keyboard at any time (thus triggering an `event.type` of `'ESC'`), `modal` stops running and returns `{'CANCELLED'}`.

Listing 9-12. The BarrelDemoTimelapse operator class (see /Ch9/
extension/barrel_pcg_demo/__init__.py)

```
class BarrelDemoTimelapse(Operator):
    bl_idname = "modal.barrel_demo_timelapse"
    bl_label = "Barrel Demo Timelapse"
    """PCG Barrel Demo Timelapse"""

    def modal(self, context, event):
        if event.type == 'ESC':
            self.cancel(context)
            return {'CANCELLED'}

        if event.type == 'TIMER':
            if self._current_step == BarrelGenSteps.Whole:
                self.cancel(context)
                return {'FINISHED'}
            else:
                self._current_step = BarrelGenSteps( ↵
                    self._current_step.value+1)

                generate_barrel(context, ↵
                    context.scene.barrel_name, ↵
                    context.scene.barrel_radius_ends, ↵
                    context.scene.barrel_radius_mid, ↵
                    context.scene.barrel_height, ↵
                    context.scene.barrel_segments, ↵
                    context.scene.cursor.location, ↵
                    self._current_step)

                update_text_obj(context, ↵
                    demo_steps_msgs[self._current_step], ↵
                    get_text_obj_loc(context))
        return {'RUNNING_MODAL'}
```

```
def invoke(self, context, event):
    hide_all_meshes(context)
    set_view(context)

    wm = context.window_manager
    self._timer = wm.event_timer_add( ↩
        time_step=1, window=context.window)
    wm.modal_handler_add(self)
    self._current_step = BarrelGenSteps.Before
    init_text_obj(context, demo_steps_msgs[ ↩
        self._current_step], ↩
        get_text_obj_loc(context))

    self.report({'INFO'}, "Barrel Demo Timelapse: Invoke.")
    return {'RUNNING_MODAL'}

def cancel(self, context):
    clear_text_obj(context)
    if self._timer:
        context.window_manager. ↩
            event_timer_remove(self._timer)
        self._timer = None
```

We'll now look at BarrelDemoTimelapse's implementations in more detail. invoke starts by hiding all meshes (Listing 9-10) and setting the desired view (Listing 9-11). It then uses a reference to context. window_manager to call event_timer_add to create a timer which ticks once a second (time_step=1). BarrelDemoTimelapse is registered as one of context.window_manager's modal handler via wm.modal_handler_ add(self), which means each time an event takes place, context. window_manager will call BarrelDemoTimelapse's modal method. With the timer set up, next, we create a variable self._current_step to keep track of which barrel generation stage we are currently at and initialize it to `BarrelGenSteps.Before`. We also call `init_text_obj` (Listing 9-13) to create a 3D text object that will provide "caption" for the generation process throughout, which we'll discuss in more detail shortly. `invoke` finishes by returning `{'RUNNING_MODAL'}` to start `modal` off in an event-detection loop.

Each time the timer ticks, `context.window_manager` calls `BarrelDemoTimelapse`'s `modal` method with the event. When `modal` detects that `event.type == 'TIMER'`, it checks whether it is at the final stage of the barrel generation (`BarrelGenSteps.Whole`)—if so, it calls `cancel` to clear the 3D text object and remove the timer and returns `{'FINISHED'}` to indicate that the operator is exiting the event-detection loop. If not, `modal` advances to the next generation stage via the line:

```
self._current_step = BarrelGenSteps(self._current_step.value+1)
```

We'll dissect this line bit by bit. Recall that in the `invoke` method, `self._current_step` is initialized to `BarrelGenSteps.Before`. Therefore, `self._current_step.value` is initially 0. When we increment this value, we get an integer that is 1 larger. `BarrelGenSteps(<integer>)` gives you the enum member in `BarrelGenSteps` that has that integer value. For example, `BarrelGenSteps(1)` gives you `BarrelGenSteps.CrossSections`. Therefore, `BarrelGenSteps(self._current_step.value+1)` gives you the enum member in `BarrelGenSteps` that is immediately after `self._current_step`.

With the generation step advanced, `modal` calls `generate_barrel` (Listing 9-8) with the new step and looks up the caption text in `demo_steps_msgs` (Listing 9-7) to call `update_text_obj` (Listing 9-15) with to update the 3D text caption.

If the user presses the Esc key at any point in time (regardless of which step the operator is currently on), `modal` is called with the event. When `modal` sees that `event.type == 'ESC'`, it will call `cancel` to clear the 3D text object and remove the timer and return `{'CANCELLED'}` to indicate that the operator is exiting the event-detection loop.

Creating 3D Text Objects

We'll now look more closely at how `BarrelDemoTimelapse` (Listing 9-12) manages the captions throughout the PCG demo. `init_text_obj` in Listing 9-13 creates and initializes the 3D text object (`text_obj`). Since `text_obj` is of internal use only by the operators, its name does not matter so we just use a hard-coded name, "`modal_text_obj`". We will also only create this object once and reuse it between operator runs.

We'll begin by creating `text_obj`'s underlying curve data, which is of type `'FONT'`. We set the curve's `fill_mode` to `'FRONT'`, its body to the passed-in `text` (the caption string), and its X and Y alignment to `'CENTER'`. We then create `text_obj` with the curve data if it does not yet exist; set its location, font size (`text_obj.data.size`), and rotation; and link it to the current context's scene collection.

Next, we'll set the font color. To do so, we temporarily make `text_obj` the active object, so we can create a new material `mat` and apply it to `text_obj`. Since `bpy.ops.material.new()` does not return the new material, we look it up by the last material created: `bpy.data.materials[-1]` and rename it after `text_obj`'s name. We set `mat`'s diffuse color to the font color we want and apply `mat` to `text_obj`, by adding a material slot to `text_obj`, setting the material at that slot to `mat` (`text_obj.material_slots[-1].material = mat`), and setting `mat`'s slot as `text_obj`'s active material slot.

To wrap up, we set the active object back to the one before, unhide `text_obj`, and assign `text_obj` to the scene variable `bpy.types.Scene.text_obj` so both demo operators can access it.

Listing 9-13. Creating a 3D text object (curve object of type 'FONT') (see /Ch9/extension/barrel_pcg_demo/__init__.py)

```
modal_text_obj_name = "modal_text_obj"
def init_text_obj(context, text, location):
    curve_name = modal_text_obj_name + "_curve"
    curve_obj = bpy.data.curves[curve_name] if ↵
```

```
    bpy.data.curves.find(curve_name) >= 0 else ↵
    bpy.data.curves.new(curve_name, 'FONT')
curve_obj.fill_mode = 'FRONT'
curve_obj.body = text
curve_obj.align_x = 'CENTER'
curve_obj.align_y = 'CENTER'

text_obj = bpy.data.objects[modal_text_obj_name] if ↵
    bpy.data.objects.find(modal_text_obj_name) >= 0 else ↵
    bpy.data.objects.new(modal_text_obj_name, curve_obj)
text_obj.location = location
text_obj.data.size = 1.5
text_obj.rotation_euler = Euler((radians(d) for d ↵
    in [90,0,90]), 'XYZ')
if context.collection.objects.find( ↵
    modal_text_obj_name) < 0:
    context.collection.objects.link(text_obj)

cur_active_obj = context.view_layer.objects.active
context.view_layer.objects.active = text_obj
bpy.ops.material.new()
mat = bpy.data.materials[-1]
mat.name = modal_text_obj_name + "_mat"
mat.diffuse_color = (1, 1, 1, 1)

bpy.ops.object.material_slot_add()
text_obj.material_slots[-1].material = mat
text_obj.active_material_index = ↵
    text_obj.data.materials.find(mat.name)
context.view_layer.objects.active = cur_active_obj

text_obj.hide_set(False)
bpy.types.Scene.text_obj = text_obj
```

During a demo, since we want the caption to go just above the barrel, we calculate text_obj's location based on the 3D cursor, which will also be the location of the barrel, as shown in Listing 9-14. Since the barrel's location is at its center, we add an additional Z offset of half the barrel's height, plus a little slack. An example of text_obj captioning a generation step is shown in Figure 9-4.

Listing 9-14. Deriving text_obj's location based on the 3D cursor position and barrel height (see /Ch9/extension/barrel_pcg_demo/__init__.py)

```
def get_text_obj_loc(context):
    z_offset = context.scene.barrel_height * 0.5 + 3
    x, y, z = context.scene.cursor.location
    return Vector((x, y, z+z_offset))
```

As a demo operator advances each generation stage, it can update the caption by setting text_obj.data.body to a new string, as shown in Listing 9-15.

Listing 9-15. Updating the 3D text object with new text and location (see /Ch9/extension/barrel_pcg_demo/__init__.py)

```
def update_text_obj(context, new_text, new_location):
    context.scene.text_obj.hide_set(False)
    context.scene.text_obj.data.body = new_text
    context.scene.text_obj.location = new_location
```

Figure 9-4. *Example of the 3D text object captioning a barrel generation step. Pictured is the third step, which corresponds to* `BarrelGenSteps.BridgeLoops` *in Listing 9-6*

When a demo operator cancels (either because it has exhausted generation stages or the user pressed "Esc"), it needs to clear the caption. Since we want to reuse text_obj between operators, as well as between operator runs, we set text_obj.data.body to an empty string then hide it, until an operator needs it again, as shown in Listing 9-16.

Listing 9-16. Clearing text_obj's text and hiding it (see /Ch9/ extension/barrel_pcg_demo/__init__.py)

```
def clear_text_obj(context):
    context.scene.text_obj.data.body = ""
    context.scene.text_obj.hide_set(True)
```

Implementing the "Barrel Demo Interactive" Operator

If you prefer to give users more control over when the next generation stage is triggered in the demo, you can replace the timed event in BarrelDemoTimelapse (Listing 9-12) with key events (i.e., when the user presses and releases keys on the keyboard).

Advancing Generation Stages with Keystrokes

We'll modify BarrelDemoTimelapse from Listing 9-12 to create an interactive demo operator BarrelDemoInteractive (Listing 9-17), which lets users advance generation stages by pressing the Down Arrow key. As you can see, aside from the new bl_idname and bl_label, there is minimal modification to BarrelDemoTimelapse to make it trigger a stage change by a key press event instead of a timer event. I've marked the modifications in **bold**. First, in the invoke method, no timer is created, and we change the caption to inform the user to press the Down Arrow key to advance. Then, the cancel method is simplified so it only calls clear_text_obj to reset text_obj. The final modification is in the modal method, where upon detecting a release of the Down Arrow key (event.type == 'DOWN_ARROW' and event.value == 'RELEASE'), the generation step is advanced and another partial mesh is produced.

Listing 9-17. The BarrelDemoInteractive operator class (see /Ch9/ extension/barrel_pcg_demo/__init__.py)

```
class BarrelDemoInteractive(Operator):
    bl_idname = "modal.barrel_demo_interactive"
    bl_label = "Barrel Demo Interactive"
    """PCG Barrel Interactive Demo"""

    def modal(self, context, event):
```

```python
    if event.type == 'ESC':
        self.cancel(context)
        return {'CANCELLED'}

    if event.type == 'DOWN_ARROW' and ↩
        event.value == 'RELEASE':
        if self._current_step == BarrelGenSteps.Whole:
            self.cancel(context)
            return {'FINISHED'}
        else:
            self._current_step = ↩
                BarrelGenSteps(self._current_step.value+1)

            generate_barrel(context, ↩
                context.scene.barrel_name, ↩
                context.scene.barrel_radius_ends, ↩
                context.scene.barrel_radius_mid, ↩
                context.scene.barrel_height, ↩
                context.scene.barrel_segments, ↩
                context.scene.cursor.location, ↩
                self._current_step)

            update_text_obj(context, ↩
                demo_steps_msgs[self._current_step], ↩
                get_text_obj_loc(context))

    return {'RUNNING_MODAL'}

def invoke(self, context, event):
    hide_all_meshes(context)
    set_view(context)

    context.window_manager.modal_handler_add(self)
    self._current_step = BarrelGenSteps.Before
```

473

```
        init_text_obj(context, demo_steps_msgs[ ↵
            self._current_step] +  "\nPress Down ↵
            Arrow to Continue and Esc to Quit.", ↵
            context.scene.cursor.location)

        self.report({'INFO'}, ↵
            "Barrel Demo Interactive: Invoke.")

        return {'RUNNING_MODAL'}

    def cancel(self, context):
        clear_text_obj(context)
```

Summary

In this chapter, you learned how to transform your Blender Python work into sellable products step by step, from licensing and packaging extensions, formulating marketing plans, to analyzing pricing models, and providing support post release. Along the way, you discovered various ways to build up a following and create a personal brand.

In addition, you learned how to create marketing materials by utilizing Blender Python itself, by taking screenshots with Python operators and preparing the viewport for video captures by hiding distractions and customizing display options. You also found out how to launch Blender from the command line and automate script runs with optional blend data.

In the final part of the chapter, you discovered how to implement a time-lapsed demo as an extension using modal operators to showcase your procedural generation algorithm, which displays intermediate stages of the mesh creation with 3D text captions. You also learned how to create an interactive version of the demo by revising the modal operator to trigger the next stage with a key event instead of a time event.

Index

A

Add-on
  extension, 36
    install, 37
    uninstall, 37
  legacy
    disable, 36, 37
    enable, 36, 37
    install, 37
    uninstall, 37
Add-on design
  assessing which tasks to
    automate, 391
  dividing tasks, 390
  turning tasks into operators, 391
  using poll to enforce
    prerequisites, 392
Autocomplete, 3

B

Background images, 269
Blender Extensions Platform, 432
blender_manifest.toml, 264, 325
bmesh, 118
  edges
    access by indices, 130, 131

accessing edges through a
  bmesh instance, 128–130
creating new edges through
  a bmesh instance, 128–130
direction, 139
end vertices, 139
end vertices
  ordering, 128–130
ensure internal lookup table
  is initialized and up-to-
  date (bm.edges.ensure_
  lookup_table()), 130
fallback vertex, 131
length, 139
midpoint, 140
removal, 131
scaling, 140
sliding end point
  by axis, 140
faces
  access by indices, 130, 131
  accessing faces through a
    bmesh instance, 128–130
  boundary vertices
    ordering, 128–130
  creating new faces through a
    bmesh instance, 128–130

I. Lupiani, *Blender Scripting with Python*, https://doi.org/10.1007/979-8-8688-1127-2

Printed in the United States
by Baker & Taylor Publisher Services